# THEORIES OF DEVELOPMENTAL PSYCHOLOGY

## Second Edition

# THEORIES OF
# DEVELOPMENTAL
# PSYCHOLOGY

## PATRICIA H. MILLER
*University of Florida*

## SECOND EDITION

W. H. FREEMAN AND COMPANY
*New York*

Library of Congress Cataloging in Publication Data
Miller, Patricia H.
   Theories of developmental psychology / Patricia H. Miller.
— 2nd ed.
      p.      cm.
   Bibliography: p.
   Includes indexes.
   ISBN 0-7167-2001-9. — ISBN 0-7167-2002-7 (pbk.)
   1. Developmental psychology — Philosophy. 2. Child psychology
— Philosophy. I. Title.
BF713.M55 1989
155 — dc19                                               88-30443
                                                              CIP

Printed in the United States of America

3 4 5 6 7 8 9 0   VB   9 9 8 7 6 5 4 3 2 1 0

*To Scott, Erica, and Kevin*

# Contents

## 2

# FREUD'S AND ERIKSON'S PSYCHOANALYTIC THEORIES  121

# Preface

In both the first and second editions of this book I tried to give the "big picture" of psychological development. Sometimes students are frustrated by fact-laden textbooks that do not provide frameworks in which to fit the facts. It is often not clear, for example, why a Swiss philosopher would be interested in children's numerical judgments after a row of objects is spread out or why it is noteworthy that an infant cries when his mother leaves the room. In this book, six theories, or approaches, provide frameworks for understanding and perceiving the significance of the research findings in developmental psychology.

The book can be used as a primary or supplementary text in undergraduate or graduate courses. In addition, it can provide perspectives on children's behavior for those who work with children in any capacity. I also hope that developmental psychologists will find something of interest in these pages.

I have used a parallel structure in the various chapters in order to help the reader compare the theories. To provide continuity, I have introduced four central issues of development that are addressed in each chapter. Finally, I have tried to convey what is exciting about each of the theories.

Probably no one, including myself, is completely satisfied with the selection of theories. Certainly, many important theories were necessarily excluded. Several of the theories included — those of Piaget, Freud and Erikson, and of social learning — appear in most books of developmental theories. This book differs from others by including several approaches that have a great deal of influence on contemporary research on development. These approaches are information processing, ethology, and E. J. Gibson's perceptual learning. Although they are not formal theories, they function as theories by identifying what to study, what questions to ask, and how to answer these questions.

The second edition updates the first. I have tried to show how each theory has changed in its emphasis or in its influence on developmental psychology over the last six years. I have added major new sections. The chapter on Piaget's theory now includes separate sections on the neo-Piagetians and on modifications that Piaget himself made in his final years. The chapter on information processing reflects researchers' growing awareness that knowledge influences memory. I also added Robert Sternberg's theory of intelligence, which illustrates the extension of the information-processing approach to the area of intelligence. Bandura's recently published book on social learning and thinking led to greater coverage of topics such as self-efficacy. With respect to ethology, recent research such as Charlesworth's studies of resource allocation in children makes that chapter more contemporary. Finally, Gibson's increasing emphasis on the affordances (utility) of surfaces, events, and objects and on infants' use of this information for locomotion and exploration is reflected in the chapter describing her view of perceptual development.

I am grateful to a number of people who read and offered comments for the first or second edition: Patricia Ashton, William Charlesworth, Eleanor Gibson, Harry Grater, Richard Griggs, Gardner Lindzey, Jack Meacham, Stuart Miller, Joy Osofsky, Anne Pick, Robert Siegler, and Robert Watson. Several undergraduate and graduate students also made helpful suggestions. Most of all, I want to thank Scott Miller, who read the entire manuscript and offered valuable advice for both editions. Finally, I am grateful to John Flavell, who guided my meanderings into theories when I was a graduate student and has continued to be a source of inspiration.

Patricia H. Miller

# THEORIES OF DEVELOPMENTAL PSYCHOLOGY

## Second Edition

# Introduction

Give us theories, theories, always theories. Let every man who has a
theory pronounce his theory.
[James Mark Baldwin]


Never trust an experimental result until it has been confirmed by theory.
[Sir Arthur Eddington]

A rchimedes is said to have run naked through the streets, shouting "Eureka, eureka!" (I have found it, I have found it!) after discovering the principle of hydrostatics. This joy and excitement of discovery, although usually more restrained than Archimedes', is the driving force behind every theoretical advance. The purpose of this book is to tell the story of theory building in developmental psychology. We will meet the grand old theories of Jean Piaget, Sigmund Freud, and Erik Erikson, the rapidly changing learning theories, and several approaches relatively new to developmental psychology— information processing, ethology, and Eleanor Gibson's perceptual learning. These theories have saved developmental psychology from drowning in the sea of data on children. They have helped psychologists keep their faith that development is a comprehensible process and a legitimate area of study.

To understand the contribution of these developmental theories, we must first look at the general nature of theories. In this introductory chapter, we ask the following questions about theories:

1. What is a theory?
2. What is a developmental theory?
3. Of what value is a developmental theory?
4. How are facts and theories related?
5. What are the main issues of developmental psychology?

## WHAT IS A THEORY?

When we ask what a theory is, we are entering the realm of metatheory: the theory of theories. Every philosophy of science is in part a metatheory. A philosophy of science specifies what a theory is and what it should do. Unfortunately, it turns out that we are not asking a simple question. A philosopher of science might "answer" our question with two more:

1. Are we asking what theories should be or what they typically are?
2. Are we asking about theories as they are stated formally or as they operate in a scientific community?

The philosopher's first question concerns the distinction between ideal and real theories and expresses the sad fact of scientific life that our theories fall short of their goal. Especially in the social sciences, theories usually do not reach a complete, formal state. An ideal, compete, formal scientific theory is a set of interconnected statements — definitions, axioms, postulates, hypothetical constructs, intervening variables, laws, hypotheses, and so on. Some of these statements, which are usually expressed in verbal or mathematical form, are deduced logically from certain other statements. The function of the set of interconnected statements is to describe unobservable structures, mechanisms, or processes and to relate them to each other and to observable events.

All writers do not define these various types of statements in the same way, but only the most widely accepted meanings are used in this book. Perhaps the best way to contrast these types of statements is to show that they occupy different levels within a theory. That is, they vary in their distance from observable behavior. The "farther" a statement is from observable behavior, the less likely it is to be supported by empirical data.

At a point farthest from observable behavior are certain assumptions (axioms, postulates) that are accepted without being tested. (For example, in Piaget's theory, an assumption is that thinking is organized.) These assumptions may be so self-evident to the theorist that he is not even aware of them. As we move to a less general level, we find hypothetical constructs — concepts that posit relationships among events, objects, properties, or variables. These constructs (such as "mental scheme" and "mental reversibility" in Piaget's theory) are unobservable themselves, but refer to behavior that can be observed. The theorist infers what he cannot see. Hypothetical constructs are translated into testable hypotheses, which are tentative statements about the relationship among events, objects, properties, or variables. (One Piagetian hypothesis is that the infant tends to repeat interesting actions, such as shaking a rattle.) A hypothesis becomes a fact when it is sufficiently supported by research. As facts accumulate, they are tied together by a law: a relatively well established general statement concerning the relationship among a set of facts.

All of these formal elements should meet certain requirements. A theory should be logically sound, that is, internally consistent, with no statements that contradict each other. A theory should also be empirically sound, that is, not contradicted by scientific observations. Furthermore, it should be testable and parsimonious, relying on as few constructs, propositions, and the like, as possible. Finally, a theory should cover a reasonably large area of a science, and it should integrate previous research.

The closest that psychology has come to having a formal theory is Clark Hull's elaborately formalized learning theory, which he developed in the 1930s and 1940s. Hull constructed a system of postulates regarding constructs such as habit strength, drives, and reinforcements. His theory, however, was not totally successful. It was logically incomplete and inconsistent and, in some cases, empirically incorrect. Perhaps psychology was not ready for such an ambitious undertaking.

Although current theories of development do not meet the formal requirements of a theory, these requirements give us a context for judging whether each theory of development is headed in the right direction. We can ask whether each theory could eventually reach the status of a formal, testable theory. In their present form, developmental "theories" serve as frames of reference for examining changes in behavior over time. (For example, Piaget's theory directs our attention to the organization of thought rather than to specific pieces of knowledge, to stagelike changes during development rather than to a gradual accumulation of knowledge, and to the child's active construction of knowledge rather than to his passive processing of information.)

Our philosopher of science would probably urge us to continue to build theories, despite their imperfect state, but to keep in mind that we are far from the promised land of formal theory. The young science of developmental psychology, with its informal theories and growing pains, may yet develop into a mature science with formal theories. The philosopher's second question distinguishes between theories as they are stated (in books such as this one) and how they actually operate in a scientific community. A theory, in its tidy and polished form in a textbook, bears only a faint resemblance to the way the theory guides the behavior of real people doing real research. A theory is both a static formulation and a social and psychological phenomenon. When a person develops or adopts a particular theory, she takes on a whole set of beliefs concerning what questions about development are worth asking, what methods for studying these questions are legitimate, and what the nature of development is. A Freudian is not likely to study how rats learn to press bars in tightly controlled experiments, and a learning theorist is not likely to ask people to describe their dreams or memories of childhood. There are unwritten rules of the game that are very much a part of the theory as it is practiced.

## WHAT IS A DEVELOPMENTAL THEORY?

At this point we can make two statements about developmental theories. First, they are somewhat informal at present. Second, like all theories, they have a dynamic, nonpublic role as well as a static, public one. Our next step is to ask what makes these theories developmental. Simply studying children does not make a theorist a developmental theorist. For example, studying learning in 6-year-olds does not necessarily lead to conclusions about development. What is critical about a developmental theory is that it focuses on *change over time*. Although developmental theories have nondevelopmental theoretical concepts such as id, mental representation, attention, and drive, they diverge from nondevelopmental theories by emphasizing changes over time in these concepts.

This concern with change presents developmental theories with three tasks. These tasks are (1) to *describe* changes *within* one or several areas of behavior, (2) to *describe* changes in the relationships *among* several areas of behavior, and (3) to *explain* the course of development that has been described. Let us look more closely at each of these three tasks.

1. A developmental theory describes changes over time in one or several areas of behavior or psychological activity, such as thought, language, social behavior, or perception. For example, a theory might describe changes in the rules of grammar underlying language in the first few years of life. Although developmental theories tend to stress changes over months or years, an adequate theory must ultimately describe changes over seconds, minutes, and days. For example, the object concept, the notion that objects exist even when we do not see them, may develop over many months, but a full description would include many "minidevelopments" that occur during the child's moment-to-moment encounters with objects.

Many people believe that description is based on neutral, objective observation and is prior to theory building. However, even direct observation is guided to some extent by theoretical notions that distort the flow of behavior in some way. The observer records certain behaviors and ignores others. She divides the stream of behavior into units. She encodes the behavior into words that add connotations. She allows inference to creep into her observations. That several degrees of inference are possible is demonstrated in the following descriptions of the same behavior:

a. The baby's hand came closer and closer to the spinning top.

b. The baby reached for the spinning top.

c. The baby wanted to pick up the spinning top.

d. The baby applied her grasping scheme to the spinning top.
(A scheme, according to Piaget, is an organized sequence of behavior that reflects an infant's knowledge in a particular area, such as grasping.)

Later in the chapter, we have more to say about the relationship between observation and theory.

Much of the early work in developmental psychology was almost exclusively concerned with description. In the 1930s, Arnold Gesell's maturational theory of development was directed toward establishing norms of physical, cognitive, and motor development through description. Although description is not sufficient for an adequate theory of development, it certainly is necessary. Without a data base, we have an "edifice without a foundation," in B. L. White's (1969) words.

2. A second task for a theory of development is to describe changes over time in the relationship among behaviors or aspects of psychological activity within one area of development and, ideally, among several areas of development. A developmental theory tries to deal with the simultaneous changes in thought, personality, and perception that we observe. A developmental theorist is a "specialized generalist" in that he is knowledgeable about many areas of psychology, but specializes in the developmental approach to studying these content areas.

In the case of the object concept described above, a theory might describe how the concept relates to the child's developing memory system and his social relationship with one particular object, his mother. A theory would outline the temporal relationships among these areas of development. For example, a theory might claim that a certain degree of memory capacity must be developed before the object concept can emerge, that the mother is the first permanent object, and that subsequent developments within the object concept are correlated with changes in the memory system and the child's attachment to his mother. Another example concerns the relationship between thought and language. One position, that of the Russian psychologist Lev Vygotsky, is that thought and language are relatively independent until they merge to produce symbolic thought. Both examples describe the organization within the child at various points in time. The descriptions refer to certain sequences (first A, and then B) and concurrences (A and B at the same time) that occur during development.

Of course, any attempt to divide behavior into parts is somewhat arbitrary because there is an interrelated system, or the famous "whole child." Nevertheless, since scientists are not superhumans, everything about the child cannot be studied at once. They do some breaking down before they can build up again.


3. Even if a theory provides a full description of development, it has not accounted for the transitions from point to point during development. Thus, a third task for a developmental theory is to explain the course of development that the other two tasks describe. In fact, the sequences and concurrences identified in the first two tasks often suggest particular explanations. If skill B always appears shortly after the development of skill A, a psychologist may hypothesize that A causes B.

With respect to the third task, a developmental theory offers a set of general principles or rules for change. These principles specify necessary and sufficient antecedents for each change and identify variables that modify or modulate the rate or nature of each change. For example, Freud proposed that the biologically based drives "move" from the oral to the anal area and that the degree of the child's accompany anxiety depends somewhat on the parents' child-rearing practices. In addition, principles of change hypothesize a set of processes for producing the change. These processes have been as diverse as dynamic equilibration in Piaget's theory, physical maturation in Freudian and ethological theory, and the strengthening of a response by reinforcement in learning theory.

One way to interpret developmental change is to hypothesize a continuity underlying the apparent change. For example, a theory might claim that dependency is expressed in different ways during development but that the underlying trait is the same. Or a theory might emphasize the underlying continuity in cognitive development by pointing to the gradual change in the understanding of number and by hypothesizing that what can be learned is limited by what number concepts the child already has. In more general terms, a theory may claim that concept, trait, skill, or behavior A is transformed into B, is replaced by B, combines with B to form C, and so forth. Most of the developmental theories we examine in this book posit an underlying continuity to the superficial changes during development.

When a theory explains why development proceeds in a certain way, it at the same time explains why certain other possible courses of development did not occur. Why did A lead to B rather than X? The significance of nonoccurrences is expressed by Sherlock Holmes:

" . . . the curious incident of the dog in the nighttime."
"The dog did nothing in the nighttime."
"That was the curious incident," remarked Sherlock Holmes.

*[Sir Arthur Conan Doyle]*

The discussion so far has avoided the question of exactly *what* should be described and explained. Should developmentalists emphasize universal change or individual differences? On the one hand, Piaget emphasizes concepts acquired in all racial and cultural groups. On the other hand, social learning theory emphasizes differences in various children's behavior that derive from the particular models, feedback, and learning situations to which the children are exposed. Throughout this book, we ask whether theorists should strive to describe and explain general, universal acquisitions or the acquisitions of any particular child or both.

It should be pointed out that listing the three tasks for developmental theories in a particular order should not imply that a theory approaches them in that order. Most commonly, a theory of development weaves back and forth among the three tasks. Progress on one of the tasks stimulates progress on another, which in turn feeds back to the first task or the third. A related point is that description and explanation are not as separate and independent as the list might imply. Attempts to describe change often bring in explanatory concepts, and the type of explanation a theorist offers is somewhat constrained by how he has described behavior.

These three monumental tasks, even if incompletely met in the near future, provide us with goals by which to measure the success of current theories of development. A more realistic expectation for the near future is that we can have theories that succeed in a more limited way. Theories may successfully describe and explain one particular area of development, such as language development, but not all areas. Or they may cover several areas, but only achieve one or two of the three tasks. For example, a theory might competently describe changes in several areas, but unsuccessfully explain these changes.

By the end of this book, it will have become clear that most theories are not equally concerned with these three tasks. Piaget is much more successful at describing the development of thought than explaining this development. In contrast, learning theory has focused on mechanisms of change rather than the content of this change. No one theory has satisfactorily handled all three tasks, but each theory has contributed to at least one. As we examine each theory, we judge how well it has accomplished each of these tasks.

## OF WHAT VALUE IS A DEVELOPMENTAL THEORY?

What does a developmental theory actually do when it describes and explains development? A theory makes two contributions: (1) it organizes and gives meaning to facts; (2) it guides further research. We examine each of these contributions in turn.

## Organizing Information

A developmental theory organizes and gives meaning to facts of development. Facts do not speak for themselves. As Jules Henri Poincaré (1908) says, "Science is built up of facts, as a house is built of stones; but an accumulation of facts is no more a science than a heap of stones is a house." Just as stones need an architect or a blueprint to become a house, so do facts need a theorist to give the facts structure and show their relationship to the overall design. Thus, a theory gives meaning to facts, provides a framework for facts, assigns more importance to some facts than others, and integrates existing facts. One by-product is that by summarizing and organizing information we are saved from "information overload." It is easier (but perhaps more dangerous) for us to refer to "defense mechanisms" than to state all the separate behaviors to which they refer.

Just as the same stones can be used to make different houses, so can a set of facts be given different meaning by different theories — by organizing them differently, emphasizing different behaviors, and inferring different hypothetical constructs. Consider the following example from McCain and Segal (1969). At one time, two theories explained the tendency of a falling rock to increase its speed as it approaches the earth. According to a popular Greek theory, rocks and earth like to be with each other because they are made of the same elements. As the rock gets closer to the earth, it travels faster because it becomes increasingly excited. The facts can also be explained by Newton's theory of universal gravitation. All particles attract each other with a force directly proportional to the product of their masses and inversely proportional to the square of their distances. These two theories are based on the same set of observations, but they assign different meaning to these facts.

When we view development through the lenses of first one theory and then another, we experience a gestaltlike shift. We see the child as seething with sexual energy or reflecting on the origins of the universe. We see the child as a bundle of conditioned responses or a highly organized system. At times, we may wonder if we are looking at the same child in these different perspectives. These theoretical shifts have been likened to shifts in the perception of ambiguous figures (Averill, 1976), such as the sudden perceptual shift of young woman to old

**FIGURE I-1** ■ *The lines in this drawing can be perceptually organized to form an old woman or a young woman.*

woman in Figure I-1. The information has not changed, but our organization of it has.

The explosion of research on children in the last two decades makes it especially important to look at current theories or develop new theories to make sense of our information about children. All too often, textbooks on developmental psychology list empirical findings, much as a phonebook lists names and numbers. Although they briefly describe theories, they typically do not use these theories to organize facts other than those directly associated with the development of each theory.

## Guiding Research

In addition to giving meaning to facts, a theory serves a second function. It is a heuristic device, a tool to guide observation and generate new information. A theory's abstract statements predict that certain empirical statements should be true. These empirical statements, then, must be tested. For example, Gibson's theory of perceptual development hypothesizes that attention to features that differentiate objects underlies much of perceptual development. In addition to organizing and giving meaning to a variety of previous research findings, this theory has led investigators to examine the roles of attention and the structure of objects and events in perceptual development. A further example comes from ethology, an approach borrowed from biology. This theory has led developmental psychologists to search for social behaviors in infancy that are innate and have contributed to the adaptation of the species to the environment.

Theories not only stimulate new observations but in some cases also cause us to reexamine familiar behavior and pay more attention to variables we have slighted. Piaget certainly was not the first person to watch babies play, but he suggested a new way of looking at this behavior: the actions themselves are creating thought, according to Piaget.

Theory's dual role as a stimulator of, and interpretor of, data is nicely illustrated in a 22-year longitudinal study of aggression (Eron, 1987). Traditional learning theory, with its emphasis on drive reduction, guided the selection of the original variables in 1960. In later years, as new learning theories emerged, investigators interpreted the data first in terms of Skinnerian operant learning (early 1970s), then according to social learning (mid 1970s), and finally by the cognitive model (mid 1980s). Thus, in these four phases of learning-theory development, the investigators sought the causes of aggression in frustration (drive reduction), reinforcement of aggression (Skinner), aggressive models (social learning), and finally the child's attitudes and interpretation of potential instigators of aggression (cognition).

Throughout our discussion, we have been flirting with the question of how facts and theories are related. It is now time to take a careful look at this question.

## HOW ARE FACTS AND THEORIES RELATED?

The psychologist is never sure that what he does is "science." And if what he does is "science" he is never sure that it is psychology.

[*Greco, 1967, p. 937*]

Facts typically are defined as statements that are based on observations and are generally agreed on by several people. We accept this definition for the present, but it has many pitfalls, as we shall see later.

Perhaps the best way to show the relationship between facts and theories is to look at how facts are involved in theory construction. M. H. Marx (1976) has described four modes of interaction between theories and facts (data) that characterize theory construction. These are shown schematically in Figure I-2. The arrows show the direction of the relationship between theory and data. The vertical lines indicate that the theory does little more than summarize the data. The diagonal lines indicate that data, theory, or both play a more dynamic role. The longer the line, the more removed the theory is from the data. Finally, the horizontal dimension represents the passage of time. We now examine the four basic ways of relating data and theory: models, deductive theories, functional theories, and inductive theories.

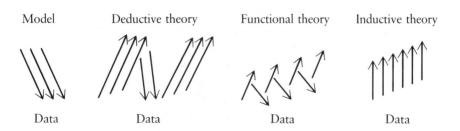

| Model | Deductive theory | Functional theory | Inductive theory |
|---|---|---|---|
| Data | Data | Data | Data |

FIGURE I-2 ■ *The relationship between theory and data defines four types of theory construction.* [*From "Formal Theory," by Melvin H. Marx. Reprinted with permission of Macmillan Publishing Co., Inc., from* Theories in Contemporary Psychology, *2nd ed., edited by Melvin H. Marx and Felix E. Goodson. Copyright © 1976, Macmillan Publishing Co., Inc.*]

## The Model

A model is a framework, structure, or system that has been developed in one field and is then applied to another, usually less well developed, field. The model stands for or represents something other than itself. It serves as an analogy or a metaphor to guide research and thinking. Examples are the early image of the nervous system as a telephone switchboard or the eye as a camera and the later notion of an instinct as a hydraulic system. More recently, thinking has been likened to an equilibration system (Piaget) or a computer (information-processing approach).

Since the model serves a heuristic function, there is a one-way influence between theory and data. The model suggests and guides research, but there is little interest in using the results of that research to modify the general model. More specific models, however, may be modified as a result of research. This is particularly true of information-processing theory, which takes the computer as a general model of thinking. This general model is not modified as a result of research, but the specific features of the processing model may change as a result of new data. These specific models often take the form of schematic diagrams consisting of boxes and arrows to represent the flow of information. The diagrammatic models are modified as a result of research. Another common example of specific models that are modified by data is the mathematical model. Although the conceptual structure is taken from mathematics, data determine the final form the model takes.

It should be mentioned that the term *model* has been used in two additional ways that should not be confused with the use of the term here. First, a model can refer to a very general "world view," one's view of reality. An example would be the view that the world, including the human, is like a machine or, in contrast, like a living organism (Overton, 1984). Second, in current usage, *model* sometimes replaces *theory*. The term connotes an undertaking that is less ambitious and less speculative than a general theory.

## Deductive Theory

The hypothetical philosopher of science we were questioning earlier had the deductive type of theory in mind when he described what a theory should be. A deductive theory is a logically organized set of propositions, stated in a formal way. These propositions include basic assumptions and definitions from which are deduced further propositions. There is a two-way relationship between data and the theory in that theoretical propositions are continually tested and the results in turn modify the theory. Hull's theory of learning is psychology's best example of a deductive theory. Deductive theories are attractive because they are elegant and because they spell out all of the assumptions and the implications of these assumptions. Good deductive theories are vulnerable simply because they cannot hide anything.

### Functional Theory

Most present-day theory construction falls into this category. Functional theory is much more informal and modest than deductive theory. Its propositions are closely related to data (as represented by the short arrows in Figure I.2) and are often restricted to a particular experimental problem. There is a continual, rapid interplay between theory and data. General statements, or hypotheses, are suggested by a set of research findings. These general statements and their implications are then tested by further research. The general statements are then modified, and the process continues. For example, one might choose smiling in infancy as an experimental problem. A first hypothesis might be that recognition of an object causes smiling. Research, however, may show that this hypothesis is true only for certain ages and particular types of situations. The hypothesis is continually refined through modification and further testing.

### Inductive Theory

An inductive theory consists of descriptive statements that summarize sets of data. Little inference is involved. An inductive theorist is someone who demands "just the facts." A one-way relationship holds between data and theory: data lead to theory. Inductive theorists argue that collecting facts unbiased by interpretation eventually leads to statements that tie together the data. The best contemporary example of inductive theory is Skinner's operant conditioning theory (despite the fact that Skinner claims to have no theory at all). Statements in Skinner's inductive theory take the following form: if a response is followed by a reinforcer for several trials, the frequency of that response increases. Because of their belief in making minimal inferences from the data, inductive theorists are likely to react to more grandiose theories with "What's a nice fact like you doing in a theory like this?"

## An Overview

These four modes of theory construction demonstrate that theories can generate research either by analogy, as in the model, or by deduction, as in deductive and functional theories. Data, in turn, generate theories by induction, test the deductions or specific models that are derived from theories, and ultimately modify theories, except in the case of general models. Empirical observation can never completely prove that a theory is true because future observations could provide disconfirming evidence.

The history of science shows that there may be a considerable lag between the gathering of data and the production of a theory. Data may not immediately suggest a particular theory. Darwin's *Origin of Species* was published more than 20 years after his voyage on the HMS *Beagle*. It took Kepler over 30 years to produce the three laws of planetary motion.

The four types of theories vary in how far the empirical observations are from the theoretical statements. Functional and inductive theories are closer than deductive theories or models to the data. For example, a learning theorist might refer to "stimulus," "response," and "punishment"—terms that are very close to observable objects or events. At the other extreme, Freud's "unconscious" process or Piaget's "equilibration" process bears at best an uncertain and distant relationship to observable behavior.

The distance between theory and behavior is of considerable importance for two reasons.

1. The greater this distance, the more difficult it is to either support or weaken the theory. Much of scientific progress comes from showing that particular theories are wrong and correcting them. If a theory is so far from possible data that it can be neither confirmed nor disconfirmed (even in the future), it is of little value for science.

2. A second, related point is that the further the distance between data and theory, the greater the number of theories that can be pro-

duced to explain the same set of facts. As we saw earlier, two theories were offered to explain observations about falling objects. Because of the distance between these theories and their observations, neither could be disproved. Sometimes theories are retained for years because their central claims are so far from possible observations that they cannot be tested and refuted.

As with all nice classification systems, this classification of types of theory building does not quite fit into the messy reality of science. Most developmental theorists actually have used all four types of theory construction at some point in their lives. For example, Piaget used models from theoretical biology, logic, and physics. Equilibration, organization, and the logicomathematical structures are all borrowed from older, respected relatives of psychology. A functional relationship characterizes his theory building in particular subareas such as the number concept or the object concept. In fact, we find research and theory focused on a particular task in much post-Piagetian work. Piaget, by nature, was not satisfied with making simple inferences from data, but the inductive mode is sometimes found in the earliest phases of his research on certain problems. Piaget did not formalize his theory into a set of theoretical propositions. Some logical deductions, however, come ready-made from the particular logical structures he adopted. (These modes of interaction between data and Piaget's theory are elaborated in the next chapter.)

To some extent, this section on theory building has presented a half-truth. In it, we have seen the conventional view of theory building presented. Theory building was pictured as an orderly, objective, logical process that involves four types of relationships between facts and theories. This is a picture of scientists in their "dress clothes." Although science sometimes does proceed in this way, more often it proceeds in a much messier, irrational fashion to produce a polished final product.

More specifically, the conventional view of theory building implies that empirical observations are objective bits of information that we can use to make more general statements or to test statements derived from a theory. In reality, observations themselves are somewhat constrained by the observer's theoretical orientation, expectations based on previous research, beliefs about "human nature," and personal motivations. Facts do not simply present themselves to the bright young scientist for developing a new theory or evaluating an existing one. For example, a scientist may hold certain assumptions that lead him to see certain facts more easily than others; in fact, it is difficult to see what we are not looking for. As an illustration, radio signals from Jupiter had been heard, but ignored, for many years before two young American astronomers "discovered" these signals in 1955 and recognized their significance.

The scientist's social and political beliefs can be especially biasing in a field such as psychology, in which people are studying people. The psychologist holds a mirror rather than a telescope. If a psychologist assumes that the human is basically rational, he is more likely to study thought than emotions, more likely to become a Piaget than a Freud. A developmental psychologist does not escape the views of children of his society at that point in its history. As Scarr (1985, p. 204) observed, "We pose questions to fit our place and time; we get answers to fit our theoretical niches." She argued that we change our scientific lenses as the culture changes. Scarr noted that in the 1950s and 1960s social scientists expected, and thus looked for, evidence that boys in "broken homes" were affected negatively by the lack of a father. The finding that these boys, when young, were observed to be low in aggression was taken as evidence for poor sex-role development. After the women's movement and the emergence of nontraditional families, it is no longer automatically assumed that negative effects accompany a father's absence. With today's less rigid view of desirable masculine and feminine traits or behavior, low aggression in a boy may not be seen as a deficit.

The individual psychologist's personality and motivations also influence the particular direction his research takes, a point demonstrated by learning theorist E. C. Tolman:

I started out . . . with considerable uneasiness. I felt that my so-called system was outdated and that it was a waste of time to try to rehash it and that it would be pretentious now to seek to make it fit any accepted set of prescriptions laid down by the philosophy of science. I have to confess, however, that as I have gone along I have become again more and more involved in it, though I still realize its many weak points. The system may well not stand up to any final canons of scientific procedure. But I do not much care. I have liked to think about psychology in ways that have proved congenial to me. Since all the sciences, and especially psychology, are still immersed in such tremendous realms of the uncertain and the unknown, the best that any individual scientist, especially any psychologist, can do seems to be to follow his own gleam and his own bent, however inadequate they may be. In fact I suppose that actually this is what we all do. In the end, the only sure criterion is to have fun. And I have had fun.

[1959, p. 152]

Because of all these influences on the scientist, when she makes an observation or discovers a fact, she is not a neutral fact finder. As mentioned earlier in the discussion about the task of describing in developmental psychology, an investigator does not simply record reality. She has already made decisions about what facet of behavior to study, what measures to use, how to divide up the "stream of behavior," how to collect the data, and how to score the data. Each decision further constrains what facts can be observed. A one-minute episode of a baby playing could be described or measured in thousands of ways. There are different levels of behavior, from heart rate to pattern of manual exploration, and different temporal units, from a fraction of a second to a behavioral unit spanning perhaps the entire minute. What facts or observations the psychologist chooses from the thousands of candidates tells us as much about the psychologist or her theory as about the episode of behavior itself. These constraints on what is observed are necessary, of course, because it is not feasible to record everything.

We have seen that theory building is objective and subjective, orderly and disorderly. This dual nature of science again claims our attention in the last chapter, when we examine Thomas Kuhn's views on the role of scientific revolutions in the history of science. At that point, we can reexamine the dual nature of science in light of the history of theories of developmental psychology.

This discussion of facts, theories, and theory construction was intended to prepare the reader for the specific theories that follow, not to serve as a crash course in the philosophy of science. It should be kept in mind that this simplified account ignores many controversies in the history of ideas. Also, we have given little attention to the disagreement among philosophers of science about the distinctions between such terms as *hypothetical constructs*, *laws*, *hypotheses*, and *postulates*. These controversies and the more subtle aspects of metatheory can be found in the suggested readings at the end of this chapter. The reader is encouraged to explore these problems.

# WHAT ARE THE MAIN ISSUES OF
# DEVELOPMENTAL PSYCHOLOGY?

Although the theories to be covered differ in their content, methods of investigation, and formal nature, they are similar in that they are forced to take a position on certain core issues of development. Developmental change, by its very nature, leads to these issues. There are four critical issues:

1. What is the basic nature of the human?
2. Is development qualitative or quantitative?
3. How do nature and nurture contribute to development?
4. What is it that develops?

These issues, which serve as a way of summarizing and contrasting the theories, reappear at the end of each chapter. First, however, some discussion of each issue is in order.

## What Is the Basic Nature of the Human?

A theorist's view of development is closely tied to his view of human nature. His view of human nature, in turn, is closely tied to his world view, or his notion about how the universe works. In the history of the Western world, there have been two basic world views of great relevance to the study of psychology (Overton, 1984): the mechanistic and the organismic. We examine each of these.

In the mechanistic view, the world is like a machine composed of parts that operate in time and space. For example, the world could be likened to a watch. Forces are applied to the parts and cause a chain reaction that moves the machine from state to state. In principle, then, complete prediction is possible because complete knowledge of the state and forces at one point in time allows us to infer the next state. This mechanistic view has its roots in Newtonian physics. It is also related to the empiricist philosophy of Locke and Hume, which pictures the human as inherently at rest—a passive robot, motivated by external sources. Development, consequently, is caused by external forces and events acting on a passive, machinelike mind composed of interlocking parts. One can almost see the wheels turning in the child's head!

In contrast, the organismic world view is modeled on living systems, such as plants or animals, rather than machines. This image derives from Wilhelm von Leibniz (1646–1716), who believed that substance is in "a continuous transition from one state to another as it produces these states out of itself in unceasing succession" (Cassirer, 1951, p. 29). Leibniz pictured the world as composed of organized "wholes" that are inherently and spontaneously active and self-regulating. This organization is necessary, or natural, given the nature of the organism. The emphasis is on the whole rather than its parts, the relations among the parts, and how the whole gives meaning to its parts. In the realm of psychology, visual perception, for example, cannot be understood by looking only at the processes of the retina, optic nerve, visual areas of the cortex, and so on. The whole must be considered, such as other perceptual systems and higher cognitive functions.

Rather than look for antecedent causes, as the mechanistic world view has done, the organismic view considers inherent properties and goals. The human, by nature, is an active, organized whole and is constantly changing, not randomly but in a particular direction. Development, then, is inherent in humans. Self-initiated behavior and thought lead to changes in both the structure and the content of behavior and thought. S. H. White describes an active organism:

> Let us define an active organism as one that gives form to its experience, a passive organism as one that receives form from its experience. Active organisms have purposes and they attend, reason, and selectively perceive. All this enables the active organism to select, modify, or reject environmental influences pressing upon it.
>
> *[1976, p. 100]*

Because so many examples of the organismic and mechanistic world views will emerge throughout this book, a single one will serve us at this point. With respect to acquiring knowledge about the world, the organismic view is that the child "constructs" his knowledge by actively formulating and testing hypotheses about categories of objects and the causes of events. In contrast, the mechanistic view is that a child passively acquires ("soaks up" like a sponge) a copy of reality.

Organismic, unlike mechanistic, theories are usually state theories, which posit qualitative rather than gradual change.

In addition to these two metaphysical views of the human and the world are more specific and limited views based on particular economic and political ideologies. For example, Riegel (1972) relates views of childhood and of development to the capitalistic and mercantilistic politicoeconomic systems in the seventeenth to nineteenth centuries.

The capitalistic system, largely Anglo-American, saw the human as competitive, as struggling for success. Thomas Hobbes' (1588–1679) pronouncement of the human as selfish and competitive and of life as "nasty, brutish, and short" expressed this notion. The roots continue through Charles Darwin, who stressed the survival of the fittest. In the economic arena, the emphasis was on free trade, competition, and entrepreneurship. The standard of success (as a result of struggle and competition) was the white, middle-class adult male engaged in manufacturing or business. By this standard, children, the elderly, mental defectives, and women were considered inferior. Childhood, considered a state of incomplete adulthood, was a "disability." Normative descriptions of each age were developed to detect "abnormal" development and chart children's progress toward the adult standard of success. Society saw children as passive beings who must be molded ("socialized") into appropriate adult roles.

The mercantilistic ideology, in contrast, was found primarily in continental Europe in the seventeenth through the nineteenth centuries. The economy was based on land ownership and state-controlled trading more than on manufacturing and free trade. Distinct social classes enjoyed specified duties and privileges, and little competition between classes occurred. Society emphasized cooperation more than competition; differences between groups were tolerated. The main philosophical spokesman, Jean Jacques Rousseau (1712–1778), saw the child as a "noble savage," basically good but ruined by the adult world. Children were not to be judged by adult standards; children and adults were seen as qualitatively different. From this point of view, the goal of education was self-realization. Consequently, a child-oriented education was developed by Maria Montessori, Eduard Spranger, and others.

From even this brief account of changing history, it is easy to see how each theory of developmental psychology must have a view of the human being that reflects philosophical, economic, and political beliefs. This view is often implicit, and sometimes the theorist himself is not even aware of these assumptions. The view influences not only theory construction but also decisions about which research problems are meaningful, what method should be used, and how data should be interpreted. Even the meanings of the terms "explanation" and "fact" are different in theories with different world views. For these reasons, it is sometimes claimed that it is impossible to integrate or reconcile theories or make crucial tests that support one or the other if they have different world views. However, integrations of mechanistic and organismic approaches have been offered (Overton, 1984).

## Is Development Qualitative or Quantitative?

Closely related to these views of the human being is the issue of the basis of developmental change: Is it qualitative or quantitative? The mechanistic and capitalistic views emphasized quantitative change, whereas the organismic and mercantilistic approaches emphasized qualitative change. Qualitative changes refer to changes in kind or type. An example from nature is the following sequence: egg → caterpillar → cocoon → butterfly (Spiker, 1966). New phenomena or characteristics emerge that cannot be reduced to previous elements. Qualitative changes typically involve changes in structure or organization. In contrast, quantitative changes refer to changes in amount, frequency, or degree. In some cases, the behavior becomes more efficient or consistent. The change is gradual and occurs in small increments. Bits and pieces of information, habits, skills, and the like, are acquired during development.

An example of the contrast between quantitative and qualitative change can be found in the development of memory. If a 4-year-old can recall three objects and a 7-year-old can recall seven objects from a set of objects seen several minutes earlier, we might infer a quantitative difference in their mental functioning. The older child can remember more. However, if the 7-year-old uses strategies such as organizing the objects into classes and rehearsing them, whereas the 4-year-old does not, we would infer a qualitative difference in their mental functioning: they process the information in a different way.

At a more general level, the issue of qualitative versus quantitative change becomes an issue of stage versus nonstage development. When there are similarities in a number of abilities or behaviors during a period of time, a theorist often infers that the child is in a particular "stage." For example, Piaget posits stagelike qualitative changes in the structure of thought from birth to adolescence. Yet stage theorists disagree about the possibility of being in more than one stage at the same time or of regressing to an earlier stage, and they argue about what can cause children to differ in how fast they pass through the stages.

Stagelike, qualitative changes have been identified by scholars other than developmental psychologists. Historians identify periods in history, such as the "industrial age" or the "age of reason," Shakespeare saw seven ages of man from the "mewling and puking" infant to the old person "sans teeth, sans eyes, sans taste, sans everything."

Despite their arguments about which developmental changes are qualitative and which quantitative, most developmentalists agree that both types of changes occur. Some behaviors involve both qualitative and quantitative changes. In some cases the periods of quantitative and qualitative change appear to alternate. Using the memory example presented earlier, one might find an increase in the number of items rotely memorized (quantitative change). This increase in memory may eventually be followed by the development of a strategy (qualitative change) of putting together items from the same category, say, foods, furniture, and toys. Subsequent increases in the speed and accuracy of this clustering would involve quantitative change.

## How Do Nature and Nurture Contribute to Development?

Regardless of the extent to which development is qualitative or quantitative, a theorist must refer to the underlying causes of development. The basic issue is whether knowledge and behavior are derived from one's genetic endowment or from experience in the world. The nature–nurture issue is known by several other labels, such as "heredity versus environment," "nativism versus empiricism," "biology versus culture," "maturation versus learning," and "innate versus acquired abilities."

This controversy has raged not only within psychology but also within philosophy. The controversy began in classical Greek times when philosophers asked whether ideas are innate or acquired through the experience of the senses. For example, Plato (427–347 BC) believed that ideas are innate because the soul, which exists before birth in the realm of ideas, is trapped by the body at birth. Later, medieval Christian philosophers proclaimed the innate depravity of man, and later still French philosopher Jean Jacques Rousseau (1712–1778) proclaimed innate goodness. On one side, René Descartes (1596–1650) believed that certain ideas are innate, while on the other side British empiricist John Locke (1632–1704) argued that the newborn's mind is a blank slate (*tabula rasa*) on which experience writes. The debate continued through the history of psychology. For example, the Gestalt school emphasized the role of innate factors in determining perception, whereas the behaviorists emphasized environmental factors in learning.

Anastasi (1958) points out that we did not ask the right question in the past. We should not have asked *which* (heredity or environment) causes a behavior or *how much* of each is needed for a given behavior. Instead, we should ask *how* (in what manner) nature and nurture interact to produce development. This is an interesting illustration of how progress in a field sometimes simply means learning how to ask the right question.

Today nearly everyone agrees that the interaction of innate and environmental factors accounts for both the development of a trait or behavior in an individual and the variations in a trait or behavior among individuals. Nature and nurture are inextricably intertwined. Both nature and nurture are fully involved in the development of any behavior. Hebb (1980) concludes that behavior is determined 100 percent by heredity and 100 percent by environment. Genes are never expressed directly in behavior. There is a long chain of events involving genes, physiological processes, and the environment. The way that heredity is expressed depends on the specific environment in which this expression occurs. In other words, a given hereditary influence can have different behavioral effects in different environments. And, conversely, a given environment can have different effects on people with different genetic makeups. A jack-in-the-box might delight a placid baby, but disturb a nervous, reactive infant who is upset by sudden change. Moreover, intense stressful events that cause disturbances in most children have little effect on so-called resilient children (Garmezy and Tellegen, 1984).

The theories presented in this book differ in whether they emphasize the nature or the nurture part of the interaction. In addition, there is disagreement about the process by which either environmental or innate factors have their influence. For example, the environment can "stamp in" associations, provide models to be imitated, or supply information to be assimilated.

There are several possible ways in which experience can have an influence. Wohlwill (1973) has proposed four models.

1. In the first, or "hospital-bed," model, the person is acted on by the environment, as if he were a helpless hospital patient. This condition is most likely in the first few months of life.

2. In the "amusement-park" model, the person selects certain features of the environment to experience. However, once he selects certain stimuli, he has little control over their effect on him: "Once he has decided to partake of the roller-coaster ride, there is little he can do to alter the experience he will derive from it" (p. 101).

3. The third, or "swim-meet," model likens experience to a swimming race in which "from the sound of the gun the individual's behavior takes its course in virtual independence from environmental stimuli" (p. 101). The environment is merely a supportive context for the person's behaviors.

4. In the "tennis-match" model, there is an interaction between the influences of the environment and the person. A tennis player must adapt to the way his opponent (the environment) returns the ball. However, he influences the opponent's behavior by hitting a lob or volleying.

As these four models demonstrate, a theory's conception of the influence of the environment is closely related to the theory's view of humans as active or passive, a distinction we noted earlier.

Finally, theories differ in how much importance they place on the timing of a particular experience. Are there "critical periods" in which the child is especially sensitive to a particular experience? Is early experience more influential than later experience?

### What Is It That Develops?

This deceptively simple question takes us to the heart of the differences among theories. Each theorist makes a claim concerning the "essence" of development, or at least the proper unit of analysis.

Throughout this book, we encounter associations, schemas, expectations, cognitive structures, psychic structures (id, ego, superego), strategies of information processing, and fixed action patterns. What a theorist sees as the essence of development depends on where his theoretical assumptions and methods of study place him along several dimensions.

1. One's level of analysis (from molecular to molar).

2. Whether one focuses on structure (organization of behavior, thought, and personality) or process (dynamic, functioning aspects of the system).

3. What content one emphasizes (for example, personality or cognition).

4. Whether one emphasizes overt behavior or covert thought and personality.

5. What methodology one uses to study development.

These five dimensions have a chicken-and-egg relationship: Which came first, ethologists' decision to study complex, molar behavior acquired by species in their struggle to adapt to the environment or their choice of a methodology, namely, observations in natural settings? This interrelationship among the dimensions will become more obvious as we examine each theory.

## SUMMARY

The traditional view of an "ideal" scientific theory is that it should be a hypotheticodeductive system and include a set of logically interconnected statements. It formally describes psychological structures and processes and relates them to each other and to observable events. However, in several ways, this picture of psychological theories is incomplete. In addition to deductive theories, there are models, functional theories, and inductive theories, which are less elaborate and formalized. Most psychological "theories" have failed to achieve the status of a theory in the strict definition of the term. Another way in which the traditional view of theories is incomplete is that a theory has not only a public, formal, static nature but also a private, informal, dynamic nature. A theory plays an important informal role as it guides the behavior of psychologists doing research. It helps the psychologist formulate questions, choose what to study, and decide how to study a problem.

We need developmental theories. They help us describe and explain developmental changes by organizing and giving meaning to facts and by guiding further research. Developmental theories have taken a stand on four issues that are of special importance to the study of development:

1. What is the basic nature of the human?

2. Is development qualitative or quantitative?

3. How do nature and nurture contribute to development?

4. What is it that develops?

We now have a framework for viewing each of the theories in turn.

## A WORD ABOUT THIS BOOK

The following six chapters describe six major theories of development. Piaget's theory is presented first because many of the current issues in developmental psychology were raised by his theory. Next come the other two big theories of development: psychoanalytic theory and social learning theory. The remaining three theories are directed toward more limited areas of development. The information-processing approach examines thinking, particularly memory. Ethology focuses on early social behavior. Finally, Gibson's theory analyzes perceptual development, especially perceptual learning. Each chapter follows roughly the same organization, in order to make comparisons among the theories easier. At the end of each chapter, the theory is evaluated in terms of its strengths and weaknesses, according to the current state of developmental psychology. That is, we ask what each theory can contribute to today's developmental researchers, professionals who work with children, and parents.

## SUGGESTED READINGS

The following books serve as helpful guides to philosophical issues in theory construction.

Bergmann, G. *Philosophy of science.* Madison: University of Wisconsin Press, 1957. Bergmann discusses issues of theory construction in various sciences.

Hempel, C. C. *Philosophy of natural science.* Englewood Cliffs, N.J.: Prentice-Hall, 1966. This book is a useful simple introduction to the nature of scientific theories.

Marx, M. H., and F. E. Goodson, eds. *Theories in contemporary psychology.* 2d ed. New York: Macmillan, 1976. This collection of reprinted papers and new essays covers a wide range of issues and problems in theory building and evaluation, especially in the field of psychology.

The following sources are oriented to issues in developmental theories.

Lerner, R. M. *Concepts and theories of human development.* 2d ed. Reading, Mass.: Addison-Wesley, 1986.

Horowitz, F. D *Exploring developmental theories.* Hillside, N.J.: Erlbaum, 1987.

Overton, W. F. World views and their influence on psychological theory and research: Kuhn-Lakatos-Laudan. In H. W. Reese, ed., *Advances in child development and behavior,* Vol. 18. Orlando, Fla.: Academic Press, 1984.

Thomas, R. M. *Comparing theories of child development.* Belmont, Calif.: Wadsworth, 1985. Chapters 1–4.

# 1

# Piaget's Cognitive-Stage Theory

*[At 7 months, 28 days] Jacqueline tries to grasp a celluloid duck on top of her quilt. She almost catches it, shakes herself, and the duck slides down beside her. It falls very close to her hand but behind a fold in the sheet. Jacqueline's eyes have followed the movement, she has even followed it with her outstretched hand. But as soon as the duck has disappeared—nothing more! It does not occur to her to search behind the fold of the sheet, which would be very easy to do (she twists it mechanically without searching it all).*
[Piaget, 1937 (1954, p. 36)]

*Hub (age 6½):* Is the moon always round?—No.—What's it like?—*Sometimes a crescent, it is very worn out.*—Why?—*Because it has done a lot of lighting.*—How does it come round again?—*Because it is made again.*—How?—*In the sky.*
[Piaget, 1926 (1929, p. 281)]

I ntriguing glimpses of children's behavior and thought, such as those on the preceding page, fired Piaget's imagination. In these unremarkable daily events, Piaget saw a remarkable process of cognitive development. In Piaget's view, moment-to-moment specific encounters with objects or people lead to general ways of understanding the world. This understanding changes during development as thinking progresses through various stages from birth to maturity. Moreover, the child himself actively constructs this knowledge.

Piaget's theory is the most widely known theory of cognitive development. His influence has spread not only throughout the disciplines of psychology, but also into areas such as education and philosophy. It is appropriate, then, to begin our look at theories with the cognitive-structural theory of Jean Piaget.

This chapter can only hint at the complexity of Piaget's theory. We first delve into Piaget's life in some detail in order to clarify his theory and to illustrate the close relationship between the personality of a theorist and the nature of his theory. After this biography comes a general orientation to the theory, then a description of the stages and other developmental changes, followed by a discussion of the mechanisms of development. The next section relates cognitive-structural theory to the critical issues of development and to the characteristics of theories presented in the introduction. Near the end of the chapter, Piaget's theory is evaluated in a contemporary context. The chapter ends with a description of Piaget's own modifications of his theory to supplement the more traditional version presented in the chapter, along with an overview of work of the neo-Piagetians.


## BIOGRAPHICAL SKETCH

Jean Piaget was born on August 9, 1896, in Neuchâtel, Switzerland.* Piaget describes his father, a historian devoted to medieval literature, as "a man of a painstaking and critical mind, who dislikes hastily improvised generalizations, and is not afraid of starting a fight when he finds historic truth twisted to fit respectable traditions" (Piaget, 1952, p. 237). Piaget remembers his mother as intelligent, energetic, and kind, but with a neurotic temperament that drove him to both imitate his father and escape to what Piaget called a "private and nonfictitious world," a world of serious work. Piaget acknowledges that the turbulent family situation aroused his interest in psychoanalytic theory.

It would be easier to list what did not interest the boy Piaget than what did. A sampling of his interests includes mechanics, seashells, birds, and fossils. One of his early writings was a pamphlet (written in pencil because he was not yet allowed to write in ink) describing an "autovap," an intriguing union of a wagon and a locomotive. Piaget's first publication was a one-page article about a partly albino sparrow he had observed in a park. This achievement came at age 10 — long before he had heard of "publish or perish"! Piaget's interest in the exhibits in the local natural history museum led to an invitation to assist the director with his mollusk (shellfish) collections. Thus, Piaget had entered the field of malacology, the study of mollusks, which captivated him for years to come. Piaget's publications on mollusks attracted notice among natural historians. He was offered, sight unseen, the curatorship of mollusks at a natural history museum in Geneva. He had to decline the offer, however, because he had not yet finished secondary school!

Piaget did not escape the typical social and philosophical crises of adolescence. Conflicts between his religious and scientific teachings stimulated him to read hungrily through Bergson, Kant, Spencer,

*Most of the material in this biographical sketch comes from Piaget's autobiography, which appears in a book edited by E. G. Boring et al., *A history of psychology in autobiography*, Vol. 4 (Worcester, Mass.: Clark University Press, 1952).

Comte, Durkheim, and William James, among others. This philosophical turmoil is expressed in a philosophical novel that was published in 1917. That this novel did not become a best-seller can be surmised from passages such as these: "Now there can be no awareness of these qualities, hence these qualities cannot exist, if there are no relationships among them, if they are not, consequently, blended into a total quality which contains them while keeping them distinct," and "positive theory of quality taking into account only relationships of equilibrium and disequilibrium among our qualities" (1952, p. 243). Piaget observed that "no one spoke of it except one or two indignant philosophers" (1952, p. 243).

Piaget continued to write on a variety of philosophical issues. He notes: "I wrote even if it was only for myself, for I could not think without writing—but it had to be in a systematic fashion as if it were to be an article for publication" (1952, p. 241). In these writings, one finds themes that are central in Piaget's later writings, for example, the logical organization of actions and the relationship between the parts and the whole.

Piaget continued his formal studies in the natural sciences and took his doctoral degree with a thesis on mollusks at the University of Neuchâtel in 1918 at age 21. Although he had published twenty papers by this time, he was not eager to devote his life to malacology. After visiting psychological laboratories in Zurich and exploring psychoanalytic theory briefly, Piaget spent 2 years at the Sorbonne. There he studied psychology and philosophy. By luck (for the field of developmental psychology), Piaget met Théodore Simon, a pioneer in the development of intelligence tests. Simon, who had at his disposal Alfred Binet's laboratory at a grade school in Paris, suggested that Piaget standardize Binet's reasoning tests on Parisian children. Piaget began the work with little enthusiasm. However, his interest was aroused when he began questioning children about the reasons underlying both their correct and incorrect answers. He became fascinated with the thought processes that appeared to lead to the answers. In these "conversations," Piaget used psychiatric techniques he had learned while interviewing mental patients for his courses at the Sorbonne. Without Simon's knowledge, Piaget continued this research for 2 years. Piaget sums up this experience:

> At last I had found my field of research. First of all it became clear to me
> that the theory of the relations between the whole and the part can be

studied experimentally through analysis of the psychological processes underlying logical operations. This marked the end of my "theoretical" period and the start of an inductive and experimental era in the psychological domain which I always had wanted to enter, but for which until then I had not found the suitable problems. . . . my aim of discovering a sort of embryology of intelligence fit in with my biological training; from the start of my theoretical thinking I was certain that the problem of the relation between the organism and environment extended also into the realm of knowledge, appearing here as the problem of the relation between the acting or thinking subject and the objects of his experience. Now I had the chance of studying this problem in terms of psychogenetic development.

[1952, p. 245]

The subsequent publication of three articles based on this research in Binet's laboratory led to an offer in 1921 to become director of studies at the Institut J. J. Rousseau in Geneva. Piaget planned to spend only 5 years studying child psychology (a plan that, happily, went awry). The freedom and research facilities of this position nurtured Piaget's productive tendencies and led to the publication of five books: *The Language and Thought of the Child* (1923), *Judgment and Reasoning in the Child* (1924), *The Child's Conception of the World* (1926), *The Child's Conception of Physical Causality* (1927), and *The Moral Judgment of the Child* (1932). To his surprise, the books were read and discussed widely. He became known as a child psychologist, even though he had no university degree in psychology. He was much sought after as a speaker, and his fame grew rapidly in Europe. This public attention was somewhat disquieting to Piaget, in part because he considered his ideas in these books to be quite preliminary and tenuous, rather than the final statement that many people considered them to be.

In the following few years, Piaget continued his research at the Institute, taught philosophy at the University of Neuchâtel, learned about Gestalt psychology, observed his own babies, and even performed some research on mollusks in his free time! From 1929 to 1945, he occupied several academic and administrative positions at the University of Geneva, as well as international posts, such as President of the Swiss Commission of UNESCO. There were productive collaborations with Alina Szeminska, Bärbel Inhelder, and Marcel Lambercier on the manipulation of objects, the development of perception, and the notions of number, physical quantity, and space. Hearing of Piaget's work, Albert Einstein encouraged him to study the concepts of time, velocity, and movement. Two provocative books emerged from this suggestion: *The Child's Conception of Time* (1946a) and *The Child's Conception of Movement and Speed* (1946b).

The 1940s and 1950s were marked by research on an amazing range of topics: various aspects of mental development, education, the history of thought, logic, and his old passion, epistemology, or theory of knowledge. His titles included Professor of Psychology at the University of Geneva and the Sorbonne, Director of the Institut des Sciences de l'Education, and Director of the Bureau International de l'Education. In addition, he founded the Centre d'Epistemologie Génétique, a meeting ground for philosophers and psychologists.

In 1969, the American Psychological Association gave Piaget the Distinguished Scientific Contribution Award "for his revolutionary perspective on the nature of human knowledge and biological intelligence" (Evans, 1973, p. 143). He was the first European to receive this award.

Piaget pursued the riddle of children's thinking until his death on September 16, 1980, at the age of 84. Even in his final years, books and articles continued to stream from his home, the Center for Genetic Epistemology. His flowing white hair, pipe, beret, and bicycle were a familiar sight in Geneva. We have the following description of Piaget at age 70: "He moves deliberately, but his blue eyes sparkle with youth, good humor and zest. Benevolent enough, but not heavy enough, to look like Santa Claus, he reminds one faintly of the pictures of Franz Liszt that have come down to us" (Tuddenham, 1966, p. 208).

One cannot help but be struck by Piaget's amazing productivity. A conservative estimate of his writing is over 40 books and more than 100 articles on child psychology alone. Adding publications in philosophy and education swells these numbers even more. Piaget attributes his productivity, in part, to his helpful colleagues, but goes on to give us an interesting glimpse into his personality:

And then, too, I owe it to a particular bent of my character. Fundamentally I am a worrier whom only work can relieve. It is true I am sociable and like to teach or to take part in meetings of all kinds, but I feel a compelling need for solitude and contact with nature. After mornings spent with others, I begin each afternoon with a walk during which I quietly collect my thoughts and coordinate them, after which I return to the desk at my home in the country. . . . It is this dissociation between myself as a social being and as a "man of nature" (in whom Dionysian excitement ends in intellectual activity) which has enabled me to surmount a permanent fund of anxiety and transform it into a need for working.

*[1952, p. 255]*

# GENERAL ORIENTATION TO THE THEORY

The wise tourist begins to explore an unfamiliar city by setting out on a guided tour, with map in hand. This experience gives the tourist a "feel" for the city — its general structure, tempo, and major landmarks. Similarly, Piaget's theory is best approached by an overviews that presents the Piagetian landscape. The quick guided tour to follow attempts to give the reader a "feel" for Piaget's theory before she explores the nooks and crannies — and perhaps becomes lost. Because Piaget's theory is complex and notoriously difficult to understand, we approach it first at a general level, then at a more specific level. We examine the following salient characteristics of the theory: genetic epistemology, the biological approach, structuralism, the stage approach, and Piaget's methodology. The orientation both describes these characteristics and relates them to Piaget's interests and goals described earlier.

As a preface to the rest of this chapter, it should be noted that Piaget acknowledges the contributions of his coworkers. Although this is a chapter on Piaget's theory, much of the work it describes was done in collaboration with a number of people, especially Bärbel Inhelder.

## Genetic Epistemology

Perhaps the most incomprehensible thing about the world is that it is comprehensible.

*[Albert Einstein]*

Piaget might well have agreed with Einstein, for he had a lifelong fascination with how humans comprehend the world. The branch of philosophy concerned with the study of knowledge is called epistemology. As Piaget views it, epistemology is "the problem of the relation between the acting or thinking subject and the objects of his experience" (1952, p. 245). Piaget tackled the same questions that have engaged philosophers for centuries: How do we come to know something? Is objective knowledge, unbiased by the nature of the knower, even possible? Are there certain innate ideas, or must all knowledge be acquired? All of Piaget's writings can be seen as attempts to answer these questions in different content areas, for example, mathematics, moral reasoning, and language. As we saw in our biographical sketch of Piaget, his philosophical quest led him through various schools of philosophy, biology, history, mathematics, and psychology. His search finally stopped at developmental psychology, which was not even an organized field of study at the time.

Piaget's journey to developmental psychology brings us to the "genetic" part of the term *genetic epistemology.* "Genetic" refers not to what is innate, the more common meaning of the term today, but to "development" or "emergence." By studying developmental changes in the process of knowing and in the organization of knowledge, Piaget felt that he could find answers to the traditional questions of epistemology. His concern with the classical issues in epistemology explains his concern with what philosophers have considered the basic categories of thought: time, space, causality, and quantity. These categories of thought are obvious to an adult but, in Piaget's way of thinking, may not be obvious to children. Piaget wondered how and when children understand that no two objects can occupy the same place, that two contiguous events can have a causal relationship and that a specific event cannot occur both before and after some other event. It may be as difficult for young children to understand these concepts as it is for adults to understand "black holes" in space or the theory of relativity.

Piaget could be called an experimental epistemologist. Unlike most epistemologists, who used logical arguments to support their views, Piaget rejected the armchair approach and formulated empirical hypotheses that could be tested. For example, he examined the question of how humans acquire concepts of time, space, and causality by tracing the development of these concepts. Thus, Piaget's brand of epistemology is a marriage of philosophy and the scientific method, of logic and fact.

Piaget's solution to the problem of epistemology is now described briefly. His simple, but revolutionary, claim is that knowledge is a process rather than a state. It is an event or a relationship between the knower and the known. A child knows or understands a ball or a rattle by acting on it—physically or mentally. In a sense, a person "constructs" knowledge. He has an active part in the process of knowing and even contributes to the form that knowledge takes. Cognitive humans actively select and interpret information in the environment. They do not passively soak up information to build a storehouse of knowledge.

The child's knowledge of the world changes as his cognitive system develops. As the knower changes, so does the known. A concrete example is the knowledge of relationships in space. An infant constructs a practical knowledge of near and far, up and down. An older child constructs a more abstract "cognitive map" of the relations among objects in his environment. The infant "knows" space by crawling in it and reaching for objects, whereas the older child knows space by manipulating mental symbols in particular ways. Note that in both cases there is a constant interaction between the knower and the external world.

One implication of Piaget's theory of knowledge is that knowledge is biased. Experience is always filtered through the child's current ways of understanding. The child's mind is not a camera that takes faithful pictures of reality. However, as the mind develops, it becomes more in tune with reality.

It is worth noting that Piaget applies his developmental approach not only to the epistemology of individual people but also to collective knowledge. This collective knowledge can be seen in the history of science and the relations between the fields of science. An example from the history of science is Piaget's discovery that both children and a scientific field progress from a view that is restricted to a single point of view and concerned with surface properties to a reflective, more deeply analytic view with a broader frame of reference. Thus, Greek mathematics, in which numbers were considered properties of the real world, progressed toward a wide variety of mathematical notions, such as negatives and irrationals, which bear varying relations to the real world. The emphasis also shifted from the results of mathematical operations to the operations themselves. With respect to the relationships among the sciences, one claim is that physiology depends on physics and chemistry, much as thought ultimately can be related to neonatal biological reflexes.

## Biological Approach

Beginning with the early boyhood interest in shells and birds, Piaget's thinking was firmly rooted in biology. Piaget's distinction is that he saw more in mollusks than did most biologists. In the humble mollusk he saw general principles of how living organisms adapt to the world. Mollusks both adjust themselves to the environment and actively assimilate it in ways allowed by their biological structure. Piaget felt that these principles also apply to human thought. His most general definition of intelligence is that it is adaptation to the environment. Just as human and nonhuman organisms adapt physically to the environment, so does thought adapt to the environment at a psychological level. Piaget hypothesized that the modes of psychological functioning involved in this adaptation are general, or universal.

Borrowing another concept from biology, Piaget proposed that cognitive growth is much like embryological growth: an organized structure becomes more and more differentiated over time. In fact, Piaget (1970) sometimes referred to cognitive development as "mental embryology."

Adaptation, organization, and structure, as well as such other biological concepts as equilibration, assimilation, and accommodation, are discussed later in the chapter, when we turn our attention to processes of development. At this point, however, it should be emphasized that these biological concepts serve as analogies for the way intelligence works. Biology did not lead Piaget to a physiology of intelligence.

## Structuralism

Along with such other luminaries as anthropologist Claude Lévi-Strauss and linguist Ferdinand de Saussure, Piaget belongs to an approach called *structuralism*. Structuralists look at the organizational properties of whatever they are studying. Piaget proposed that a small set of mental operations underlies a wide variety of thinking episodes. Thus, there is an underlying structure to the apparent diversity of the content. Structuralists look at how parts are organized into a whole, and they abstract patterns of change. In particular, they are concerned with relationships—between parts and the whole and between an earlier and a later state. For example, the thinking of younger and older children has similar elements, but these elements are combined in different ways to form the organized whole of thought.

According to Piaget the structuralist, the nature of mental structures changes as they develop. An infant's cognitive structures are labeled "schemes" (sometimes translated "schemas" or "schemata"). A *scheme* is an organized pattern of behavior; it reflects a particular way of interacting with the environment. For Piaget, a scheme is whatever is repeatable and generalizable in an action. The sucking scheme, then, describes the way the child puts various objects in his mouth and sucks them. As the scheme becomes more differentiated, the child classifies objects into "suckables" and "nonsuckables," with various subcategories such as hard suckables, soft suckables, pliant suckables, and hairy suckables (daddy's leg).

In contrast, the cognitive structures of the older child, from roughly age 7 on, are described in terms of abstract mental operations organized into logicomathematical systems. The structuralist framework can be seen in the way these schemes and operations mediate content and function and organize themselves into an organized whole. For example, addition, subtraction, multiplication, and division are operations that are coordinated in a concept of number that underlies (mediates) much mathematical behavior. (We return to the notion of cognitive structures later.)

## Stage Approach

> Milestones, phases, and ages
> render general gauges
> While periods, levels, and stages
> require pages and pages.
>
> *[Leland van den Daele, 1969, p. 303\*]*

Perhaps the boldest and most controversial of Piaget's claims is that cognitive development proceeds through a series of stages. For Piaget,

---

\*From "Qualitative Models in Developmental Analysis" by Leland van den Daele, *Developmental Psychology, 1*, 303–310. Copyright © 1969 by the American Psychological Association.

a *stage* is a period of time in which the child's thinking and behavior in a variety of situations reflect a particular type of underlying mental structure. Piaget's emphasis on stages is not surprising, considering his years of careful observing and classifying while a student of zoology. The stages can be thought of as sequential levels of adapting. Just as various species have different ways of adapting to the environment, so do various cognitive levels provide different ways of adapting to the environment. Because stage theories abound in developmental psychology, it would be well to characterize Piaget's particular brand of stage theory. There are five salient characteristics.

1. *A stage is a structured whole in a state of equilibrium.* Piaget the structuralist sees a stage as an integrated whole that organizes the parts. The schemes or operations of each stage are interconnected to form an organized whole. Each stage has a different structure, which allows a different type of interaction between the child and the environment, and consequently provides fundamentally different views of the world. The essence of Piaget's stage approach is that movement through the stages involves structural changes that are qualitative (changes in type or kind) rather than quantitative (change in degree, amount, speed, or efficiency). For example, there is a qualitative change when the child moves from structures based on actions in infancy to structures based on mental representation in the preschool years. At the *end* of each major period of development, the cognitive structures are in a state of balance, or equilibrium. (We have more to say about the equilibration process later in this chapter.)

2. *Each stage derives from the previous stage, incorporates and transforms that stage, and prepares for the next stage.* The previous stage paves the way for the new stage. In the process of achieving this new stage, the previous stage is reworked. Thus, once a child achieves a new stage, he no longer has the previous stage available. Although previous skills remain, their position or role in the organization changes. For example, an elementary schoolchild can still roll or hit a ball (a skill acquired during infancy), but he now imbeds this skill in a number of other skills. Furthermore, a more advanced level of thought controls the old skills of rolling and hitting. Rolling and hitting are now combined with other actions to win the game. One implication of this characteristic is that regression to an earlier stage is impossible because the previous stage is no longer present. This notion is in

contrast to Freud's theory of stages, in which a person overwhelmed with anxiety may regress to an earlier stage.

3. *The stages follow an invariant sequence.* The stages must proceed in a particular order. No stage can be skipped. In other words, since the first stage does not have all the building materials needed for the third stage, the second stage is required. This claim that stages follow an invariant sequence is implied by the second claim that each stage is derived from the preceding stage.

4. *Stages are universal.* Because Piaget was interested in how humans as a species adapt psychologically to their environment, he focused on the structures and concepts acquired by humans everywhere. Of course, because of mental retardation from brain damage, severe deprivation, or other sources, some people may not progress through all the stages or may progress through them more slowly. The crucial claim is that the stages they do achieve are achieved in the predicted order by everyone. Even people who are not retarded vary in how fast they proceed through the stages. Again, the crucial claim is that the same order is found in children of the African jungle, the American suburb, or the Swiss mountainside.

5. *Each stage includes a coming-into-being and a being.* There is an initial period of preparation and a final period of achievement in each stage. Unstable, loosely organized structures mark the initial period of transition from the previous stage. The description of each stage later in this chapter refers to the final, stable, generalized, tightly organized structure of each stage.

In summary, stages are structured wholes that emerge from and transform a previous stage, follow an invariant and universal sequence, and proceed from an unstable period of transition into a final stable period.

## Methodology

One message from the introductory chapter was that the scientist, the theory, and the methods for gathering data both facilitate and constrain one another. The three develop together in particular directions. Piaget the sparrow watcher and mollusk collector used his observation and classification skills when watching infants master the objects around them and when observing toddlers struggle to express their thoughts in spontaneous speech. Piaget as the Sorbonne student interviewing mental patients soon became known as the man who asked questions about dreams, the origin of the universe, and quantity. Piaget's early work with preschool and schoolchildren typically involved the *clinical method*, which refers to a chainlike verbal interaction between the experimenter and the child. The experimenter begins by posing a problem or asking a question, but his subsequent questions are guided by the answer the child gave to the previous question. Through this interchange, the experimenter tries to understand the line of reasoning underlying the child's answers. A talented interviewer avoids biasing the child's answers by giving too much suggestion.

The following exchange between Piaget and a 5-year-old illustrates the clinical method:

Where does the dream come from? — *I think you sleep so well that you dream.* — Does it come from us or from outside? — *From outside.* — What do we dream with? — *I don't know.* — With the hands? . . . With nothing? — *Yes, with nothing.* — When you are in bed and you dream, where is the dream? — *In my bed, under the blanket. I don't really know. If it was in my stomach(!) the bones would be in the way and I shouldn't see it.* — Is the dream there when you sleep? — *Yes, it is in my bed beside me. . . .* Is the dream in your head? — *It is I that am in the dream: it isn't in my head(!). When you dream, you don't know you are in the bed. You know you are walking. You are in the dream. You are in bed, but you don't know you are. . . .* Where do dreams come from? — *I don't know. They happen.* — Where? — *In the room and then afterward they come up to the children. They come by themselves.* — You see the dream when you are in the room, but if I were in the room, too, should I see it? — *No, grownups (les Messieurs) don't ever dream. . . .* When the dream is in the room, is it near you? — *Yes, there!* (pointing to 30 cms. in front of his eyes).

[1926 (1929, pp. 97–98]*

In Piaget's later work, these interviews were often combined with the manipulation of objects by the experimenter or child. This was

---

*The references to Piaget's works in this chapter are to the publication dates of the original works, usually in French. The page numbers are those of the translations (given in parentheses).

especially likely when Piaget studied numerical and physical concepts or perceptual development. For example, Piaget might spread out a row of objects and ask whether the number had changed.

Infants, of course, cannot fruitfully be questioned about their thoughts. Piaget carefully observed his own infants as they went about their normal activities. At times he became a participant-observer by inventing little experiments on the spot, such as hiding a toy and observing whether the infant searched for it.

Because these verbal protocols and behavioral observations were seen through the eyes of Piaget the philosopher and theoretical biologist, their description became more and more abstract. Piaget saw general structures of thought in these varied, concrete behaviors. This process of abstraction, or generalization, is evident in his writings, which often have a high proportion of theoretical interpretation to actual observation.

One of the challenges to someone encountering Piaget's theory for the first time is to relate the many elusive, abstract features of the theory to the abundant specific behaviors found in each stage. For the moment the reader may simply have to have faith that the abstract and the concrete actually fit together somehow. Perhaps the best way to grasp the relationship between the abstract and the concrete is to swing back and forth between the two. Following this strategy, we now swing from the preceding abstract orientation to a description of specific stagelike changes, then swing back to a new set of abstract features: the mechanisms of change.

## DESCRIPTION OF THE STAGES

In the introductory chapter of this book, it was proposed that a developmental theory should both describe and explain development. The present section describes the prototypic Piagetian child making his way through the stages of cognitive development. The subsequent section tackles the questions of how and why this particular course of development occurs.

To understand each stage, we need to know not only where it came from, but also where it is going. Each stage holds both the fruits of the past and the seeds of the future. Here, then, is an overview of the stages, followed by a more detailed account. The ages listed with each stage are approximate because children vary somewhat in the ages at which they proceed through the stages.

1. *Sensorimotor period* (roughly birth to 2 years). The infant understands the world in terms of his overt, physical actions on that world. He moves from simple reflexes through several steps to an organized set of schemes (organized behaviors).

2. *Preoperational period* (roughly 2 to 7 years). No longer does the child simply make perceptual and motor adjustments to objects and events. He can now use symbols (mental images, words, gestures) to represent these objects and events. He uses these symbols in an increasingly organized and logical fashion.

3. *Concrete operational period* (roughly 7 to 11 years). The child acquires certain logical structures that allow him to perform various mental operations, which are internalized actions that can be reversed.

4. *Formal operational period* (roughly 11 to 15 years). Mental operations are no longer limited to concrete objects; they can be applied to purely verbal or logical statements, to the possible as well as the real, to the future as well as the present.

The following description of the stages of development should be prefaced by a word about Piaget's terminology. Although Piaget refers to "stages" of development, each of the four major stages is designated a "period," for example, the "sensorimotor period." When Piaget identifies substages within one of these four major periods, they are designated "stages."

## Sensorimotor Period (Roughly Birth to 2 Years)

In Piaget's view, a human starts life with a set of reflexes, a particular physical makeup unique to the human species, and inherited ways of interacting with the environment. These inherited ways of interacting refer to the tendency of thought to be organized and adapted to the environment. The thinking of even an Einstein has these humble beginnings. Although the infant knows almost nothing about the world, he has the potential to know everything. Indeed, one of Piaget's books on infancy is aptly titled *The Origins of Intelligence in Children* (1936).

We now trace the infant's construction of a model of the world by means of the sensory (perceptual) and motor (physical movement) systems. The infant progresses through six stages in the construction of a sensorimotor system of thought.

## *Stage 1: Modification of Reflexes*
## *(Roughly Birth to 1 Month)*

A newborn is a bundle of reflexes, or "wired-in" responses that are triggered by particular stimuli. Touch a newborn's lips and she sucks, prick her foot and her knee flexes, place a finger in her hand and she grasps it. As these reflexes are activated a number of times, they very gradually are modified. The infant adjusts them slightly to meet the requirements of slightly different circumstances. For example, the infant's mouth must search out the nipple from different angles on different occasions. In addition, the way the mouth and tongue fit around a hard, plastic rattle differs from the way they fit around a finger.

As an expanding number and type of objects serve as "grist" for the reflex, the category of "suckables" grows to include objects ranging from nipples to blankets to bars of the crib. However, at the same time that the infant is generalizing her sucking behavior to many objects, she is also increasing her discrimination between objects. A hungry infant never confuses a finger with a nipple. In a sense, she "recognizes" objects.

Behaviors such as sucking, grasping, and looking do not remain reflexes; they can be produced spontaneously. In fact, the baby sometimes sucks when there is nothing to suck. Piaget claims that there is an innate tendency for humans to exercise their skills. A baby sucks because she *can* suck. Sucking strengthens the sucking skill and leads to further sucking in a like-begets-like fashion.

In short, in stage 1, the baby strengthens, generalizes, and differentiates behaviors that began as reflexes. At this point, Piaget begins to use the term "scheme," which was introduced in the earlier section on structuralism. These schemes — organized patterns of behavior — continue to strengthen, generalize, and differentiate throughout the rest of the sensorimotor period. The infant is constructing a world of things to suck, grasp, look at, hit, feel, listen to, and so on. The primitive schemes of the first stage are a small, but significant step in this construction.

## Stage 2: Primary Circular Reactions
### (Roughly 1 to 4 Months)

The behaviors in stage 1 can be called schemes only in a very limited sense because there is so little modification of the reflex. In stage 2, there is widespread and rapid development of schemes because primary circular reactions can now occur. A circular reaction is a behavior that is repeated over and over again and thus becomes circular. By chance, the baby discovers an interesting result from some behavior and then attempts to recapture this result. As the behavior and its results are successfully repeated, it can be said that a "habit" is formed. These circular reactions are called "primary" because they involve response consequences that are centered on or around the infant's body rather than other objects.

Piaget observed many cases of primary circular reactions in his own infants. Consider the following example (the three numbers refer to the child's age in years, months, and days):

From 0;2(3) Laurent evidences a circular reaction which will become more definite and will constitute the beginning of systematic grasping; he scratches and tries to grasp, lets go, scratches and grasps again, etc. On 0;2(3) and 0;2(6) this can only be observed during the feeding. Laurent gently scratches his mother's bare shoulder. But beginning 0;2(7) the behavior becomes marked in the cradle itself. Laurent scratches the sheet which is folded over the blankets, then grasps it and holds it a moment, then lets it go, scratches it again and recommences without interruption. At 0;2(11) this play lasts a quarter of an hour at a time, several times during the day. At 0;2(12) he scratches and grasps my fist which I placed against the back of his right hand. He even succeeds in discriminating my bent finger and grasping it separately, holding it a few moments. At 0;2(14) and 0;2(16) I note how definitely the spontaneous grasping of the sheet reveals the characteristics of circular reaction — groping at first, then regular rhythmical activity (scratching, grasping, holding and letting go), and finally progressive loss of interest.

[1936 (1952, pp. 91–92)]

One primary circular reaction that is probably universal is thumb sucking. Although thumb sucking has occurred since (or before) birth, it now has developed into a systematic, coordinated behavior. The infant efficiently brings the thumb to the mouth and keeps it there. Other examples of primary circular reactions include active visual exploration of objects and listening to one's own vocalizations.

The performance of the circular reactions seems to be accompanied by feelings of pleasure. Piaget describes a baby who "played with his voice, not only through interest in the sound, but for 'functional pleasure,' laughing at his own power" [1945 (1951, p. 91)].

### Stage 3: Secondary Circular Reactions (Roughly 4 to 8 Months)

Infants are never content with the status quo; they continue to expand their world. This expansion is especially striking in the movement from primary to secondary circular reactions. Whereas primary circular reactions are centered around the infant's body, secondary circular reactions are oriented to the external world. By chance, the infant does something that leads to an interesting effect in the environment: he shakes a rattle, which produces a noise; he slaps a ball, which causes it to roll. In the previous stage, the shaking or slapping itself was of interest; now the environmental consequences are.

When the secondary circular reactions generalize, Piaget calls them "procedures for making interesting sights last." If kicking one's legs vigorously leads to a jiggling mobile a number of times, the infant may make this kicking procedure a part of his repertoire. On future occasions when an interesting movement occurs, he may make kicking movements in an attempt to sustain or recreate this movement. Sometimes these procedures produce the desired result; sometimes they do not. On one occasion, after watching, in fascination, his father drum on a tin box, 7-month-old Laurent first stares at it, then shakes his arm, raises himself, strikes his covers, and shakes his head in an attempt to capture the box—all to no avail!

One of Piaget's novel observations is the "motor recognition" that emerges during this stage:

> What happens, in effect, is that the child, confronted by objects or sights which habitually set in motion his secondary circular reactions, limits himself to outlining the customary movements instead of actually performing them. Everything takes place as though the child were satisfied

to recognize these objects or sights and to make a note of this recognition, but could not recognize them except by working, rather than thinking, the schema helpful to recognition.

[1936 (1952, pp. 185–186)]

For example, when Piaget's infant daughter, Lucienne, sees a doll that she has often swung in the past, she simply opens and closes her hands or shakes her legs; this is a reduced, effortless version of the original behavior.

During stages 2 and 3, the infant achieves some simple coordinations of his schemes. The integration of vision and grasping is especially useful for developing circular reactions. Now the infant can see an object, reach for it, and run through his repertoire of "things to do to objects." This coordination of the schemes of looking, grasping, sucking, hearing, and so forth continues throughout the sensorimotor period. In this way, the cognitive structures are becoming increasingly integrated and organized.

## Stage 4: Coordination of Secondary Schemes (Roughly 8 to 12 Months)

In this stage, the infant can combine his schemes in complex ways. In particular, planning and intentionality emerge. This new behavior sequence is made up of an instrumental (or means) behavior and a goal behavior. The infant knows what he wants and can use his skills to achieve that goal. He has differentiated between means and end. In contrast, in stage 3, the infant's discovery of interesting results was fortuitous; only *afterward* did the infant try to achieve the outcome again. A special feature of the means–end behavior found in stage 4 is that it is applied to *new* situations. The schemes are now mobile; they are freed from their original contexts and can be used at will to achieve a variety of goals.

Piaget relates various occasions on which he places his hand in front of a desirable matchbox. Whereas in stage 3 Laurent simply applied (unsuccessfully) his familiar grasping scheme toward the matchbox, in stage 4 he hits his father's hand (means) and grasps the box (end). Laurent has removed a barrier in order to achieve a goal.

In addition to coordinating schemes to remove barriers, the infant can now use objects as instruments to obtain a goal. A modern example is the infant who places his mother's hand on the television knob in order to see the dark screen come alive.

Another outcome of the differentiation between means and ends is the anticipation of events:

> At 0;9(16) . . . she likes the grape juice in a glass, but not the soup in a bowl. She watches her mother's activity. When the spoon comes out of the glass she opens her mouth wide, whereas when the spoon comes from the bowl, her mouth remains closed. Her mother tries to lead her to make a mistake by taking a spoon from the bowl and passing it by the glass before offering it to Jacqueline. But she is not fooled.
>
> *[1936 (1952, p. 249)]*

### Stage 5: Tertiary Circular Reactions
### (Roughly 12 to 18 Months)

In this stage, we see the infant scientist at work. The environment is his laboratory. He performs miniature experiments in which he deliberately varies an action in order to see how this variation affects the outcome. He exploits each object's potential. He seems to be asking, "Is there anything new about this object?" As in earlier circular reactions, there is repetition with variation.

Again Laurent thoughtfully provides us with a nice example:

> At 0;10(11) Laurent is lying on his back but nevertheless resumes his experiments of the day before. He grasps in succession a celluloid swan, a box, etc., stretches out his arm and lets them fall. He distinctly varies the positions of the fall. Sometimes he stretches out his arm vertically, sometimes he holds it obliquely, in front of or behind his eyes, etc. When the object falls in a new position (for example on his pillow), he lets it fall two or three times more on the same place, as though to study the spatial relation; then he modifies the situation. At a certain moment the swan falls near his mouth: now, he does not suck it (even though this object habitually serves this purpose), but drops it three times more while merely making the gesture of opening his mouth.
>
> *[1936 (1952, p. 269)]*

Through deliberate trial-and-error exploration, the infant is extending the means – end behavior of the previous stage to develop new means. He no longer simply coordinates old schemes. In fact, Piaget often characterizes stage 5 as "the discovery of new means through active experimentation." Examples of new means might include pulling a blanket to obtain an object resting on the blanket or positioning a long, thin object in such a way that it can be slipped through the bars of a crib.

## Stage 6: Invention of New Means Through Mental Combinations (Roughly 18 to 24 Months)

Stage 6 both closes the curtain on the sensorimotor period and raises it on the preoperational period. The achievements of one period always make it possible for the child to begin the next period. In stage 6, thought begins to go underground. Up to this time, the child has displayed his thinking to the world; now the overt is becoming covert. External exploration gives way to internal mental exploration. All of this is possible because the child now can use mental symbols to *represent* objects and events.

Let us see how this mental representation leads to a new way of solving problems:

> At 1;6(23) for the first time Lucienne plays with a doll carriage whose handle comes to the height of her face. She rolls it over the carpet by pushing it. When she comes against a wall, she pulls, walking backward. But as this position is not convenient for her, she pauses and without hesitation, goes to the other side to push the carriage again. She therefore found the procedure in one attempt, apparently through analogy to other situations but without training, apprenticeship, or chance.
>
> *[1936 (1952, p. 338)]*

This episode illustrates the critical features of stage 6 behavior:

1. The child abandons overt trial and error because it no longer is necessary.

2. She creates new solutions (means to an end) on the spot.

3. She manipulates mental images that correspond to (stand for, represent) external events.

The emergence of a mental symbol can be seen in what is perhaps the most stunning of Piaget's observations. Piaget has been playing a game with Lucienne at age 1 year, 4 months, in which he hides a watch chain inside an empty matchbox. Lucienne has attained the chain by applying old schemes — turning the box upside down so the contents spill out through the opening or, with a smaller opening, sliding her fingers into the slot to grasp the chain. (It should be noted that Lucienne has not observed her father sliding the box to change the size of the opening.) Then Piaget slips the chain through an even smaller opening, which, as Lucienne discovers, is too small to permit her fingers to reach the chain. Now we see the behavior of interest:

> She looks at the slit with great attention; then, several times in succession, she opens and shuts her mouth, at first slightly, then wider and wider! Apparently Lucienne understands the existence of a cavity subjacent to the slit and wishes to enlarge that cavity. The attempt at representation which she thus furnishes is expressed plastically, that is to say, due to inability to think out the situation in words or clear visual images she uses a simple motor indication as "signifier" or symbol.
>
> *[1936 (1952, p. 338)]*

When faced with a problem that past methods do not solve, Lucienne thinks through the problem, partly by means of movements of the mouth and partly by thinking. She is in transition to a true use of mental symbols. The movements of the mouth represent the idea of widening the opening of the matchbox.

One achievement of this stage is that an event that has been represented can be evoked at a later time. This absent event is reproduced in part, as seen in the following observation:

> At 1;4(3) J. had a visit from a little boy of 1;6, whom she used to see from time to time, and who, in the course of the afternoon got into a terrible temper. He screamed as he tried to get out of a play-pen and pushed it backwards, stamping his feet. J. stood watching him in amazement, never having witnessed such a scene before. The next day, she herself screamed in her play-pen and tried to move it, stamping her foot lightly several times in succession. The imitation of the whole scene was most striking. Had it been immediate, it would naturally not have involved representation, but coming as it did after an interval of more than twelve hours, it must have involved some representative or pre-representative element.
>
> *[1945 (1951, p. 63)]*

## Comment

The sensorimotor period has been presented in some detail because it provides a concrete illustration of the following general characteristics of all four periods:

1. The child learns about properties of objects and relations among them. In the sensorimotor period, the child achieves this knowledge through overt actions.

2. Cognitive structures become more tightly organized. The child coordinates schemes and applies them as solutions to new situations.

3. Behavior gradually becomes more intentional. The child differentiates between means and ends, invents new means, and applies them to new ends in new situations.

4. The self is gradually differentiated from the environment. The child discovers the boundaries of his own body and sees himself as one object in a world of objects.

If this book were devoted entirely to Piaget's theory, the next step would be to show how various important concepts develop as a result of the six stages of the sensorimotor period. Because we still have many theorists to meet, there is time only to hint at some of these developments. A description of these developments would not seem unfamiliar, however, because the concepts are simply extended applications of the general sensorimotor abilities of each stage already outlined.

Perhaps the most important concept acquired during the sensorimotor period is the notion of *object permanence*. This concept is the knowledge that there are entities that have a reality of their own, independent of the child's actions. Thus, an object continues to exist even when the child cannot see, hear, or feel it. Piaget proposes that the essence of the development of the object concept is that the child gradually comes to understand that his actions on the object are separate from the object itself. The assumption that objects exist even when not seen is without doubt one of the most basic assumptions in the adult's conception of a stable, predictable physical world. Briefly, according to Piaget, the concept develops as follows:

During the first few months of life, if an object disappears, the infant does not search for it (stages 1 and 2). Her behavior follows the rule "out of sight, out of mind."

Later, she searches if the object is only partially hidden or if she was doing something with the object when it disappeared (stage 3). However, she gives up easily if the object does not reappear quickly. She still thinks of the object as an extension of her actions on it.

Still later, as schemes are coordinated, the child has the skills needed to look for hidden objects (stage 4). However, she persists in searching in the place where she searched previously. Thus, when Piaget hides a toy parrot twice under a mattress to his daughter's left, then hides it to her right (as she watches), she immediately searches to the left — in the original hiding place. Piaget's interpretation of her persistence is that the child defines an object partly in terms of its position, as in the case of a "ball-under-the-sofa."

The next advance is that the child can appropriately search for an object, even if there are several displacements, but only if they are visible (stage 5). There is a problem with invisible displacements, as when Piaget puts a coin in his hand and moves it under a cushion, then under a coverlet, then out again.

However, in the final stage, Jacqueline continues to search for the coin because she now knows that it has to be somewhere (stage 6). She can represent the object mentally, so is not dependent on seeing, or otherwise acting on, the object. At last she understands that objects, including herself, are things that exist in and of themselves.

In addition to the object concept, Piaget traces the development of concepts of time, space, and causality. This should come as no surprise, given Piaget's interest in these classical philosophical problems of epistemology. The details of the sensorimotor evolution of these concepts can be found in Piaget's *Construction of Reality in the Child* (1937). The concepts of time, space, and causality are closely linked to the object concept because objects exist, move, and affect other objects in a spatiotemporal field. As in the case of the object concept, these concepts are variations on a (sensorimotor) theme by Piaget.

## Preoperational Period (Roughly 2 to 7 years)

Ending the first period and beginning the next can be likened to climbing a mountain, only to discover that it is merely a foothill to Mt. Everest. The achievements of the sensorimotor period, although monumental, are also preparation for what is to come. In a sense, the child starts all over again. What he has achieved in the realm of actions on the world is redeveloped, now in the realm of mental representations. He transfers notions about objects, relations, causality, space, and time to a new medium (mental representation) and a more highly organized structure.

### *Semiotic Function*

As we noted earlier, the emergence of mental representations in stage 6 of the sensorimotor period provides a bridge to the preoperational period. These mental representations are made possible by a more general developmental milestone: the *semiotic function,* or ability to use one object or event to stand for another. Stated more formally, a *signifier* evokes a *significate.* Words, gestures, objects, and mental images can serve as signifiers. A 4-year-old may use the word "airplane," a swooping hand, a mental picture of an airplane, or a toy airplane to stand for a real airplane.

There are precursors to the true use of signifiers. One precursor, which was mentioned in the description of stage 6, is imitation. Lucienne's solution to the problem of the watch chain in the matchbox illustrates the transition between overt behavior and a mental symbol. These reduced imitations become internal symbols during the course of development.

There are two types of signifiers: *symbols* and *signs.* Symbols bear some similarity to the objects or events they stand for. They have lingering traces of their origins in imitation. Symbols often appear in *symbolic play,* as when Jacqueline pretends that a cloth is a pillow and feigns sleep, laughing hard all the while.

In contrast to symbols, signs are arbitrarily related to certain events or objects. There is no relationship between the world "table" and the four-legged thing at which we sit, except that our language has assigned a relationship between them. This notion that words or other signs are arbitrarily assigned to objects is not easy for a child to grasp. Young children think that an object's name is as intrinsic to the object as are its color and form. When asked why spaghetti is called spaghetti, a young child may say that it looks like spaghetti and feels like spaghetti and tastes like spaghetti, so we call it spaghetti!

Representational thought has some obvious advantages over sensorimotor thought. It is faster and more mobile. It can deal with the past, present, and future in one grand sweep and can recombine its parts to create ideas that refer to nothing in reality (for example, monsters that go bump in the night). In contrast, Piaget describes sensorimotor intelligence as a motion picture in which the action is slowed down so that "all the pictures are seen in succession but without fusion, and so without the continuous vision necessary for understanding the whole" [1947 (1950, p. 121)].

It should be noted that Piaget does not hold the common view that the source of representational thought is the ability to use words. He believes that the opposite is true. The development of representational thought makes it possible to use words as well as other signifiers. Thus, thought is both prior to language and broader than language. Language is primarily a mode for expressing thought. Throughout development, thought is prior to language. For example, teaching a child to use the words "more," "taller," and "same" does not teach him the quantitative concepts underlying these utterances.

Although thinking is not dependent on language, language can aid cognitive development. Language can direct the child's attention to new objects or relationships in the environment, introduce him to conflicting points of view, and impart abstract information that is not easily acquired directly. Language is one of many tools available to the cognitive system.

## Characteristics of the Period

Although thinking through symbols and signs is a tremendous advance over sensorimotor thought, such thinking is limited in a number of ways. As the term *preoperational* suggests, children in this period have not yet acquired reversible mental operations, which characterize the thinking of the next period, called concrete operations.

In many ways, this period is a time of preparation for the next stage, and Piaget himself described preoperational children in terms of what they cannot do, rather than what they can do. However, he also identified a number of positive acquisitions such as identity, functions, and regulations, all described later. Even if one emphasizes deficits, it is important to keep in mind that it is an accomplishment even to reach the point at which these errors are made. The main characteristics of preoperational thought are egocentrism, rigidity of thought, semilogical reasoning, and limited social cognition.

1. *Egocentrism.* Egocentrism does not refer to selfishness or arrogance, and Piaget does not use it in a derogatory way. Rather, the term refers to (a) the incomplete differentiation of the self and the world, including other people, and (b) the tendency to perceive, understand, and interpret the world in terms of the self. One implication is that the child cannot take another person's perceptual or conceptual perspective. For example, the preoperational child does not realize that a person viewing a display from a position different from his own sees the display from a different perspective. A child holding a book upright points to a picture and asks, "What is this?" He is unaware that his mother, who is facing him, can see only the back of the book. Egocentrism makes it difficult to take the role or point of view of another person. This can be seen in a card game when a 5-year-old giggles upon receiving the "old maid" card. A 5-year-old does not perceive the need for a "poker face" as card-playing strategy.

Because the child cannot easily take another person's role, he makes little effort to tailor his speech to meet the needs of the listener. In fact, Piaget notes that the child "feels no desire to influence his hearer nor to tell him anything; not unlike a certain type of drawing-room conversation where everyone talks about himself and no one listens" [1923 (1926, p. 9)]. He may tell his mother that at a birthday party "he hit her with it," without bothering to explain to what "he," "her," and "it" refer. His account may also have an incorrect ordering of events, which makes it impossible for his mother to understand how "he cried" and "he blew out the candles" are related.

Egocentric speech is rampant in children's play groups. Children who apparently are talking together while playing in a group may actually be talking, but not necessarily together. Each child's remarks are unrelated to anyone else's. There is a collective monologue, of sorts, rather than a conversation. For example, one child's statement, "I think I saw Superman in a phonebooth yesterday," might be followed by "this sweater makes me itch" from another child.

Although the preoperational child is considered to be egocentric, he is less egocentric than he was in the sensorimotor period. Early sensorimotor functioning reflects a lack of differentiation between one's own actions and properties of objects. After the preoperational period, egocentrism continues to decline, but never disappears completely, even in adulthood.

2. *Rigidity of thought.* Piaget characterizes preoperational thought as frozen. One example is *centration*, the tendency to attend to or think about one salient feature of an object or event and ignore other features. If two identical containers have equal amounts of water and the contents of one container are poured into a taller, thinner container, the child centers on the heights of the liquids, while ignoring their widths. Consequently, he erroneously concludes that there is now more liquid because the water level is higher. Centration and egocentrism are similar in that they both reflect an inability to deal with several aspects of a situation at the same time and that they both cause a biased view of the world.

We also find a rigidity, or lack of flexibility, of thought in the tendency to *focus on states* rather than on the transformations linking the states. When faced with the task concerning quantity of liquid in the containers, the child thinks about the "before" and "after" states, but ignores the process of changing from A to B as the liquid is poured.

Perhaps the clearest example of the rigidity of thought is its *lack of reversibility*. The preoperational child cannot mentally reverse a series of events, transformations, or steps of reasoning. For example, he is unable to return the poured liquid to its original container mentally. His ability to internalize action is not yet complete because it is not bidirectional.

Toward the end of the preoperational period, we begin to see "the great thaw," as the child partially corrects the tendency of thought to be centrated, focused on states, and irreversible. We now see three positive achievements of the preoperational period: function, regulation, and identity.

A *function* is the notion that there is a covariation between factors, as expressed in the equation, $y = f(x)$. For example, the more one pulls a curtain, the farther a curtain opens. Or when the rope on a pulley is pulled, there is an increase in the length of one section of rope as the other section decreases in length. However, the child cannot yet work out the precise and quantitative nature of the relationship.

A *regulation* is a mental act that is partially decentered. Again using the test of liquid quantity, we find that the child switches back and forth between using liquid height and width to make his judgments about quantity. A glass may contain more than another glass because it has a higher water level, or it may contain less because it is thinner.

The third achievement, *identity*, is the notion that an object can change its appearance without changing its basic nature, or identity. Water may look different after it is poured from one container to another, but it is the same water. Putting on a Halloween mask does not change a person into a witch, contrary to the belief of younger children. Thinking has become less rigid because a concept can be maintained despite superficial physical changes.

3. *Semilogical reasoning.* As a young psychologist, Piaget questioned children about their beliefs concerning the world. These interviews revealed various fascinating characteristics of preoperational reasoning. The conversations provide many examples of egocentrism and rigidity of thought. We treat them separately because they demonstrate some specific, and somewhat surprising, properties of semilogical reasoning.

The following protocol illustrates several facets of semilogical reasoning in a 6-year-old child.

> How did the sun begin? — *It was when life began.* — Has there always been a sun? — *No.* — How did it begin? — *Because it knew that life had begun.* — What is it made of? — *Of fire.* — But how? — *Because there was fire up there.* — Where did the fire come from? — *From the sky.* — How was the fire made in the sky? — *It was lighted with a match.* — Where did it come from, this match? — *God threw it away.* . . . How did the moon begin? — *Because we began to be alive.* — What did that do? — *It made the moon get bigger.* — Is the moon alive? — *No . . . Yes.* — Why? — *Because we are alive.*
>
> [1926 (1929, pp. 258–259)]

The child tries to explain the mysterious natural events of everyday life. One solution is to explain natural events in terms of human behavior. The sun and moon, like people, are alive, are created by a humanlike action (a god lighting a match) and are tied to human activities (the moon began because people began to exist). Similarly, a preoperational child may assert that snow is made for children to play in and clouds move because they are pulled when people walk.

Thoughts are often linked together in a loose way rather than in a logical relationship. For example, one afternoon when Lucienne had no nap, she reasoned that it could not be afternoon because she had not had her nap. Or a child might say that his friend fell down because he got hurt. The child reasons from the particular to the particular.

4. *Limited social cognition.* Piaget argues that his description of thought applies to social objects and events as well as physical ones. Our description of preoperational thought hints at this parallel between the physical and the social realms. Examples are deficits in role taking and communication resulting from egocentrism, confusions between natural events and human events, and notions about the identity of persons when physical appearances are changed. In addition, Piaget specifically examines social thought in his work on moral judgments. A preoperational child judges the wrongness of an act according to external variables, such as how much damage was done and whether the act was punished. He ignores internal variables, such as the person's intentions. Thus, the boy who breaks fifteen cups while trying to help his mother set the table is considered to be more guilty than the boy who breaks only one cup while trying to steal cookies from the cabinet.

## Concrete Operational Period (Roughly 7 to 11 Years)

Piaget sometimes combines ages 2 to 11 and labels this period as "preparation for and achievement of concrete operations." Despite the considerable accomplishments in the preoperational period, in many ways the period is simply preparation for the pinnacle of cognitive development: the operation. Regulations, functions, and identities turn into operations as they become more complete, differentiated, quantitative, and stable. Let us now turn to these operations.

An *operation* is an internalized action that is part of an organized structure. With the ability to use these operations, or concepts, the child's representations are no longer isolated or simply juxtaposed, as in the preoperational period. They are brought to life.

We can most easily see operations at work in Piaget's famous *conservation* task, which we described as the problem of liquid quantity. Let us consider this task in more detail. The child sees two identical containers equally filled with water and judges them to contain the same amount of water. As the child watches, one container is poured into a container with different dimensions or into several small containers. A "nonconserver" claims that the amount has changed, usually because the water level has changed. Since the water rises higher in a taller, thinner container, the child concludes that the amount has increased. In contrast, a "conserver" believes that the amount has not changed. He realizes that quantity remains the same despite changes in appearance. Piaget usually requires the child to give a logical explanation for this judgment before he considers the child to be a true conserver.

Both the nonconserver and the conserver have a basis for their answers. Both think their conclusions are quite reasonable. In fact, if a tester happens to test the same child twice — once when the child is a nonconserver and later when she is a conserver — he may face the child's scorn on both occasions. The child on both occasions is likely to think that the tester is dumb to ask a question when the "correct" answer is so obvious!

Conservation is an important concept because it gives a certain stability to the physical world. In addition, Piaget assigns a great deal of importance to the conservation task because it reveals the presence or absence of mental operations. It is a diagnostic tool that probes the cognitive structures. Piaget asserts that a child cannot conserve unless he has certain mental operations. These operations can be illustrated by the explanations the children give:

"If you pour it back where it was, they will have the same amount." (*reversibility*)

"The water goes up higher, but the glass is thinner." (*compensation*)

"You didn't add any water or take any away." (*addition – subtraction*)

The preoperational child who lacks these operations centers on states, especially the water level.

Other examples of operations are the common mathematical operations of multiplying, dividing, ordering (greater than, less than), and substituting (one thing equals another thing). Each operation is related to and obtains its meaning from the entire structure of which it is a part. Thus, addition is coordinated with subtraction, multiplication, and division to form a system of mental actions. Piaget's interest in logic and mathematics appears in his attempt to describe these systems of operations in terms of logicomathematical structures. These structures serve as a model for characterizing concrete operational thought. (We examine Piaget's use of this model when we discuss the formal aspects of the theory.)

The various operations are applied to a wide variety of physical and social situations, of which only a few can be described here. For example, various properties are conserved in addition to liquid quantity. The number of objects in a collection remains the same when they are spread out; the total length of a stick remains the same if the stick is pushed ahead of another stick; and the weight of clay remains the same if the clay is broken into pieces.

Operations are evident in another basic acquisition: *class inclusion.* The experimenter shows the child 20 wooden beads, 17 of them brown and 3 white. He asks whether the child could make a longer necklace with the brown beads or the wooden beads. The preoperational child claims that there are more brown beads than wooden beads. She can deal only with the parts (brown or white beads) or the whole (wooden beads), but not with both of them simultaneously. She does not understand that the parts and the whole are reversible. In contrast, the concrete operational child has the underlying operations necessary to derive the correct answer.

Operations apply not only to classes but also to *relations.* If a concrete operational child knows that John is taller than Bill, and Bill is taller than Henry, she can infer that John has to be taller than Henry. In addition, she can order a row of dolls according to height and give the dolls sticks ordered according to length.

Operations are also applied to *temporal-spatial representations.* For example, a preoperational child draws liquid in a container in such a way that it remains parallel to the base or a side (as in Figure 1.1). Her perceptions are influenced by the immediate surroundings. In contrast, a concrete operational child keeps the liquid parallel to the larger context, the surface of the earth.

Turning to the social realm, we see that the child is overcoming many of the limitations in her reasoning about the social world. She is less egocentric, but sometimes still has difficulties with role taking and communication. She is beginning to take intentions into account in her

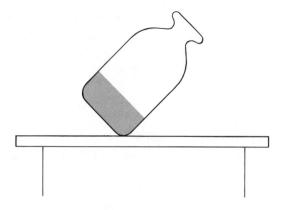

**FIGURE 1-1** ■ *A typical error on the water-level problem occurs during the preoperational period.*

moral judgments. She is increasingly aware of the subtle social relationships in the family, peer group, and larger society.

This list of acquisitions could continue to the end of this book, but the examples we have considered are representative. Two observations about these acquisitions should be kept in mind. First, the various concepts or operations do not develop at the same time. In fact, some concepts, such as conservation of weight, often do not appear until near the end of the period. Second, each cognitive acquisition develops over a period of time. At first, it is transitional in nature and is demonstrated only part of the time. It gradually strengthens, stabilizes, and generalizes to a variety of situations.

We have seen the child move from an understanding of the world based on action schemes, to one based on representations, to one based on internalized, organized operations. Thought now is decentered rather than centered, dynamic rather than static, and reversible rather than irreversible. For the first time, the lawful nature of the world seems to be reflected in a logical system of thought. Thought is in tune, in equilibrium, with the environment. However, the concrete operations are still "concrete." They can be applied only to concrete objects — present or mentally represented. They deal with what "is" rather than what "could be." The final step is to apply the operations to purely verbal or logical statements and to the possible as well as the actual. This story unfolds as we turn to formal operations.

## Formal Operational Period (Roughly 11 to 15 Years)

During the concrete operational period, mental operations are applied to objects and events. The child classifies them, orders them, and reverses them. During formal operations, the adolescent carries concrete operations one step further. He can take the results of these concrete operations and generate hypotheses (propositions, statements) about their logical relationships. Thus, we now have operations on operations: thought has become truly logical, abstract, and hypothetical.

Formal operational thought resembles the kind of thinking we often call the scientific method. The child formulates a hypothesis about a present or potential event and tests this hypothesis against reality. If necessary, he can generate all possible outcomes or all possible combinations at the beginning. Piaget typically presents a problem from physics or chemistry and observes how the adolescent goes about solving it. The problem-solving process, rather than the correct answer itself, is what is of interest.

A prototypic task is the pendulum problem. An adolescent observes an object hanging from a string and attempts to discover what determines how fast the object swings. He is shown how to vary the length of the string, the height from which the pendulum is released, the force of the push on the pendulum, and the weight of the object. One or several of these variables could control the speed of the swing. A concrete operational child experiments with the variables and may even arrive at the correct answer, but his approach is haphazard; he has no overall plan. He does not vary one factor while holding the other factors constant. For example, he may compare a long, light pendulum with a short, heavy one and conclude that both factors are important. In fact, the length of the string is the main determinant of the rate of oscillation.

In contrast to the concrete operational child, the formal operational adolescent imagines all possible determinants of the rate of oscillation before he begins, systematically varies the factors one by one, observes the results correctly, keeps track of the results, and draws the appropriate conclusions (identifies which factor controls the rate of oscillation). He has systematically isolated the critical factor and dealt all the while with propositions, not objects. By testing predictions from each hypothesis, he has demonstrated hypotheticodeductive thought. More generally, as Flavell expresses it, "Reality is thus conceived as a special subset within the totality of things which the data would admit as hypotheses; it is seen as the 'is' portion of a 'might be' totality, the portion it is the subject's job to discover" (1963, pp. 204–205).

Piaget posed several other problems.

1. Determine which mixture of five colorless liquids produces a yellow color.

2. Discover which variables (for example, weight, length, types of material) cause a rod suspended over water to bend down far enough to touch the water.

3. Discover and state the law governing the relationship between the angle at which a billiard ball hits the table wall and the angle of its rebound.

4. Solve a geometric proof.

5. Discover proportional relationships (for example, 16 is to 4 as 4 is to 1).

6. Evaluate syllogisms, such as "All children hate spinach; girls are children; therefore, girls hate spinach."

It should be noted that direct instruction in scientific thought is not necessary for the development of formal operations. Years of common, unremarkable experiences contribute to this achievement. As Einstein remarked: "The whole of science is nothing more than a refinement of everyday thinking."

As in the concrete operational period, Piaget applies logicomathematical models to the child's thought. He identifies 16 underlying mental operations that he believes are necessary for solving the various problems he presents to adolescents. This *system of 16 binary operations* forms a tightly knit organization of logical relations. Although his complex model is beyond the scope of this chapter, we look at two examples: conjunction and disjunction. *Conjunction* is an operation that refers to the co-occurrence of $x$ and $y$. Another operation is *disjunction*, which refers to three possible outcomes: $x$ and $y$, $x$ and *not y*, and $y$ and *not x*. In the problem of discovering what causes rods to bend, we consider two of many possible outcomes: (1) great length, great bending (conjunction) and (2) great length, great bending; short length, great bending; great length, little bending (disjunction).

In addition to the binary operations, a system of rules for manipulating the logical relations identified by the binary operations is included in Piaget's logical model. For example, in a weight-balance problem, an imbalance can be negated by subtracting the extra weight from the heavier side or adding more weight to the lighter side.

The ability to consider abstract ideas, the future, and various possibilities is evident in the adolescent's social world. She dreams about her future and imagines herself in various occupational and social roles. She may experiment with some of these roles just as she experiments with hypotheses about physical events. She is concerned with the world of ideas. In sessions with friends, she debates various moral and political issues, such as whether wars can ever be moral, whether abortions should be legal, whether there are basic inalienable human rights, and what an ideal community would be like. She can consider these issues from a number of different perspectives and see how the issues are related to a larger set of social relationships. However, there is still a lingering egocentrism. The adolescent is impressed with the power of thought and naively underestimates the practical problems involved in achieving an ideal future for herself or for society. She feels that the sheer force of her logic will move mountains. Piaget notes that this starry-eyed egocentrism is squelched when the adolescent undertakes her first real job!

One further difference between concrete and formal operational thought has implications for both social and physical development. The adolescent can reflect on her own thinking (and that of others). For example, she can think about propositions, which are thoughts. Or, in the social realm, we find the following line of thought: "He's thinking that I'm thinking that he's thinking about her."

By achieving formal operations, the adolescent completes her cognitive structures. The various concrete operational logical systems have been combined to create a single, tightly organized system of thought —a unified whole. Thought is logical, abstract, and flexible. Thinking continues to develop throughout adulthood as the formal operations are applied to more and more content areas and situations. Egocentrism continues to decline as the person broadens her experiences in the world of work and social relationships. However, these changes after age 15 entail a change not in the structure of thought but only in its content and stability.

## An Overview

Now that we have reached the height of Piaget's theory, it would be well to look back over our climb. Perhaps the best way to highlight the differences between periods is to see how a typical child in each period would understand several aspects of reality. First, what is an "object" for a child in each stage? During the sensorimotor period, an object that at first is simply a stimulus for feeding a reflex becomes something on which one can act. Then an object becomes an independently existing entity that is separate from one's actions and can be mentally represented. For a preoperational child, an object can represent other objects, can undergo physical changes while maintaining its identity (if not its amount), and can be joined with other objects to form a class of objects. During the period of concrete operations, various operations manipulate the representation of an object; for example, any changes in the object can be reversed, and the object can be fit into a series of objects ordered according to some dimension. Finally, during the period of formal operations, higher-order operations allow further mental manipulations of the representation of the object. All the object's possibilities can be examined scientifically.

Another way of slicing the periods vertically is to consider how a child in each period would attack a specific problem. Consider what would happen if we gave a child in each stage a tub of water and various small objects of various densities, sizes, weights, shapes, and colors. An infant would immediately splash, throw the objects, push the objects to the bottom of the tub, and probably attempt to eat the objects. Toward the end of the sensorimotor period, the child might drop the objects from various heights and note that the bigger, heavier objects make bigger splashes than do the smaller, lighter objects. He might also notice that some objects sink, while others do not. A preoperational child might imagine that the objects are boats or fish. He would notice that some objects float, while others sink, but would be content to change his reasons from case to case. He might claim that one object floats because it is little, another because it is dry, another because it is a boat, and so on. The concrete operational child is bothered by inconsistencies that did not bother him in the previous stage, such as the fact that some small objects sink, while other small objects float. He makes comparisons between objects, but they are neither systematic nor exhaustive. For example, he does not hold their amounts constant while varying their weights. However, he does develop several categories of "sinkability," for example, always floats (light weight), always sinks (heavy), and sinks or floats depending on the circumstances (small objects, lids). The formal operational adolescent has both a plan and the necessary operations to solve the problem. He systematically varies the factors to determine their influence and uses the results to test his hypotheses. He knows that density is the proportion of weight to volume and that the relative density of the object to the water is the critical factor. The adolescent is able to form a proportion made up of two other proportions: the density for the objects and for the water. These are operations on operations. This general law allows one to predict whether any particular object will sink or float.

## OTHER DEVELOPMENTAL CHANGES

Although we have carefully made our way through a wide range of cognitive skills and concepts, we have nearly ignored two traditional topics in the field of cognitive psychology: perception and memory. Our necessarily brief coverage of perception and memory should not imply that Piaget considers them unimportant. He and his coworkers produced a substantial body of work on both topics. The perception book is titled *The Mechanisms of Perception* (1961), and much of the memory work can be found in *Memory and Intelligence* (Piaget and Inhelder, 1968).

### Perception

Flavell (1963) suggests that Piaget's scholarly "major" is intelligence and his "minor" is perception. We cover this minor separately, rather

rather than in the section describing stages, because its developments do not seem to proceed in a qualitative, stagelike manner. Perceptual, compared with cognitive, development seems to be a more continuous, quantitative process. Piaget makes a sharp distinction between perception and cognition in terms of what each can achieve. The most advanced level of perception allows the semireversible regulations we saw in the preoperational period. Perception can never achieve the reversible operations eventually developed by the cognitive structures. It follows, then, that perception can never give certainty; it can give only approximations. Furthermore, perception always remains a subsystem of intellectual structures. Consequently, its functioning is always influenced by the intellectual structures.

Most of Piaget's work focuses on a few tasks such as visual illusions and the estimation of lengths of lines or sizes of objects. Using these tasks, Piaget finds developmental changes in perception as the child becomes more active in his perceptual processing and more advanced cognitively. Some of the perceptual errors resulting from centration on one part of the stimulus are corrected as the child explores more of the stimulus; for example, Piaget proposed that perceptual centration on a line causes overestimation of its length, an error that decreases during development as the child scans other parts of the array as well. Much of the published work on perception is presented in a precise, mathematical form, unlike the looser reports of most of Piaget's work. In fact, Wohlwill (1960) speaks of "two Piagets," one for perception and one for cognition.

Piaget's work on the development of perception contrasts with most contemporary approaches to this topic. For example, later in this volume, we see that Gibson stresses the child's growing ability to detect differences between stimuli. Both Gibson and Piaget, however, place great importance on the active nature of the perceiver.

## Memory

Perhaps Piaget's most dramatic claims stem from his work on memory. Consider the following typical experiment by Piaget and Inhelder (1968). They showed children an array of 10 sticks of various sizes that were ordered according to size. A week later they asked the children to draw from memory the array of sticks they had seen. Developmental differences emerged. In general, 3- and 4-year-olds lined up a few sticks having the same length. The 5- and 6-year-olds tended to draw some tall and some short sticks. By 7 years of age, most children could draw the original array correctly. Piaget and Inhelder concluded that the children had processed and interpreted the original array in terms of their present understanding of ordered relations. Only when this understanding is fully achieved can the child accurately remember the array. Thus, memory reflects and depends on the entire cognitive structure. Memory is active understanding rather than a static, passive state.

Although this is an interesting set of results, it is less surprising than that found 6 months later when the children returned. Although the children were not shown the sticks again, this time 75 percent of the children drew arrays that were more advanced cognitively than those they had produced 6 months earlier. For example, a child who originally lined up three tall sticks of the same height and three short sticks of the same height later made a row of three tall sticks, three medium-size sticks, and three short sticks. Piaget's interpretation is that such improvements are reasonable if one assumes that the children have developed cognitively during those 6 months. If the child's cognitive structures are expressed in his memory, then changes in these structures should produce changes in memory.* Note that improvement in memory over time is the *opposite* of what one would expect from most theories of memory or from common sense. The typical view is that a memory trace fades over time or its recall is blocked by newer memories.

Piaget's claim that memory is not always reliable is seen in the following intriguing account of a memory from his second year of life:

> I was sitting in my pram, which my nurse was pushing in the Champs Elysées, when a man tried to kidnap me. I was held in by the strap fastened around me while my nurse bravely tried to stand between me and the thief. She received various scratches, and I can still see vaguely those on her face.
>
> *[1945 (1951, p. 188)]*

---

*It should be mentioned that there are many methodological problems involved in this type of study. Furthermore, other researchers have not always replicated Piaget's results (see Liben, 1977, for a review).

When Piaget was 15, his parents received a letter from the nurse shortly after she had joined a religious order. She said she wanted to return the watch that had been given to her as a reward for protecting little Jean from the kidnapper. The truth was that she had made up the story and had even faked the scratches that Piaget so vividly "remembered"! Piaget believes that what he remembered was a visual memory that he created from the story his parents had told him as a child.

In addition to studying memory performance, Piaget examined children's concepts of memory. This topic was rediscovered by American and English psychologists 50 years later and labeled "metamemory," which is described in Chapter 4. A sample of Piaget's work is the following interview with an 8-year-old innatist:

> *Memory is something in the head which makes us think.* — What do you think this memory is like? — *It is a little square of skin, rather oval, and inside there are stories (les histories).* — What are they like? — *They are written on the flesh.* — What with? — *Pencil.* — Who wrote them? — *God, before I was born, he put them there.*

> [1926 (1929, p. 52)]

## MECHANISMS OF DEVELOPMENT

The previous two sections described the stages of cognitive development and the development of perception and memory. We now turn to Piaget's explanation of the development through those stages. In other words, by what processes does the child's thinking progress? What are the rules of transition from step to step? Our attempt to answer these questions both expands our coverage of Piaget's theory and integrates the earlier sections that oriented us to the theory and described developmental changes. The abstract and the specific ultimately do fit together — at least for Piaget.

Emphasizing the grand stages, which span several years each, can make us forget that thought actually develops in the moment-to-moment, everyday encounters between the child and her environment. Stagelike changes ultimately are due to millions of these minidevelopments. An adequate theory of cognitive development must explain these small, but significant steps.

In Piaget's theory, these small steps are spurred by certain functional invariants. The *functional invariants* are intellectual functions that do not change during development. The two basic functional invariants are organization and adaptation. In yet another tie to biology, these invariants are also found in physiological activities. In both physiological and intellectual functioning, there are certain abstract properties (functional invariants) that define the relationship between the organism and the environment. These functional invariants are part of the general heredity of living organisms. We are born with tendencies to organize our thinking into structures and to adapt to our environment. With apologies to Descartes, it could be said that "I am, therefore I think."

## Cognitive Organization

Cognitive *organization* refers to the tendency for thought to consist of systems whose parts are integrated to form a whole. These systems, in turn, are coordinated; there are interrelationships among cognitive activities. The mind is not a grab bag of facts. Rather, it is a coherent view of the world. This view becomes more and more coherent and interrelated as the child develops. For example, the young infant has separate structures for sucking objects and for grasping them. Only later are these two structures organized into a higher-order structure that allows coordinated reaching for an object and bringing it to the mouth to suck.

Development through the stages involves changes in the nature of cognitive organization as the structures of thought change from stage to stage. As development proceeds, thought may be organized into schemes, regulations (partial reversibility), functions, concrete operations, or formal operations. Thus, the infant's sucking on a toy and Einstein's insights into relativity both reflect cognitive organization. In principle, one could trace a line of development from the former to the latter.

Again, Piaget sees parallels between psychological and physical activity. The human body is composed of systems, such as the digestive system, circulatory system, and nervous system. Each is organized within itself and interacts with other systems. A change in one system has repercussions for other systems. For example, digesting a meal changes not only the temporary state of the digestive system but also the flow of blood and body temperature.

## Cognitive Adaptation

We do not live to think, but, on the contrary, we think in order that we may succeed in surviving.

*[José Ortega y Gassett]*

The other basic functional invariant, cognitive *adaptation,* refers to the interaction between the organism and the environment. Piaget claims that all organisms have an innate tendency to adapt to the environment. Intelligent behavior is behavior that is appropriate to the demands of the environment. The following passage by Piaget expresses the close relationship between adaptation and organization:

> Organization is inseparable from adaptation: They are two complementary processes of a single mechanism, the first being the internal aspect of the cycle of which adaptation constitutes the external aspect. . . . The "accord of thought with things" and the "accord of thought with itself" express this dual functional invariant of adaptation and organization. These two aspects of thought are indissociable: It is by adapting to things that thought organizes itself and it is by organizing itself that it structures things.

> *[1936 (1952, pp. 7–8)]*

Adaptation involves two complementary processes: assimilation and accommodation. *Assimilation* is the process of fitting reality into one's current cognitive organization. In every cognitive encounter with objects or events, there is a degree of "bending" or distorting of experience as a person attempts to incorporate, understand, or interpret this experience. In other words, the person is applying what he knows in order to understand properties of objects and events as well as relationships between properties and events.

The four types of assimilation occur in all the periods and stages, but they are observed most easily in the sensorimotor period:

1. *Reproductive (or functional) assimilation.* The infant exercises his schemes by repeating them again and again. Consequently, they become stronger.

2. *Generalizing assimilation.* The range of stimuli that can be assimilated to a scheme increases.

3. *Recognitory assimilation.* Various objects are differentiated even as the schemes generalize. The infant "recognizes" an object when he assimilates it appropriately; he sucks a nipple when he is hungry and sucks a rattle when he is full.

4. *Mutual assimilation of schemes.* Schemes can assimilate each other (become coordinated) to form a larger, more organized scheme.

We can see these four kinds of assimilation in the sucking scheme. The baby tends to suck repeatedly (*reproduction*) his fingers, nipples, blankets, and toys (*generalization*) but sucks each one in a slightly different way (*recognition*) and often combines sucking with watching objects, reaching for them, grasping them, and bringing them to his mouth (*coordination*).

*Accommodation* is the other side of the coin. This term refers to adjustments in cognitive organization that result from the demands of reality. Every object or event has special characteristics that must be taken into account sooner or later. In a sense, accommodation occurs because the current structures have failed to interpret a particular object or event satisfactorily. The resulting reorganization of thought leads to a different and more satisfactory assimilation of the experience. A particular stimulus is never again experienced in quite the same way. As Oliver Wendell Holmes tells us: "Man's mind stretched to a new idea never goes back to its original dimensions."

Assimilation and accommodation are closely intertwined in every cognitive activity from birth to death. Attempts to assimilate reality necessarily involve slight changes in the cognitive structures as these adjust to the new elements. Assimilation and accommodation are so related, in fact, that Piaget sometimes defines adaptation as an equilibrium between assimilation and accommodation. In a state of equilibrium, neither assimilation nor accommodation dominates.

In true Piagetian style, both a biological example and a psychological example are needed. In the biological realm, food is assimilated into the body as it is changed into a form the body can use. As Piaget expresses it, "A rabbit that eats a cabbage doesn't become a cabbage; it's a cabbage that becomes rabbit—that's assimilation" (Bringuier, 1980, p. 42). The digestive system accommodates to food by adjusting the mouth opening, chewing, secreting digestive juices, contracting the muscles of the stomach, and so on. Thus, the digestive system both changes and is changed by an environmental event: the presentation of food.

In the psychological realm, consider the infant who has happened onto a sheet of newspaper for the first time. In an attempt to make sense out of this new experience, the infant runs through her repertoire of actions on objects. She applies her current structures (habitual patterns of behavior). She grasps the paper, hits it, sucks it, turns it over, shakes it, puts it over her head, and so on, in her attempts to fit this new object into something she already knows. However, a newspaper has certain characteristics foreign to her existing schemes. She is forced to stretch or reorganize (accommodate) these schemes in small ways. Her ideas about the way things sound when they are shaken must be altered to include the rustle of a newspaper. Similarly, the light weight and the new feel and sight make further demands on her comprehension of the world.

Most of the characteristics to be assimilated and accommodated to in our example are at least related to previous experiences, but some characteristics (for example, ripping the paper) may be quite foreign — and startling. These varying degrees of discrepancy between current schemes and the experience at hand raise the issue of what the limitations are to accommodation. Piaget's answer is that only moderately discrepant events or characteristics can be accommodated to; great leaps are not possible. If reality is too different from the person's current level of understanding, she cannot bridge the gap. There can never be radical departures from the old. Thus, development necessarily proceeds in small steps.

To illustrate this gradual, continual development, consider what would happen if children of various ages were given a metal magnet for the first time. The 6-month-old might accommodate to the unfamiliar metallic taste, the peculiar (horseshoe) shape, and the sound of the magnet being dropped. However, he cannot accommodate such features as magnetic properties. The 3-year-old, if given an assortment of objects, might accommodate to the fact that some of the objects cling to the magnet and might entertain explanations such as "stickiness" and "wanting to stay together." At 9 years, the child might hypothesize that only objects with certain characteristics are attracted to the magnet and might test out the conditions in which magnetism occurs — through glass, water, and certain distances. Only in adolescence could the child accommodate by formulating an abstract theory of magnetism and simultaneously consider all of the variables involved, such as the size and shape of the magnet and the distance from the object. Thus, accommodation always occurs in small steps and is relative to the present cognitive level. Infants do not accommodate to the property of magnetism.

In summary, the functional invariants of assimilation and accommodation are simultaneously present in every act and stimulate cognitive development. Attempts to apply one's current intellectual structures typically are only partially successful because most encounters with the environment are new in some way. As a result of this failure to "understand" the object or event, minor cognitive adjustments or accommodations are made. These push the child to a slightly more advanced cognitive level. She is one step closer to reality. However, this new level of understanding makes the child aware of other discrepancies in experience, and again assimilation presents new elements and again accommodation occurs. Each accommodation makes new accommodations possible in the future. This spiral continues in our moment-to-moment encounters with the environment throughout development.

## Cognitive Equilibration

The two basic functional invariants, organization and adaptation, imply a third functional invariant: equilibration. In Piaget's view, every organism strives toward *equilibrium* with the environment and equilibrium within itself (among cognitive elements). When assimilation and accommodation are in balanced coordination so that neither one is dominant, equilibrium is achieved. This balance is achieved through the development of organized structures that provide ways of interacting with the world. A change in either the organism or the environment leads to a state of disequilibrium, which must be corrected. It should be clear from other parts of Piagetian theory that equilibrium is dynamic rather than static. There is constant activity, but there is a balance, a pattern, to this activity. Equilibration has been likened to "the self-regulatory processes which keep missiles on target despite changes in the world outside such as the movement of their prey" (Meadows, 1983, p. 10).

Piaget often uses the liquid-conservation task to illustrate the equilibration process. The child proceeds through four steps:

1. Centering on the heights of the liquids.

2. Centering on the widths of the liquids and eventually switching back and forth between heights and widths.

3. Considering heights and widths at the same time.

4. Applying mental operations such as compensation of height and width, which lead the child to assert that the amount is conserved.

In this final step, the child achieves equilibrium by bringing several pieces of information into balance. His interaction with the world is no longer distorted by centration.

Equilibration, while one of the most important concepts in the theory, is probably also the most difficult and evasive. Part of the difficulty may lie in the fact that equilibration can refer to several spans of time, ranging from a fraction of a second to a number of years. In each case, there is a period of equilibrium, followed by a state of disequilibrium, followed by equilibration, which leads again to equilibrium.

Piaget seems to have at least three spans of time in mind when he applies the notion of equilibrium.

1. The moment-to-moment equilibration process occurs as assimilation and accommodation operate in the course of adaptation. Temporary disequilibrium occurs when the child encounters new properties of objects that do not fit into his present cognitive structures. Once the assimilation–accommodation process occurs and discrepancies are resolved, equilibrium is once again achieved. Assimilation and accommodation are brought into balance once again. At this level, the equilibration process is continually operating in the child's daily activities, no matter how mundane and specific.

2. Equilibration refers to moving toward the final level of achievement of each period or stage. A child enters a new period in a state of relative disequilibrium because the new cognitive organization is in the process of formation and therefore is incomplete and unstable. By the

end of this new period, the child has achieved equilibrium with respect to the structures of the period. For example, at the end of the sensorimotor period, a child is in equilibrium with the environment in terms of action schemes, but not in terms of operations. Each period achieves a different kind of equilibrium state. Equilibrium is reachieved in each period at a higher and higher level of abstraction.

3. The entire course of cognitive development can be seen as a process of equilibration as the child proceeds through increasingly "better" forms of equilibrium. The most complete equilibrium is achieved when formal operations bring fully reversible and abstract thought. Piaget sees a directionality to development toward a generalized, mobile, stable set of relations between the subject and the object. The earlier states of equilibrium, because they are incomplete, inevitably break down at some point. In a sense, each period or stage eventually self-destructs.

For Piaget, equilibration is the grand process that puts together all of the elements of development. Equilibration integrates and regulates the other three main factors of development: physical maturation, experience with the physical environment, and the influence of the social environment. All of these factors together propel the child through the stages. These factors are stage-independent forces that make cognitive development possible.

## Comment

Perhaps the best way to summarize this section on mechanisms of development is to relate it to the earlier sections of this chapter. Knowledge of the world develops through a series of discrete states of equilibrium (stages) between the organism and the environment. This is the essence of Piaget's genetic epistemology. Mental structures, in equilibrium, are acquired as the organism interacts with objects in an organized way. Here we see Piaget's structuralism. In the innate tendencies toward organization and adaptation (assimilation and accommodation), we see Piaget the biologist. Finally, the particular stages that characterize human cognitive development are an inevitable outcome, given the nature of the human organism (its physical structures and cognitive functions) and the nature of the environment.

## POSITION ON DEVELOPMENTAL ISSUES

The introductory chapter identified four basic developmental issues on which each theorist takes a stand. Using these issues, we can view Piaget's theory from a new perspective. The issues also provide a means for cutting across the diverse theories covered in this volume.

### Human Nature

Piaget's world view clearly fits into the organismic rather than the mechanistic view. He posits an inherently active organism. The child tirelessly explores, hypothesizes, tests, and evaluates; he does this either overtly (particularly in the sensorimotor period) or covertly (as in the manipulation of symbols, concrete operations, and formal operations).

No external motivation is necessary. The motivation for this activity is intrinsic to the organism. Schemes are used simply because they exist. Once activated, they tend to be repeated. In other words, "to be is to do." The Piagetian child is a self-regulating, organized whole as he strives to maintain an equilibrium within himself and with the environment. He corrects any cognitive imbalance to the extent he is capable. The tendencies toward inherent activity and self-regulation produce an organism that is constantly changing.

Finally, the organismic world view can be seen in the fact that the parts can be understood only in terms of the whole. Any one behavior, scheme, or operation is influenced by and derives its meaning from the whole structure. The same behavior (for example, a child swinging a pendulum) obviously has a different meaning when observed in a 2-year-old than in a 12-year-old.

### Qualitative Versus Quantitative Development

Although Piaget sees both qualitative and quantitative changes, he emphasizes the qualitative changes that occur when the overall cognitive structure changes. These structural changes occur, of course, when the child moves from period to period or from stage to stage. Just as the colored plastic fragments rearrange themselves when a kaleidoscope is turned, so does the organization of thought change to form new patterns as the child develops.

In contrast to qualitative change, quantitative changes occur as schemes, operations, or other cognitive skills become stronger, more easily activated, more efficient, and more consistent. One could also say that there is quantitative development in the increase in the number of schemes or habits in the child's repertoire or the number of "facts" available. The child who can name the capitals of all the states has more information at hand than the child who can name only five capitals. Of course, it should be kept in mind that this information is always assimilated into structures that undergo qualitative changes. Thus, qualitative and quantitative changes go hand in hand.

Qualitative and quantitative changes build on each other during development. A qualitative change in structure makes possible certain quantitative changes. For example, once class inclusion is understood, the child can quickly learn about the classifications and relationships in many different content areas, such as animals, people, trees, shapes, and colors. Quantitative increases in amount of information, in turn, may pave the way for further qualitative change as new information challenges the present structures. For example, talking with peers and adults rapidly expands the child's knowledge and challenges his present understanding. This new information can stimulate subsequent qualitative change as the system attempts to resolve the contradictions in the child's knowledge.

Whether we see quantitative or qualitative change in Piaget's theory depends, in part, on the unit of time we select. If we look at changes over minutes, days, and weeks, we are struck by the gradual nature of development. If we look at changes over months and years, we are struck by the qualitative changes from stage to stage or period to period. For example, from age 4 to $4\frac{1}{2}$, a child may become more consistent in his grouping of objects according to shape. That is, during those 6 months, he is increasingly likely to keep the same basis of sorting from the beginning to the end of the task. This gradual improvement contrasts with the qualitative change in the basis of sorting, as when the child at age 7 can sort objects into hierarchies of classes — for example, animals, mammals, brown mammals, and so forth.

## Nature Versus Nurture

Piaget is an interactionist through and through. All psychological phenomena, from the most specific and concrete sensorimotor behavior to the most general and abstract formal thought, are a result of the inextricable influences of innate and experiential factors. Innate factors include physical structures (for example, the structure and positioning of the particular species' eyes), reflexes, physical maturation, and the invariant functions (organization and adaptation). Given these innate factors and the nature of the physical and social world, development inevitably proceeds in the way it does. It could not be otherwise.

Piaget would agree with Anastasi (1958) that the proper question to ask is *how* innate and environmental factors interact. Piaget has proposed the following "formula" for development:

Development = Physical maturation + Experience with the
    physical environment + Social experience + Equilibration

1. It is obvious that physical maturation — of the nervous system, the muscular system, and the like — creates new possibilities for the cognitive system and requires certain adjustments of that system. For example, when physical maturation permits walking, new vistas open up for the toddler. As the child actively exploits this new skill, he is forced to assimilate and, whenever possible, accommodate to new experiences.

2. The second factor in the formula, experience with the physical environment, refers to three kinds of experience: exercise, physical experience, and logicomathematical experience. *Exercise* simply refers to the use of intellectual skills, such as reflexes, schemes, or operations. These skills become consolidated and strengthened as a result of exercise. For an understanding of how new information is acquired, however, we must look primarily at physical and logicomathematical experience.

*Physical experience* involves actions that extract the attributes of an object or event. In contrast, *logicomathematical experience* refers to reflecting on one's own actions on the objects rather than on the objects themselves. To illustrate these two types of experience, Piaget refers to a friend's recollection from childhood:

He was seated on the ground in his garden and he was counting pebbles. Now to count these pebbles he put them in a row and he counted them one, two, three up to 10. Then he finished counting them and started to count them in the other direction. He began by the end and once again found he had 10. He found this marvelous. . . . So he put them in a circle and counted them that way and found 10 once again.

[1964, p. 12]

The child considered the results of repeatedly counting and arranging the pebbles and concluded that number is constant despite physical rearrangements. He discovered something (number) that is not intrinsic to the objects themselves. In contrast, physical experience in this situation might include noting the color, shape, size, and weight of the pebbles.

3. The third factor, social experience, refers to the effect of the cultural or educational environment. For example, other people transmit knowledge, either directly or through books and television. In this way, a child can benefit from the experience of others. Of course, as always, the child must be cognitively advanced enough to assimilate the information if it is to be of value.

These three factors, taken together, can address the question of what is universal about cognitive development. Given the similarities among cultures in the course of physical maturation, the nature of the physical world, and, to a lesser extent, the nature of the social environment, it is not surprising that the four major periods proceed in the same order in all cultures studied. However, it is not clear whether the development of steps *within* the major periods occurs in an invariant sequence in all cultures. The methodological problems in doing cross-cultural research cloud the issue (see Ghuman, 1981, for a review). Even if some or all of the sequences identified by Piaget prove to be universal, we would still expect some variation in the rate of progress through the cognitive stages in various content areas. This variation can arise from differences in physical maturation, physical experience, or social experience. We would expect some variation within a culture and some overall differences between cultures. An example of how experience in particular cultural settings can influence development comes from a study by Price-Williams, Gordon, and Ramirez (1969). They found that experience with clay promotes the development of conservation of substance (in which clay is the medium). Mexican children aged 6 to 9 who had grown up in pottery-making families were more likely to be conservers of substance than were Mexican children who had grown up in families engaged in other activities. In addition, Piaget recalls that his daughter Jacqueline, who was born in the winter, was often bundled up in a carriage, so did not have as much opportunity as children born in warmer weather to develop eye-hand coordination.

4. The fourth factor, equilibration, ties together and controls the interaction of the innate and experiential factors. Maturation, experience with the physical environment, and the influence of the social environment constantly cause momentary disequilibrium. In this way, they force the cognitive system to change, to adjust. Through reestablishing equilibrium, the cognitive system reaches a higher level. Thus, it is in the interplay of forces within the equilibration process that experiential and innate forces together finally have their effect on cognition.

From this account, it is obvious that experience does not write upon a passive, blank slate. Intelligence is always active and self-regulating, from the first modification of a reflex to the formal operations of adolescent thought.

A final claim about the role of experience is that the timing of the experience is important. Here we see the notion of "readiness." A child can profit from a given experience only if she is ready for it. She must be able to assimilate it to her present cognitive structures or accommodate her structures to the experience. Instruction in calculus would not be successful with most 5-year-olds.

## What Develops

Piaget tells us that the essence of cognitive development is structural change — change in the schemes, regulations, functions, and various logicomathematical structures of the concrete and formal operational periods. Structural change gives meaning to and influences change in the content of thought. Thus, Piaget emphasizes change on a molar level, which leads to change at various more molecular levels.

Piaget is concerned with not only the structure of thought but also the process of thought. The cognitive processes are the functional invariants: organization and adaptation (assimilation and accommodation). They function in essentially the same way throughout development, but their relationship changes. For example, assimilation and accommodation become both more differentiated and more in balance (through equilibration).

The question of what develops is tied to Piaget's methodology. He relies on observations, interviews (the clinical method), and assessment situations in which the experimenter participates. In this way, he keeps the organization of the thought processes as intact as possible; too much experimental interference or control would distort the child's normal line of reasoning.

## THEORETICAL NATURE OF THE THEORY

We have essentially completed our description of Piaget's theory. It is now time to look back to our discussion of the nature of theories in the previous chapter and see what kind of theory Piaget has. This metatheoretical overview prepares us for the final section, which is an evaluation of the theory.

Does Piaget deduce, induce, model, or describe functional relationships? The best answer to this multiple-choice question is "all of the above." At one time or another in his life, Piaget could be found doing each kind of theory building. Let us look at what aspects of the theory could be classified as a model, a deductive theory, a functional theory, and an inductive theory.

### Models

There are two main models in the theory: the equilibration model and the logicomathematical model. Both were described earlier in this chapter, but are now examined in terms of what they do for the theory. Recall from the previous chapter that a model is a framework, structure, or system that has been developed in one field and is applied to another field. A model is a heuristic device that guides research and theory building, but is not itself modified by the outcome of this research and theorizing.

Of the many types of equilibration systems in nature, Piaget chose a system that maintains a dynamic, rather than a static, balance. The dynamic model of equilibrium comes from the fields of physics (thermodynamics and mechanics) and biology. For example, a thermostat and a mollusk are self-regulating equilibration systems. For Piaget, systems of psychological actions maintain equilibrium, despite constant activity and change, to maintain a steady state. Built-in corrective devices counteract new forces acting on the system. In contrast to Piaget's active system is a static system, exemplified by a balance scale with equal weights in the two paths. It is a closed system at rest, with no method of exchange between the system and the environment.

The equilibration model has been used by many theorists, including Freud, Gesell, and the cognitive-dissonance theorists. However, Piaget more than anyone else has given it a central, unifying role in cognitive development. Equilibration unifies the theory by providing a general, overall regulatory function. The various experiential and maturational forces are tied together and organized by the process of equilibration. The model also unifies the theory by outlining the causes and nature of the transitions from state to state. Cognitive imbalance motivates the system to activate cognitive actions, and these move the system to a higher state of equilibrium. A final way in which the model has unified the theory is that it gives Piaget a way to compare and contrast the various cognitive levels or various domains within a cognitive level. Cognitive levels or domains can vary in their stability and mobility.

The second main model is the logicomathematical model, which is most clearly seen in the logicomathematical structures applied to concrete and formal operational thought. Logic and algebra are purely formal, nonpsychological systems; however, they have certain characteristics that are similar to characteristics of cognitive structures. Piaget felt that many aspects of thought approximated these abstract logicomathematical structures and that it would be fruitful to look for various types of thinking suggested by the model. Furthermore, logical models are often clearer and more specific than verbal statements.

Since a complete description of the various logicomathematical structures is beyond the scope of a single chapter on Piaget, an example may illustrate how the model is used. In the concrete operational period, there are nine groupings — logical structures that describe certain logical operations and relationships among these operations. Let us look at the psychological concept of class inclusion, which corresponds to what Piaget calls grouping I. This grouping describes the primary addition of classes and is the simplest grouping. For example, modes of transportation form a classification hierarchy, in which modes of transportation (C) at the top of the hierarchy have two subheadings: ground vehicles (B) and other classes of vehicles (B'). B, in turn, contains cars (A) and other ground vehicles (A'). The system's elements (A, A', B, B', C) can be manipulated according to certain rules. In the case of grouping I, the rules refer to the following properties of the grouping: composition $(A + A' + B)$; association $[(A + B) + C = C]$; general identity $(A + 0 = A)$; negation $(A - A = 0)$; and special identities $(A + A = A$ or $A + B = B)$. These properties, stated in formal, nonpsychological terms, serve as a model for the properties of thought that underlie the concept of class inclusion. They are logical representations that describe the essence of thought.

The grouping probably should be considered an idealized version of what cognitive structures the child must have in order to solve class-inclusion problems. As Flavell (1963) expresses it, a child who understands class inclusion is like a computer with a grouping program. The grouping supplies the necessary operations for the computer to solve the problem, and children solve the problem in an analogous way. The actual process of thinking, however, may differ in various ways from that expressed by the grouping. Several different computer programs can produce the same answer. In other words, grouping I is a logically possible cognitive structure, but is not necessarily the child's actual cognitive structure. In short, this is the nature of models. They are heuristic devices. They tell us what to look for, and they provide a framework for interpreting behavior. However, they may or may not reflect reality.

## Deductive Theory

Recall that a deductive theory is a formalized network of logically related propositions. Hypotheses, which are derived from the propositions, are subjected to empirical tests, and the outcomes of these tests serve to support or modify the theory. It is clear that Piaget's theory as a whole does not meet the requirements for a deductive theory. At best, the theory provides a set of loosely connected verbal propositions. For example, we could translate Piaget's claims about stages into a set of propositions and derive certain hypotheses about behavior during each of these stages. However, we cannot trace a logically tight series of steps from the general propositions about stages all the way down to specific hypotheses. Certain steps in the logical progression are missing, and certain propositions are vague (for example, claims about equilibration). As a result, we only know in general what to predict about behavior in each stage. The consequence is that the empirical results do not always clearly support or refute the more general claims about stages.

This state of affairs does not mean that the theory can never be presented in a deductive fashion. It merely means that at present, like most developmental theories, Piaget's theory is not satisfactorily formalized. This lack of formalization is both a disadvantage and an advantage. It is a disadvantage in that the more general claims are difficult to test. On the other hand, it is an advantage in that the theory is still open to change.

It should be noted that in more limited ways the theory could be considered a deductive system. The logicomathematical model, in particular, may play this deductive role. Most models do not have a hierarchic, organized structure that lends itself to making deductions. The logicomathematical model, however, consists of sets of logically interrelated formal propositions. Because the various logical operations are logically interconnected, if certain logical operations are found in the child's thought, then one can predict (deduce) that the child should possess certain other logical operations. For example, Piaget's model would predict a particular type of logical relationship between the operation of classifying objects and the operation of ordering them along some dimension.

## Functional Theory

If we were to leaf through recent developmental journals, we might conclude that Piaget's theory is a functional one. American psychologists have focused on certain experimental problems or tasks about which Piaget made a limited set of claims. Conservation is the best example, but other problems, such as the object concept and egocentrism, would also qualify. In the case of conservation, Piaget claims that conservers should demonstrate certain concrete operations, such as mental reversibility and compensation, and that conservation training should be most successful for children who are "ready" to develop conservation naturally. These claims and others have been tested in hundreds of experiments. In these experiments, there is a close interplay between the explanatory hypotheses and the data. It appears that the emphasis is increasingly on the conservation problem itself rather than on the theory. To some extent, the question has changed from "What implications does conservation have for the development of general logical structures?" to "What causes conservation to develop?" In short, the example of the conservation task demonstrates that in contemporary developmental psychology Piaget's theory is often treated as though it were a functional theory.

## Inductive Theory

There is little in Piaget's theory that can be termed inductive theory building: developing descriptive statements that merely summarize sets of data and involve little inference. It is true that the theory includes some low-level descriptive statements that are closely tied to the data. However, as we have seen, Piaget constantly leaps from empirical observations to the abstract upper levels of the theory. Inductive theorists simply do not talk about cognitive structures, equilibration, and the like. Moreover, unlike inductive theorists, Piaget moves from theory to data as easily as from data to theory.

## Comment

In summary, Piaget's theory contains elements of each of the four types of theories. However, his theory depends primarily on models, both for analogies of the structure of thought and for a source of theoretical deductions. The theory depends least on the inductive and functional modes.

# EVALUATION OF THE THEORY

As we saw earlier, when Piaget's first writings on children appeared, he was appalled that people evaluated them as though they were final statements on certain cognitive problems rather than the tentative solutions he intended them to be. Even in his final years, over half a century later, Piaget probably would have reacted to evaluations of his theory in much the same way. The theory continued to expand and undergo modifications as Piaget continued to work into his mid-eighties. We should keep the theory's potential for change in mind as we sit in judgment. We now look at the most salient strengths and weaknesses of the theory.

## Strengths

We focus on five strengths of Piaget's theory: its recognition of the central role of cognition in development, its value as an integrative and heuristic theory, its discovery of surprising features of young children's thinking, its wide-ranging scope, and its ecological validity.

### *Recognition of the Central Role of Cognition*

Piaget transformed the field of developmental psychology. If a developmental psychologist were somehow plucked out of the 1950s and set down today, he would be like a man without a country. He would hear psychologists discussing strategies, rule-governed behaviors, cognitive structures, schemes, plans, and readiness, instead of stimulus generalization, mean length of utterance, attention span, mental age, reversal shifts, discrimination learning, and learning set. To a great extent, Piaget is responsible for this change. He altered the course of psychology by asking new questions that made developmentalists wonder why they had ever asked the old questions in the first place. Once psychologists looked at development through Piaget's eyes, they never again saw children in quite the same way. Before we go into the specific notions that transformed developmental psychology, we must glance at the state of the field that received and assimilated Piaget.

Both the state of academic psychology and the history of developmental psychology in the United States provided fertile ground for change in the 1950s and 1960s. Academic psychology had pushed behaviorism in general and learning theory in particular to their limits and found them wanting. Even when learning theory was modified by such notions as verbal mediation, social reinforcement, modeling, intrinsic reinforcement, and attention, it did not completely satisfy psychologists. There was dissatisfaction with the notion of drives, with the explanation of language development in terms of imitation, practice, and reinforcement, and with the formal theory building of Hullian psychology. Along with these dissatisfactions, there were promising approaches from several directions: Noam Chomsky's transformational grammar, Donald Broadbent's filter model of attention, and the computer scientists' work on information processing. All these were cognitive approaches. The winds of change were sweeping the field of psychology. America was ready for Piaget.

We must look at not only the readiness of American academic psychology for cognitive theories, but also the particular history of developmental psychology in the United States. Until the 1950s, researchers interested in children could be found less often in departments of psychology than in "child institutes" or departments of home economics, pediatrics, public health, education, clinical psychology, and nursing. The real-life problems of children's physical and mental welfare often meant that developmentalists worked in child institutes that were physically and ideologically isolated from departments of psychology. At the very least, most developmental psychologists were forced to keep one foot in real-life settings and one foot in the laboratory. Thus, concern with poor nutrition, physical and mental retardation, learning disabilities, and emotional disturbances prevented many developmental psychologists from becoming completely immersed in the behaviorist–experimental zeitgeist of academic psychology of the 1940s and 1950s. In addition, developmental psychologists at that time were primarily interested in collecting normative data — descriptions of the kind of behavior that could be expected at each age. For all these reasons, there was room for Piaget's naturalistic, descriptive approach. For developmentalists, problems resulting from Piaget's lack of uniform testing procedures and statistical analysis and his small number of subjects were more than offset by his remarkable naturalistic observations.

A newcomer to developmental psychology might wonder why Piaget had produced almost a lifetime of work before American academics became interested in him. Certainly the state of academic psychology at that time provides part of the answer. A further reason is the language barrier. Until the 1960s, much of Piaget's work had not been translated into English. An additional language problem is that Piaget's writings are difficult to understand in any language. Fortunately, John Flavell, David Elkind, Hans Furth, and Joachim Wohlwill, among others, served as psychological translators of Piaget's work in the late 1950s and early 1960s. In particular, Flavell's timely book, *The Developmental Psychology of Jean Piaget* (1963), made Piaget understandable to English-speaking psychologists.

The rest, as they say, is history. Psychology witnessed both a flurry of Piagetian replication studies and an attempt to fit Piaget into the existing field of developmental psychology. For example, Berlyne (1965) attempted to integrate learning theory and Piagetian theory. Next came efforts to train children to acquire various Piagetian concepts, especially conservation. At the same time, there emerged American-style laboratory studies of variables such as the nature of task materials and instructions, the scoring criteria, and the socioeconomic level of the children. In fact, interest in Piaget's theory became so intense that nearly 20 percent of all articles published in the journal *Developmental Psychology* from 1969 to mid-1972 cited books by or about Piaget (Looft and Svoboda, 1971). Finally, we can see an extension of Piaget's theory in areas such as social development, clinical psychology, and education. For example, educators applied Piaget's notions that learning is most likely to occur when the child actively participates, when problems are approached in a concrete rather than an abstract way, and when the child is cognitively ready to learn. In short, the 1960s and 1970s became the "Piagetian stage" of developmental psychology.

The purpose of this historical side trip has been to show the impact of a theory that recognized the central role of cognition in development. Piaget searched for the modes of thinking underlying the overt behavior studied by behaviorists and by child psychologists constructing norms of development. This focus on cognition provided a new perspective for a generation of developmental psychologists.

## Value as an Integrative and Heuristic Theory

The introductory chapter asserted that a theory has two functions. First, it should integrate and give meaning to facts. Second, it should serve as a heuristic device for further research. Piaget's theory passes both tests. With respect to its integrative function, it postulates an underlying continuity and organization to a range of seemingly unrelated behaviors. Continuity and organization exist at any one point in time by means of stages and at different points in time by means of the invariant functions. For an example of the integrative nature of the stage notion, we can turn to the logical structures that underlie notions about number, time, causality, and people in the concrete operational period. For an example of the integrative nature of the invariant functions, we turn to the gradual, selective changes in the concept of spatial relations. There is moment-to-moment continuity over time as schemes or operations are slowly stretched to incorporate new information. Longer, cross-stage continuity occurs as the understanding of spatial relations is transformed from physical actions to symbols, then concrete operations, and finally formal operational systems.

Piaget's theory has also served well in its second function, as a heuristic device for the generation of new research. Its specific empirical contributions to research are outlined later in this list of strengths; the heuristic value is mentioned here. One influential notion is Piaget's view that the child actively constructs his knowledge. This view has colored research not only in general cognitive development, but also in memory, attention, learning, language, and social perception. Researchers in these areas are sensitive to children's strategies and plans. The "active child" has become a cliché. Piaget, of course, is not solely responsible for this focus on the child's active participation, but he at least reinforces this view.

A second notion that has had heuristic value is that development follows an invariant sequence, in which later forms use and build on earlier forms. Psychologists studying Piagetian-inspired concepts, such as classification, number, and causality, search for intellectual precursors to the mature forms of these concepts. A psychologist studying number automatically looks for earlier subskills, such as counting or attending appropriately, that eventually lead to a mature understanding of number.

In addition to serving integrative and heuristic functions, the theory makes some novel specific proposals about development:

1. Children inherently seek stimulation, rather than try to escape it (as proposed by the stimulus–response learning and Freudian theories).

2. The thinking of elementary schoolchildren resembles that of logicomathematical structures.

3. The "wrong" or "cute" notions the preschool children have about the world are a symptom of a complex, probing intellectual system that is trying to understand reality.

4. Much of cognitive development does not depend on our ability to use language.

5. To a great extent, children teach themselves.

The list could go on.

### Discovery of Surprising Features of Children's Thinking

Piaget's main legacy may be his rich description of what it is we develop. The thousands of observations by Piaget himself, combined with the thousands of studies inspired by him, constitute a remarkable body of information. Regardless of the final judgment on his theoretical claims, his detailed, sensitive, and astute observations remain with us.

Piaget revealed new developmental phenomena, many of which strike us as surprising or as running counter to common sense. Especially notable are the following: Infants apparently do not expect objects to be permanent. Preschoolers believe that rearranging objects can change their number and assert that the wrongness of an act depends on how much damage resulted. More generally, most concepts not only take longer to develop than we might think, but also go through a number of interesting steps along the way. A further surprise is that children think about such a wide variety of things. Children's thinking ranges from pondering the origin of the universe to solving the problem of how to open doors without dropping what they are holding, from penetrating the nature of society's moral system to determining the speed of the swing of a pendulum. In a discipline that has few real "discoveries" to rival the discovery of a new planet or the structure of DNA, Piaget's surprises about cognitive development are refreshing and his observations remarkable, considering that they came from seemingly mundane, everyday behavior. He showed us that developmental descriptions can be profoundly intriguing.

## *Wide-ranging Scope*

Piaget's theory is ambitious, drawing its net over behavior ranging from playing with pebbles to causal reasoning, from the sucking reflex to formal operational structures. The theory attempts to describe and explain both cognitive states and transitions between those states. Piaget not only tackles cognitive development, but also follows up on its implications for other areas of development, such as social and emotional development and learning. In addition, he speaks to other disciplines, such as epistemology, philosophy of science, and education. In short, Piaget's theory addresses itself to more areas of behavior than does any other developmental theory. In Piaget we catch a glimpse of how a complete theory of development might look.

The theory's wide scope obviously increases its attractiveness. At the same time, it increases its vulnerability. The theory may try to do too much too soon.

## *Ecological Validity*

Every psychologist has an intuitive list of what a good theory should do. Many lists would include the requirement that the theory tell us about the real world of children. Although even the most basic research in laboratories has some relevance for day-to-day behavior, some approaches have a closer relationship than others to common, everyday behavior. Piaget's theory seems to rate well in this respect. The focus is on the child's adaptation to the world he encounters every day. Infants try to grasp a rattle just out of reach, replace a pacifier, and figure out where a ball has rolled. Preschoolers divide their cookies with friends, try to express their ideas to others, and chastise those who break the rules of games. Schoolchildren struggle with math problems, try to make sense of social rules, and find their way around their neighborhood or city.

Ecological validity arises from three intermingling, mutually dependent facets of the theory: a theoretical emphasis on adaptation to the environment, a methodology that includes observations of ongoing behavior, and the resulting data concerning the behavior of everyday life.

The ecological validity of the theory is more striking for infancy than for the later stages of development. When studying children beyond infancy, Piaget tends to interrupt the flow of behavior with questions or even pose problems from the beginning. The reason is that the infant's thinking is expressed in her overt actions, whereas an older child's thinking is more covert and must be prodded.

## Weaknesses

The excitement and inspiration generated by Piaget's theory fade into a feeling that the theory is not all that it could be. Although we may feel presumptuous in criticizing a theory that has broken so much new ground, it is necessary to ask whether the theory deserves all of the attention and energy it has attracted in the last two decades. We now look at some of the weaknesses of the theory.

It has become fashionable to criticize Piaget. He provides an easy target in many ways. His unusual methodology, his wide scope, and his ties to biology and philosophy encourage psychologists to expose the inadequacies of the theory. Our goal in this section is to point out these inadequacies and determine which are most easily corrected. We examine the following weaknesses: Unclear links between constructs and behavior, inadequate support for the stage notion, inadequate account of mechanisms of development, need for a theory of performance, slighting of social and emotional aspects of development, and methodological and stylistic inadequacies. In addition, we review some of the recent research in North America and Great Britain stimulated by notice of these weaknesses.

### *Unclear Links Between Constructs and Behavior*

Piaget gifted us with a useful framework for studying cognitive development. He did not, however, give us a final, rigorous, tightly knit set of theoretical constructs with clear ties to empirical events. Such critical concepts as *assimilation, accommodation, equilibration,* and *stage* strike us as somewhat vague and imprecise. Furthermore, it is not clear how these notions are related to behavior. How do we know when a child is in temporary "disequilibrium"? What behavior could tell us if a child is or is not "accommodating" to new information? Can we assess the child's attainment with respect to "stages" accurately enough to predict whether he should profit from a particular type of training? Piaget's theory does not yet give us clear answers to these and other questions. Hypotheses generated by the theory relate only in a general way to higher-order levels of the theory. In other words, the structural model is simply too far from the data. Future empirical and theoretical work, however, could tighten up the definitions, specify their links with behavior, and fill in necessary logical steps within the theory. In short, the theory *could* have a good deal more logical integrity and testability than it now has.

## Inadequate Support for the Stage Notion

The inadequacies just mentioned come into focus when we look at the notion of stages, the heart of the theory. Are there, in fact, broad stretches during development that have characteristics that apply to all the psychological events during that period? Or does the notion of stages simply confuse and mislead by oversimplifying development and claiming more coherence among concepts than there actually is? A basic issue here is how stages are related to the child's actual intellectual functioning. Although Piaget sometimes treats the stages, particularly their logical structures, as idealized models of thought, he usually claims that the stages have a psychological reality. They are not merely models or heuristic devices. That is, the stages describe the actual psychological organization of the child's knowledge and predict the child's knowledge about a range of objects and events. His main evidence for the reality of stages is the similarity in thought over a variety of content areas and the feeling of necessity that accompanies the acquisition of a cognitive structure. For example, he quotes a child who said, "Once one knows, one knows forever and ever" (1971, p. 5). Piaget asserts that the logical structures give this feeling of logical necessity.

There are, however, some doubts about Piaget's claim that there are general structures that characterize stages. For example, there is only limited evidence for the existence of the logicomathematical structures of the concrete and formal operational periods. The main problem is that there is no clear correspondence between each component of the logical model and a particular unit of behavior. More specifically, it is not clear which behaviors would unambiguously demonstrate the presence or absence of each logicomathematical grouping and reveal the structural relationship among the groupings. There appear to be several types of plausible logical structures that would predict the same set of cognitive data (Osherson, 1975). In addition, some of the logical operations considered necessary for acquiring a particular concept may not be necessary. Compensation, for example, does not seem to be closely involved in the acquisition of conservation (Gelman and Weinberg, 1972). For all these reasons, we must wonder whether Piaget's logico-mathematical structures are the best way to characterize the knowledge that underlies the various cognitive skills of middle childhood. Piaget later turned to other types of logicomathematical models that seemed more satisfactory.

In addition to the theoretical inadequacies of the stage notion, there also is uncertain empirical support. Four types of inconsistencies in performance raise questions. First, a child may appear to understand a specific concept when tested with certain materials or types of transformations, but not others. For example, Uzgiris (1968) assessed conservation of substance, using plasticine balls, metal cubes, wire coils, or plastic wire. Conservation emerged earlier on some tasks than others. Second, different manifestations of the same general concept, such as conservation, emerge at different times during the same stage. Piaget noted this type of inconsistency and referred to it as a *horizontal décalage*. For example, conservation of substance typically develops a year or two before conservation of weight. The décalages are not satisfactorily related to any changes within the stages themselves. Piaget's claim that these lags are caused by differences in how various stimuli "resist" the application of the cognitive structures is both incomplete and unconvincing. These first two types of unevenness in development are problematic for a strong stage notion because the mental operations underlying a concept should be content-free, so that the theory applies across a variety of cases and materials.

Third, there is not overwhelming consistency across tasks that are claimed to reflect the same underlying cognitive structure for a particular stage. For example, various concrete operational concepts, such as class inclusion and conservation, in fact are often acquired at different ages (Brainerd, 1978; Flavell, 1971b), and there are not strong correlations among various concrete operational tasks (Klausmeire and Sipple, 1982). And at the level of formal operations, Piaget acknowledges that an individual may attain formal operational thought in some content areas but not in others. Fourth, there are child prodigies whose cognitive achievements in one particular area, such as math, are much more advanced than they are in other areas of thinking. This challenges Piaget's theory because the theory does not describe how cognitive structures limited to one domain can be isolated from the child's overall cognitive structure (Feldman, 1980). These anomalies challenge, but do not critically damage, Piaget's stage notion. Piaget's theory is concerned mainly with knowledge per se, not with how it is applied to a particular task. Thus, some inconsistency in the level of knowledge in various content areas is expected and is not necessarily incompatible with the stage notion. However, it is reasonable to require a stage theory to account for these inconsistencies, which Piaget's theory does not.

We have seen several ways in which the stage notion is inadequate. In each case, however, it is difficult to decide whether the notion of stages is wrong or simply incomplete. Are the logicomathematical structures a philosopher's dream or, as described at present, are they simply too vague, general, and distant from behavior? Looft and Svoboda voice some of these doubts:

> While reading Piaget's most recent writings one sometimes acquires an eerie, cold feeling that something very strange is going on in this man's work. In his early writings we read about delightful children playing on the banks of Lake Geneva, expressing their surprise and exhilaration as they make new discoveries about their little worlds. Today we are presented with some sort of cybernetic automata, regulating themselves and pushing themselves to ever higher levels of differentiation and complexity. In short, it would seem that as Piaget's theory has evolved over the past five decades to higher and higher levels of abstraction, people have somehow dropped out and have been replaced by sterile logico-mathematical structures.
>
> *[1971, p. 15]*

Unfortunately, our dilemma is that we cannot test the notion of stages until they are described more clearly and tied more closely to behavior.

Analyses of the stage notion by Flavell (1971b; 1982) demonstrate both its incompleteness and the potential for revision within the theory. Flavell suggests several modifications of Piaget's conception of stages:

1. Stagelike, qualitative changes appear to be causally linked to more gradual, quantitative sorts of developmental changes, such as an increasing attentional capacity or an increasing stability and generality of concepts.

2. The development of a cognitive skill is an extended process. In fact, children may not achieve the "full functional maturity" of a stage until after that stage has officially ended.

3. Concepts or structures that characterize a stage are often only roughly synchronous in their development. For example, two concepts might begin their development at the same time, but complete it at different times. Or they might begin and end their development at different times, but have a considerable temporal overlap. There are other possible temporal relationships as well. The temporal relationships among various developments are especially important for an adequate account of the logicomathematical structures. In what sense are they a simultaneously developing, tightly knit system of structures?

4. The cognitive items of a particular stage may *eventually* become tightly organized and interrelated into a true stage, even if there is not synchrony throughout the stage.

5. In cognitive performance, there are several different types of homogeneity and heterogeneity, and these vary in their implications for Piaget's theory. For example, there may be more cognitive homogeneity in spontaneous, everyday thinking than in testing situations and more in some cognitive domains than in others.

Although Flavell reveals the ambiguity and complexity of the notion of stages, he also shows that Piaget's theory can generate interesting and testable hypotheses. Even though the stages may be less coherent units than Piaget would have us believe, they are still useful ways to organize a large number of diverse behaviors. They are convenient points of reference for accounting for the orderliness of thought. As Flavell and Wohlwill conclude, "To paraphrase Voltaire's dictum concerning the deity: if there were no such structures in the mind of the child, we should have to invent them, to account for the degree of consistency and orderliness that we do find in his cognitive development" (1969, p. 94)

The most reasonable way to use Piaget's notion of stages may be to look for stagelike changes limited to a particular content area (Feldman, 1980). Each domain may develop somewhat independently of the others. This possibility will be discussed in a later section on the neo-Piagetians.

## Inadequate Account of Mechanisms of Development

We need clarification not only of the criteria for stages but also of the transitional mechanisms both within a stage and from stage to stage. Piaget more successfully describes than explains the course of development. The functional invariants, such as assimilation and accommodation, provide at best a general framework with which to examine cognitive change. There are not specific, precise statements as to how sensorimotor thought becomes preoperational thought or how preoperational thought becomes operational thought. Furthermore, although the equilibration process is an intuitively appealing idea, it is not clear how the child's awareness of a contradiction would lead her to the solution that resolves the contradiction (Bryant, 1986). Simply knowing that something is wrong does not identify the cause of the problem.

Piagetians, especially Inhelder, have attempted to provide empirical support for the mechanisms of change by studying how training studies stimulate learning (Inhelder, Sinclair, and Bovet, 1974). In addition, hundreds of training studies have been conducted by American and British psychologists. Many of these have successfully taught a new concept by creating cognitive conflict, teaching underlying operations such as reversibility or compensation, verbalizing the rule for the child, or providing a model who illustrates the new concept. Other approaches focus on removing barriers to the child's performance by redirecting attention to the relevant feature, such as number, or by ensuring memory of relevant information.

Obvious methodological problems in this area of research spring from issues we have already discussed. For example, the issue of the appropriate way to assess whether the child "really has" the concept before and after training is critical. In addition, there is the issue of how much generalization to different materials we can reasonably expect, in order to conclude that the child has acquired a general concept rather than a specific response. In addition to these general issues, however, are issues more specific to training studies:

1. Even if we find that training based on one of Piaget's mechanisms of development (for example, cognitive conflict) causes the child to acquire the concept, there is no guarantee that children progress by this mechanism in real life. Spontaneous, natural development may proceed in other ways.

2. When a training study succeeds, that success may be based on mechanisms other than those the experimenter thought he was providing. Gelman's (1969) training procedure was intended to redirect the child's attention from irrelevant dimensions to the relevant dimension, for example, number. However, as Beilin (1971) points out, this procedure's success could have stemmed from cognitive conflict created when the child's initial answer did not consistently lead to reinforcement.

3. A third main issue arises from the finding that there are limits to how early a concept can be acquired by training. No one claims that 6-year-olds are formal operational. There is general agreement that the closer a child is to acquiring the concept naturally, the more likely he is to benefit from training. This notion of readiness, however, is not easy to support experimentally. It is true that the older the child, the more likely he is to acquire the concept as a result of training. However, more refined predictions are more difficult. Most critically, it is not clear how to assess degree of readiness in children of the same age. We need a more refined analysis of the cognitive precursors leading to the target concept.

Beyond these issues about the limitations of training studies rises a broader question: What is the impact of training on the child? Piaget cautioned that "each time one prematurely teaches a child something he could have discovered for himself, that child is kept from inventing it and consequently from understanding it completely" (Piaget, 1983, p. 113). We know little about this important issue.

One problem in evaluating Piaget's use of stages and transitional mechanisms is that there is little longitudinal research applied to this issue. Such research, which could involve repeated measures on the same children from the time they enter one stage until they enter the next stage, would provide a detailed picture of cognitive change and reveal the temporal relationships among concepts. Sequences and concurrences would emerge. Unfortunately, virtually all Piagetian and post-Piagetian cognitive research is cross-sectional; it provides measures of children of different ages at a single time. Cross-sectional research obviously gives us less information about cognitive change than does longitudinal. Thus, we cannot accept or reject several of Piaget's most central claims until we have more appropriate evidence.

## Need for a Theory of Performance

Piaget created an elaborate system of cognitive structures that represent children's knowledge about the world. He also provided a rich description of behavior. There is, however, a missing link: a detailed account of exactly *how* the structures are translated into behavior. This account could be called a theory of performance — a theory of how a child's knowledge is expressed in his behavior at any particular time. A theory of performance takes heed of cognitive processes such as memory, attention, and verbal comprehension. In this undertaking, the theory must deal with variables that influence these processes. This list of variables would include, for example, the salience of each attribute (shape, color) in the materials, familiarity of the materials, the amount of information to remember, and the complexity of instructions about the task.

The conservation-of-number task can supply us with a concrete example of how a theory of performance would analyze the way children use their cognitive structures. A test of conservation of number requires that the child proceed through a number of steps as the stimuli (objects and instructions) make contact with the mental operations relevant to conservation. A partial list of steps is as follows: (1) understanding that the task concerns the number of the objects rather than some other feature and (2) attending to the relevant attribute (number) while ignoring irrelevant attributes (color, length, and orientation). Other steps include (3) counting the objects, (4) encoding information about the number of objects, (5) observing the experimenter move the objects, and (6) remembering the initial equality and the lack of addition or subtraction during the transformation. In addition, the child may (7) recall previous experiences with counting or moving objects, (8) search for an appropriate rule or mental operation, and (9) carry out the appropriate operation, for example, mentally reversing the transformation. Final steps involve (10) inferring the correct answer and (11) translating this answer into words, including a logical explanation. It should be noted that some of these steps may occur at the same time rather than in sequence.

Piaget did not deny the importance of these cognitive activities. He simply was less interested in them than in the more general cognitive structures. In contrast, other theoretical approaches, such as information processing, Gibson's perceptual learning, and learning theory, focus on the nature of performance. We encounter these theories in later chapters; they may eventually provide the missing link between structures and behavior in Piaget's theory.

It should be noted that in his later years Piaget [Inhelder and Piaget, 1980; Piaget, 1981 (1987)] began to give more attention to a performance model, as seen in his work on procedural knowledge. He saw procedural knowledge as distinct from, but complementary to, structural knowledge. Procedures, or mental actions carried out in a sequence, provide the means used to reach a goal. They include strategies for gathering relevant information or processing it further during problem solving. Thus, procedures help the child use his structures.

Developmental psychologists have given some attention to performance variables in Piagetian cognitive development. Flavell and Wohlwill (1969) make a distinction between competence (knowledge) and performance in cognitive development and outline a set of issues involved in this distinction. Empirical research has revealed the importance of memory (Trabasso, 1977), attention (Gelman, 1969), stimulus complexity (Gzesh and Surber, 1985), encoding (Siegler, 1978), language used in the testing procedures (S. A. Miller, 1976c), stimulus variables (P. H. Miller, 1978), and information-processing capacity (Case, 1985). For example, with respect to stimulus variables, materials for conservation have included even classmates and live crickets (S. A. Miller, 1982).

It is interesting to note that these performance factors may account, in part, for the extended, gradual development described in the papers on stages by Flavell (1971b, 1982) mentioned earlier. For example, it may be that the early, fragile form of a concept can be used only if there are not large demands on the child's memory, attentional capacity, and verbal ability.

### Slighting of Social and Emotional Aspects of Development

Piaget gave relatively little attention to (1) how sociocultural-historical influences and emotions shape cognitive development and (2) the nature of the development of cognitions concerning people and social events. With respect to the first criticism, it has been said that Piaget's epistemic subject has no social class, sex, nationality, culture, or personality—and also has no fun (Murray, 1983b, p. 231). Chapter 3, on social learning theory, will show that social influences must be addressed. Piaget's neglect of social factors may have affected even his assessment of physical concepts. For example, the standard Piagetian procedure, in which an adult asks children about quantity twice (before and after the transformation), may cause children to think that they should change their answer because of the adult's actions on the materials. More conservation is revealed when the question is asked only once (Samuel and Bryant, 1984).

Curiously, emotional factors continue to be slighted by contemporary developmentalists. Piaget considers cognition and emotion to be parallel and interdependent: "Feelings express the interest and value given to actions of which intelligence provides the structure" [1945 (1951, pp. 205–206)]. He suggests that, in a sense, emotions provide the energetic force behind behavior. For example, feelings influence the content to which structures are applied. A child with a passion for airplanes is likely to learn a great deal about them.

Regarding children's thinking about social objects and events, Piaget claimed that the development of cognitive structures can be seen in the realm of social as well as physical objects and events. Yet he had little interest in working out the implications of the theory for social and emotional development. We can hardly say that Piaget was lazy. We can say instead that his philosophical and biological interests led him toward concepts such as time, space, and causality. His main contributions to social development are his work on moral judgments, egocentrism, and communication. Kohlberg (1969) adopted Piaget's stage approach to moral judgments, but has expanded and modified the model considerably. Inspired by Kohlberg and Piaget, psychologists publish studies on moral judgments at a steady rate. Recently, there has been a flurry of interest in what is called "social cognition." This term refers to how children understand the thoughts, intentions, feelings, and points of view of other people. The inspiration for this work comes from both Piaget and social attribution theory based primarily on research with adults. To some extent, then, others are correcting Piaget's omissions in the area of social development. It remains to be seen how successfully the results of this recent research are integrated into Piaget's theory.

## Methodological and Stylistic Inadequacies

Probably the most common criticisms of Piaget are directed toward certain inadequacies in how he conducted and reported his research. With respect to his infancy research, Piaget observed his own three children. Unfortunately, he did not have 40 or 50 children of his own to give us a more respectable sample size! The small number of subjects, the possible biases in interpreting the behavior of one's own children, the absence of measures of reliability by having two independent observers, and the lack of control over the children's immediate environment, possible only in a laboratory, did not endear Piaget to American experimental psychologists. However, subsequent studies, with more subjects and better-controlled testing situations, generally have replicated the sequence of development within infancy, if not always the exact ages at which the changes occur.

In his work with older children, Piaget usually employed the clinical method. Although the clinical method has certain advantages, such as flexibility in tailoring questions to the particular answers given by each child, it also has a number of disadvantages. Two main disadvantages are the danger that the examiner may be too leading in his questions or not leading enough and that different children may be asked slightly different questions. Uniform instructions, stimuli, and measures of response are the backbone of testing in experimental psychology. We are asked to make the leap of faith that Piaget was in fact a sensitive and accurate observer. Piaget himself seemed aware of these problems:

> It is so hard not to talk too much when questioning a child, especially for a pedagogue! It is so hard not to be suggestive! And above all, it is so hard to find the middle course between systematisation due to preconceived ideas and incoherence due to the absence of any directing hypothesis!
>
> [1926 (1929, p. 9)]

With respect to the verbal nature of the testing, one concern has been that children may not completely understand the instructions, for example, the meaning of "same number" and "amount." Another concern is that children may not be able to express in words their ideas about quantity, the origin of the universe, the nature of dreams, and so forth. In particular, some psychologists (Brainerd, 1973) believe that a child may have the concept of conservation, but not be able to give an adequate reason for his answer—one of Piaget's criteria for conservation. Children's knowledge may, therefore, be underestimated, even with Piaget's "revised clinical method," which provides concrete objects about which to question the child.

This concern with the considerable verbal requirements has led to a number of interesting attempts to devise nonverbal, or at least less verbal, procedures. Psychologists have cleverly devised ways of using expressions of surprise (Gelman, 1972), heart rate (T. G. R. Bower, 1974), and choice of candy (S. A. Miller, 1976b) to test for the presence or absence of certain concepts. For example, Gelman (1972) found that 3-year-olds notice, and are surprised, when the number of toy mice changes (because the experimenter has surreptitiously removed one). There is considerable debate whether these studies demonstrate that some of Piaget's concepts develop earlier than he thought or whether the nonverbal procedures are revealing earlier, less advanced versions of these concepts. It should be noted that even if concepts are developed earlier than Piaget found, this finding is not necessarily damaging to his theory. His concern is with the order in which concepts are acquired, not the particular ages.

Another basic concern with Piaget's methods is that his procedures may be too complex and consequently underestimate the child's knowledge. One way to simplify the task is to use simpler materials. For example, young children demonstrate more knowledge about counting when there are only a few objects than when there are many (Gelman and Gallistel, 1978). The importance of such modifications of Piaget's methodology may lie less in the fact that the concepts may be acquired earlier than Piaget thought than in the unearthing of precursors to the concepts examined by Piaget. Gelman and Gallistel found a sequence of simple principles of counting, such as the principle that numerals must always be used in the same order. That is, a child who says "1, 2, 6, 9" follows this counting principle correctly if he always uses these numerals in this order for counting. These early principles supplement Piaget's account of the full-blown concept of number acquired several years later. Techniques that simplify the Piagetian tests are more sensitive to earlier forms of concepts than are Piaget's procedures.

The differences in the methodology of Piagetians on the one hand and North American and British psychologists on the other reflect different goals of assessment. Piaget especially wanted to avoid "false positive errors," namely, concluding that the child has the concept when in fact he does not. Thus, he sometimes even considered it desirable to have complex materials, a misleading visual array, and heavy verbal demands. In contrast, the other camp is more concerned about "false negative errors," concluding that the child does not have the concept when in fact he does.

The inadequacies of Piaget's methodology carry over to his reporting of his experiments. His reports do not allow the reader to evaluate the research. He typically does not report the number of subjects, the exact ages and socioeconomic level of the children, and details of the testing procedure. Sometimes it is even difficult to tell whether Piaget is referring to hypothetical children or children he has actually tested! He is not impressed with statistical analysis. In his words, "Acute observation, especially when made by [a good observer] . . . , surpasses all statistics" [1936 (1952, p. 72)]. Instead of presenting statistical summaries of the findings, Piaget provides sample protocols, which he interprets at great length. The reader has no idea whether these protocols are representative of all children tested. The data from the entire group of subjects are needed to evaluate Piaget's claims that children typically go through stages of cognitive development. Flavell (1963) suggests that if Piaget had reported his research more adequately, there would have been less need for the extensive replications of Piaget's research in the 1960s. Or at least it would have been clearer what aspects of the theory needed to be replicated.

What are we to make of these shortcomings in Piaget's methodology? Flavell (1963) concludes that Piaget was primarily interested in satisfying his own curiosity, not the requirements of the scientific community. Consequently, he played by his own rules when doing research and wrote almost as though he were talking to himself.

Although the inadequacies in Piaget's methodology and reporting are annoying to anyone trying to understand and evaluate his theory, they may be somewhat responsible for Piaget's success. It could be argued that when a psychologist explores new areas and develops tentative hypotheses to guide his research, he should be flexible in his methods. If Piaget had used standardized procedures from the beginning, he might have missed some fascinating facets of cognitive development. In fact, as Ginsburg and Opper suggest, "If Piaget had attempted to establish every point with the maximum of certainty, then he probably would not have advanced beyond the study of children's verbal communication (one of his first research topics)" (1979, pp. 94–95).

## PIAGET'S OWN MODIFICATIONS OF HIS THEORY

As Piaget's recent papers are translated and made accessible to researchers in other countries, the "classic Piaget" presented in this chapter must be modified. Many of these changes in Piaget's thinking are described in a recent chapter by Beilin (in press). Three main areas are discussed below: equilibration, the logicomathematical model, and the stage notion.

In recent years, Piaget [1978 (1985)] increased his attention to mechanisms of cognitive change, especially the equilibration process. His collaborators, particularly Inhelder, conducted training studies in an attempt to create cognitive conflict and observe whether it brought about cognitive change. Piaget differentiated three levels of equilibrium. In the first, equilibration occurs between the child's mental scheme (for example, sucking) and external events or objects (physical characteristics of the object sucked); the object is assimilated and there is accommodation of the scheme. In the second, more internal level, schemes (grasping and sucking) are combined. In the third, schemes are integrated into a total, more general system of knowledge; that is, equilibration occurs between the whole (concrete operations) and its parts (seriation and classes).

An important aspect of equilibration is contradiction. An example of Piaget's [1974 (1980)] research in this area involved a row of seven disks, each of which was slightly, but imperceptibly, larger than the one before it. Because the last and largest disk was unattached, it could be moved to, and compared with, each of the six disks attached to the board. Thus, the contradiction facing the child was that any two adjacent disks appeared to be equal in size, but the disk at the end of the series was obviously larger than the first disk. Three stages of understanding contradiction emerged. In the first stage, young children were unaware of the contradiction. Next, children had some awareness of the contradiction but their attempted solutions were not satisfactory. For example, a child might categorize the disks as small ones and large ones, thereby accounting for some of the perceived equivalences between adjacent disks and also explaining the difference in size of the first and last disk. Finally, by age 11 or 12 children resolved the contradiction and reestablished equilibrium by creating a new structure—quantified seriation of size.

Other topics related to equilibration that interested Piaget in his later years were possibility and necessity. Young children seem aware of only a few possible solutions to a problem, such as various ways to make a toy car go from point A to point B. The awareness of possibility increases, and by age 11 or 12 a child realizes that the number of possibilities can be essentially unlimited for many problems. One reason that this development is interesting is that the concept of unlimited possibilities cannot be observed in the environment. It must be constructed internally. As for necessity, a sense of necessity occurs in young children because they can imagine so few possibilities, but it reflects an understanding of logical conditions in older children. For older children, mental operations are accompanied by feelings of logical necessity; if A is greater than B, and B is greater than C, then A *must* be greater than C. Possibility and necessity are intertwined during development because each arises from the other in a back-and-forth manner: "A new necessity emerges only after its having been made possible by earlier states and it generates, in turn, new possibilities" (Piaget, 1986, p. 302).

In light of the problems with Piaget's logicomathematical model mentioned earlier, it is interesting that he introduced changes in the model in his later years (Beilin, 1986). He tried to incorporate a "logic of meanings" and "category theory," a branch of mathematics developed since the 1960s. A logic of meanings is described in a forthcoming posthumous publication (Piaget and Garcia, in press). Briefly, Piaget felt that a logic of meanings could lead to a logic of operations. Assimilation of an object generates meaning, as when an infant's grasping a rattle implies relations between grasping and seeing. This meaning is preparation for the later logical operations described in classical Piagetian theory. In category theory, Piaget's previous emphasis on action in the form of mental transformations is supplemented with "correspondences" (Piaget, 1979). Examples of correspondences include (1) seeing the similarity between a currently perceived object and a previously encountered one, and thereby assimilating the former, and (2) relating a mental operation to its inverse, for instance, addition to subtraction (Beilin, 1980). Thus, comparisons are central. The current object or event is recognized, categorized, or characterized; it therefore "corresponds" (is seen as similar) to other objects or events. Detecting correspondences can lead the child to notice a transformation. For example, when a picture corresponds to the same picture hung upside down, a mental rotation links the two states and underlies their correspondence.

A final modification concerns the stage notion. In his last years, Piaget put less emphasis on stages. He began to view development as less steplike, with longer transition periods between stages. In fact, Vuyk (1981, p. 192) concludes that Piaget "now considers development a spiral and though one may call a stage 'a detour of the spiral,' this indicates that periods of equilibrium are relatively unimportant."

Piaget's final contributions concerning equilibration, the logico-mathematical model, and stages raise enough important questions to occupy cognitive theorists and researchers for years to come. Only after this critical examination will we be able to judge the ultimate value of these new ideas.

## THE NEO-PIAGETIANS

Many of the problems and limitations in Piaget's theory have been addressed by a group of developmental psychologists labeled "neo-Piagetians." They are Piagetian in their belief in stages, sequences, and structural change but new in their inclusion of constructs such as skills, limited memory capacity, and automaticity and in their focus on domain-specific concepts. Domain-specific concepts or stages are those that pertain only to a particular area or areas, such as role taking or number. In contrast, Piaget emphasized the domain-general application of cognitive structures.

The neo-Piagetians will be represented here by Robbie Case (1985), a major theorist and researcher. His work draws heavily on the construct of memory capacity, or, in his words, *executive processing space*: "the maximum number of independent schemes a child can activate at any one time" (Case, 1985, p. 289). Capacity is emphasized by information-processing psychologists. In fact, because Case attempts to integrate Piagetian and information-processing theory, his views could have been presented instead in the later chapter on information processing. For Case, an increase in available capacity, rather than the logical equilibration process, is the major mechanism for development.

The total amount of capacity does not increase, but the amount of *available* capacity increases as activities, because they are carried out more efficiently, require less capacity for their operation. The freed capacity then can be used for new or additional cognitive activities. For example, the faster a child can count objects, the better she is at remembering the number of objects in sets in a counting span test (Case, 1985).

The increased efficiency of mental activities is due to two factors: biological maturation and increased automation of activities. Case hypothesizes that increased myelinization (insulation of neurons) during development increases the efficiency of the conduction of neural impulses. He presents evidence that different systems of the brain are myelinated at different times during development. Thus, changes in biological maturation could account for the transitions from one stage to another, in particular, because these changes tend to occur at the ages of the movement from one stage to another. The other cause of greater capacity is increased automaticity of activities or skills as they are practiced. A relatively automatic activity requires little effort, and consequently little capacity.

Case and Piaget differ in their views of how children's mental structures can be modeled. Rather than draw on symbolic logic, Case uses constructs from the information-processing framework, particularly *executive control structures* that represent the existing state in the problem situation, the desired goal state, and strategies for achieving that goal. He views the child as a problem solver, with mental structures as her tools. Changes in these mental structures are spurred by innate processing abilities. The processes include the ability to set goals, to activate procedures (scheme-sequences) in novel ways for reaching these goals and to evaluate the results of these procedures. They also include restructuring successful procedures so that they later can be produced intentionally, and practicing and integrating successful procedures until they are consolidated. For example, with respect to counting, the child sets a goal (determining the number of objects), generates counting procedures for attaining it, evaluates her success, "marks" the successful sequence, and integrates the successful counting procedures.

The child who experiments during attempts to solve problems uses these general processes: he explores objects, observes and imitates other people, and interacts with others as together they solve a problem. For example, a child might learn about counting by using his own verbal labels as he touches each object during problem solving, counting different types of objects during exploring, observing others count, and trying to count a large set with the help of an adult.

In summary, if a child has the necessary processing capacity, he can use his innate processing abilities to take advantage of these experiences to construct more advanced executive control structures (for example, procedures for determining quantity). Consequently, in Case's (1985, p. 415) words, "The problem of décalage can be resolved by pointing out that different forms of the same logical insight may require executive control structures of differing complexity and may therefore entail a different executive processing load."

Although Piaget and Case offer very different mechanisms for change and propose different models for mental structures, they both view development as structural change resulting in a series of stages. In both theories, lower-order concepts are differentiated and coordinated into higher-order concepts. Case proposes four stages, which will sound very familiar to someone who has just read a description of Piaget's theory. Each stage has a different type of executive-control structure.

1. *Sensorimotor control structures* (birth to $1\frac{1}{2}$ years). Infants' mental representations are linked to physical movements.

2. *Relational control structures* ($1\frac{1}{2}$ to 5 years). Children detect and coordinate relations among objects, events, or people. For example, children eventually understand the relation between the difference in weight of two objects and the effect of this difference on the arms of a balance scale; that is, the heavy object makes the arm go down more than the light one does. For a child, this dimension is bipolar, for example, heavy and light. In contrast to Piaget, who sees this stage primarily as preparation for the concrete operational stage, Case sees a distinct stage, equal to the others in importance.

3. *Dimensional control structures* (5 to 11 years). Children extract the dimensions of significance in the physical and social world. They learn to compare two dimensions, such as height and width in a logical quantity task, in a quantitative way: liquid poured into a narrower container rises proportionately higher.

4. *Abstract control structures* (11 to 18½ years). Children acquire abstract systems of thought that allow them to use proportional reasoning, solve verbal analogy problems, and infer psychological traits in other people. Children's dimensional control structures serve as a foundation for this final stage.

Although Piaget and Case posit similar stages, Case sees stagelike change as less general and more domain-specific when some tasks make greater demands on the child's capacity than do others. For example, Case (1984, p. 41) refers to changes in "a particular framework for dealing with a particular class of situations" caused by a "set of processes that are oriented toward achieving particular results, in particular physical and social environments."

Case also is interested in changes within a stage. His analysis of Noelting's (1980) orange juice problem for the third stage will serve as an illustration. There are two sets of small glasses. In each set some glasses contain orange juice and some contain water. Children must predict which pitcher would taste more strongly of orange juice if the liquid were poured from one set of glasses into one pitcher and that of the other set into a second pitcher. Thus, children must determine which pitcher would have the higher proportion of orange juice.

The following sequence of strategies, or rules, were revealed: 3- to 5-year-olds judged solely on a perceptual basis, on whether one set looked as if it had a lot of juice and the other set did not. Five- to 7-year-olds believed that whichever set had more glasses of juice would taste more strongly of juice. Thus, they were correct when there was an equal total number of glasses in the two sets but were incorrect when, for example, set A contained four glasses of juice and four of water and set B contained three glasses of juice and two of water. That is, the children chose set A. Seven- to 9-year-olds could consider the number of water glasses if the number of juice glasses was about the same in the two sets. Nine- to 11-year-olds noted the difference in the number of water glasses in the two sets and the difference in the number of juice glasses in each set. If the juice difference was greater, they picked the set with more juice as "juicier," and if the water difference was larger they picked the set with more water as less juicy. With this task, as well as others used by Case, what changes during the stage is that (1) more elements are considered (because processing capacity has increased), and (2) these elements become more organized into a structure. In addition to tasks that are similar to those in Piaget's research, Case has examined a variety of tasks, such as eating with utensils in infancy, using vocalizations for social purposes, manipulating other people's feelings, story telling, and judging intelligence in others.

Case's theory is an exciting attempt to supplement a logical-structural model of development with a processing model. That is, he shows how limits in processing capacity limit logical reasoning and constrain what the child can learn at any developmental level. By the same token, increases in capacity create a new opportunity for the further development of logical thinking. Because Case's theory is still being developed, criticisms generally point to the need for more supporting evidence, for example, in the role of myelinization in increasing mental efficiency, and for a clearer criterion for assessing how much capacity a particular strategy requires (Flavell, 1984). Case is continuing to develop his theory, most recently in work on emotional development (Case, Hayward, Lewis, and Hurst, 1988).

The interested reader is urged to read the work of other theorists considered neo-Piagetians. For example, Kurt Fischer (Fischer, 1980; Fischer and Pipp, 1984) uses "skill theory" to describe 10 cognitive levels organized into several tiers that are similar to Piaget's stages. During development, these skills, for example, role playing or mathematical reasoning, become increasingly complex. Because skills are acquired in the context of particular experiences, a skill may not be applied to all domains. As a result, a child may be at different cognitive levels in different domains. Thus, Fischer attempts to account for Piaget's décalages by emphasizing the role of specific experiences in the environment; he concludes that development is somewhat domain specific, that is, restricted to a particular type of knowledge. In addition, like Case, Fischer considers limits in processing capacity at each developmental level to be an important constraint on development. He views development as the coordination of relations among objects, events, and people (like Case), as well as the coordination of skills. He has tested his theory in a variety of knowledge domains, ranging from math to the Oedipus conflict.

Other theorists that are not as clearly classified as neo-Piagetian have also focused on the issue of whether cognitive development is domain specific or domain general. Keil (1986), for example, argues that much of cognitive development is domain specific. Different knowledge domains, such as the classification of animals versus the activity of cooking, have different structures, perhaps because of biologically based constraints.

The two main contributions of the neo-Piagetians have been to propose a promising set of processes to account for developmental change and to clarify and refine the notion of stages, for example, by attempting to differentiate domain-general and domain-specific achievements. As Flavell (1982, p. 1) has observed, "Cognitive development might appear to be more general-stage-like than many of us believed, if only we knew how and where to look."

In addition to these large-scale neo-Piagetian theoretical accounts, many neo-Piagetian studies have emerged. Although many psychologists claim that the influence of Piaget's theory is waning, this decline may be more apparent than real. Perhaps there are fewer studies with such Piagetian tasks as conservation and class inclusion, but so many of Piaget's assumptions about the nature of cognitive development are assimilated into the thinking of researchers that Piaget's ongoing influence often is not recognized. For example, the search for a general concept underlying several different behaviors and for the process by which a new concept arises from a previous one continues in most cognitive developmental research.

Several particularly active new areas of research clearly are neo-Piagetian. One is children's "theory of mind" (Astington, Harris, and Olson, 1988) — their notions of the nature of the mind, particularly the distinction between mind and reality, which includes the realization that the mind mediates (embellishes, interprets, distorts) our perceptions of the world. For example, 3-year-olds do not understand that a person can possess a false belief. That is, they do not realize that a person would look for an object in its usual location rather than in the place it was moved to in the person's absence, and without his knowledge (Perner, Leekam, and Wimmer, 1987). Other vigorous neo-Piagetian research areas include the acquisition of mathematical skills (for example, Resnick, 1987), the role of social interaction in learning and cognitive development (for example, Berkowitz, 1984), the distinction between appearance and reality (Flavell, 1986), and cognitive maps of large-scale spaces, such as classrooms (Cohen, 1985).

# SUMMARY

Piaget's theory is the most influential stage theory in developmental psychology. These invariant stages describe changes in how children acquire knowledge about the world (genetic epistemology). In the first 2 years of life, the child constructs sensorimotor schemes based on physical action upon the world. The schemes become more intentional and more intercoordinated during that time. During the preoperational period, approximately ages 2 to 7, the child exploits his newly acquired symbolic ability. Despite the limitations of egocentrism, rigid thought, and limited role-taking and communication abilities, the child combines symbols into semilogical reasoning. During the concrete operational period, roughly ages 7 to 11, the child acquires logicomathematical structures. Now thought is operational and consequently more flexible and abstract. Finally, during the formal operational period, ages 11 to 15, these operations are no longer limited to concrete objects. Operations can be performed on operations, verbal propositions, and hypothetical conditions.

These stagelike changes involve changes in the structure of thought. Thought becomes increasingly organized, always building on the structure of the previous stage. Evidence for these structural changes comes from observations of infants and from interviews or problem-solving tasks with older children.

Movement through the stages is caused by four factors: physical maturation, experience with physical objects, social experience, and equilibration. Experience brings cognitive progress through assimilation and accommodation. These functional invariants help the child adapt to the environment by strengthening and stretching his current understanding of the world.

Piaget views children as active and self-regulating organisms that change by means of interacting innate and environmental factors. He emphasizes qualitative change, but identifies certain quantitative changes as well. The essence of cognitive development is structural change.

With respect to the theoretical nature of the theory, it is possible to discern all four types of theory building: models, deductive theory, functional theory, and inductive theory. In particular, Piaget draws on the equilibration model and the logicomathematical model.

The theory's main strengths are its recognition of the central role of cognition in development, value as an integrative and heuristic theory, discovery of surprising features of young children's thinking, wide scope, and ecological validity. The main weaknesses include its unclear links between constructs and behavior, inadequate support for the stage notion, inadequate account of mechanisms of development, need for a theory of performance, slighting of social and emotional aspects of development, and methodological and stylistic inadequacies. Some of these problems have been addressed by the neo-Piagetians. In addition, Piaget himself continued to modify his theory in his later years.

What should be our final judgment on Piaget's theory? This flawed but amazingly productive theory gives us a framework for viewing the richness and complexity of cognitive development. Even when it has failed, for example, where an adequate explanation for conservation cannot be found despite hundreds of studies, the theory has revealed interesting facets of development, such as the role of attention in conceptual development or rudimentary numerical skills that may lead to conservation. Furthermore, the theory has raised developmental issues that all subsequent theories must address. All new theories for years to come will inevitably be compared to Piaget's theory. In short, we have not made a mistake by paying attention to this "giant in the nursery" (Elkind, 1968).

## SUGGESTED READINGS

We now have a vast number of books written about Piaget. An especially notable effort is the following.

Ginsburg, H., and S. Opper. *Piaget's theory of intellectual development.* 3d ed. Englewood Cliffs, N.J.: Prentice-Hall, 1988. This book presents an up-to-date account of the theory.

The following books by Piaget are two of his more readable and clearly written publications.

Piaget, J. *Six psychological studies.* New York: Random House, 1967.
Piaget, J., and B. Inhelder. *The psychology of the child.* New York: Basic Books, 1969.

Piaget's research has stimulated a number of thoughtful publications on issues raised by his theory. Four influential publications are mentioned here.

Case, R. *Intellectual development: Birth to adulthood.* Orlando, Fla.: Academic Press, 1985.

Flavell, J. H. Stage-related properties of cognitive development. *Cognitive Psychology,* 1971, 2, 421–453.

Flavell, J. H. An analysis of cognitive-developmental sequences. *Genetic Psychology Monographs,* 1972, 86, 279–350.

Levin, I., ed. *Stage and structure: Reopening the debate.* Norwood, N.J.: Ablex, 1986.

# 2

# Freud's and Erikson's Psychoanalytic Theories

*I dreamt that it was night and that I was lying in my bed. . . .*
*Suddenly the window opened of its own accord, and I was terrified*
*to see that some white wolves were sitting on the big walnut tree in*
*front of the window. There were six or seven of them. The wolves*
*were quite white, and looked more like foxes or sheep-dogs, for they*
*had big tails like foxes and they had their ears pricked like dogs*
*when they pay attention to something. In great terror, evidently of*
*being eaten up by the wolves, I screamed and woke up.*
[Freud, 1918 (1955, p. 29)]

*The most significant sex difference was the tendency of boys to erect*
*structures, buildings, towers, or streets . . . the girls tended to use*
*the play table as the interior of a house with simple, little, or no use*
*of blocks. . . . Simple enclosures with low walls and without*
*ornaments were the largest item among the configurations built by*
*girls. However, these enclosures often had an elaborate gate. . . . A*
*blocking of the entrance or a thickening of the walls could on further*
*study be shown to reflect acute anxiety over the feminine role.*
[Erikson, 1963, pp. 102–105]

**P** sychoanalytic theory and Piagetian theory are the giant theories of developmental psychology. To meet the source of psychoanalytic theory, we move from Geneva to Vienna, where Freud spent most of his life. The development of the theory followed a tortuous course, full of dazzling insights, diverging ideas, and clashing personalities. Although many figures are responsible for the psychoanalytic movement, we must limit our attention to Sigmund Freud, who began the movement, and Erik Erikson, who more recently constructed a life-span view of development. Both proposed that personality development proceeds through a series of stages. In each stage, the child copes with certain conflicts stimulated, to a great extent, by biological changes in development. The presentation of these theories follows the order of the previous chapter: a biography, a general orientation, a description of stages of development, an account of mechanisms of change, the theory's stand on critical issues, the theoretical characteristics of the theory, and an evaluation.

# FREUD

## BIOGRAPHICAL SKETCH

Sigmund Freud was born in Freiberg, Moravia, in 1856.* When he was 4, his family moved to Vienna, where he lived for nearly eighty years. He was the eldest of eight children born to a wool merchant and his wife. Freud believed that he was a favored child and that great things were expected of him. As he expressed it, "A man who has been

---

*Much of the material in this section comes from Ernest Jones' biography, *The life and work of Sigmund Freud*, in three volumes (1953, 1955, 1957), and abridged in 1961 by L. Trillig and S. Marcus (New York: Basic Books).

the indisputable favorite of his mother keeps for life the feeling of a conqueror, that confidence of success that often induces real success" (Jones, 1961, p. 6). He had a voracious appetite for books on history and philosophy, as did Piaget. He and a friend taught themselves Spanish so that they could read *Don Quixote* in the original. In secondary school, he read an essay by Goethe on nature that awakened an interest in science. He entered medical school with the expectation that he would devote his life to scientific research. In retrospect, it is interesting that his first major research project was on the structure of the testes in eels.

The goal of becoming a research scientist had to be set aside when his poor economic situation and the barriers against advancement for a Jew in academia forced him to enter private practice. Freud's longstanding interest in neurology led him naturally into the treatment of nervous disorders. At the time, this branch of medicine was at a very primitive level, and its practitioners could give little help for the mentally ill. Patients typically received hydrotherapy (various types of baths) and electrotherapy (mild electric currents passed through the body).

Freud was fascinated with hysteria, a disorder characterized by such symptoms as paralysis, numbness, squinting, and tremors. His interest in a possible new treatment, hypnosis, was aroused by his contact with the French neurologist Jean Charcot and the Viennese physician Josef Breuer. The fact that Charcot could produce symptoms of hysteria in people by means of hypnotic suggestion was evidence that the malady had a psychological basis. As Freud began to use hypnosis with his patients, he was impressed that they could recall important incidents and feelings while under hypnosis that were otherwise inaccessible. Despite the general belief among neurologists that hypnotism was both fraudulent and dangerous, Freud enthusiastically experimented with this technique: "There was something positively seductive in working with hypnotism. For the first time there was a sense of having overcome one's helplessness; and it was highly flattering to enjoy the reputation of being a miracle-worker" [1925a (1959, p. 17)].*

---

*The references to Freud's works in this chapter are to the publication dates of the original works in German. The page numbers are those of the translations (given in parentheses): J. Strachey, ed. and trans., *The standard edition of the complete psychological works of Sigmund Freud.* 24 vols. (London: Hogarth Press, 1953–1966).

Freud was also influenced by Breuer's discovery that symptoms of hysteria could be alleviated simply by having his patients talk about (and "relive") their emotion-laden experiences from early life. It eventually became clear that hypnosis was often not even necessary in order to remove hysterical symptoms. With a sense of excitement, Freud experimented with what Breuer called the "talking cure." In a letter to his friend Wilhelm Fliess in 1895, he described how psychology possessed him: "A man like me cannot live without a hobbyhorse, a consuming passion — in Schiller's words a tyrant. I have found my tyrant, and in his service I know no limits. My tyrant is psychology."

Freud's study of his patients' dreams and childhood memories led to his first major publication, *The Interpretation of Dreams*, in 1900. Although this book was ignored by medical and scientific circles, as well as the general public, Freud was not discouraged. A succession of fascinating books appeared in the following years. Although he worked almost completely in isolation for years, he eventually began to attract a small following.

Carl Jung and Alfred Adler, in particular, strengthened the new psychoanalytic movement even while the European medical establishment spurned it. This rejection drew the psychoanalysts closer together, and they formed the International Psycho-Analytical Association, which exists even today. A turning point came in 1909, when the eminent American psychologist G. Stanley Hall invited Freud to speak at the twentieth-anniversary celebration of the founding of Clark University in Worcester, Massachusetts. Freud described his feelings on this occasion: "In Europe I felt as though I were despised; but over there I found myself received by the foremost men as an equal. As I stepped on to the platform at Worcester to deliver my *Five Lectures on Psycho-Analysis* . . . it seemed like the realization of some incredible daydream: psycho-analysis was no longer a product of delusion, it had become a valuable part of reality" [1925a, (1959, p. 52)].

Freud began to achieve international recognition, especially in the years following World War I. Psychoanalysis began to influence not only psychiatry and the social sciences, but also fields such as literature, art, ethics, and education. "Subconscious" and "ego" became household words. It should be noted that much of the reaction was far from positive. Many people were shocked at the claim that children have a sexual nature. The attacks on psychoanalytic theory continued throughout Freud's lifetime. In addition, Freud's success was marred by the later defections of Jung and Adler and other prominent leaders within psychoanalysis.

Freud continued to develop his theory over the years. In fact, he made some basic changes in his views when he was in his seventies. By the end of his life, his psychoanalytic writings filled 23 volumes. In his last years, he worked while in considerable pain from cancer of the jaw. When the Nazis took over Austria in 1937, he was forced to flee to England. He died in 1939 in London.

## GENERAL ORIENTATION TO THE THEORY

The neophyte faces certain frustration when he attempts to understand Freud's theory because various sources give contradictory accounts. The problem stems from the fact that Freud revised his ideas over the years. Although revision is a sign of a healthy theory, it is discouraging to anyone struggling to understand the theorist's writings. Fortunately, despite certain changes in the details of the system, there is constancy in the general approach. Six general characteristics emerge from the details of Freud's work: a dynamic approach, a structural approach, a topographic approach, a developmental stage approach, a normal–abnormal continuum, and the psychoanalytic methods. We look at each of these characteristics and, when useful for clarifying the theory, compare them with those of Piaget's theory.

### Dynamic Approach

Freud described his theory as "a sort of economics of nervous energy" (Jones, 1953, p. 345). This nervous energy is variously termed *psychic energy, drive energy, libido,* and *tension.* In an analogy to energy in the field of physics, nervous energy builds up and can be distributed, tied to certain images, transformed, and discharged. Just as mechanical, electrical, or thermal energy performs physical work, so does psychic energy perform psychological work.

It is possible to identify several laws of energy in Freud's system with its commonsense physics. For example, in the same way that physical energy is transformed but not destroyed, psychological energy is transformed into anxiety, displaced into a physical structure that causes a symptom, such as paralysis, transformed into a thought, such as an obsession, and so on. Another law of energy comes from the famous *pleasure principle*, which states that whenever possible, energy is discharged without delay. The organism strives toward the immediate, direct reduction of tension, which reduces pain and produces pleasure. Hunger leads to eating; the need to suck leads to sucking one's thumb. A final example is the *principle of least action*, in which small amounts of energy are discharged, but only after a delay and only after following an indirect route. The *reality principle* rules here. The mental apparatus scans reality and evaluates various possible courses of action before allowing energy to be discharged. For example, an angry child may tell his friend he is angry with him rather than hit him and risk punishment.

Where does this psychological energy come from? The human body has certain instincts that make demands on the mind. Instincts (or biological drives, as they often are called) involve excitation in some region of the body. This internal excitation stimulates the mind and creates a "need." Thus, psychic energy is derived from biological energy. Freud maintained that "mind" and "body" have a constant interplay:

An 'instinct' appears to us as a concept on the frontier between the mental and the somatic, as the psychical representative of the stimuli originating from within the organism and reaching the mind, as a measure of the demand made upon the mind for work in consequence of its connection with the body.

*[1915 (1957, pp. 121–122)]*

In Freud's final account, the two basic instincts were *Eros* (sex, self-preservation, love, life forces, striving toward unity) and the *destructive instinct* (aggression, undoing connections, the death instinct, hate). Freud assigned the term *libido* to the available energy of Eros. There is no analogous term for the energy of a destructive instinct. In Freud's earlier and best-known writings, he emphasized the sexual nature of Eros and did little toward developing ideas about the destructive instinct. His later interest in the destructive instinct is attributed to his horror at the atrocities of World War I and the anti-Semitic feelings of his times. In Freud's words, "the aim of all life is death" [1920 (1955, p. 38)].

We can use the sex drive to illustrate four characteristics of an instinct: its source, aim, object, and pressure.

1. The sex drive has its *source* in bodily needs, as described above. Sexual excitation arises from erogenous zones in the body, particularly the oral, anal, and genital areas. This change in the site of excitation underlies the movement from stage to stage, as we shall see later.

2. The *aim* of the sex drive, or of any instinct, is to remove this bodily need. This ultimate goal is achieved through such subordinate goals as finding and investing energy in sexual objects. An instinct, in Freud's words, is "an urge inherent in organic life to restore an earlier state of things" [1920 (1955, p. 36)]. This return to a state of mental and physiological equilibrium (or lack of excitation) is achieved by satisfying the need.

3. Tension mounts, an appropriate sex *object* is found, tension is discharged, and the person experiences pleasure. The object may be a real person (the self or another) or object or a representation of a person or an object. There are many ways to satisfy a drive. Libido becomes attached or, in Freud's terminology, "cathected" to an object. An infant cathects his mother and other objects that satisfy his needs.

4. Finally, the *pressure* of the sex drive is determined by the degree of force (amount of sexual energy). The more energy, the stronger the drive.

Diverse human behaviors can ultimately be traced to the two general instincts, with their various subinstincts. Freud would claim that writing a book, jogging, watching television, and making a bookcase have their origins deep in human needs. The route between the instinct and the behavior may be very indirect because of the mobility of the instincts. Psychic energy is a general energy source that can be likened to an electricity supply, which can be used to toast bread, shave, bake, and so forth (Hall, 1954, p. 84). Freud spoke of the many ways that instincts can be expressed and combined. Drives can be fused; for example, playing soccer may satisfy both aggressive and cooperative needs, or eating, both hunger and destructiveness (by biting and chewing). Drives can be satisfied in a partial and roundabout way, as when a person gossips about an enemy instead of physically attacking him. Freud believed that da Vinci's interest in painting Madonnas was a way of partially satisfying his desire for his mother, from whom he had been separated early in life. Drives also may be substituted, as intense hate turns into love or sexual desire becomes platonic love. Finally, one object can substitute for another object, as when an adult's oral needs are satisfied by playing a trumpet. In some cases, a culturally or morally "higher" goal object is substituted for the truly desired object. This is labeled *sublimation.* An angry person might sublimate his desire to attack other people by painting violent scenes. Another common type of object substitution is *compensation,* in which a person makes up for his failure in one area by applying himself in another area. A five-foot, six-inch basketball player may eventually become a sports announcer.

Both Freud and Piaget have a dynamic approach, but in different ways. Freud was concerned with drive *forces* that energize behavior, whereas Piaget was concerned with mental *actions* — schemes, operations, assimilation, and accommodation. Piaget contended that emotions are the energizers behind thought, but he did little to develop this idea further. Both Piaget and Freud were enamored of another aspect of dynamics: the notion of equilibrium from physics. The process of equilibrium, followed by disequilibrium and subsequently by equilibrium again is central in both theories. However, crucial differences in the nature of equilibrium divide the theories, as we shall see in the section on mechanisms of development.

## Structural Approach

The previous section creates the image of a human hydraulic system with powerful forces surging through the body and the mind. We now look at the psychological structures through which these forces flow. These structures mediate between the drives and behavior; drives do not lead directly to behavior. There is, then, an architecture of the mind. Mental processes take place within the structures, between the structures, and by means of the structures. There are three major structures: the id, ego, and superego. Roughly speaking, the *id* is the seat of biologically based drives, the *ego* is the mechanism for adapting to reality, and the *superego* is analogous to the conscience. We examine each "province of the mind" [1933a (1964, p. 72)] in turn and then portray their overall organization.

## Id

In Freud's words, the id is the "dark, inaccessible part of our personality. . . . a chaos, a cauldron full of seething excitations" [1933a (1964, p. 73)]. Furthermore, the id

contains everything that is inherited, that is present at birth, that is laid down in the constitution — above all, therefore, the instincts, which originate from the somatic organization and which find a first psychical expression here [in the id] in forms unknown to us.

*[1940 (1964, p. 145)]*

As the novelist Peter De Vries humorously expresses it in *Forever Panting*, " 'Id' isn't just another big word." The id is the seat of innate desires and is the main source of psychic energy. It wants immediate satisfaction, in accordance with the pleasure principle described earlier. The energy of the id is invested either in action on an object that would satisfy an instinct or in images of an object that would give partial satisfaction. For example, an infant may satisfy his oral-hunger drive directly by sucking a nipple and receiving milk or partially and indirectly by imagining a bottle of milk. This hallucinatory wish fulfillment is called *primary-process thought*. The id's energy is so mobile that it is easily discharged or transferred from object to object or image to image.

In contrast to young infants, older infants, children, and adults have an ego and a superego in addition to an id. The id, however, continues to operate throughout life, especially in our nighttime dreams, daydreams, imagination, and impulsive, selfish, and pleasure-loving behavior. The id has been called the "spoiled child of the personality" (Hall, 1954, p. 27). Deep down inside of us, we want total satisfaction — a state of nirvana.

Much of Freud's knowledge about the id came from his study of dreams. The desires of the id appear in dreams in either an obvious or a disguised fashion. One does not need psychoanalytic training to interpret a hungry man's dream about a thick steak. However, some urges are so threatening that they must be rendered less obvious. According to Freud, clothes and uniforms sometimes represent nakedness; water can stand for birth; a journey can mean death. (The interpretation of dreams is discussed in a later section.)

## Ego

In the beginning, there is id. The id, armed with primary-process thought (hallucinatory wish fulfillment), makes its demands. However, the baby soon discovers that thinking something does not make it so. The image of the mother and milk and the memory of warmth do not quiet the pangs of hunger. He is learning that there is a difference between images and reality, between the self and the outer world.

The id's inability to always produce the desired object leads to the development of the ego.* The ego, the mind's avenue to the real world, is developed because it is needed for physical and psychological survival. It aids in survival because it possesses *secondary-process thought*. Secondary-process, or rational, thought is more organized, integrated, and logical than primary-process thought, in which contradictions abound. The ego's activities include such intellectual ones as perception, logical thought, problem solving, and memory. Most of the intellectual abilities studied by Piaget would fall into Freud's ego domain. The ego is the director who must make the tough, high-level decisions. It evaluates the present situation, recalls relevant decisions and events in the past, weighs various factors in the present and future, and predicts the consequences of various actions. The ego's decisions are aided by feelings of anxiety, which signal that certain actions would be threatening. Above all, the ego's decision making involves the *delay* of energy discharge, the reality principle mentioned earlier. Freud described the thinking of the ego as "an experimental action carried out with small amounts of energy, in the same way as a general shifts small figures about on a map before setting his large bodies of troops in motion" [1933a (1964, p. 89)].

These small quantities of energy at the disposal of the ego come from the id. As the ego acquires more and more energy and gains experience using secondary-process thought during development, it becomes stronger and more differentiated. Of course, the ego, with its

---

*Near the end of his life, Freud softened his claim that the ego developed out of the id. He began referring to an early, undifferentiated ego–id.

secondary-process thought, does not replace the primary-process thought of the id. Rather, it simply adds another level to thought. Gratification can be achieved either by finding appropriate real objects in the environment after a delay or by hallucinating and dreaming. Throughout life, we use a mixture of primary- and secondary-process thought. However, as development proceeds, the secondary-process aspects of thought become more dominant.

The ego serves "three tyrannical masters": the id, superego, and external world [1933a (1964, p. 77)]. Freud described the ego's position in an analogy:

> The ego's relation to the id might be compared with that of a rider to his horse. The horse supplies the locomotive energy, while the rider has the privilege of deciding on the goal and of guiding the powerful animal's movement. But only too often there arises between the ego and the id the not precisely ideal situation of the rider being obliged to guide the horse along the path by which it itself wants to go.
>
> *[1933a (1964, p. 77)]*

The ego mediates between the id and the external world:

> Thus the ego is fighting on two fronts: it has to defend its existence against an external world which threatens it with annihilation as well as against an internal world that makes excessive demands. It adopts the same methods of defence against both, but its defence against the internal enemy is particularly inadequate. As a result of having originally been identical with this latter enemy and of having lived with it since on the most intimate terms, it has great difficulty in escaping from the internal dangers. They persist as threats, even if they can be temporarily held down.
>
> *[1940 (1964, p. 200)]*

These constant threats and dangers from the id and the environment arouse anxiety. When possible, the ego tackles the problem in a realistic way, using its problem-solving skills. However, when the anxiety is so strong that it threatens to engulf the ego, *defense mechanisms* come into play. They control and thereby alleviate anxiety by distorting reality in some way. Although defense mechanisms allow only partial satisfaction of the drives, for the organism in a state of tension, some satisfaction is better than none at all. Freud's list of defense mechanisms changed in number from time to time as they were combined or further differentiated in his writings or those of his daughter, Anna Freud. We limit our discussion to five main defense mechanisms: repression (denying or forgetting the danger), reaction formation (acting the opposite from the way one feels), projection (attributing one's unacceptable impulses to others), regression (returning to an earlier form of behavior), and fixation (remaining at the present level).

1. *Repression* is preventing a threatening thought from emerging into awareness. The principle seems to be "What we don't know can't hurt us" (Hall, 1954, p. 85). If anxiety-arousing thoughts cannot surface, we do not experience anxiety. A thought may be anxiety-arousing because it threatens a breakdown in self-control or arouses frustration or guilt. To avoid anxiety, we forget the name of someone who has hurt us or forget to pay a bill that would put a severe strain on the budget and cause worry.

Often a whole constellation of memories must be repressed because recalling neutral memories would elicit associated painful memories. One of Freud's patients feared going out in the street because it aroused her earlier fear that she would become a prostitute, which in turn was related to her desire for sexual experience. Furthermore, according to Freud, there is massive repression of memories of childhood sexuality once children reach grade-school age. Only with great difficulty could Freud help his adult patients recover these memories.

Freud's ideas about repression developed from his observations in therapy. When a patient freely reported her thoughts during "free association," she would often stop abruptly and claim that her mind had suddenly gone blank, just at the moment when important memories of the past seemed about to emerge. Perhaps Friedrich Nietzsche was correct in his remark, "One's own self is well hidden from oneself: of all mines of treasure one's own is the last to be dug up."

If a person depends too heavily on this defense mechanism, she may develop a repressed personality: withdrawn, inaccessible, nonspontaneous, and rigid. Also, there can be some loss of contact with reality as the person makes serious and frequent mistakes in remembering, speaking, and perceiving or develops symptoms of hysteria. For example, hysterical deafness may prevent a person from hearing something she does not want to hear.

2. In *reaction formation*, the ego masks an unacceptable emotion by focusing on its opposite, often in an exaggerated way. A child's jealousy and hatred for a newborn sibling is experienced as love, extravagantly displayed. A toddler who wants to soil his diapers and do "dirty" things may become compulsively clean, frequently washing his hands. Chastity may hide unacceptable sexual desires; purity may hide evil.

3. *Projection* is the attribution of anxiety-arousing thoughts to people and objects in the external world, rather than the self. "I want to kill him" is changed to "He wants to kill me." Consequently, any violence against the other is permissible because it is done in self-defense. It is easier for the ego to handle objective, external dangers than internal dangers.

4. In *regression*, a person reverts to an earlier level of development. If the anxiety of the present is too much to handle, one retreats to simpler times, when there were fewer controls. Thus, people act in childish ways. They fight, play practical jokes, eat too much ice cream, yell obscenities at the referee at a football game, seek cuddling, and get drunk.

5. In *fixation*, one component of personality development comes to a halt. A portion of the libido remains tied to an earlier period of development and does not allow the child to proceed fully to the next stage. Fixation can occur when the present mode of satisfaction, for example, sucking a breast or bottle, is so gratifying that the child does not want to give it up, even under pressures to become weaned. Fixation can also occur when the next step appears to be too frightening or demanding or unsatisfying. The initiation of toilet training, if too harsh, may cause the toddler to remain partially in the oral stage rather than progress through the anal stage. The toddler may be fixated on a particular mode of satisfaction (sucking), object (mother), or type of thinking (primary process). Fixation is tied to regression in that a person is more likely to regress in the face of a barrier if there has been fixation at an earlier point in development.

Other psychological processes discussed elsewhere in the chapter are sometimes considered defense mechanisms. These include sublimation of an unacceptable desire to a more socially accepted activity, identification with the aggressor (usually a boy's father), and displacement of drives.

Defense mechanisms are a necessary evil. We need them to deal with high anxiety, but at the cost of "wasting" our energy when it could be put to better use in ego development, for example, for creative thought or the development of problem-solving skills. Furthermore, if too much energy is tied up in the defense mechanisms, personality may not develop normally because the person distorts reality and deceives himself. This situation makes subsequent adjustments to reality even more difficult.

### Superego

The superego is the last to develop. It arises when children resolve their Oedipus complex and develop identification with their parents. That story is told in the section on stages.

The superego is composed of two parts: the conscience and the ego ideal. In general, the conscience is negative, and the ego ideal is positive. The *conscience* is composed of the parents' prohibitions, their "Thou shalt nots." Just as the parent has punished the child for his transgressions, so does the conscience punish the person with feelings of guilt, "accidentally" cutting one's finger, or intentionally self-destructive behavior. Curiously, the superego often becomes even more severe than the parents were. A person with a particularly strong conscience may lead a "strait-jacket existence" (Hall, 1954, p. 46) or be extremely moral-idealistic rather than realistic in his thinking.

The term *ego ideal* refers to standards of conduct toward which the child strives. Just as the child has been rewarded for certain behavior by the parents, she is rewarded by the ego ideal with feelings of self-esteem and pride. These are echoes of early years when a parent said "Good girl!" to the young child.

The superego opposes both the id and the ego. It rewards, punishes, and makes demands. It tries to do away with both the pleasure principle and the reality principle. The superego watches over not only behavior but also the thoughts of the ego. Thinking is as bad as doing, from the superego's point of view. As in the case of the id, the superego does not distinguish between the subjective and the real.

The superego is society's way of achieving order. Unrestrained sexual and aggressive behavior would destroy the always tenuous social structure. Freud notes that if the ego represents the "power of the present" and the id represents the "organic past," then the superego represents the "cultural past" [1940 (1964, p. 206)].

## Structural Relationships

We have dissected the personality into id, ego, and superego. However, personality is an organized whole—a unique constellation of forces and structures. Freud sketched out the relationship among the mental "areas," as seen in Figure 2.1. He cautions that we should not regard the id, ego, and superego as sharply defined areas. Rather, they are "areas of colour melting into one another as they are presented by modern artists" [1933a (1964, p. 79)]. The superego, for example, blends into the id and, in fact, is intimately related to the id. This close relationship is most clearly seen in the Oedipus complex, discussed later, in which strong urges in the id necessitate the development of the superego and are subsequently controlled by the superego. Or in another instance, the id and superego may join forces in attacking

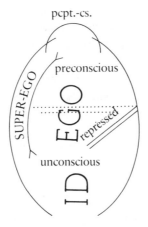

**FIGURE 2-1** ■ *In Freud's sketch of the structure and topography of the mind, which also depicts the process of repression, the label "pcpt.-cs." refers to the perceptual-conscious, usually termed the conscious. [Reproduced from* New Introductory Lectures on Psycho-Analysis, *by Sigmund Freud, translated and edited by James Strachey, with the permission of Hogarth Press and W. W. Norton & Company, Inc. Copyright © 1965, 1964 by James Strachey.]*

supposedly "immoral" persons as in witch-burning or the cruelty of the Inquisition (Hall, 1954, p. 48).

The energy of the three structures is also not rigidly separated. If the id's energy cannot be discharged, it can be used to energize the ego or superego. Sexual energy might be transformed into artistic activities, creative scientific thought, or piety. In fact, the ego has no energy of its own; all energy is derived from the id. Just as the energy can go from the id to the ego, it can return to the id if the ego does not successfully satisfy the needs of the id. This return of energy to the id is common in normal personalities during dreams or during wishful thinking when awake.

These structures contain a closed energy system, in which a certain amount of energy is distributed to the three parts. A gain in energy in one part strengthens that part, but at the same time weakens the other parts.

Finally, the id, ego, and superego lack separation, in that they combine to produce a behavior or a thought. Nearly every activity reflects the combined action of the id, ego, and superego. Licking an ice-cream cone reflects the hunger and oral-sucking drives of the id, the successful search for a suitable object by the ego (adults do not normally suck on lollipops in public), and the reward for good behavior by the superego. Under ordinary circumstances, the three systems work together as a team in relative harmony rather than war against each other.

The ego is central in this structural relationship. It is brought into all conflicts between the id and superego because each is trying to use the ego to meet its own needs. The ego must both obey and control the id, superego, and external reality. It survives by compromising. If the id says "yes" and the superego says "no," then the ego says "wait" (Hall, 1954, p. 47). Freud summed up this relationship as follows:

Thus the ego, driven by the id, confined by the super-ego, repulsed by reality, struggles to master its economic task of bringing about harmony among the forces and influences working in and upon it; and we can understand how it is that so often we cannot suppress a cry: 'Life is not easy!'

[1933a (1964, p. 78)]

Yet Freud remained optimistic about human reason:

> The voice of the intellect is a soft one, but it does not rest till it has gained a hearing. Finally, after a countless succession of rebuffs, it succeeds. This is one of the few points on which one may be optimistic about the future of mankind, but it is in itself a point of no small importance.
>
> *[1927 (1961, p. 53)]*

There are two possible misconceptions of Freud's model that should be corrected. The reader may be struck by the anthropomorphizing of the id, ego, and superego. Freud spoke of them as if they were three homunculi, or little men — one passionate and spoiled, one rational, and one moral — constantly at each other's throat. He was displeased with these humanlike images, but felt they helped give both the clinician and the layman an intuitive understanding of the three systems: "Analogies, it is true, decide nothing, but they can make one feel more at home" [1933a (1964, p. 72)]. The other possible misinterpretation is that the three systems refer to particular physical regions of the brain. The structures are simply a way of summarizing three aspects of the personality.

## Topographic Approach

> Everyone is a moon and has a dark side which he never shows to anybody.
>
> *[Mark Twain]*

Freud's early writings portray a geography (or topography) of the mind. In a metaphorical sense, the "parts" of the mind have spatial relationships to each other. This geography was later supplemented by the structural notions of id, ego, and superego described earlier. Turning again to Figure 2.1, we see that the map of the mind displays three topographic regions: the unconscious, preconscious, and conscious (or perceptual conscious, as labeled in Figure 2.1). The unconscious is largely unknown territory; the preconscious and, especially, the conscious have familiar terrains.

1. The *unconscious* refers primarily to thoughts and feelings that are repressed and therefore unknown. This material is incapable of breaking into consciousness without certain changes or interventions, such as an increase in the drive, a weakening of ego defenses, or the guidance of a therapist.

2. The *preconscious* is capable of becoming conscious because it is not actively barred from consciousness. It is a great deal closer to the conscious than is the unconscious. Preconscious thought becomes conscious by forming mental images or linking up with language.

3. The *conscious* (or perceptual conscious) is synonymous with what a person is aware of at the moment. It is a "highly fugitive state" [Freud, 1940 (1964, p. 159)] because thoughts can rapidly slip back and forth between the preconscious and the conscious. Since energy is required for a thought to enter into consciousness, only a few thoughts can be conscious at any one time.

Freud used a metaphor to describe the relationship between the unconscious and the preconscious and conscious:

> Let us therefore compare the system of the unconscious to a large entrance hall, in which the mental impulses jostle one another like separate individuals. Adjoining this entrance hall there is a second, narrower, room — a kind of drawing-room — in which consciousness, too, resides. But on the threshold between these two rooms a watchman performs his function: he examines the different mental impulses, acts as a censor, and will not admit them into the drawing-room if they displease him.
>
> *[1917 (1963, p. 295)]*

Returning to Freud's sketch, we see how the id, ego, and superego (structures) are related to the unconscious, preconscious, and conscious (topography). All the id resides in the unconscious. The unconscious id is a large area, and in fact Freud corrected his drawing by noting that the space taken up by the unconscious id should have been much greater than that of the ego or the preconscious. If the mind is like an iceberg, then the conscious is only the exposed tip of the iceberg; most of the iceberg (the unconscious) remains hidden. Both the ego and the superego span the three layers. For example, the ego is unaware of the action of its defense mechanisms.

Developmental changes also occur in the relative size of the unconscious, preconscious, and conscious. The infant's mind is almost completely unconscious. With increasing age, the preconscious and conscious occupy more and more of the mental territory. Even among adults, however, the unconscious is the largest area.

Although Freud described the unconscious, preconscious, and conscious as though they were separate entities, he constantly noted that no such separation exists. Rather, he was simply abstracting three aspects of mental functioning. These three aspects of functioning operate together in a holistic fashion to produce behavior. Reading obituaries in the newspaper can be traced to both unconscious (fear of death) and conscious (keeping track of elderly friends) motivations.

Freud placed great importance on the role of the unconscious: "For the property of being conscious or not is in the last resort our one beacon-light in the darkness of depth-psychology" [1923 (1961, p. 18)]. The notion that there is a vast unconscious that controls behavior emerged from Freud's early psychoanalytic sessions with his patients. Patients had sexual fantasies or impulses of which they were unaware, but which led to certain inexplicable behavior. For example, a patient with a healthy visual system was unable to see because seeing was too painful; seeing activated painful memories in the unconscious. Additional evidence for the existence of an unconscious came from post-hypnotic suggestion, in which the patient performs some action that was suggested to him while under hypnosis or from slips of the tongue, accidents that were not really accidental, selective forgetting (as when someone forgets a dental appointment), and dreams.

## Stage Approach

Freud makes two bold claims about human development. One is that the first few years of life are the most important years for the formation of personality. The other claim is that this development involves psychosexual stages.

The notion that early experience is crucial seems obvious and non-controversial to the modern student of development. This idea, however, had not really been taken seriously until Freud systematically developed it. According to Freud, a behavior can be understood only if one knows how it developed in the person's early history. Both normal behavior and abnormal behavior have their roots in the early years, when the basic structure of the personality is laid down. The early interactions between the child's drives and his social environment set the pattern for later learning, social adjustment, and coping with anxiety. The child truly is father of the man.

It is interesting that a therapist who studied and treated adults would develop a theory of child development. Early in his work, Freud discovered that attempts to trace the cause of a disturbed personality usually led to traumatic, unresolved sexual experiences of childhood. The distant past was very much alive in his patients' current lives in dreams, anxiety from repressed childhood desires, and defense mechanisms acquired in childhood. From information revealed in sessions with the patient, Freud was able to reconstruct the sequence of stages of childhood.

Freud and Piaget are the grand stage theorists of developmental psychology. Freud, like Piaget, focuses on qualitative changes during development. We look at the general nature of the stages here and leave a description of the content of each stage for later.

Four distinct stages and a period of latency mark developmental time. Each stage is defined in terms of the part of the body around which drives are centered. The eye of the storm shifts from the oral to the anal to the phallic area during the first five years. Then a period of latency in middle childhood is followed by the genital stage of adolescence. Each stage presents new needs that must be handled by the mental structures. The way in which these needs are met (or not met) determines not only how sexual satisfaction is achieved, but also how the child relates to other people and how he feels about himself. He develops characteristic attitudes, defenses, and fantasies. Unresolved conflicts in any stage may haunt the person throughout his lifetime.

Because the movement from stage to stage is biologically determined, it occurs whether or not there is unfinished business in the stage that is ending. This notion of stage development is very different from Piaget's, in which one stage must be essentially completed before the next stage may begin. The two theories, however, coincide in their claim that the stages follow an invariant order. For Freud, the invariant order comes almost entirely from physical maturation. For Piaget, it comes not only from physical maturation, but also from physical and social experiences and innate ways of functioning mentally.

The two theories differ in the relationship between the stages. In Freud's theory, each stage is characterized by one dominant trait (for example, anal concerns) but does not form a tightly knit, structured whole, as does a stage in Piaget's theory. Freud's stages form layers, with each stage only loosely integrated into the next. The reorganization of previous knowledge that characterizes each of Piaget's stages is much less apparent in Freud's stages. Furthermore, one stage does not contain the germ of the next, as it does in Piaget's theory. The oral stage does not *become* the anal stage, in the way that concrete operations become (are transformed into) formal operations.

Although a stage builds upon and is dominant over the previous stage, it does not completely replace that stage, according to Freud. No stage is ever given up entirely. Freud offered a simile of an army that advances into new territory but leaves forces en route to send on supplies or provide a place to retreat if difficulties arise. In the same way, a child can escape unbearably tense experiences by regressing to earlier behavior, such as sucking the thumb or hallucinating the desired object.

We can see many remnants of earlier stages in later stages. Earlier modes of satisfaction may be retained, as when thumb sucking persists throughout the preschool years. Or these earlier modes of gratification may be integrated into later sexual gratification, as when kissing becomes a subordinate part of adult sexuality. Anal concerns may still be present, but are suppressed, sublimated, and displaced until they bear little resemblance to their earlier form (for example, giving gifts in adulthood). There is a partial integration in the last stage, the genital, when the component instincts (oral, anal, and phallic) merge to form adult genital sexuality.

## Normal–Abnormal Continuum

Psychologists often study the unusual or exotic in order to understand the usual or mundane. The unusual may include the mentally ill, the retarded, another culture, or deprived environments. Even more commonly, the medical profession, of which Freud was a part, studies diseased or malfunctioning organisms in order to understand normal organisms. Strokes and injuries to various areas of the brain cause characteristic changes, such as paralysis of one side of the body, loss of speech, or loss of balance. These data clarify the role of each area of the brain in its undamaged stage.

Freud's first evidence about the normal functioning of the unconscious arose from his early study of hysteria. Much more evidence came later. For example, certain patients suffered from delusions of being observed by unknown persons who distrusted them and expected them to transgress and be punished. This abnormal behavior revealed the workings of the conscience in normal people. The only difference was that the internal was projected to the external in abnormal cases. Freud explains the value of studying abnormal behavior:

> Pathology, by making things larger and coarser, can draw our attention to normal conditions which would otherwise have escaped us. Where it points to a breach or a rent, there may normally be an articulation present. If we throw a crystal to the floor, it breaks; but not into haphazard pieces. It comes apart along its lines of cleavage into fragments whose boundaries, though they were invisible, were predetermined by the crystal's structure. Mental patients are split and broken structures of this same kind. . . . They have turned away from external reality, but for that very reason they know more about internal, psychical reality and can reveal a number of things to us that would otherwise be inaccessible to us.
>
> *[1933a (1964, pp. 58–59)]*

So far, we have followed Freud's argument that his study of the abnormal heightens our understanding of the normal. Freud, however, makes a further claim. He sees no sharp cleavage between the abnormal and the normal. Instead, abnormal and normal personalities obey the same principles and merely occupy different positions along a continuum ranging from the very disturbed to the very healthy. In an abnormal personality, psychological processes are exaggerated or distorted. A melancholic patient has an overly strong superego. A sadistic killer has a strong, uncontrolled aggressive drive. An amnesiac must repress all of a painful past. Yet every normal personality has traces of melancholia, sadism, and unaccountable forgetting, as described in a publication appropriately titled *The Psychopathology of Everyday Life* [1901 (1960)]. When reality becomes too painful or impulses of the id intensify, the ego's frantic attempts to keep in touch with reality or fortify the barriers against the id or superego ultimately fail. Neurotic symptoms or even a psychosis results. In Freud's words, "The threatened ego throws itself into the arms of the unconscious instinctual forces in a desperate revolt" [1933a (1964, p. 16)].

## Methodology

It might seem odd that Freud did not study children directly as he built a theory of development. His rationale was that our childhoods remain with us always, in that our adult personalities are residues of our childhoods. In addition, his patients happened to be adults rather than children. For these reasons, he devoted his efforts to developing methods for eliciting information about childhood from adults.

Freud's methodology has aroused as much interest and controversy as has the content of the theory. Free association, dream analysis, and transference at first shocked the psychiatric profession and the public but eventually won the acceptance of many therapists.

### *Free Association*

The method of free association requires that the patient verbally report his ongoing stream of thought. During the free-association sessions, the patient relaxes, usually on the famous couch, in a quiet room. Freud sat near the patient's head, but out of sight. He instructed his patients to report every thought, regardless of how trivial it seemed, omitting or censoring nothing. This relaxed, accepting state promoted the relaxation of control by the ego over unconscious thoughts. Repressed thoughts might then emerge, though often in disguise. Occasionally, if the patient fell silent, Freud would ask a question or even "lay on hands" — put his hand on the patient's forehead — and tell him that new memories would come! Freud analyzed the patient's sequence of thoughts and discovered relationships between certain ideas. He abstracted common themes underlying seemingly unrelated thoughts or behaviors. More generally, he tried to describe the organization of the patient's mind. The organization usually did not follow the rules of logic. Thoughts and feelings were typically organized around strong drives or conflicts. For example, objects that satisfy the oral drive, such as food, cigars, and one's mother (in infancy), might be closely connected in the mind. The patient might be overeating because he associated food with his mother's love. Since the free-association sessions often spread over several years, Freud could recheck his earlier interpretations and revise his conclusions if necessary.

The theoretical rationale for the free-association technique is as follows. Freud believes that every psychological event has a meaning. That is, a thought or feeling is caused; it does not occur randomly. If one thought typically leads to another, there is a reason for it. If the patient talks about her deceased father, then abruptly changes the subject to a trip she is thinking about taking, Freud may infer that she is troubled by her father's death. (Freud found that a journey is often a symbol for death.) The patient may not be aware of these anxious feelings.

The central concepts of Freud's theory arose from the free-association sessions. Freud found that patients' thoughts often turned to sexual memories of childhood. At first, Freud thought that these early sexual experiences had actually happened. Eventually, however, he concluded that it was unlikely there were so many Viennese parents who had seduced their children. Freud then viewed the sexual memories as fantasies or perceptions distorted by sexual desire. The fact that the experiences were not based on fact does not, however, diminish their importance. Our early perceptions and memories, true or false, affect the course of development of our personality. Furthermore, the way in which the patient distorts memories provides the therapist with a clue about her personality.

It might seem difficult for a therapist to elicit repressed thoughts and correctly infer the connections between sentences during free-association sessions. Freud, however, claims that the task is not so difficult:

> I thought the task was a harder one than it really is. He that has eyes to see and ears to hear may convince himself that no mortal can keep a secret. If his lips are silent, he chatters with his finger tips; betrayal oozes out of him at every pore. And thus the task of making conscious the most hidden recesses of the mind is one which it is quite possible to accomplish.
>
> [1905a (1953, pp. 77–78)]

A final comment about Freud's use of free association is that he conducted a self-analysis, beginning in 1897 and continuing throughout his life. He spent the last half hour of each day for this purpose. This increased his confidence, if not that of the scientific community, in his theory of personality.

### Dream Analysis

As one aspect of the free-association method, dream analysis deals with the patient's verbal reports of his own mental activity. If all thoughts are causally related and significant, then psychologists cannot ignore dreams. In fact, Freud concludes that more unconscious material may emerge when one is asleep than awake. During dreams, the usual psychological controls are "sleeping" and allow disturbing thoughts to be expressed and wishes to be fulfilled. These thoughts, however, are often disguised until they are unmasked during psychoanalysis. Since both the dream itself and the patient's associations to the dream influence the therapist's interpretation, dream analysis becomes very complex and difficult. The therapist might find that a house with smooth walls stands for a man, a house with balconies and ledges represents a woman, kings and queens are parents, little animals or vermin are siblings or other children, water refers to birth, and snakes and trunks stand for the sex organs [Freud, 1916 (1963, pp. 153–157)].

Freud was struck by the similarity between hysterical symptoms and the content of dreams. Both express, in a symbolic way, threatening unconscious impulses. Surface, or manifest, content (a twitch or an image of a fire) is linked to latent content (repressed thoughts).

### Transference

As the psychoanalytic sessions proceed, a particular type of relationship develops between the patient and the analyst. In Freud's words, in the analyst the patient sees "the return, the reincarnation, of some important figure out of his childhood or past, and consequently transfers on to him feelings and reactions which undoubtedly applied to this prototype" [1940 (1964, p. 174)]. This important figure from the past is usually the father or mother. It is not surprising, then, that the patient has both positive and negative feelings toward the analyst. The patient strives to please the analyst, as he would a parent, but also lashes out in anger at times.

Transference is a useful technique for both the analyst and the patient. Its value for the analyst is that it helps him discover the nature of the patient's relationship with his parents in childhood. Certain patterns of social interaction are repeated throughout life in various settings, including the therapist's office. The patient acts out these interactions from childhood instead of giving a verbal account, which might be inaccurate. The value of transference for the patient is that it can aid in the healing process. The therapist can point out similarities between the patient's relationship with him and with the father. Furthermore, the patient can express or "act out" feelings toward the surrogate parent (the therapist) that he did not allow himself to express during childhood. The patient's catharsis ("getting it out of his system") of his pent-up feelings and his development of a new relationship with the surrogate father can relieve his neurotic symptoms.

## Comment

In summary, Freud's methodology was to listen to troubled adults talk. These reports ranged from being spontaneous to being somewhat directed by Freud's questions. He did not perform controlled experiments and, unlike Piaget, did not observe children's behavior in natural situations. Instead, he studied single individuals in depth, sometimes spending hundreds of hours with a single patient. As if putting together a jigsaw puzzle, he put together pieces of information from patients' free associations, dreams, expressions of emotion, use of defense mechanisms, slips of the tongue, and so on.

Freud organized this information into a coherent picture in his case studies. Several long case studies were published and became well known. For example, the "Rat Man" (1909b) had the obsession that his father and girl friend would be punished with hungry rats fastened to their buttocks. The "Wolf Man" (1918) reacted to viewing the "primal scene" (sexual intercourse between his parents) by dreaming about wolves (see the dream report at the beginning of this chapter).

## DESCRIPTION OF THE STAGES

Earlier we saw that Freud's stage approach is based on the belief that development through the psychosexual stages early in life lays the foundations of personality. This claim was startling because it challenged the common belief that children are sexually innocent until puberty. According to Freud, oral sexuality (birth to 1 year) changes to anal sexuality (1 to 3 years), which in turn becomes phallic sexuality (3 to 5 years). After a period of latency, in which sexual feelings are repressed (5 years to the beginning of puberty), adult "true" genital sexuality emerges. Each stage, except latency, centers on a particular *erogenous zone*, an area of the body that, when stimulated, produces sexual tensions that need to be relieved. This section describes each of the psychosexual stages. As in Piaget's theory, the ages are approximate.

### Oral Stage (Roughly Birth to 1 Year)

During infancy the mouth rules. Oral experiences introduce the baby to both the pleasure and the pain of the world. Pleasure flows from the satisfaction of the oral drives. Sucking, chewing, eating, and biting give sexual gratification by relieving uncomfortable sexual excitations. The oral activities cause pleasant sensual feelings in the lips, tongue, and membranes of the mouth. These pleasant feelings need not be linked with the satisfaction of hunger because the oral activities themselves are satisfying. The outcome of all of this, in Freudian terminology, is that libidinal energy is cathected (invested) in the oral erogenous zone. The salient social and nonsocial experiences in the oral stage center around oral concerns.

In addition to experiencing oral pleasure, the infant meets pain from frustration and anxiety. Sexual tensions are pleasant if they are satisfied, but painful if they are not and continue to intensify. A preferred object, such as a nipple, may not be present at the moment the infant wants it. She must wait, which she finds frustrating. She may lapse into hallucinatory wish fulfillment as she imagines the desired nipple. Or she may suck her fingers, a blanket, or a soft toy. Still, satisfaction is not complete. Other frustrations come when parents demand that the nighttime feeding be given up, that certain objects not be chewed because they are unsanitary or unsafe, and, especially, that the breast or bottle be given up for the cup. The cultural demands of one's society are expressed through the parents. Parents teach the infant how to satisfy her drives in ways that are acceptable to the society. Conflict is inevitable. In small ways, the infant discovers that life has its frustrations as well as its pleasures, its "downs" as well as its "ups." She develops ways of coping with these frustrations that will form the basis for her later personality.

Another unpleasant feeling, closely related to frustration, is anxiety. Anxiety originates in birth, when the newborn is overwhelmed with stimulation as she emerges from the calm, warm womb. She reacts with fear to this traumatic experience. Thereafter, the infant becomes anxious whenever stimulation, especially sexual stimulation, mounts. The infant feels anxious not only when sexual urges become too intense, but also when the object of gratification is not present or when she fears that the object might leave. Thus, the perception that the mother will leave or has left is a common source of anxiety. Anxiety during birth, then, is a prototype for later anxieties.

As the baby seeks gratification and valiantly struggles to overcome barriers to this satisfaction, there is an important psychological principle at work: the infant is in trouble if he obtains either too little or too much oral gratification. The side effects of too little gratification are obvious: frequent anxiety, continual seeking of oral gratification in later years, and pessimism. The outcome of too much gratification is less obvious. If oral satisfaction is especially gratifying, the child may find it difficult to shift his cathexes to new objects, as demanded by a new stage. In this case, fixation can occur. Furthermore, relatively minor anxiety in a later stage may cause regression to highly cathected objects of the oral stage. For example, the initiation of toilet training during the anal stage may cause a child to return quickly to thumb sucking. The goal, then, is to achieve an optimal level of oral gratification so that he need not carry unfulfilled needs into later stages or feel unwilling to move on to a new stage.

Our description of the oral stage has emphasized the infant's search for objects that satisfy his sexual needs. During the oral stage, however, we also have our first glimpse of the darker side of human nature. The young infant passes from the oral passive–receptive phase to the oral sadistic phase when teeth appear. Biting and spitting out unpleasant substances are destructive, rejecting behaviors. As we shall see later, these behaviors have their counterparts in adult aggressive behavior. In infancy and throughout life, people often feel ambivalence toward other people and objects. Both positive and negative emotions arise, often in quick succession. Just as the infant both sucks and bites a nipple, the man both loves and hates his wife.

Freud claims that the way the infant develops during the oral stage forms the foundation for his personality as an adult. This claim is now elaborated. There are at least five oral "modes of functioning":(1) taking in, (2) holding on, (3) biting, (4) spitting out, and (5) closing (Hall, 1954, p. 104). Each of these modes forms a prototype (model, plan, or blueprint) for later personality characteristics. The infant learns certain oral reactions to situations he encounters. These characteristic reactions lead to certain attitudes, behaviors, and life goals in adulthood:

1. The infant who found pleasure from taking in food becomes an adult who voraciously "takes in," or acquires, knowledge or power and who incorporates or identifies with significant other people.

2. Holding on to the nipple when it is removed may lead to determination and stubbornness.

3. Biting is the prototype for destructiveness, "biting" sarcasm, cynicism, and dominance.

4. Spitting out becomes rejection.

5. Closing the mouth firmly leads to rejection, negativism, or introversion.

Note that these adult behaviors range from the literally oral, as in smoking, nail biting, and eating, to the metaphorically oral, as in being gullible (swallowing anything) and obstinate (holding on).

All these characteristics are found in every personality to some degree. However, some people have a personality structure that is dominated by one or several of these prototypes from the oral modes. In particular, certain traits may dominate because of extremely pleasant or unpleasant experiences in infancy. For example, an infant with an unaffectionate mother may become an adult who seeks to "take in" love symbolically by acquiring power or vast amounts of money.

Each of these personality traits has certain defense mechanisms associated with it. For example, a person who feels anxious about his oral aggressive ("biting") behavior may become, by means of reaction formation, overly pleasant in his face-to-face conversations with people.

Perhaps the most momentous event of the oral stage is the formation of attachment to the mother. Freud proclaims that the mother's importance is "unique, without parallel, established unalterably for a whole lifetime as the first and strongest love-object and as the prototype of all later love-relations" [1940 (1964, p. 188)].*Because the mother typically satisfies needs such as food, sucking, and warmth, she becomes the primary love object in the infant's life. The infant invests a good deal of libidinal energy in her. The notion of an emotional attachment to the mother is one of Freud's main legacies to the field of developmental psychology. This work inspired Spitz's (1945) work on disturbed mother–infant relationships. After observing that many infants left in foundling homes became depressed and that some even died, Spitz concludes that the lack of mothering contributes to psychological and health problems in infants. Subsequently, Bowlby's (1958) seminal work on attachment led to research by many other investigators in recent years. (Research on attachment is discussed in detail in Chapter 5.)

Although it may seem counterintuitive, attachment seems to lead to the infant's healthy sense of separateness from his mother. Winnicott (1971) stresses that this gradual differentiation is necessary for a clear sense of self and for normal interpersonal relations later. Before this differentiation, an infant–mother matrix gives little sense of a separation of the self and the world: "The mother, at the beginning, by an almost 100 percent adaptation affords the infant the opportunity for the *illusion* that her breast is part of the infant" (Winnicott, 1971, p. 11).

What Winnicott calls "good-enough mothering" involves a synchrony, or match, between the infant's needs and spontaneous behaviors and the caretaker's activities. Consequently, the infant feels omnipotent because he can magically obtain his every desire. Gradually, the baby's ego develops as he encounters delays in gratification,

---

*The obsession with mothers, which characterized not only Erikson and Freud but most developmental psychologists before the 1970s, is fading somewhat as fathers are beginning to be given some attention (for example, M. Lamb, ed, *The father's role: Cross cultural perspectives*, Hillsdale, NJ: Erlbaum, 1987).

interacts with various "not-me" objects, and discovers his own resources for interacting with the world. The "holding environment" with the mother provides a secure base for this threatening process of individuation. Mothers also design "play dialogues," which involve a mutual regulation of the interaction between themselves and their infants. The mother uses the infant's gaze and state of arousal as cues for the timing and intensity of her facial expressions and talking (Stern, 1974). Thus, the ideal mother tries to avoid both stimulus overload and boredom. The important outcome is that in the context of a social relationship, the child uses feedback regarding his effect on the mother to construct his self-concept. In other words, the baby expresses and defines his true self by being with his mother and seeing the effects of his spontaneous actions toward the mother.

The individuation process continues during development as the child uses "security blankets" or other cuddly, comforting objects to ease his separation from his mother (Winnicott, 1953). In addition, Mahler, Pine, and Bergman (1975) describe a series of steps in the differentiation of the self from the mother. The toddler has ambivalent feelings about this growing independence and, in severe cases, child psychosis results from a faulty individuation process. These and other psychoanalysts have identified object loss, particularly the real or perceived loss of the mother, as one of the most significant events that can occur in early life.

Attachment is a vital process for development because it serves as a building block for later social relationships. Furthermore, it facilitates the mother's attempts to socialize the child by using her attention to reward desirable behavior. However, in Freud's somewhat pessimistic theory, all silver linings are covered by clouds. Thus, attachment has its dangers. If the attachment is too strong, the infant may become overly dependent on the mother or anxious about her possible rejection of him. Then, later in life, he may depend on others to do things for him and even do his thinking for him. He may develop a generally passive personality.

## Anal Stage (Roughly 1 to 3 Years)

By the end of the oral stage, the infant has developed the rough outlines of a personality. This personality consists of attitudes toward himself and other people, mechanisms for achieving gratification within the demands of reality, and interests in certain activities and objects. As maturation moves the infant to the anal stage, the concerns of the child move from the oral area to the anal area. The new needs of this stage set in motion new conflicts between the child and the world. The way in which the child resolves these new conflicts further differentiates and crystallizes the rudimentary personality structure. The expression of oral needs does not stop, of course. The child simply faces a new set of needs and demands that require his immediate attention.

The physiological need to defecate creates tension, which is relieved by defecation. This anal stimulation and subsequent reduction of tension produces pleasure. As in the oral stage, the erogenous zone brings frustration and anxiety as well as pleasure. Society, as represented by the parents, demands that involuntary expulsion be replaced by delayed, voluntary expulsion. Thus, the child faces toilet training. His desire for immediate gratification is frustrated. In a small but momentous way, the child enters into conflict with authoritarian adult society. Children all over the world face and resolve this conflict in some way. Obviously, many variables affect how much conflict the child feels and how he adapts to the demands placed on him. These variables include the age at which toilet training is begun, how strict or relaxed the training is, and the mother's attitude toward defecation, control, and cleanliness.

If toilet training is particularly harsh or premature or overemphasized by the parents, defecation can become a source of great anxiety for the child. This anxiety can generalize to other situations in which an external authority makes demands or the child must control his own impulses. Some children react to strict toilet training by holding back elimination and becoming constipated or by defecating at inappropriate times or places, such as the supermarket.

Activities and events surrounding the anal area serve as prototypes for a variety of behaviors during both this stage and subsequent stages. Explosive, uncontrollable elimination is a prototype for temper tantrums or vigorous, demanding, physical exercise. In reaction against overly strict toilet training, the child may become messy, dirty, and irresponsible. Or, at the other extreme, the child may become a compulsively neat, frugal, and overly controlled adult. The mother's praise of the child's success at the toilet may create a link between giving a gift (feces) and receiving love. In this case, the child may become "giving" and generous. If the mother places great value on the child's productions at the toilet, the child may become creative and productive, or, on the other hand, become depressed due to a feeling of loss. If the child balks at giving up his prized possessions at the toilet, he may become retentive and stingy and may gain pleasure from collecting objects. This list of personality characteristics reflects the child's ambivalence between giving and retaining.

Freud coined the term *anal character* to describe a person who is orderly, pedantic, and obstinate. Such a person has a distorted perception of the world as he tries in vain to make everything clearcut, neat, and unambiguous.

The list of potential negative outcomes in the anal stage certainly is not comforting to the prospective parent! As in the oral stage, the goal is to allow enough, but not too much, gratification, and to develop enough, but not too much, self-control. If this goal is adequately achieved, the child will have developed a more mature ego because it has been sharpened by its confrontation with reality. The child who survives the anal period relatively unscathed is ready to tackle the third stage, the phallic stage, when it arrives.


### Phallic Stage (Roughly 3 to 5 Years)

The child's solution to problems of the oral and anal stages sets a pattern for solving later problems of adjustment. This development is continued in the phallic stage, so named because the possession of the phallus in boys and its absence in girls is a major concern of children, according to Freud. In this stage, pleasures and problems center on the genital area. Stimulation in the genital area brings tensions and, if the tensions are relieved, pleasure. The problem of the stage arises when the sexual urge is directed toward the parent of the opposite sex. This situation is the well-known *Oedipus complex*. (In Greek mythology, Oedipus killed his father and married his mother.)

Since the Oedipus complex is somewhat different for boys and girls, each sex is considered separately here. Freud emphasizes the development of boys more than girls in the phallic stage because he believes that the conflict is more intense for boys. A young boy has sexual desires for his mother and does not want to share her with his father. At the same time, the boy fears that the father, in retaliation, will castrate him. As a way out of this highly anxious situation, the boy represses both his desire for his mother and his hostility toward his father.

The most important outcome of the Oedipus complex is that the boy comes to identify with his father. That is, he develops a strong emotional bond with the father, strives to be like him, and "internalizes" him — his beliefs, values, interests, and attitudes. Identification serves as a basis for much of socialization. In particular, the development of the superego and behavior appropriate to one's sex are by-products of this identification. The superego increases the child's self-control and adherence to the parents' morality.

Identification is a reasonable solution to the demands of the ego and id in this stage. The ego is partially satisfied because anxiety is reduced. The id is partially satisfied because the child can "have" the mother vicariously through the father. Again, as the child tries to cope with both his drives and the prohibitions of society, he achieves a compromise solution that advances his psychological maturity.

In comparison with boys, girls face a similar, but much less intense, conflict during the phallic stage. The father, of course, is the object of the girl's sexual longings. Part of this longing involves penis envy as the girl realizes that the father has a prized object that she does not have. In Freud's words, "She makes her judgment and her decision in a flash. She has seen it and knows that she is without it and wants to have it" [1925b (1961, p. 252)]. The girl begins to prefer her father to her mother. She feels that she has been castrated and blames her mother for this loss because she "sent her into the world so insufficiently equipped" [1925b (1961, p. 254)]. This anger toward the mother weakens the cathexis with her.

As in the case of boys, society does not allow the full expression of the sexual desire for the parent. However, the girl feels less threat from the mother than the boy does from the father. The girl has less to fear because castration is not possible. Freud claims that since there is less anxiety and consequently less repression, the girl has a weaker identification with the mother than does the boy with the father. Freud then concludes that girls have a weaker conscience than do boys. In girls, the Oedipus complex usually continues to some extent for many years, but may slowly weaken or be repressed.

It should be noted that there is a basic difference in the role of feelings about castration in boys and girls. In boys, fear of castration leads to the abandonment of the Oedipus complex. In girls, the belief that castration has already occurred partially causes the Oedipus complex, through penis envy.

This account of the Oedipus complex is somewhat over-simplified. In actuality, there is always identification with both parents. The relative strengths of the two identifications vary from child to child, depending on variables such as the balance of feminine and masculine components in the physiological makeup of the child (because all people are bisexual to some extent, according to Freud) and the intensity of the castration anxiety or penis envy. In addition, both sexes retain a strong cathexis for the mother because she is the most important object in the two previous psychosexual stages.

In psychoanalytic sessions, Freud found powerful and lasting influences from the phallic stage. For example, women often had disturbing sexual fantasies about their fathers that had never been resolved. Another common problem was the inability to overcome one's attachment to one's parents and establish independence. More generally, lasting attitudes toward the opposite sex and toward people in authority could be traced to this stage.

With the achievement of identification and the waning of the phallic stage, the influential early years come to an end. Thereafter, conflicts are resolved in characteristic ways. Personality changes, but primarily by further differentiation of the basic structure. It is rather awesome that these important early years are only dimly remembered by the adult because of massive repression.

## Period of Latency (Roughly 5 Years to the Beginning of Puberty)

After the *Sturm und Drang* of the first three stages, there is a period of relative calm, when sexual drives are repressed and no new area of bodily excitement emerges. The child conveniently "forgets" the sexual urges and fantasies of his earlier years. He turns his thoughts to school activities and plays primarily with children of the same sex. This is a time for acquiring cognitive skills and assimilating cultural values as the child expands his world to include teachers, neighbors, peers, club leaders, and coaches. Sexual energy continues to flow, but it is channeled into social concerns and into building defenses against sexuality. Thus, the ego and superego continue to develop. The small amount of space allotted to describing this period and the next stage reflects Freud's emphasis on the first three stages.

## Genital Stage (Adolescence)

The sexual impulses, which were repressed during the latency stage, reappear in full force as a result of the physiological changes of puberty. These sexual impulses are fused with the earlier ones, but are now directed toward a peer of the opposite sex. The goal is mature, adult sexuality, with the biological aim of reproduction. Love becomes more altruistic, with less concern for self-pleasure than in earlier stages. The choice of a partner is, of course, not independent of the person's earlier development. A woman may choose a "father figure," a passive man she can dominate, a sadistic male, and so on, depending on the attitudes and social patterns developed in the early years.

Although some internal conflict is inevitable throughout life, a relatively stable state is achieved by most people by the end of the genital stage. Typically, the individual achieves a fairly strong ego structure that makes coping with the reality of the adult world possible. One important achievement is a balance between love and work.

## Case Study of "Little Hans"

The above outline of the psychosexual stages cannot capture the vivid, powerful conflicts that operate in an individual child's life. Thus, we turn to one of Freud's most famous case studies, the "Analysis of a Phobia in a Five-Year-Old Boy" (1909a) or, as it is more commonly known, "Little Hans." This case study was unique because it was Freud's only analysis of a child and because Freud conducted the analysis by mail in a series of letters with the boy's physician-father, who made the observations. Nevertheless, the study was a central force in the formation of one of Freud's most important developmental concepts: identification.

When Hans was 5 years old, anxiety attacks, a phobia, and a fantasy appeared. His phobia, the fear that a horse would bite him or fall down, was so strong that he would not leave his house. He was especially afraid of horses that pulled heavy loads in carts or vans or were white with a black muzzle and wore blinders. In Hans' fantasy, during the night "there was a big giraffe in the room and a crumpled one; and the big one called out because I took the crumpled one away from it. Then it stopped calling out; and then I sat down on top of the crumpled one" [1909a (1955, p. 37)].

After sifting through this evidence, Freud identified three themes: an Oedipus conflict, sibling rivalry, and fear of punishment for masturbation. Thus, in the phobia, the horse represented Hans' father, who had a mustache (a black muzzle around the horse's mouth) and eyeglasses (blinders) and was, as Hans remarked, "so white" (like the white horse). Hans feared that the horse would bite (castrate) him because of his sexual longing for his mother and his masturbating. Anxiety about masturbation may have been prompted by his mother's threat that if his masturbation continued, she would send him to the doctor to cut off his "widdler." The fear that a horse might fall down was interpreted as a fear that his father might die or go away, as he sometimes wished when he wanted his mother alone. Significantly, Hans had remarked, "Daddy, don't trot away from me" (p. 45). The giraffe fantasy might be interpreted as a wish for possessing the mother, as Hans imagines he sits on the smaller giraffe (mother), which he has taken from the larger giraffe (father). Note the phallic symbol in the giraffe's long neck.

Hans' feelings of loss of attention and love after the birth of his sister are expressed in the fear that a cart might be upset and spill its contents (his mother might give birth again). In the fantasy, Hans destroys his younger sister when he sits on her (the small giraffe).

Hans eventually identified with his father, thereby resolving his conflicts and recovering from his fear of horses. He continued to develop a healthy personality.

## MECHANISMS OF DEVELOPMENT

The section on psychosexual stages presented the "what" of development, but not the "how" or "why." Our next task is to examine the mechanisms that propel the child through these stages. One similarity between the theories of Freud and Piaget is striking in this respect. Both have a "trouble" theory of development. Development proceeds because of disturbances or perturbations to the system. Development is hard work. The child must continually try to reestablish a state of relative calm. There are, however, important differences in how the two theorists conceptualize the disturbances and their removal. Piaget posits a dynamic equilibration system that orchestrates and brings into harmony three inputs: physical maturation, social experience, and physical experience. These inputs produce new information that may contradict, or at least not fit into, current schemes. Equilibrium is reachieved when actions (operations or schemes) are in balance once again. Although Freud also sees equilibration as a process of reducing disturbing elements, he stresses different inputs: emotion-laden thoughts rather than objective information about the physical world. He is more concerned with psychological pain than logical inconsistency, with energy in repose than mental actions in balance.

Another difference between the theorists is that Freud's equilibration system is less open (less responsive to external information) than Piaget's. Piaget speaks of continual assimilation and accommodation as new experiences are encountered. In Freud's system, there is more resistance to change. The system is also closed, in that there is a certain amount of energy that can be changed in form, but never amount.

Now that we have examined the general nature of equilibration in Freud's theory and compared it with Piaget's use of the term, we look more specifically at how equilibration is a mechanism of development. Freud identifies several sources of conflict or psychological disruption: physical maturation, external frustrations, internal conflicts, personal inadequacies, and anxiety (Hall, 1954, p. 72).

1. *Maturation* refers to changes in the nervous system, motor development, hormonal changes, drives, and so on. Each of these maturational changes brings new possibilities and new problems. As we saw earlier, the drives are particularly important. These maturational forces both propel the child into activity as he tries to satisfy the drives and move him from stage to stage as the bodily site of pleasure changes.

2. *External frustrations* come from people or events that do not allow the immediate expression of needs. These cause a painful buildup of tension and force the child to delay and detour his discharge of energy.

3. *Internal conflicts* arise from battle among the id, ego, and superego or, more specifically, between drives and forces of repression.

4. *Personal inadequacies* refer to certain skills, knowledge, expertise, or experience that the person needs but lacks. For example, a child may want to join a peer group, but be too shy to enter the group or too clumsy at the game they are playing.

5. Finally, *anxiety* is an unpleasant feeling that occurs when the child anticipates physical or psychological pain. The fear of losing a valued love object is a common example.

All these elements cause an unpleasant state of tension, which the child attempts to rectify in accordance with the pleasure principle and the reality principle. Thus, these disturbances to the system are one mechanism of personality development. These disturbances, however, merely initiate change. Other mechanisms actually accomplish change. The ego has the primary responsibility for guiding the course of change. Its perceptual and cognitive systems gather relevant information about the current situation, recall useful information from past experiences, and use whatever defense mechanisms are most appropriate. The ego develops methods for keeping distressing sexual thoughts from becoming conscious and placates the id and superego. The ego, then, mediates change from moment to moment. The accumulation of these small changes adds up to long-term change. Over time the ego gathers strength, and personality crystallizes and becomes further differentiated into complex attitudes, interests, and behaviors.

Several developmental "products" also serve as mechanisms of development. The most notable are attachment and identification. As mentioned earlier, both lead to other important acquisitions, such as sex typing and moral development in the case of identification.

## POSITION ON DEVELOPMENTAL ISSUES

### Human Nature

Hall and Lindzey summarize Freud's view of the person as

a full-bodied individual living partly in a world of reality and partly in a world of make-believe, beset by conflicts and inner contradictions, yet capable of rational thought and action, moved by forces of which he has little knowledge and by aspirations which are beyond his reach, by turn confused and clearheaded, frustrated and satisfied, hopeful and despairing, selfish and altruistic; in short, a complex human being.

[*1957, p. 72*]

This description of the conflicted, contradictory nature of humans stands in sharp contrast to Piaget's rational person, calmly searching for epistemological truth in a world that can be comprehended. Freud is concerned with emotions, particularly their role in forcing the development of personality and thought as the child strives to cope with these emotions. By nature, man has strong passions that color his perceptions throughout life.

Although not all interpreters of Freudian theory would agree, Freud's world view seems to fit more comfortably into the organismic than the mechanistic camp. The classification, however, is less clear than for Piaget. For Freud, psychological man is a loosely organized whole that is, in most ways, active and self-regulating. Freud's holistic approach is clearest in his claim that a given behavior is caused by several aspects of personality. The id, ego, and superego, organized into a structured whole, together cause a particular behavior. An action is not "pure" id, ego, or superego. Of course, the relative influence of each varies from behavior to behavior.

Although the human being is passive, in that drives force him into action, he is active in his attempts to cope with these drives and maintain a state of equilibrium. The ego, in its executive role, is the most active agent of the personality. It organizes incoming information from the self (for example, anxiety about some impending event) and the social environment and directs the behavior chosen.

Although both Freudian and Piagetian theory can be considered organismic theories, two important differences should be noted. First, it is clear that Freud's psychological whole is not the tightly knit, integrated, equilibrated whole described by Piaget. Freud posits a looser organization. Still, his thinking is in line with the Gestaltists' claim that the whole is more than the sum of the parts. Second, the Piagetian child acts because she is inherently active and self-regulated; the Freudian child acts because drives force her to act.

## Qualitative Versus Quantitative Development

As in Piaget's theory, the stagelike changes proposed by Freud imply that development involves qualitative change. There is a change in which aspect of the sexual drive is dominant: the oral, anal, phallic, or genital. There is also qualitative change in the psychological organization as new acquisitions, such as defense mechanisms and the superego, appear.

Although Freud emphasizes qualitative change, he does not slight quantitative change. The developing child exhibits a gradual strengthening of the ego, superego, and various defense mechanisms.

## Nature Versus Nurture

It is sometimes claimed that Freud has a biologically based theory of development. Although he emphasizes maturation and the biologically based drives, he is, in fact, an interactionist: "The constitutional factor must await experiences before it can make itself felt; the accidental factor must have a constitutional basis in order to come into operation" [Freud, 1905b (1953, p. 239)]. Although drives derive from the human's biological nature, their expression is always modified by the social milieu. The people or objects available and the behaviors allowed by parents or other authorities direct the satisfaction of the drives. The demands of civilization are as real as the demands of one's body.

Within the category of nurture, not all experiences make an equal impact. The experiences of the first five years of life are especially important. These experiences need not be traumatic in order to be influential. In fact, many intense, violent events of childhood have only a fleeting effect. In Freud's words, "harsh rulers have short reigns" [1905b (1953, p. 241)]. The recurrent, day-to-day enduring patterns of satisfying one's drives in a socially and psychologically acceptable way have the most influence on later life.

Variations in either the social environment or the physical constitution can cause personality differences among people. Although it is easy to imagine the former, the latter may be less obvious. Freud suggests that there are innate differences from person to person in the strength of the various components of the sex drive (oral, anal, phallic) and in the time at which each psychosexual stage emerges.

## What Develops

The essence of development is the emergence of structures—the id, ego, and superego—that channel, repress, and transform sexual energy. These structures and their dynamic processes are both affective (emotional) and cognitive. The tendency to criticize Freud for slighting cognition is somewhat unfair. Thought—whether unconscious, preconscious, or conscious and whether primary or secondary process in nature—always accompanies feeling.

## THEORETICAL NATURE OF THE THEORY

Freud was a practicing therapist concerned with the real problems of real people. He entered a field that offered few tools for helping him solve these problems. Therefore, he had to develop ideas about personality that helped him develop therapeutic tools. This pragmatic concern left little time for formal theory building. Nevertheless, we can sort out various theoretical characteristics of the theory.

There have been attempts to systematize Freud's theory, especially the fruitful efforts of Rapaport (1960). However, there is no organized, formal, axiomatic account of his theory. Thus, it certainly is not a deductive theory. Likewise, Freud's formulations bear only traces of an inductive or a functional theory. As with Piaget, there is data gathering based on observations—a characteristic of the inductive approach. However, Freud was quick to jump far beyond these facts. Superficially, there are functional aspects, as when he researched specific problems, such as hysteria or the infant's attachments to objects. In these cases, there is a close interplay between data gathering and theory developing. Despite these traces of inductive and functional theory, the theory is most marked by the use of models. We now turn to these.

## Models

Rapaport (1960) describes four models implicit in Freud's theory: reflex arc, energy, Darwinian (genetic), and Jacksonian (neural-integration hierarchy).

1. The *reflex-arc model* comes from neurology, Freud's original field. A reflex refers to an innate connection between a particular type of stimulation and a particular response. For example, when the infant's foot is pricked, the knee flexes. The model, then, refers to the tendency for organisms to respond when stimulated. This simple "in-and-out" or S-R (stimulus–response) model is useful for describing the relationship between various types of stimuli and various types of responses. Stimulation can come from the external world or the internal world, particularly the unconscious. Drive excitations in the unconscious usually lead to behavior but may stop in the preconscious or conscious.

2. The *energy model* was outlined in the earlier sections on Freud's dynamic approach and mechanisms of development. In an attempt to reduce drive tension, people are forced to do something. As tension associated with hunger mounts, the baby may act (suck a bottle), hallucinate (imagine a bottle of milk), or discharge affect (cry). As the internal pressure builds up, the release of energy becomes more and more necessary. If one possible outlet is "plugged," the person seeks another. This model, of course, comes from physics and draws on many physical laws concerning the distribution, transformation, and discharge of energy. The goal of this energy system is to maintain a homeostatic (equilibrated) state, in which energy buildup is corrected by energy discharge.

3. The *Darwinian*, or *genetic, model* presents the biological, evolutionary viewpoint. In Freud's interpretation of the model, development proceeds according to instincts, which we share with animals. These instincts express themselves in the psychosexual stages. Both evolution over many generations and developmental changes within a lifetime are due to organisms' attempts to adapt to the environment. Modes of adaptation developed early in life influence personality and behavior later in life. Psychological adaptation can parallel physical adaptation. For example, mental flight from a dangerous thought or impulse can be likened to physical flight from a dangerous predator.

4. Freud borrowed the *Jacksonian*, or *neural-integration hierarchy, model* from the study of the nervous system. According to this model, the nervous system is organized into a hierarchy. Higher levels control (facilitate or inhibit) lower levels. If the higher levels are unable to

function, because of injury or other problems, the lower levels run unchecked. Freud posits an analogous organization in the psychological system. Higher psychological levels (for example, the ego) control lower psychological levels (the id) unless the higher levels are unable to function, for example, because anxiety has overwhelmed the ego.

## EVALUATION OF THE THEORY

Although clinical psychology is still influenced by psychoanalytic theory, an anti-Freudian attitude has pervaded experimental psychology in recent years. The world of academic developmental psychology has its fads and fashions, as does the larger world. In the 1980s, Freudian theory is no longer popular. To illustrate, if one looks through the major journals of developmental research, it is clear that "tests" of the theory are almost nonexistent and references to psychoanalytic work are scarce. The psychoanalytically oriented developmental psychologist is an endangered species. There are many reasons for the theory's falling stock in recent years. Some of these are discussed in the section on weaknesses and include an inadequate methodology for identifying developmental processes, the uncertain testability of central claims concerning development, and the overemphasis on sexuality. In addition, the theory's incorporation into "pop culture" and the recent focus on cognition in developmental research surely contributed to the trend.

Although rejection of certain aspects of Freud's theory is reasonable, experimental psychologists' overall rejection of the theory may have deprived the field of a valuable perspective on development. In the belief that the Freudian approach can provide some insights into current concerns of developmental psychologists, the following section presents some strengths of the theory. The focus is on contemporary relevance.

### Strengths

Of the many strengths of Freud's theory, three seem most central to present-day developmental psychology: the theory's uncovering of the unconscious as a powerful shaper of development, its lasting contributions to developmental research, and its particular relevance for contemporary research on cognitive development.

## Uncovering of the Unconscious as a Powerful Shaper of Development

This section focuses on the historical impact of one of Freud's most important conclusions: that development is directed by powerful unconscious drives. The expression of these unconscious forces spurs the development of the ego and superego, which in turn operate unconsciously for the most part. Freud's revelations of the drive-driven nature of human beings struck twentieth-century thought with force. Concepts such as infantile sexuality, the anal personality, and the teeming desires of the unconscious jarred a Victorian society that covered piano legs to hide their nakedness. That the theory eventually was partially accepted may reveal more about changes in society than anything about the theory itself. Freud's view of the human potential for destructive behavior could not be so easily dismissed after two world wars and the political crimes of the times. It was a theory whose time had come.

Regardless of how one judges the scientific merit of the theory, it is, without doubt, the most widely influential psychological theory in history. Its impression on society may equal that of Marx and Darwin. The theory's influence reaches into nearly every area of twentieth-century thought. Freud described unconscious motivation in the areas of anthropology (*Totem and Taboo*, 1913), art ("The Moses of Michelangelo," 1914), religion (*The Future of an Illusion*, 1927), literature ("Dostoevsky and Parricide," 1928), sociology (*Civilization and its Discontents*, 1930), and history (*Why War?*, 1933). Freud also touched these disciplines indirectly in his more general writings. Many neo-Freudians developed further the implications of psychoanalysis for other disciplines. For example, Ernst Kris drew fascinating conclusions in *Psychoanalytic Explorations in Art* (1952). In addition to professionals in the various areas, the general public became familiar with many of his ideas. Slips of the tongue became more embarrassing than before, and millions of people began to take their dreams seriously. The belief that weaning and toilet training should not be sudden and harsh is often attributed to Freud's ideas.

Within psychology and psychiatry, the influence of Freud's work on emotional and nonrational aspects of personality was also far-reaching.

He left his mark on every area from social psychology to sensory processes, from adult therapy to child therapy. This effect was not immediate, because many rejected his ideas. Eventually, however, his ideas spread throughout Europe and, later, North America. The great diversity of viewpoints among psychoanalysts today can be traced to the various followers of Freud who further developed his theory and, in some cases, broke away from Freud. Some of the best-known neo-Freudians were Carl Jung, Otto Rank, Alfred Adler, Karen Horney, Harry Stack Sullivan, Erik Erikson, Melanie Klein, Anna Freud, Heinz Hartmann, and David Rapaport. Freud and his descendants have been prolific writers. *The Index of Psychoanalytic Writings* (Grinstein, 1956–1971) lists over 100,000 books, articles, and monographs relevant to psychoanalysis.

Freud's influence on academic, research-oriented psychologists came slowly. His theory only peripherally dealt with the topics central to academic psychology in his time: perception, learning, and psychophysics. Eventually, however, there were scattered experimental studies on topics such as the effect of emotions on perception and memory. Hartmann's (1958) work on ego functions — memory, thought, and perception — helped to bring psychoanalytic theory and academic psychology closer together.

Since Freud's theory is thoroughly developmental, it is not surprising that it deeply influenced developmental psychology. The initial reaction of developmental psychologists was varied. It was not until the late 1930s that there was considerable interest in the theory. This increasing attention to psychoanalytic theory was due in part to the growth of child-guidance clinics in the 1920s and 1930s. It became clear that emotional forces are an important part of development. Salient psychoanalytic developmental work in the 1940s and 1950s included Erikson's stage of psychosocial development; direct observations of children by Anna Freud, Ernst Kris, Sybill Escalona, and René Spitz; John Whiting and Irvin Child's cross-cultural work; and John Bowlby's early studies on infant social attachment. Psychoanalytic theory also touched the early work of other theoretical approaches. Social learning theorists, especially Robert Sears, Neal Miller, and John Dollard, brought psychoanalytic content into learning theory. A concern with unconscious motivation was very clear in Sears' work on defense mechanisms, dependency, identification, and parent–child relations. Today, Freud's theory remains a vital force within child clinical psychology, child psychiatry, and counseling psychology. Both the therapeutic techniques and the theoretical notions, such as the normal–abnormal continuum, the unconscious–conscious distinction, and the psychic structures (id, ego, superego) are very much alive.

## Lasting Contributions to Developmental Research

Certain general theoretical notions and some empirical content from Freud's theory continue to influence developmental psychology. Particularly influential general notions include developmental stages, psychological structures, unconscious motivation, and the importance of early experience. In addition, the theory stimulated research in the areas of moral development, sex typing, identification, parent–child relations, attachment, aggression, and dependency. These remain active areas of research even today. Although a number of Freud's specific claims may be inaccurate, he told us what is important in development. Researchers have found something of value in the theory, even if they have not accepted it in its entirety.

## Relevance for Contemporary Research on Cognitive Development

The major change in developmental psychology from the late 1960s to the present has been the increasing interest in cognitive development. This trend may be responsible, in part, for the waning interest in Freudian theory in recent years. After surveying the results of this era of research on cognitive development, we may conclude that certain shortcomings could be remedied by a renewed interest in psychoanalytic theory. The theory's relevance for the current research scene in cognitive development is outlined here.

In the last 15 years, cognitive developmentalists have focused on rational problem solving: how thought becomes increasingly organized, efficient, abstract, and objective. This type of thought characterizes that of an adult scientist. It is assumed that this is the end goal of developing thought. This viewpoint emerges clearly in Piaget's emphasis on logical operations and on concepts of the physical world. The information-processing approach, described in a later chapter, also subscribes to this perspective, as seen in the study of how memory encoding becomes more efficient as strategies develop, how rules generate hypothesis testing, and how thought is organized like a computer program. Both the Piagetian and the information-processing approaches picture a developing child as an organism that relentlessly searches for truth in an increasingly efficient and rational way. Although this view characterizes part of cognitive development, it does not tell the whole story. Humans probably are not as rational as these theories propose. As Wason and Johnson-Laird (1972, p. 245) express it, "At best, we can all think like logicians; at worst, logicians all think like us."

Psychoanalytic theory's focus on "irrational" thought processes can expand and enrich our current concepts of children's thinking. Freud's work suggests that much thought is motivated by reasons unknown to the child. She may be intellectually capable of inferring that she hates her younger brother for the attention he receives from her parents; yet, because of the psychological pain and guilt that such knowledge would produce, she may instead believe that she feels only love for her brother. Even the intelligent adult is guided by emotions when he buys resort property without seeing it first, daydreams, supports corrupt politicians on faith, and marries someone he knows has a personality incompatible with his. In other words, thought distorts reality and ignores relevant information.

These irrational thought processes are as important as the more frequently studied rational ones; in fact, the former may occur more frequently than the latter. Thus, Freud's theory poses two challenges for developmentalists. One challenge is to study how emotions affect thinking in children. Does the child reason differently when he is angry or frustrated than when calm? A second challenge is to examine whether the mental processes underlying primary- and secondary-process thought and the defense mechanisms (such as projection, reaction formation, repression, and sublimation) differ from the mental processes described by Piaget and the information-processing psychologists. For example, how is Piaget's notion of mental reversibility related to Freud's notion of reaction formation, in which a negative attitude toward a person or an object is transformed into a positive attitude? Are conflicting feelings and logically contradictory ideas resolved in the same way? What are the mental processes underlying self-deception? What cognitive acquisitions are necessary for understanding displaced aggression (taking one's anger out on an innocent person)? Do the notions of repression and the preconscious have any relevance for the distinction between short-term and long-term memory?

So far, the suggestion has been that the *processes* of thought identified by psychoanalytic theory could fruitfully become an object of developmental research. They could supplement, and perhaps modify, our view of logical thought. A further suggestion is that the *content* of children's thought is more wide-ranging than recent research would indicate. Freud would point out that children do not think only about quantity, spatial relationships, justice, objects, and causality. They also try to understand, and mentally adjust to, the violence on television or in their home, hunger, their parents' physical and emotional relationship, their own sexual or aggressive feelings, the tendency of adults to say one thing and do the opposite, rejection by their peers or parents, failure in social interactions, and so on. Other psychological content given little attention by current cognitive research includes dreams and fantasies. Adding this content to that considered by cognitive developmentalists would give a more balanced view of children's thinking.

This suggested new direction for research on cognitive development is particularly promising because it is compatible with two new interests within the field: social cognition and metacognition. *Social cognition*, thinking about people and their behavior, obviously should take into account such problematic or troublesome content of thought as we have just described. Thus far, social-cognitive research has given almost no attention to this area. *Metacognition* refers to a person's understanding of the nature of thinking, memory, language, attention, and comprehension. The study of metacognition would provide a foundation for studying the developing understanding of the psychological defenses used by others as well as oneself, the nature of dreams, the distinction between fantasy and reality, and so forth.

### Weaknesses

Freud made it difficult for anyone to criticize his theory: "No one has a right to join in a discussion of psycho-analysis who has not had particular experiences which can only be obtained by being analysed oneself" [1933a (1964, p. 69)]. Nevertheless, we intend to "crash" the Freudian party and examine several weaknesses of the theory: inadequate methodology for identifying developmental processes, uncertain testability of central claims concerning development, and overemphasis on childhood sexuality.

## Inadequate Methodology for Identifying Developmental Processes

The scientific community requires that theories be based on empirical observations that can be replicated by scientists other than the theorist. Freud's methodology makes this type of data gathering nearly impossible. His primary methods — free association, dream analysis, and transference — pose three major difficulties.

1. According to Freud, these methods require that the experimenter be trained in psychoanalysis. Because such training is a long, expensive process, few people are even qualified to test the theory. Furthermore, those who are psychoanalytically trained tend to be "believers," who can hardly be expected to supply objective data. (Of course, this criticism can be leveled against any researcher who has a theoretical bias.) If one believes that there are strong psychosexual forces in childhood, one can see them in every word or action.

2. Freud's methods lend themselves to experimenter error. Freud made notes about the psychoanalytic sessions after they occurred, often hours later. It is ironic that someone who demonstrated the distortions of memory in his patients should be so oblivious to that possibility in himself. There is a danger that he selectively remembered only that which fit into his theory. Another source of experimenter error is the possibility that the patient's line of thought is influenced by the nature of the therapist's questions or even the timing of his grunts and silences.

3. Adults' recollections of childhood and recent dreams are unlikely to be completely accurate. Introspection has a poor reputation in psychology. It is not easy to report objectively even one's current mental state or recent dream states; mental states from 50 years earlier pose even more difficulties. Childhood and dream experiences are filtered through the patient's memory, which is selective, and his linguistic system, which supplies a structure. Freud himself knew that these verbal reports are not reliable, but felt that even fantasies and distortions are revealing. The patient's experience of these earlier events, whether accurate or distorted, is what is most relevant to therapy. Still, the fact that the therapist usually does not have the means to discern when the reports are real and when they are not limits his assessment of the patient's perception of reality.

## Uncertain Testability of Central Claims Concerning Development

Perhaps the most common criticism leveled against Freud's theory is that it is inherently untestable or at least difficult to test. In part, this problem stems from the methodological inadequacies outlined above. An involved, possibly biased participant-observer, who records only a portion of the patient's responses, is a dubious source of objective data for testing the theory. In addition, it is uncertain whether the critical developments during childhood can be clarified by data coming from adults. Furthermore, the problem of definition poses a challenge to the experimental psychologist. There are many vague, imprecise, poorly defined terms. Because Freud relies heavily on analogies to communicate the meaning of the terms, the meaning conveyed is intuitive. Freud's reply to this criticism was that terms are imprecise in the early years of any science. For example, when physics was a young science, the notions of force and mass were elusive.

One facet of the problem of definition is that many of Freud's notions have an uncertain relationship to observable behavior, in part because of the considerable distance between the two. The therapist takes verbal reports and, to a lesser extent, nonverbal behavior (e.g., facial expressions, crying, and physical accidents) and interprets them in terms of distant theoretical concepts, such as defense mechanisms, drives, and unconscious motivation. In particular, the evidence for the unconscious from dreams, forgetting and puns sometimes seems rather farfetched. For example, Freud made a large jump from a report of a dream about an oven to the interpretation that this image represents the uterus. One way to state the problem is that a psychological attribute can refer to several different behaviors, or conversely, a particular behavior can stem from several different psychological attributes. As an example of the former, an "anal personality" can be expressed in either a compulsively neat or an overly messy person. Or a patient's problem can be diagnosed as an Oedipus complex if he either talks constantly about his mother or never mentions her (due to repression). As an example of a relationship in which a behavior can have several possible causes, the inability to eat can stem from hysteria (perhaps caused by a fear of seeming to be pregnant) or paranoia (perhaps a fear of being poisoned). It is unclear how one would "test" these notions. The theory must be stated more systematically before it is clearly testable. Rapaport (1960) has taken a significant step in that direction.

There have been numerous attempts to test Freud's theory either clinically, often with hypnosis or projective tests in which the subject must interpret inkblots or pictures, or experimentally.* The latter approach, however, has been criticized for not adequately testing the theory. For example, exposing a boy to an aggressive, hostile male adult and subsequently observing how much the boy imitates the male's behavior is not a fair test of the notion that the Oedipus complex leads to identification with the aggressor. The long-term, emotionally powerful experiences of real life may not be translated easily into brief, simplistic, experimental episodes. In short, psychologists are in a bind. They cannot adequately test the most crucial theoretical notions outside of the psychoanalytic session, but the psychoanalytic session does not lend itself to experimental procedures.

If the theory itself cannot be tested scientifically, perhaps the best use of the theory is as a springboard for more limited, testable hypotheses. For example, in the 1950s, learning theorists took Freudian notions such as sex typing, dependency, identification, and defense mechanisms and studied their development within a learning framework. More recently, hypnosis has been used to test hypotheses concerning the unconscious (Hilgard, 1965). Reyher (1967) provides an example. Hypnotized college students were told a story designed to arouse unconscious oedipal feelings. They were told they would not remember anything about the story after awakening, but would have strong sexual feelings when certain words were mentioned after they awakened. As predicted, the critical words, but not neutral words, aroused sweating, trembling, and guilt. Thus, it is possible to test hypotheses about unconscious conflicts. Finally, there have even been attempts to formulate computer models based on information-processing constructs (see Chapter 4) of Freud's notions concerning the repression of painful memories (Wegman, 1985).

It should be recognized that Freud's notion of the scientific approach differed from that of the scientific community. He looked for converging evidence for a particular interpretation. If dream reports,

*For reviews of research on Freudian theory, see S. Fisher and R. P. Greenberg, *The scientific credibility of Freud's theories and therapy* (New York: Basic Books, 1977 and M. N. Eagle, *Recent developments in psychoanalysis: A critical evaluation.* (New York: McGraw-Hill, 1984).

memories from childhood, physical symptoms, slips of the tongue, and accidents all suggested that the patient had not resolved her feelings of sibling rivalry in childhood, then Freud believed he had proved his case. He integrated facts from several sources to form a consistent picture. He felt that his interpretations were further bolstered if several patients illustrated the same relationship between variables. For example, patients with paralysis of a limb (hysteria) often reported unresolved sexual conflicts from childhood. We are not, however, told how many patients exhibited these two behaviors. Furthermore, we cannot know whether the co-occurrence of the variables would be statistically significant or was simply coincidental. However, this lack of experimental rigor was not of great concern to Freud. His goal, after all, was to provide clinical insights that would help him formulate a theory that would improve therapy.

## Overemphasis on Childhood Sexuality

Freud's emphasis on sexuality brings to mind the greeting card that begins, "SEX — Now that I have your attention. . . . " Not surprisingly, claims about childhood sexuality both captured the attention of psychologists and the public and alienated many. Freud's answer to those who saw little evidence that sexuality pervades childhood was that his critics were repressing their own strong sexual memories from childhood! If we criticize the theory, we risk being recast as a patient.

For most developmental psychologists, claims about infantile sexuality in normal children strain the theory's credibility. The bulk of the developmental research of the last 20 years portrays infants and children as curious, self-motivated, social creatures who seek stimulation, rather than driven, anxiety-ridden beings who seek the reduction of tension. Recent research on attention and thinking in infants demonstrates that even a young infant is much more than id. Of course, the Freudian and cognitive views are not necessarily incompatible. Decarie's (1965) study of parallels in the development of Freud's object relations and Piaget's object permanence, neo-Freudian advances in ego psychology (for example, Hartmann, 1958), and Furth's (1987) integration of Freudian and Piagetian theory are particularly notable attempts to bridge the two areas.

Developmentalists certainly would not deny that most children are curious about sex, just as they are curious about much of their world.

The issue is how much emphasis to place on sexuality. Freud's theory demonstrates the mutual constraints among method, data, and theory mentioned in the Introduction. His data on the sexual fantasies of neurotic middle- and upper-class adults during the sexually repressive Victorian era may have little generality to children developing today. Furthermore, the specific claims about sexuality may reflect the biases of a male-oriented society. For example, Horney (1967) suggests that one could find as much evidence for womb envy in boys, due to their inability to have children, as for penis envy in girls.

Freud's emphasis on sexuality slights the social influences on development. Although he believes that social factors are important, he did not work out their role in any detail. Erikson and other neo-Freudians have remedied this oversight to some extent. Even this work, however, pays little attention to children's prosocial behavior, such as empathy and altruism, which is an active topic of research today. It should be mentioned that some of the early research on social factors stimulated by Freud's theory did not totally support the theory. For example, among the Trobrianders, Malinowski (1927) found little evidence of the type of Oedipus conflict described by Freud.

It is possible to reject Freud's focus on sexual content without rejecting the entire theory. The structures (id, ego, superego), processes (repression, unconscious motivation), and stage notion can retain their validity even if replaced with other content.

## Comment

What is Freud's heritage for developmental psychology? He began by asking why his patients suffered and ended by giving us a new perspective on human development. The theory has been a rich source of hypotheses for developmental research and has untapped relevance for today's research on cognitive development. The breadth and richness of the theory is impressive; it includes what other psychologists ignored: dreams, slips of the tongue, humor, and fantasies. Freud's loose, informal manner of gathering data and developing the theory poses problems, but that style is typical of pioneering theorists in many of the sciences. Hall and Lindzey note that whereas Freud may not have been the most rigorous scientist or theorist, "he was a patient, meticulous, penetrating observer and a tenacious, disciplined, courageous, original thinker" (1957, p. 72).

# ERIKSON

Powerful theories spawn "neo"s: neo-Piagetians, neo-Freudians, neobehaviorists, and so on. Freud's theory, despite its limitations, inspired a diverse group of brilliant and creative theoreticians, researchers, and therapists. They stretched, patched, and rearranged Freud's vision in two main ways that had consequences for developmental psychology.

First, several neo-Freudians, especially Hartmann (1958), stress the development of conflict-free ego functions, such as perception, memory, and logical thought. Whereas Freud's ego defends and inhibits, the neo-Freudian's ego integrates and organizes personality. Hartmann describes an ego that is partly independent of the id and its drives. The ego derives not from the id but from an undifferentiated matrix from which both the id and the ego develop. The emphasis on the ego's cognitive processes as a way of adapting to reality can be found in works by Rapaport (1960), Gill (1959), and Klein (1970). Furthermore, White (1963) identifies such ego satisfactions as exploration and competence at performing tasks well. These satisfactions are independent of satisfactions of the id. It is clear that psychoanalytic theory has become increasingly concerned with explaining normal, as much as abnormal, behavior.

Second, many neo-Freudians moved away from Freud's biological approach and considered the vast influence of society on development. These trends toward ego and social concerns came to developmental psychology largely through the work of Erik Erikson, who now commands our attention.

## BIOGRAPHICAL SKETCH

Erik Erikson was born in 1902 in Frankfurt, Germany, and grew up in Karlsruhe. His wanderlust and desire to be an artist drew him away from formal schooling. After several years of drifting, studying art, and painting children's portraits, Erikson was hired to teach art and other subjects to children of Americans who had come to Vienna for Freudian training. This accidental entry into the vigorous Freudian circle resulted in his admittance into the Vienna Psychoanalytic Institute. His own psychoanalysis, part of the usual training program, was conducted by Anna Freud. Erikson also learned from Freud himself, Heinz Hartmann, Ernst Kris, Helene Deutsch, and other gifted analysts.

The threat of fascism brought Erikson to the United States in 1933. He became Boston's first child analyst and obtained a position at the Harvard Medical School. Later he held positions at several eminent institutions, including Yale, Berkeley, and the Menninger Foundation. During the McCarthy era, Erikson's concern that California's loyalty oath was a danger to personal and academic freedom (Erikson 1951) precipitated his move back to the East Coast and to the Austen Riggs Center at Stockbridge, Massachusetts, Harvard, and several other eastern universities. Finally, he returned to California to the Center for Advanced Study in the Behavioral Sciences at Palo Alto and later the Mount Zion Hospital in San Francisco, to serve as a clinician and psychiatric consultant.

These diverse settings, from clinicians's chair to professor's podium, fueled an energy that spread Erikson's interests over a remarkable area. He studied combat crises in troubled American soldiers in World War II, child-rearing practices among the Sioux in South Dakota and the Yurok along the Pacific Coast, the play of disturbed and normal children, the conversations of troubled adolescents suffering identity crises, and social behavior in India. These observations molded his ideas, which he expressed in many publications, including the well-known *Childhood and Society* (1950a) and *Identity: Youth and Crisis* (1968). He was constantly concerned with the rapid social changes in America and wrote about issues such as the generation gap, racial tensions, juvenile delinquency, changing sexual roles, and the dangers of nuclear war. It is clear that psychoanalysis had moved far from a doctor's couch in Vienna.

## GENERAL ORIENTATION TO THE THEORY

Erikson accepts the basic notions of Freudian theory: psychological structures, the unconscious and conscious, drives, psychosexual stages, the normal–abnormal continuum, and psychoanalytic methodology. Because this orientation is described earlier in the chapter, this section concentrates on Erikson's additions to psychoanalytic theory. Erikson expanded Freud's theory by developing a set of eight psychosocial stages, which span a lifetime, by studying the development of identity, and by developing methods that reach beyond the structured psycho-analytic setting used with adults. A look at these three contributions serves as an orientation to the theory. When reading the following account of his theory, keep in mind Bruner's (1987, p. 8) observation that "there are two Eriksons: one a surprisingly doctrinaire psychoana-lyst, embracing the received doctrines of the master; the other a moral-ist, artist, and intellectual trying to deal with a culture that has begun to lose its power as an instrument for fulfilling the potential and the aspirations of those who live within it."

## Psychosocial Stages

Erikson's work in various cultures convinced him of the need to add a psychosocial dimension to Freud's theory of psychosexual develop-ment. In Table 2.1, columns A to D describe several aspects of Erik-son's theory, and column E names the Freudian psychosexual stage corresponding to each of Erikson's psychosocial stages. To illustrate the psychosexual and psychosocial components, Erikson (1959, p. 115) contrasts a toddler's oral pleasure when making speech sounds (psy-chosexual component) with the role of speech communication in shaping his relationship with his parents and significant others (psy-chosocial component). In the psychosocial view, physical maturation has personal and social repercussions. Maturation brings a new skill that opens up new possibilities for the child but also increases society's demands on him, in this case pressures to talk instead of cry when he wants something. There is a "fit" between the child and his culture. Societies have evolved agreed-upon ways of meeting the child's new needs in each step of his maturation. These include parental care, schools, social organizations, occupations, a set of values, and so on. Erikson speaks of a "cogwheeling" of life cycles, as when adults' needs to become caretakers coincide with children's needs for caretaking. In other words, each child is a life cycle in a "community of life cycles" (1959, p. 121). The child is surrounded by others who are also passing through various stages. While the culture, over many generations, has adapted itself to the child, the child in turn adapts himself to the culture, as when a new kindergartener adjusts to a bewildering new set of experiences called "school."

**TABLE 2.1** ■ Erikson's "worksheet" summarizing the eight stages of development

| Stage | A<br>Psychosocial crises | B<br>Radius of significant relations | C<br>Related elements of social order | D<br>Psychosocial modalities | E<br>Psychosexual stages |
|---|---|---|---|---|---|
| 1 | Trust vs. mistrust | Maternal person | Cosmic order | To get<br>To give in return | Oral-respiratory, sensory-kinesthetic (incorporative modes) |
| 2 | Autonomy vs. shame, doubt | Parental persons | "Law and order" | To hold (on)<br>To let (go) | Anal-urethral, muscular (retentive-eliminative) |
| 3 | Initiative vs. guilt | Basic family | Ideal prototypes | To make ( = going after)<br>To "make like"<br>( = playing) | Infantile-genital, locomotor (intrusive, inclusive) |
| 4 | Industry vs. inferiority | "Neighborhood," school | Technological elements | To make things<br>( = completing)<br>To make things together | "Latency" |
| 5 | Identity and repudiation vs. identity diffusion | Peer groups and outgroups; models of leadership | Ideological perspectives | To be oneself<br>(or not to be)<br>To share being oneself | Puberty |
| 6 | Intimacy and solidarity vs. isolation | Partners in friendship, sex, competition, cooperation | Patterns of cooperation and competition | To lose and find oneself in another | Genitality |
| 7 | Generativity vs. self-absorption | Divided labor and shared household | Currents of education and tradition | To make be<br>To take care of | |
| 8 | Integrity vs. despair | "Mankind"<br>"My kind" | Wisdom | To be, through having been<br>To face not being | |

Psychosocial development is culturally relative in two ways. First, although children in all cultures go through the same sequence of stages, each culture has its own idiosyncratic way of directing and enhancing the child's behavior at each age. For example, Erikson observed that the Sioux allowed nursing for several years in the spirit of an overall generosity that pervaded the Sioux value system. They also thumped the teething male babies on the head for biting the mother's nipples in the belief that their crying rage would turn them into good hunters, and they trained their girls to be bashful and afraid of men in preparation for serving their hunter-husbands. Second, there is cultural relativity within a culture as it changes over time. Institutions that meet the needs of one generation may prove inadequate for the next. Industrialization, urbanization, immigration, the Depression, and the civil-rights movement brought changes in what children needed to be taught in order to develop a healthy personality at their time in history.

Psychosocial development proceeds according to the *epigenetic principle*, a term derived from *epi*, which means "upon," and *genesis*, which means "emergence." This principle is borrowed from fetal development:

> Somewhat generalized, this principle states that anything that grows has a ground plan, and that out of this ground plan the parts arise, each part having its time of special ascendency, until all parts have arisen to form a functioning whole. At birth the baby leaves the chemical exchange of the womb for the social exchange system of his society, where his gradually increasing capacities meet the opportunities and limitations of his culture.
>
> *[Erikson, 1968, p. 92]*

Like the fetus, the personality becomes increasingly differentiated and hierarchically organized as it unfolds in, and is shaped by, a particular environment. As summarized in Table 2.1, this unfolding involves several dimensions. There is movement through a set of psychosocial "crises" or issues as the child matures, and there is an expansion of his radius of significant relations. Other dimensions include the translation into the child's terms of certain elements of social order or structure and the progression through a set of psychosocial modalities or ways of "being" and interacting in society. Put succinctly, the child has inborn laws of development "which create a succession of potentialities for significant interaction with those who tend him" (1968, p. 52).

We now look at the general nature of the eight stages and leave a specific description of each stage for a later section. Maturation and society's expectations together create eight crises, or issues, that the child must resolve. Each issue is most evident at a particular stage in the life cycle, but appears in some form throughout development. For example, autonomy is the dominant concern of the second year of life, but is prepared for in the first year and elaborated on in later stages.

Erikson describes each crisis in terms of a dimension with both positive and negative outcomes possible, for example, autonomy versus shame and doubt. Ideally, the child develops a favorable ratio, in which the positive aspect dominates the negative. For instance, a person needs to know when to trust and when to mistrust, but generally should have a trusting attitude toward life.

If the childhood crises are not handled satisfactorily, the person continues to fight his early battles later in life. Many adults are still struggling to develop a sense of identity. Erikson optimistically claims that it is never too late to resolve any of the crises.

With respect to the integration of successive stages, Erikson's theory lies between that of Piaget, with his tight integration, and Freud, with his loose integration. Each stage builds on the previous stages and influences the form of later stages. As Erikson expresses it, "Each stage adds something specific to all later ones, and makes a new ensemble out of all the earlier ones" (Evans, 1967, p. 41).

### Emphasis on Identity

In contrast to Freud's concern with how people defend themselves from unpleasant tensions—a somewhat negative approach—Erikson's concern is more positive. He holds that a main theme of life is the quest for *identity*. This term refers to "a conscious sense of individual identity . . . an unconscious striving for a continuity of personal character . . . a criterion for the silent doings of ego synthesis . . . a maintenance of an inner solidarity with a group's ideals and identity" (Erikson, 1959, p. 102). Stated differently, identity is the understanding and acceptance of both the self and one's society. Throughout life, we ask "Who am I?" and form a different answer in each stage. If all goes well, at the end of each stage, the child's sense of identity is reconfirmed on a new level. Although the development of identity reaches a crisis during adolescence, Erikson notes that it begins when the baby "first recognizes his mother and first feels recognized by her, when her voice tells him he is somebody with a name and he's good" (Evans, 1967, p. 35).

Thus, identity is transformed from one stage to the next, and early forms of identity influence later forms. This process is similar to the reworking of a concept (such as causality) in each successive stage in Piaget's theory.

Erikson, the wandering youth and the American immigrant, had lived with the need to establish an identity: "As an immigrant . . . I faced one of those very important redefinitions that a man has to make who has lost his landscape and his language, and with it all the 'references' on which his first sensory and sensual impressions, and thus also some of his conceptual images, were based" (Evans, 1967, p. 41). His conversations with Huey P. Newton (Erikson, 1973) demonstrate that he was particularly sensitive to the problems that minority groups have when trying to form an identity. He began using the term "identity crisis" to describe the loss of identity he observed in World War II soldiers. He saw a similar problem among troubled adolescents "who war on their society" (1968, p. 17). Eventually, Erikson realized that the problem of identity appears, though usually on a smaller scale, in all lives. Furthermore, he recognized that identity is a central problem of our times: "If the relation of father and son dominated the last century, then this one is concerned with the self-made man asking himself what he is making of himself" (Evans, 1967, p. 41).

## Expansion of Psychoanalytic Methodology

Erikson contributed to three methods for studying development: direct observation of children, cross-cultural comparisons, and psychohistory. His early experiences with children and his contact with Anna Freud, who was developing child observations and play therapy, immersed him in the world of both normal and disturbed children from the beginning of his career. In moving from the couch to the playroom, he asserted that "we must study man in action and not just man reflecting on reality" (Evans, 1967, p. 91).

Erikson's writings are sprinkled with contrasts between cultures. He is fascinated with how the solutions to the universal stages vary from culture to culture. His forays into cultural anthropology point out the inherent limitations to basic Freudian theory, which was based almost completely on psychologically troubled patients in turn-of-the-century Vienna.

Some of Erikson's most interesting writing is found in his "psycho-histories." These are analyses of the psychosocial development of well-known people, based on their own writings and their conversations and behaviors as reported by others. Erikson believes that Hitler's rise illustrates the meshing of an individual's particular needs for identity and a nation's need for a more positive identity (Erikson, 1950). In *Young Man Luther* (1958), Erikson describes a troubled youth who defied his strict father who wished him to study law, rebelled against the authority of the church, and followed a belief that gave him an honest sense of identity. Other historical "patients" include Maxim Gorky (1950a) and George Bernard Shaw (1968). His biography, *Gandhi's Truth* (1969), won a Pulitzer Prize and the National Book Award in philosophy and religion.

## DESCRIPTION OF THE STAGES

Erikson divides the entire life cycle into "the eight ages of man." These eight ages refer to eight critical periods, when certain lifelong ego concerns reach a climax. (Table 2.1 provides an overview of each stage.)

### Stage 1: Basic Trust Versus Basic Mistrust (Roughly Birth to 1 Year)

In Table 2.1, we see that the main task of infancy is to acquire a favorable ratio of trust to mistrust. If this balance is weighted toward trust, the child has a better chance of weathering the later crises than if it is weighted toward mistrust. Erikson defines *basic trust* as "an essential trustfulness of others as well as a fundamental sense of one's own trustworthiness" (1968, p. 96) and the sense that "there is some correspondence between your needs and your world" (Evans, 1967, p. 15).

The infant with an attitude of trust can predict that his mother will feed him when he is hungry and comfort him when he is frightened or in pain. He will tolerate having his mother out of sight because he is confident she will return. The mother, then, is all-important: "Mothers create a sense of trust in their children by that kind of administration which in its quality combines sensitive care of the baby's individual needs and a firm sense of personal trustworthiness within the trusted framework of their culture's life style" (Erikson, 1963, p. 249). The baby develops trust in himself from the feeling that others accept him and from increased familiarity with his bodily urges. This faith in himself and his small world corresponds to religious faith in the "cosmic order" of the universe (column C).

From the mother's side of the interaction, there must also be trust —trust in herself as a parent and in the meaningfulness of her caretaking role. Erikson (1950b) refers to a remark from Benjamin Spock: "To be a good parent you have to believe in the species—somehow."

Some mistrust is necessary at all ages in order to detect impending danger or discomfort and to discriminate between honest and dishonest persons. However, if mistrust wins out over trust, the child, or later the adult, may be frustrated, withdrawn, suspicious, and lacking in self-confidence.

The specifically oral experiences—sucking, biting, teething, and weaning—are prototypes for the psychosocial modality of getting and given (column D). The baby "takes in," or "incorporates," stimulation through all the senses, much as a Piagetian child "assimilates." By taking from the mother and the world, the baby is laying the foundation for his later role as a giver to others.

### Stage 2: Autonomy Versus Shame and Doubt (Roughly 2 to 3 Years)

With further neurological and muscular development come walking, talking, and the potential for anal control. As the child becomes more independent physically and psychologically, there are new possibilities for personality development. At the same time, however, there are new vulnerablities, namely, anxiety over separation from the parents, fear that anal control may not always be possible, and loss of self-esteem when failure does come.

A clash of wills is inevitable. Erikson refers to the "sinister forces which are leashed and unleashed, especially in the guerrilla warfare of unequal wills; for the child is often unequal to his own violent drives, and parent and child unequal to each other" (1959, p. 66). Ideally, parents create a supportive atmosphere in which the child can develop a sense of self-control without a loss of self-esteem.

While the positive component of this stage is autonomy, the negative components are shame and doubt: "Shame supposes that one is completely exposed and conscious of being looked at—in a word, self-conscious. . . . 'with one's pants down.' Shame is early expressed in an impulse to bury one's face, or to sink, right then and there, into the ground" (1959, pp. 68–69). Doubt has to do with the unknown "behind" that the child cannot see, yet must try to control. Shame and doubt about one's self-control and independence come if basic trust was insufficiently developed or was lost, when bowel training is too early or too harsh, or when the child's will is "broken" by an overcontrolling parent.

The culture, expressed through the parents, shapes and gives meaning to the toddler's new competencies. For example, cultures vary in how seriously they take training for anal control. Erikson points to the machine age's ideal of a "mechanically trained, faultlessly functioning, and always clean, punctual, and deodorized body" (1959, p. 67), in contrast to the lack of concern with such matters in the Sioux culture. By simply imitating older children, Sioux children achieve bowel control by the time they begin school.

The psychosocial modality is holding on versus letting go, the counterpart to retention and elimination. This ambivalence pervades the child's behavior and attitude. For example, toddlers often zealously hoard toys or other objects and anxiously guard them in their hiding place, then causally throw them out the window of a moving car or give them to a friend. One morning a mother is late to work because her two-year-old adamantly has insisted on buttoning every single shirt button himself, while the next morning the young Dr. Jekyll–Mr. Hyde screams with rage because his mother has not helped him get dressed. Failure to coordinate the opposing tendencies to hold on and let go can lead to the "anal personality" described by Freud— overcontrolled, compulsive, messy, stingy, or rigid.

In this second stage, the child encounters such rules as when he can have bowel movements or which areas of the house he is allowed to explore. These rules are an early hint of the "law and order" society he will face (column C of Table 2.1). The issue here, according to Erikson, is "whether we remain the masters of the rules by which we want to make things more manageable (not more complicated) or whether the rules master the ruler" (1959, pp. 72–73). In a well-functioning society, the sense of autonomy encouraged in children is maintained throughout their lives by that society's economic and political structures.

### Stage 3: Initiative Versus Guilt (Roughly 4 to 5 Years)

"Being firmly convinced that he *is* a person, the child must now find out *what kind* of a person he is going to be. And here he hitches his wagon to nothing less than a star: he wants to be like his parents, who to him appear very powerful and very beautiful, although quite unreasonably dangerous" (1959, p. 74). The theme of this stage is the child's identification with his parents, who are perceived as big, powerful, and intrusive. Erikson accepts the basic outline of Freud's account of how children achieve identification through the Oedipus complex, but emphasizes the social components more than the sexual. As we saw in Freud's theory, identification brings with it a conscience and a set of interests, attitudes, and sex-typed behaviors.

The basic psychosocial modality is "making," namely, intrusion, taking the initiative, forming and carrying out goals, and competing. After T. S. Eliot, we might conclude that the stage-3 child dares to disturb the universe. The child intrudes "into other bodies by physical attack . . . into other people's ears and minds by aggressive talking . . . into space by vigorous locomotion . . . into the unknown by consuming curiosity" (Erikson, 1959, p. 76). This initiative is supported by advances in mobility, physical dexterity, language, cognition, and creative imagination.

The child settles somewhere along a dimension ranging from successful initiative to overwhelming guilt due to an overly severe conscience that punishes sexual fantasies and immoral thoughts or behavior. In addition to guilt, another danger is that the child may forever feel that he must always be doing something, always competing, always "making," in order to have any worth as a person.

For this stage the related elements of social order are "ideal prototypes" (column C). These refer to social roles, such as policeman, teacher, astronaut, president, and "hero."

## Stage 4: Industry Versus Inferiority (roughly 6 years to puberty)

The "industrial age" begins. The child now wants to enter the larger world of knowledge and work. Her theme is "I am what I learn" (1959, p. 82). The great event is the entry into school, where she is exposed to the technology of her society: books, multiplication tables, arts and crafts, maps, microscopes, films, and tape recorders. Learning, however, occurs not only in school but also on the street, in friends' houses, and at home.

Successful experiences give the child a sense of industry, a feeling of competence and mastery, while failure brings a sense of inadequacy and inferiority, a feeling that one is a good-for-nothing. The child strives to make things well and complete what she has begun. The years spent establishing basic trust, autonomy, and initiative were preparation for this energetic entry into our technological society. Erikson notes that this stage differs from the first three in that "it does not consist of a swing from a violent inner upheaval to a new mastery" (1959, p. 88). It is a calmer period, a time of psychosexual latency.

## Stage 5: Identity and Repudiation Versus Identity Diffusion (Adolescence)

Erikson quotes a saying that hangs in a cowboys' bar in the West: "I ain't what I ought to be, I ain't what I'm going to be, but I ain't what I was" (1959, p. 93). In an earlier section, we saw that the quest for identity is the undercurrent running through all the stages:

> The process of identity formation emerges as an *evolving configuration* — a configuration which is gradually established by successive ego syntheses and resyntheses throughout childhood; it is a configuration gradually integrating *constitutional givens, idiosyncratic libidinal needs, favored capacities, significant identifications, effective defenses, successful sublimations, and consistent roles.*
>
> [1959, p. 116]

Trust, autonomy, initiative, and industry all contribute to the child's identity. In the fifth stage, however, this concern reaches a climax. Rapid physiological changes produce a "new" body with unfamiliar sexual urges. These changes, along with social pressure to make occupational and educational decisions, force the youth to consider a variety of roles. The basic task for the adolescent is to integrate the various identifications he brings from childhood into a more complete identity. Erikson emphasizes that this whole (the identity) is greater than the sum of its parts (previous identifications). This reassembled identity is appropriate for the new needs, skills, and goals of adolescence. If the adolescent cannot integrate his identifications, roles, or selves, he faces "identity diffusion." His personality is fragmented, lacking a core. Erikson quotes Biff in Arthur Miller's *Death of a Salesman*, "I just can't take hold, Mom, I can't take hold of some kind of a life" (1959, p. 91). The problem may be exacerbated by one's minority-group status, doubts about one's sexual orientation, an overly strong identification with a parent, or too many occupational roles from which to choose.

The psychosocial modality of this stage is to be oneself or not to be oneself. Hamlet's "to be or not to be" soliloquy voices his alienation and role confusion (Erikson, 1968). Youths seek their true selves through peer groups, clubs, religion, political movements, and so on. These groups provide opportunities to try out new roles much in the way the youth tries on jackets in a store until he finds one that fits. The ideology of society, this stage's counterpart in the social order, guides this role playing by conveying which roles are valued by society.

## Stage 6: Intimacy and Solidarity Versus Isolation (Young Adulthood)

Only if a reasonably well integrated identity emerges from stage 5 can psychological intimacy with other people (or even oneself) be possible. If a youth fears that she may lose herself in someone else, she is unable to fuse her identity with someone else. Although young people usually form important relationships with the opposite sex during this time, their friendships with the same sex and even their access to their own intimate feelings and thoughts also mark this stage. These relationships, by enhancing one's own identity, further the growth of personality. One aspect of intimacy is the feeling of solidarity of "us" and the defense against "them," the threatening "forces and people whose essence seems dangerous to one's own" (1959, pp. 96–97). If the youth's attempts at intimacy fail, she retreats into isolation. In this case, social relationships are stereotyped, cold, and empty.

### Stage 7: Generativity Versus Stagnation and Self-Absorption (Middle Adulthood)

*Generativity* refers to "the interest in establishing and guiding the next generation" (1959, p. 97) through child rearing or creative or productive endeavors. Simply bearing children does not, of course, ensure that the parent will develop a sense of generativity. Faith in the future, a belief in the species, and the ability to care about others seem to be prerequisites for development in this stage. Instead of having children, one may work to create a better world for the children of others. Stage 7, then, provides the mechanism for the continuity of society from generation to generation. A lack of generativity is expressed in stagnation, self-absorption (self-indulgence), boredom, and a lack of psychological growth.

### Stage 8: Integrity Versus Despair (Late Adulthood)

In this final stage, a person must live with what he has built over his lifetime. Ideally, he will have achieved integrity. *Integrity* involves the acceptance of the limitations of life, a sense of being a part of a larger history that includes previous generations, a sense of owning the wisdom of the ages, and a final integration of all the previous stages. The antithesis of integrity is despair—regret for what one has done or not done with one's life, fear of approaching death, and disgust with oneself. A recent book, *Vital Involvement in Old Age* (Erikson, Erikson, and Kivnick, 1986), describes the importance of a person's continuing to stimulate and challenge the environment as the environment simultaneously has that effect on the person.

### Comment: Contemporary Eriksonian Research on Stages

Marcia (1980) has expanded two of Erikson's notions, crisis and commitment: "Crisis refers to times during adolescence when the individual seems to be actively involved in choosing among alternative occupations and beliefs. Commitment refers to the degree of personal investment the individual expresses in an occupation or belief" (1967, p. 119). The presence or absence of crisis or commitment defines four *identity statuses*. The *identity-diffused* person, because she has experienced neither an identity crisis nor a commitment, is easily influenced by others and changes her beliefs often. The *foreclosure* person has made commitments without experiencing an identity crisis. She unquestioningly accepts beliefs, attitudes, and an occupation based on the views of others. The *moratorium* person is in a severe state of identity crisis and is not yet able to make commitments. Finally, the *identity-achieved* person has successfully passed through an identity crisis and has made a set of personal commitments.

Erikson's sequences may not be universal. For example, the stage sequence may differ for men and women and across various cultures. Although identity may precede intimacy for men, Gilligan points out that "for women these tasks seem instead to be fused. Intimacy goes along with identity" (1982, p. 12).

A final example of contemporary Eriksonian work is the renewed interest in ego development. Snarey, Kohlberg, and Noam (1983) provide a useful framework for comparing theories of ego development; they see three types of such theories. The first type includes structurally defined stages, such as Piaget's cognitive stages. In the second, stages are culturally defined in terms of ages, for example, starting school at ages 5 through 7. The third type, exemplified by Erikson's theory, has functionally defined stages that arise because of the interaction between structural and cultural factors. For example, children start school and are faced with the task of establishing their competence both because they generally have the requisite cognitive structures to deal with this task and because society says they are at the age when children must begin school. Other recent theoretical work aimed at refining or clarifying Erikson's stages of ego development includes that of Coté and Levine (1987) and Meacham and Santilli (1982).

## MECHANISMS OF DEVELOPMENT

The epigenetic principle describes the forces that underlie movement through the stages. Physical maturation writes the general timetable for development. Within these limits, one's culture pushes, slows down, nurtures, and destroys. In Erikson's view, society exerts its influence on the developing organism at many levels, ranging all the way from its abstract ideology to a parent's caress. Many of Freud's mechanisms of development can join Erikson's list of mechanisms of development: drives, frustrations from external and internal forces, attachment, and identification. However, Erikson makes little use of Freud's tension-reduction equilibration process. Instead, he seems to view development as the resolution of conflict from opposing forces. The child integrates holding on and letting go, initiative and guilt, the biological and psychological, and so on.

Erikson has elaborated on a more specific mechanism of development: play (*Toys and Reasons*, 1977). Play is used in a broad sense to mean the use of imagination to try out ways of mastering and adapting to the world, to express emotions, to recreate past situations or imagine future situations, and to develop new models of existence. Problems that cannot be solved in reality can be solved through doll play, dramatics, sports, art, block play, "playing house," and so on. Play, however, is not limited to children. Play includes Einstein visualizing a model of time and space, an adolescent fantasizing about entering various occupations, or a man rehearsing what he will say to his boss the next day. Play is often ritualized and becomes a somewhat formal, enduring, culturally agreed-upon way of interacting with others. For example, an adolescent who is "messing around" with his friends is acquiring culturally approved patterns for interacting with other people. Or the child-care rituals of infancy pass on "proper" ways of recognizing and greeting other people. Rituals are mechanisms of development because they bring humans in every stage into the cultural mainstream and provide ready-made solutions to the problems of everyday life.

## POSITION ON DEVELOPMENTAL ISSUES

In general, Erikson's position on the four issues is close to Freud's, except for differences in emphasis. Erikson, like Piaget, has a more optimistic view of human nature. Children and adults not only seek to avoid pain but also actively seek to develop a positive sense of identity. Existential man is in a process of "becoming" throughout life. This development is primarily qualitative because changes are stagelike, but it is also somewhat quantitative, considering that one's identity becomes stronger and one's convictions solidify.

Like Freud, Erikson believes that nature determines the sequence of the stages and sets the limits within which nurture operates. If heredity ensures that certain crises arise, then the environment determines how they are resolved. Erikson, however, more than Freud, emphasizes the role of culture in nurturing and shaping the developing child or adult. Not only the person's past and present but also society's past and present influence the developing person. In addition, Erikson does not accept Freud's claim that development is essentially complete after the first 5 years of life. Development is a lifelong process; sometimes childhood conflicts are not resolved satisfactorily until adulthood. Finally, for Erikson, the essence of development is the formation of an identity that gives coherence to one's personality.

## THEORETICAL NATURE OF THE THEORY

Erikson presents his theory as would a novelist or an artist rather than a scientist. At most, the theory is a loosely connected set of ideas and observations that could not, strictly speaking, be called a deductive, an inductive, or a functional theory. Two models are implicit in the theory. The Darwinian evolutionary model describes the development of social institutions that ensure the physical and psychological survival of the species. In addition, the dialectic model of history is evident in the resolution of opposing forces in each stage of development and the integration of each stage into the next.

## EVALUATION OF THE THEORY

Because Erikson's theory is an extension of psychoanalytic theory, the earlier evaluation of Freud's theory is relevant here. Instead of reiterating those comments, the present section focuses on the unique strengths and weaknesses of Erikson's theory.

## Strengths

### *Expansion of Psychoanalytic Theory*

By widening the empirical base of psychoanalytic theory, Erikson increased its credibility and application. He added the psychosocial to the psychosexual, the cultural to the biological, the ego identity to the ego defenses, the normal to the abnormal, the cross-cultural to the culture-specific, child observations to adults' reconstructions from childhood, and adult development to child development. The theory is remarkable in its power to integrate a wide variety of situations. Erikson's version of development seems well grounded in the everyday lives of the majority of people, as they struggle to find coherence and meaning in their lives. He "looks for the hopeful and active part of the person and for how human experience and human potential are organized in the communal environment, within a radius of significant social encounters" (Schlein, 1987, p. xxv). This broadened psychoanalytic framework has been a valuable heuristic for counseling and therapy, especially with adolescents. Erikson influenced the field of developmental psychology in a general way, in that he provided a new view of development. His emphasis on cultural factors and life-span development were especially important. However, his work stimulated little research on the specific claims of his theory, such as the ordering of the stages or, at a more concrete level, sex differences in children's play.

### *Broad Perspective*

Erikson's relevance for contemporary views of development lies in the broad perspective he gives to a child's behavior. A specific behavior of a specific child is influenced by his past history, the present situation, and the past and present history of his own culture and even the world society. All levels of society, from international relations to the nation's political structure to the interaction within the family, influence behavior. Erikson's writings conjure up the image of a system of interlocking forces uniting the child and the universe, the distant past and the distant future. Although many developmentalists pay lip service to this position, with few exceptions (for example, Riegel, 1972) they do not seriously examine these social and historical variables. Instead, the behavior of children is typically studied in isolation.

## Weaknesses

### Lack of Systematicity

Erikson's theory is a loose connection of observations, empirical generalizations, and abstract theoretical claims. Consequently, it is difficult to state his claims in a way that can be tested or relate his empirical findings to the more abstract levels of the theory. As with Freud, much of the problem lies in the methodological inadequacies, particularly the lack of controlled experimentation. In Erikson's case, the observations are laden with interpretations that are difficult to evaluate. For example, in Erikson's observation at the beginning of this chapter, do boys build towers because of this phallic, intrusive orientation, as Erikson claims, or simply because they like to knock tall things down? His psychohistories are fascinating but are necessarily speculative. A related problem is that the terms he selects often mislead rather than elucidate. For example, *generativity* and *integrity* do not have their usual meanings. It is not surprising, then, that many of Erikson's concepts are often misunderstood.

### Lack of Specific Mechanisms of Development

It became clear in the earlier section on mechanisms of development that Erikson does not explain in any detail how a child moves from stage to stage or even how he resolves the crisis within a stage. He states *what* influences the movement (for example, physical maturation, parents, cultural beliefs, to what extent earlier crises were resolved), but not specifically *how* the movement comes about. By what mechanisms does an infant learn when to trust and when to mistrust? Why does the resolution of the initiative–guilt polarity lead to the industry–inferiority conflict rather than to some other conflict? The validity of many of Erikson's notions, such as the conflict-resolution model, rests on the ability to describe in detail the mechanism of development.

## SUMMARY

Two of Freud's ideas have formed the backbone of developmental psychology. First, he proposes that the first few years of life are critical because the basic personality is formed during that time. Second, he believes that personality is developed as the child copes with an invariant sequence of conflicts. Each conflict involves a different domain: the oral, anal, phallic, and adult genital. The way the child satisfies the drives in each stage forms the basis of his personality. Although Freud's psychosexual focus is less influential today in academic psychology, the notion of stages has greatly influenced research and therapy with children in this century.

Using an energy model from physics, Freud describes a system of psychological energy that is distributed, transformed, and discharged within a psychological structure. This structure consists of the id, ego, and superego in a delicate balance. The ego considers its available defenses, its perceptions of reality, the demands of the id for drive reduction, and the prohibitions of the superego before deciding on a course of action. Most of the "mind" is unconscious because knowledge of the thoughts and wishes hidden in the id, ego, and superego would cause unbearable anxiety.

Most of Freud's evidence came from his patients' free associations concerning their childhood, dreams, and present concerns. Freud believes that the workings of the abnormal mind clarify the nature of normal personality because there is a continuum of behaviors ranging from the abnormal to the normal.

Freud views humans as being driven by instincts, but actively trying to cope with various internal and external conflicts. He stresses qualitative, stagelike changes in development, but also includes quantitative change. Although he emphasizes biological influences, especially drives, he also recognizes the role of experience, particularly in the first five years of life. The essence of development is the emergence of psychological structures that mediate all experience and behavior. Freud's theory uncovered the powerful unconscious and made several lasting empirical and theoretical contributions to developmental psychology. In addition, the theory has the potential to broaden future research on cognitive development by including emotion-laden thoughts and defense mechanisms. However, the theory has methodological inadequacies, and its claims may not be testable. In addition, its focus on infantile sexuality has limited its acceptance in academic psychology.

Erikson's psychosocial theory of development modified Freudian theory in two important ways. First, he identifies important social influences on development. His research in various cultures and various social settings within a culture suggests that every society tries to deal with the biologically based changes occurring during development. Ideally, there is a fit between the child's needs and the society's needs at each point in development. In each of eight stages, there is a psychosocial crisis in which there are two possible extreme outcomes: (1) trust versus mistrust, (2) autonomy versus shame and doubt, (3) initiative versus guilt, (4) industry versus inferiority, (5) identity and repudiation versus identity diffusion, (6) intimacy and solidarity versus isolation, (7) generativity versus stagnation and self-absorption, and (8) integrity versus despair.

Erikson's second major contribution to psychoanalytic theory is his notion that life is a quest for identity. Thus, he focuses on ego processes. The work on both social and ego processes greatly expanded psychoanalytic theory and provided a broad perspective on development. However, the theory is rather unsystematic and lacks specific mechanisms of development.

Freud and Erikson produced unique yet complementary perspectives on development. A remark by Kierkegaard expresses an integration of the two views: "Life can only be understood backwards; but it must be lived forwards."

## SUGGESTED READINGS

This paperback is a short, lucid introduction to Freud's theory.

Hall, C. S. *A primer of Freudian psychology*. New York: World, 1954.

For a metatheoretical look at Freud's theory, the reader should consult David Rapaport's writings, especially the following.

Rapaport, D. *The structure of psychoanalytic theory: A systematizing attempt. Psychological Issues*, Monograph 6. New York: International Universities Press, 1960.

For an account of recent developments in psychoanalysis, the following is recommended.

Eagle, M. N. *Recent developments in psychoanalysis: A critical evaluation.* New York: McGraw-Hill, 1984.

Because Freud is a talented and provocative writer, his ideas should be explored in his own writings.

Strachey, J., ed. and trans. *The standard edition of the complete psychological works of Sigmund Freud.* 24 vols. London: Hogarth Press, 1953–1966. Particularly recommended are "An Outline of Psycho-Analysis" (Vol. 23, pp. 144–207), "New Introductory Lectures on Psycho-Analysis" (Vol. 22, pp. 5–182), and any of the case studies.

Two of Erikson's books and a recent collection of his papers provide a comprehensive look at his ideas.

Erikson, E. H. *Childhood and society.* New York: Norton, 1950.
Erikson, E. H. *Identity: Youth and crisis.* New York: Norton, 1968.
Schlein, S., ed. *A way of looking at things: Selected papers from 1930 to 1980. Erik H. Erikson.* New York: Norton, 1987.

Erikson's psychohistories are a source of fascinating reading. Especially recommended is the following.

Erikson, E. H. *Young man Luther.* New York: Norton, 1958.

A biography clarifies some of Erikson's ideas.

Coles, R. *Erik H. Erikson: The growth of his work.* Boston: Little, Brown, 1970.

# 3

# Social Learning Theory

*Subjects were tested for the amount of imitative learning. . . . Three measures of imitation were obtained:* Imitation of physical aggression: *This category included acts of striking the Bobo doll with the mallet, sitting on the doll and punching it in the nose, kicking the doll, and tossing it in the air.* Imitative verbal aggression: *Subject repeats the phrases, "Sock him," "Hit him down," "Throw him in the air," or "Pow."* Imitative nonaggressive verbal responses: *Subject repeats, "He keeps coming back for more," or "He sure is a tough fella."*
[Bandura, Ross, and Ross, 1961, p. 33]

*The experimenter introduced the training task as follows: "Now let's give this lady (model) a chance to play the game. Then you (child) can play the game. Here are some cards. Which ones are the same? Which ones go together?" The model grouped the stimuli according only to the size dimension. The experimenter queried the model, "Why are they the same?" and the model responded, "Because these two are pictures of big things (pointing) and these two are little things (pointing)." Then the same item was presented to the child in identical fashion (asking about only one dimension). "Now it's your turn to play the game. Play the game just like the lady did."*
[Zimmerman, 1974, p. 1035]

M ark Twain once remarked, "Training is everything. The peach was once a bitter almond; cauliflower is nothing but cabbage with a college education." This optimistic view of learning captures learning theorists' belief that development comes primarily from experience. Children acquire new behaviors and modify old behaviors as they encounter their social and physical world. As specific learning experiences accumulate, the child develops, but not in the stagelike way described by Freud and Piaget.

The previous two chapters presented the "great man" theories of developmental psychology. The third sweeping movement in the field came not from a single person but from a number of researchers working over a span of more than 60 years. More than any other theoretical approach, learning theory was responsible for bestowing scientific respectability on developmental psychology. The theory's rigorous, objective research methods made laboratory studies of children possible in the 1950s and early 1960s, developmental psychology's formative years. Thus, learning theory changed the course of developmental psychology. This experimental orientation survives today, even though the content of studies has shifted from learning to a wide range of cognitive processes, such as memory, attention, and reasoning.

Learning theory is the most truly American theory. Most of the theories in this volume began and developed in Europe and only later influenced North American psychology. Although early Russian work on reflexes and conditioning had already begun and Hermann Ebbinghaus' verbal-learning studies were already history, learning theory developed and had most of its influence on American soil. To a great extent, the history of American psychology and the history of learning theory were synonymous until the 1960s. Learning theory has become part of our culture and has entered our language as "behaviorism," "rat psychology," "behavior modification," "Skinner box," and "reinforcement."

This chapter focuses on social learning theory because it is the version of learning theory that most clearly influences current developmental thinking and research. Work by Albert Bandura (born 1925) will be highlighted. However, in order to understand the assumptions and goals of social learning theory, it is necessary to take an extended look at its heritage in "classical" learning theory. Therefore, the first section, the history of the theory, is more extensive than in other chapters. The second section, the general orientation, is subdivided into traditional learning theory and social learning theory. The next section, on mechanisms of development, focuses on social learning theory. The final topics include the theory's position on developmental issues, its theoretical nature, and its strengths and weaknesses.

## HISTORY OF THE THEORY

Learning theory up to the time of social learning theory raised many of the issues to which social learning theory responded. This history, then, is critical to our understanding of social learning theory. As Henri Bergson noted, "The present contains nothing more than the past, and what is found in the effect was already in the cause."

### Behaviorism

Around the turn of this century, psychologists and philosophers were struggling with such weighty issues as the mind–body problem: Are the mind and body two distinct entities? If so, how are they related? There were muddled, tortuous dialogues about trivial distinctions, reminiscent of the old metaphysical arguments over how many angels could dance on the head of a pin. Psychologists' attempts to examine systematically the structure of the mind and the nature of consciousness relied on introspection: verbalizing one's own thoughts or feelings. This unsatisfactory state of affairs led to John Watson's "declaration of behaviorism" in 1913. In this strongly worded statement, he asserted that the goal of psychology should be to predict and control overt behavior, not to describe and explain conscious states. Thus, Watson redefined the field of psychology. If one studies only behavior, the mind–body problem becomes a meaningless issue. He even suggested, in his presidential address to the American Psychological Association in 1915, that the conditioned reflex could take the place of introspection in psychology. The behaviorists' reform movement had begun.

In 1917, Watson was awarded the grand sum of 100 dollars to study reflexes in infants. In his most famous study, he conditioned a fear response in "Little Albert" (a feat we describe later). Watson, like Skinner and certain other behaviorists to follow, had visions of a better society. If changing the environment can change behavior, there are exciting possibilities for human society. Watson carried his ideas to the public, especially parents. The follow excerpt comes from his manual, *Psychological Care of Infant and Child:*

There is a sensible way of treating children. Treat them as though they were young adults. Dress them, bathe them with care and circumspection. Let your behavior always be objective and kindly firm. Never hug and kiss them, never let them sit in your lap. If you must, kiss them once on the forehead when they say goodnight. Shake hands with them in the morning. Give them a pat on the head if they have made an extraordinary good job of a difficult task. Try it out. In a week's time you will find how easy it is to be perfectly objective with your child and at the same time kindly. You will be utterly ashamed of the mawkish, sentimental way you have been handling it.

*[1928, pp. 81–82]*

It speaks well for the wisdom and common sense of parents that they did not adopt his philosophy wholeheartedly. In fact, Watson had only limited direct influence on the study of children's psychological development. It is interesting that behaviorism in the United States began with studies of children, but did not really influence the field of developmental psychology until the 1950s and early 1960s, following its tremendous influence on psychology in general. One probable reason for this early resistance to behaviorism was the physical separation of departments of psychology and the interdisciplinary institutes for child study with their pragmatic social-welfare concerns. In addition, developmentalists in the 1930s and 1940s focused on physical maturation and biological models of development (Arnold Gesell, G. Stanley Hall, Heinz Werner, Freud). They gathered facts for the purpose of establishing norms of development.

Even without a developmental following, learning theory nearly engulfed the field of psychology from the 1920s through the 1950s. Although Watson left the field and became an advertising executive, the movement continued through the leadership of Edward Thorndike, Edward Tolman, Edwin Guthrie, Clark Hull, Kenneth Spence, B. F. Skinner, and others. Hull even developed a formal, deductive theory of learning, complete with postulates.

These theorists asked questions that could be answered and provided a fruitful methodology for examining these questions. Central questions included the following: Can learning occur if a stimulus and a response simply occur together, or is reinforcement always necessary? Why is a learned response more persistent if it has been reinforced only part of the time rather than all of the time? Is there "latent" learning — knowledge that is acquired simply by being in a particular environment without any immediate reinforcement? In Sheldon White's words, learning theories were so influential "because they found for Psychology a reasonable species of psychological reality, and because they then laid down a paradigm of cooperative research procedures which might search that reality with a hope of significant findings. . . . one could stop the hair-splitting and throat-clearing and one could move into intensive scientific development" (1970, p. 662). Thus, learning theory served a need at a particular point in history.

After several decades of great research activity, learning theory ran into trouble in the 1960s. Part of the discontent came from within; hundreds of studies of verbal learning had not led to a satisfactory account of memory or learning. In addition, new evidence suggested that biological predispositions limit or modify the laws of learning. For a given species, some kinds of learning are easier than others. For example, rats learn to associate nausea with a certain taste, but not with a light or a sound (Garcia and Koelling, 1966). At the same time, learning theory faced external challenges. Noam Chomsky's (1959) attack on Skinner's account of language acquisition was a serious blow because it showed that learning approaches could not explain the acquisition of a skill as complex as language. In addition, alternate conceptions of learning were developing. Information processing (see Chapter 4), Chomsky's transformational grammar, and Piaget's cognitive theory provided attractive opposing explanations of behavior: they characterized learning as a change in knowledge rather than as a change in the probability of response. Attempts to patch up learning theory by positing verbal mediation, generalized rules, and complex hierarchies of mental associations did not halt the declining influence of the theory. With the entrance of cognitive psychology, psychology began what Hebb (1960) called its second American revolution, the first being the routing of any psychology based on introspection.

A parallel, but delayed scenario unfolded within developmental psychology. The learning studies with children in the first few decades of this century were simply translations of paradigms used with animals and college students. The experiments differed from the earlier ones only in that the subjects happened to be children. Children underwent operant and classical conditioning (Fattu, Auble, and Mech, 1955). They also solved simple discrimination-learning problems and even wandered through mazes seeking prizes rather than cheese at the end (Hicks and Carr, 1912). It should come as no surprise that children learned faster than rats, but more slowly than college sophomores. In 1954, a review of children's learning concluded that the laws of learning are the same in children and other populations (Munn, 1954). However, this conclusion was changed by three important lines of research that emerged and developed from the 1950s through the 1960s. One was a theoretical approach descended from Hull and Spence concerning how children learn simple discrimination-learning problems. A second was an empirical approach stimulated by Skinnerian operant conditioning. The third lineage was social learning theory. Each provided an important context for the creation of modern social learning theory.

## Discrimination Learning

In the 1960s, the theoretical group descended from Hull and Spence turned to several laboratory tasks that (1) challenged animal-based accounts and (2) provoked clashes among alternative hypotheses of how children learn. The discrimination-learning task was particularly important. In a typical version of this task, there are numerous trials with pairs of objects that differ in one or more features. For example, a large blue square and a small red triangle might appear on one trial, a large green square and a small yellow circle on another, and so on. The child chooses the object he thinks will lead to a reward—a trinket or piece of candy. In our example, let us say that the small one always leads to reinforcement. Thus, size is relevant, and color and shape are irrelevant. The number of trials needed to solve this problem becomes fewer as children get older, of course. The controversy, however, was over the mechanism that underlies this developmental change. Developmental psychologists challenged the prevailing view, based on animal research, that at all ages learning involves the gradual strengthening of S–R (stimulus–respect) associations. Proponents of the *verbal-mediation hypothesis* (Kendler and Kendler, 1962; Kuenne, 1946) thought that children learn to use verbal labels to solve discrimination-learning problems after about age 7. If the child could use labels, he would say "little" aloud or to himself. For these older children, then, learning is a two-step process. By using words, the child first learns the relevant dimension and then learns which value along that dimension is always rewarded. Preschoolers do not mediate. Instead, they learn a response to a stimulus, much as a rat does. Language is grafted onto these simple S–R associations made by rats and young children. It almost seems that the verbal-mediation hypothesis implied that a rat with language would think the way the other child does. Evidence that words mediated the child's response came from a set of clever and complex variations of the discrimination-learning task. These tasks could be solved in a verbally mediated or a nonverbal, S–R way. From the pattern of the child's responses, it was possible to infer which mode of solving the problem he used.

Although there was agreement that at some point in development children are no longer limited to simple S–R learning, the controversy over which process was involved in this more mature learning was never completely resolved. It was suggested that attending to the relevant dimension (for example, color or shape) or learning to tell the stimuli apart may be more important processes than verbal mediation. The important outcome of this entire controversy was a wealth of evidence that learning comes more and more under cognitive control during development. Thus, there finally emerged hypotheses proposing that learning does change as a function of development.

One aspect of this cognitive control was the growing use of strategies, rules, and hypotheses during development. This was illustrated in a set of studies by Weir (1964). The child saw a display with three buttons in front of him and was told to try to win as many marbles as he could. The child did not know at this point that pushing one button led to reinforcement only 66 percent of the time and pushing either of the other two buttons never led to reinforcement. Preschoolers fairly quickly settled for partial reinforcement, perhaps because they did not expect to be correct all the time or because they were simply following the old S–R rule that the response receiving the most reinforcement is the one that is learned. Grade-school children formulated simple strategies, such as pushing the left, then middle, then right-hand button, and persisted with this strategy even though it did not consistently lead to a reward. Older children devised a variety of ingenious strategies, some quite complex (1 right, 2 left, 1 right, 2 middle, 1 left). Eventually, however, they concluded that there was no consistent way to obtain reinforcement and resorted to continually pushing the button that produced a reward 66 percent of the time. Thus, the use of strategies becomes more prevalent and skillful with increasing age.

The marble-winning task nicely illustrates an interesting feature of learning research: a rather simple task often elicits very complex behavior because it taps a variety of processes, such as abstract thought, memory, expectations concerning success and failure, and motivation. A seemingly simple task can thus reveal critical developmental differences in learning.

Although few studies of discrimination learning are conducted today, there remains an interest in children's strategies of learning, particularly in an approach called *hypothesis theory* (Tumblin and Gholson, 1981). This theory proposes that the child has a repertoire of hypotheses from which he samples during problem solving. He tests hypotheses in some organized way, ideally until he finds one that consistently produces the correct response. Investigators have identified a number of types of strategies used by children and observed that strategies become more complex with increasing age. In addition, the child's cognitive level, as assessed on Piagetian tasks, accounts in part for the degree of complexity of the child's strategy (Gholson, Theobald, and Yarbourgh, 1980). Preoperational children usually use a simple strategy, such as alternating between objects in two spatial positions. Disconfirmation (lack of consistent reinforcement) does not necessarily cause the child to abandon the hypothesis. Concrete operational children can systematically check on the two cues in each dimension — for example, choose the big one, then the small one — before rejecting the size dimension. These checks confirm or disconfirm the hypothesis that a particular dimension is relevant.

Current research on strategies of learning focuses on the cognitive skills needed for hypothesis testing. Even verbal-mediation theory has been broadened by Kendler (1979), who includes hypothesis testing and information-processing mechanisms such as encoding (see Chapter 4). There is, then, some blending of learning and information-processing approaches today.

Two main conclusions came from several decades of research on children's discrimination learning. One is that children are active in their attempts to learn. They do not simply react to the environment and passively form associations between stimuli and responses. They try to solve a problem rather than simply learn a response. Children use their language or attentional skills to help themselves learn, and they form hypotheses or tentative rules while trying to solve the problem. They come to the learning task with certain biases concerning what to attend to and certain expectations about how problems are solved and how often rewards will be forthcoming.

A second conclusion is related to the first. The main changes in learning during development do not have to do with learning per se as much as they have to do with other aspects of development, such as language, attention, thinking, and social behavior. Learning, in the sense of choosing the correct stimulus, is rather trivial and anticlimactic. It comes after all the developmentally interesting processes have occurred. For example, mentally retarded children can form the correct association between a stimulus and a response about as quickly as do children of normal intelligence. Retarded children's deficiencies lie in processes such as attention, verbal mediation, and strategy selection.

The assumption of early learning researchers that children are halfway between rats and college sophomores turned out to be a gross oversimplification. Although children learn faster than rats and more slowly than college sophomores, there are important qualitative differences among the three groups. Development involves changes in the configuration of the many facets of development. The child's growing facility with language, his use of strategies, and his experience with social interaction are not isolated skills but an interrelated set of behaviors. This configuration at any point in development guides the child's learning. This configuration is not simply a watered-down version of adult behavior and knowledge; it is qualitatively different. Although learning theory is not a stage theory, there do seem to be certain points in development when the child's way of learning changes noticeably. Sheldon White's (1965) highly influential paper pointed out a large number of psychological changes between the ages of 5 and 7. Learning does not simply become better during this time, it becomes different, as far-reaching linguistic, social, and neurological changes occur. For example, learning becomes less impulsive and more under cognitive control.

The history of discrimination-learning research with children holds a certain irony. As we saw earlier, investigators used simple tasks, with the "correct" answers arbitrarily chosen. For example, choosing the black object might always be reinforced. As Flavell and Hill note, the response is "correct for today only in this specific situation. The 'organismic change' thus amounts to a temporary pairing of two items which are already in the cognitive repertoire rather than any genuine and substantive modification of the repertoire itself" (1969, p. 44). No significant or meaningful learning occurred during the task. Responses already available were temporarily paired with stimuli they had not been paired with before. Furthermore, abstract, meaningless stimuli were used, usually colored, geometric shapes. Psychologists used such tasks because they wanted to measure "pure" basic processes of learning, uncontaminated by previous learning. The irony comes from the fact that the most interesting information from learning research has to do with children's use of their previously acquired cognitive, linguistic, and social abilities as they attempt to make sense of the simple, meaningless task put before them. The "contamination" was interesting indeed.

By the late 1960s, the attitude of many developmentalists toward learning research was that it is probably more fruitful to study the development of attention, language, or thinking directly rather than indirectly, through learning tasks. There was also dissatisfaction with the simplistic characterization of thinking as a mediated response or, at most, a new chain of associations. Piaget's more complex description of thought was attracting the attention of developmentalists. His approach provided an attractive theoretical alternative at a critical point in the history of developmental psychology.

## Operant Conditioning

The theoretical learning approach was paralleled by a Skinnerian-based empirical line of research. Skinner (born 1904) is probably the most well-known psychologist in the world. In a survey conducted by a popular magazine, he was ranked fortieth in a list of the 100 most important people who ever lived, with Jesus Christ in the number-one spot. He considered thoughts and feelings inappropriate for empirical study and therefore examined only observable behavior. Skinner's work concerned the way rats' behavior could be shaped and controlled by schedules of reinforcement. In operant conditioning, a particular behavior becomes more frequent if it is reinforced. This work led psychologists to wonder if children's behavior could be similarly influenced. In fact, in a novel, *Walden Two* (1948), Skinner proposed that children in his utopian society would be raised by behavioral engineers, specialists in operant conditioning. Such desirable behaviors as self-control and independence would be fostered by reinforcement, whereas such undesirable behaviors as jealousy and poor work habits would be extinguished because of lack of reinforcement from the environment.

In the 1960s, there were demonstrations that a wide variety of behaviors in infants and children could become more frequent if they were reinforced. There was particular interest in the fact that social reinforcers, such as attention, smiles, and praise from other people, were especially potent. There also were many studies of *behavior modification*, the application of principles of operant conditioning to naturally occurring undesirable behaviors, such as temper tantrums, avoidance of social interaction, and autistic children's lack of spoken language. The approach assumes that a common set of learning principles underlies both normal and abnormal behavior. The essence of the approach is to change the reinforcement contingencies so that desirable behavior is reinforced and thereby maintained, while undesirable behavior is ignored and thereby weakened. That is, in operant conditioning, you try to catch the child doing something right and reinforce it. The area of behavior modification is still quite active today.

During the last three decades, Bijou and Baer (1961, 1978) and Gewirtz (1967) have championed an operant analysis of development. They have attempted to account for changes in social and motor behaviors of everyday life in terms of shaping, schedules of reinforcement, and the interaction between biological and environmental changes.

## Social Learning

Social learning theory was born in the 1930s at Yale University, perhaps when Hull offered a graduate seminar on relating learning theory to psychoanalysis. Many of those who would become the pioneers in social learning theory — O. H. Mowrer, Neal Miller, John Dollard, Robert Sears, Leonard Doob, and John Whiting — attended this seminar. One of the seminar topics led to the group's first major publication, *Frustration and Aggression* (Dollard et al., 1939), which explored the causes of aggression. This book presented evidence that aggression is an outgrowth of frustration.

The young group of scholars, trained in learning theory by Hull but also inspired by Freud, combined these two traditions. In fact, one of their publications, *Personality and Psychotherapy* (Dollard and Miller, 1950), was dedicated to both Freud and Pavlov. Psychoanalysts did not welcome this reworking of Freudian concepts into learning terms. They protested that social learning theory distorted Freudian theory by ignoring important concepts such as the unconscious, psychosexual development, and ego controls. In general, social learning theorists took interesting and important content from Freudian theory, such as the concepts of dependency, aggression, identification, conscience formation, and defense mechanisms, but sought explanations for behavior in principles of S–R learning, which could be observed, rather than hydraulic models, which could not. In Dollard and Miller's words, "The ultimate goal is to combine the vitality of psychoanalysis, the rigor of the natural-science laboratory, and the facts of culture" (1950, p. 3). The guiding belief of social learning theorists was that personality is learned. They brought the parts of Freudian theory that were testable into the laboratory and ignored the rest. Thus, social learning theorists extended learning theory and changed its focus. By extending learning principles to important real-life social behaviors, they increased the plausibility of the theory.

Social learning theorists explored much territory in the 1940s and 1950s: imitation, neuroses, cross-cultural influences on personality, identification, and parental attitudes toward child rearing. Dollard and Miller were interested in developing psychotherapy based on social learning theory:

> If neurotic behavior is learned, it should be unlearned by some combination of the same principles by which it is taught. . . . we view the therapist as a kind of teacher and the patient as a learner. In the same way and by the same principles that bad tennis habits can be corrected by a good coach, so bad mental and emotional habits can be corrected by a psychotherapist. There is this difference, however. Whereas only a few people want to play tennis, all the world wants a clear, free, efficient mind.
>
> *[1950, pp. 7–8]*

A major focus of social learning theory was socialization, the process by which society attempts to teach children to behave like the ideal adults of that society. As Dollard and Miller observed, "A system of child training built on the laws of learning might have the same powerful effect on the neurotic misery of our time as Pasteur's work had on infectious diseases" (1950, p. 8). Research examined correlations between characteristics of parents (for example, authoritarianism) or their child-rearing practices (early toilet training) and the child's personality at a later time. The interest in socialization, cross-cultural comparisons, Freudian concepts, and learning processes can be seen in a study by Whiting and Child (1953). Much of socialization involves giving up pleasurable activities. For example, during weaning, the child learns to inhibit his desire to nurse. Cultures differ in whether their socialization practices are harsh or gentle, gradual or abrupt. Whiting and Child reasoned that socialization practices ought to be related to the culture's belief system, such as beliefs concerning illness: "In any system of behavior, variations in the severity of socialization will give rise to variations in the degree of anxiety associated with that system, and through continuation of this anxiety into adult life will give rise to variations in the extent to which that system of behavior is a focus of worry or concern in the adult" (1953, p. 149).

Two hypotheses followed. In cultures in which infantile behaviors, such as nursing, behaving dependently, and expressing aggression directly, are considered highly pleasurable and are given up reluctantly, behavior similar to these in adults, such as eating, should be considered therapeutic for illness. In contrast, cultures in which children are harshly forced to give up these behaviors rapidly should associate these activities with anxiety and consider them causes of illness. The results of their research were mixed. The results did not support the first hypothesis but provided some support for the latter hypothesis that cultures with harsh socialization of a particular behavior tend to use that system of behavior to explain illness.

There were methodological breakthroughs, such as the assessment of guilt in an experimental setting. In a classic social learning study of dependency, identification, and conscience formation (Sears, Rau, and Alpert, 1965), a child, placed in a roomful of attractive toys, is asked to watch a hamster, which is in a box with no lid. The experimenter leaves the room to finish making the lid for the box. When the temptation to take a closer look at the toys becomes too great and the child takes his eyes off the hamster for a moment, the hamster silently disappears through a false floor in the box. Measures of conscience, specifically guilt, in the study included the length of time before deviating, the child's emotional reaction to the deviation, whether the child confessed, and on what the child blamed the disappearance.

Social learning theorists proposed that there are important learned drives, such as aggression and dependency. Learned drives are derived from primary biological drives. Thus, the need for food leads to a dependency drive, a need to be near the mother and nurtured by her. The presence of the mother is reinforcing, and the withdrawal of her love, even temporarily in response to a misdeed, is a form of punishment. In addition, the possibility of a general social drive was suggested by the fact that children are more receptive to social reinforcement after a period of social deprivation (Gewirtz and Baer, 1958). There was also evidence that children learn in order to receive social reinforcement (a reply of "Good girl!" from the experimenter).

Two major theoretical changes in social learning theory involved imitation. The first change was introduced by Miller and Dollard (1941). They set out to show that one of the most powerful socialization forces is imitation. They proposed that a general tendency to imitate is learned because various imitative behaviors are reinforced, a process of operant conditioning. A boy may be praised for being "just like his father." Or the child may reinforce his imitations himself by repeating adults' words of praise. Models, such as parents or siblings, who have been rewarding to the child in the past are most likely to be imitated. Bandura and Walters (1963) caused the second major shift in social learning theory. They carried the concept of imitation one step further by demonstrating that relatively new behaviors can be acquired by simply watching a model. The observer need not make an overt response or be reinforced. The punishment or reinforcement of the model's behavior has the same effect on the observer as it does on the model. A child who sees a hard-working classmate praised by the teacher learns to try that behavior. Bandura and Walters called this process *vicarious reinforcement.* They argued that social learning theory based on S-R notions could not account for learning that occurs without overt behavior—"no-trial learning," in Bandura's words.

Bandura and Walters' theory became influential in developmental psychology in the 1960s and 1970s. It guided the majority of laboratory and observational studies of aggression, sex typing, and resistance to temptation. There was great interest in discovering which characteristics of models, such as warmth, power, and similarity to the observer, encouraged imitation. In addition, the list of social reinforcers was expanded to include peers.

In recent years, Bandura has moved even further from a traditional S-R account of imitation. His theory, as presented in *Social Learning Theory* (1977) and *Social Foundations of Thought and Action* (1986), has become more cognitive than his earlier statement. Bandura now calls his theory a "social cognitive theory" and defines learning as "knowledge acquisition through cognitive processing of information" (1986, p. xii). He is less concerned with the literal duplication of behavior (imitation) than with observational learning as a more general process of acquiring information from another person, verbally or visually. In 1980, Bandura's contributions were recognized by a Distinguished Scientific Contribution award from the American Psychological Association "for masterful modeling as researcher, teacher, and theoretician" (*American Psychologist*, 1981, p. 27). His current account of social learning, along with contributions by Rosenthal and Zimmerman and others, is the focus of the rest of the chapter.

Bandura's work on social learning continues to influence research on social development but no longer dominates the field. His current theoretical position is becoming increasingly difficult to distinguish from a more influential body of current research labeled "social cognition." This approach was stimulated by Piaget, Kohlberg, and social-attribution theory based on adult social psychology. This approach, even more than Bandura's, emphasizes the role of cognitive development in social development. The two approaches certainly are compatible. For example, television's effects on children depend on both cognitive and imitative processes. Whether the child can comprehend the story (infer the protagonist's motives, relate the outcome to the earlier conflict) affects the child's perceptions of the model and his tendency to imitate the model.

## An Overview

At the time of the rumblings concerning learning theory within most areas of psychology in the early 1960s, studies of learning were at their peak within developmental psychology. However, developmental psychology was not immune to the internal and external events that led to the demise of traditional learning theory in the field of psychology. Since the late 1960s, research on learning has been guided by Piaget and information-processing models much more than by learning theory. Today, the most common laboratory study of learning and thinking is a memory experiment, whereas in the early 1960s it was a discrimination-learning experiment. Currently, there is almost no research on what traditionally has been considered children's learning. Because learning now is viewed as the acquisition of new knowledge, it is virtually indistinguishable from cognitive change over short periods of time. When current developmental psychologists refer to learning, they usually have in mind topics such as instruction in math or reading, the training and transfer of general study strategies (monitoring and planning), error-correction strategies, and the novice-to-expert shift in knowledge or motor skills.

The hope that studies of children's learning would lead to an adequate account of developmental changes in learning was not fulfilled. Research produced a complex literature, and investigators sometimes became so involved in examining parameters of a small set of tasks that they lost sight of the developmental issues that caused them to choose these tasks in the first place. Finally, one limitation, not unique to learning theory, was that much of the research was conducted with bright, upper-middle-class children in university towns. (Some 4-year-olds greeted experimenters with "What reinforcement do I get this time?") Despite the problems, this phase in the history of developmental psychology was an exciting and fruitful time. The discipline was becoming a laboratory science, and "facts" were accumulating rapidly. A number of astonishingly productive and enthusiastic researchers conducted programmatic research using cleverly designed experimental tasks. Studies built on previous research in an organized way. Variables were varied, and hypotheses were modified. There was confidence that developmental psychology was progressing.

## GENERAL ORIENTATION TO THE THEORY

Fashioning a general orientation is difficult because learning theory is actually many theories, including some approaches, particularly Skinner's, that claim not to be theories at all. It is outside the scope of this chapter to explore the differences among these theories. Fortunately, despite their differences, they share important assumptions or characteristics that create a common orientation to psychology. These characteristics include an emphasis on learned behaviors, an emphasis on the environment's control of behavior, a breakdown of behavior into simple units, a focus on observable behavior, and a particular methodology. Within each section, discussion centers first on traditional learning theory, then on modern social learning theory, especially Bandura's position. Although social learning theory shares the overall assumptions of traditional learning theory, there are important modifications that should be highlighted. The following characteristics describe both early and recent learning theory, but they have been revised somewhat over time. In particular, learning theory has gradually added some cognitive processes. As each characteristic is described, we will note how the emphasis has shifted over the years.

### Emphasis on Learned Behaviors

#### Traditional Learning Theory

Only a straw-man learning theorist would claim that all behavior is completely learned. Biology clearly sets limits on what each species can learn, when it can learn the behavior, and how quickly it can learn it. Species-specific behaviors sometimes intrude on learned behaviors. This influence of biology on learning was demonstrated dramatically by two of Skinner's former students, Breland and Breland (1961), who trained animals commercially. While trying to train raccoons to drop tokens into a slot, the Brelands found that the animals stopped to "wash" the tokens, as if they were food, even though there was no water around.

Although learning theorists acknowledge biological contributions, they always have chosen to study the environmental, nonbiological influences on behavior: they clearly demarcate their field of study. This focus contrasts with that of Piaget and Freud, who incorporate both innate and experiential influences into their theories and consider how they interact.

Although there are many definitions of learning, a common one is "a more or less permanent change in behavior which occurs as a result of practice" (Kimble, 1961, p. 2). At its simplest, this learning consists of some sort of association or connection between a stimulus and a response. At its most complex, learning involves acquiring abstract rules or a chain of reasoning.

Traditionally, learning has been divided into two types: *operant conditioning* (also called instrumental conditioning) and *classical conditioning*. Operant conditioning has been most thoroughly explored by Skinner. This type of learning begins with a behavior that the child spontaneously produces. He "operates" upon the environment. This behavior becomes conditioned when it comes under the control of a particular stimulus. Some stimulus leads the child to produce a certain behavior in order to receive a reinforcement. The baby learns that when a parent appears, if he smiles at the parent (the operant behavior), he will be picked up and played with (the reinforcement). If this sequence occurs a number of times, smiling can be said to be operantly conditioned as it increases in frequency. As this example illustrates, the role of the reinforcer is to increase the frequency of smiling by occurring immediately after that behavior. The traditional example of operant conditioning is, of course, the rat who learns to press a bar to release a food pellet every time a light comes on.

There are other schedules of reinforcement possible in addition to the schedule of continuous reinforcement just described. For example, every fifth response or the response occurring after each 20-second interval might be reinforced. As Skinner demonstrated, the frequency and timing of the organism's behavior vary from schedule to schedule. In natural settings, partial reinforcement schedules are common. If the child asks for candy every time he goes to the grocery store, but receives it only part of the time, this behavior is sure to continue.

Thousands of behaviors can be operantly conditioned in the same way as smiling or bar pressing. These behaviors range from children drooling (Johnston, Sloane, and Bijou, 1966) to pigeons guiding missiles to their targets in Skinner's Project Pigeon during World War II. Even problem behaviors can be modified operantly. Harris, Wolf, and Baer (1967) observed an extremely withdrawn child who spent 80 percent of the time at nursery school in solitary activities. Their observations revealed that the teachers had unintentionally reinforced this behavior by talking to him and comforting him when he was alone. The child was ignored by the teachers when he played with others. The program of operant conditioning reversed the above contingencies. The boy received the teachers' attention when he joined a group and was ignored when he withdrew. He soon spent 60 percent of his time playing with other children.

In contrast to operant conditioning, classical conditioning begins with a reflex—an innate connection between a stimulus and a response. Behaviors that can be classically conditioned include salivating when food is placed in the mouth, sucking when a nipple is placed in the infant's mouth, and constricting the pupil when a light is shone into the eye. The response is elicited, rather than spontaneously emitted, as was the case in operant conditioning. In Ivan Pavlov's famous dog experiment, the *unconditioned stimulus* (meat powder) elicits the *unconditioned response* (salivating). To establish classical conditioning, a *conditioned stimulus* (ringing a bell) occurs just before the food powder is given. After repeated pairing of the bell ringing and the food powder, simply ringing the bell produces salivating. A new stimulus substitutes for an old one. Salivation has become a *conditioned response*.

Examples of naturally occurring classical conditioning in humans are not difficult to find. We all salivate to the smell of bacon cooking before a weekend brunch. More exotic cases are patients who experience asthmatic attacks triggered by stimuli such as elevators, children's choirs, bicycle races, political speeches, and the national anthem (Dekker and Groen, 1956). A common example from infancy is the baby who begins to suck as soon as she sees her bottle. The conditioned stimulus (sight of the bottle) is habitually paired with the unconditioned stimulus (the nipple in the mouth) to produce the unconditioned response (sucking). Eventually, sucking becomes a conditioned response.

In some cases, classical conditioning can result after just one trial. A person who once became ill while eating at a restaurant may experience a mild wave of nausea every time he passes that restaurant. Such one-trial learning appears to be possible when the species is biologically predisposed to connect the stimulus and response.

The most famous case of classical conditioning is the "Little Albert" experiment. Watson and Rayner (1920) conditioned a fear response in 11-month-old Albert. A white rat was placed in front of the toddler. As he reached for it, a steel bar behind him was struck with a hammer, producing a noxious, painful sound. Albert started violently and cried. After several repetitions of this pairing of the rat and the sound, Albert cried and crawled away when the rat alone was presented. Albert's fear was a conditioned response to the conditioned stimulus, the white rat. The initial reflex was that the noxious sound (unconditioned stimulus) produced pain (unconditioned response). The conditioned response generalized to objects such as a rabbit, a fur coat, and a Santa Claus mask. Unfortunately for Albert, his family moved away before Watson had a chance to decondition him.*

At a later time, one of Watson's students, Mary Cover Jones (1924), found that a naturally acquired fear of animals in a 2-year-old child, Peter, could be eliminated by extinguishing this response, which presumably was a conditioned response. Peter was seated in a highchair and given a snack, which produced a positive response. As he ate, a white rabbit in a cage was brought closer and closer. The conditioned stimulus (the white rabbit) was not allowed to become powerful enough to evoke the response of fear, for example, by suddenly bringing it near. As the stimulus occurred without the related fear response, this association was weakened. At the same time, the negative fear

---

*Harris (1979) points out that although the Little Albert experiment is one of psychology's most famous, it apparently was not as successful at establishing a conditioned fear response as is commonly believed. Over the years, textbook writers have "improved" the results of this now-famous case. In addition, there were methodological problems that muddy any interpretation of the results.

response to the rabbit was being replaced by the positive response, eating. The procedure was quite successful. By the end of the study, Peter was stroking the rabbit and letting it nibble his fingers. This treatment obviously requires a skillful experimenter who does not inadvertently teach the child to associate eating with fear.

There is an interesting footnote to this research. Peter had to enter a hospital for treatment of scarlet fever. As Peter was leaving the hospital, an unfortunate incident occurred. A large dog lunged at him, frightening him terribly. When Jones then retested Peter, he had reacquired his fear response to animals and had to be deconditioned again.

This deconditioning technique for overcoming fears contrasts with Freud's psychoanalytic study of Little Hans' fear of horses (see page 156). Whereas Freud was concerned with the deep-seated, underlying anxieties, learning theorists try to change the behavior. By very gradually approaching horses and at the same time establishing some positive response to horses, Hans' conditioned fear response should be weakened. In Freud's view, these procedures would treat only the symptoms, not the cause of the problem. If one symptom is removed, another may appear in its place.

Phobias are not easy to extinguish without intervention because they are self-perpetuating. By avoiding the feared situation, the person reduces the rising anxiety. Thus, the phobia is reinforced. In addition, he has no opportunity to extinguish the fear because he does not allow the feared stimulus to be present. There is an old joke about a man who is asked why he always holds a banana in his ear. His answer is that it keeps the lions away. When told there are no lions around, he replies, "See? It works!" Behaviors that are perceived to bring reinforcement are difficult to unlearn.

This simple classification of learning into two types—operant and classical conditioning—turned out to be too simplistic. For example, some reflexes can be operantly conditioned. In *biofeedback*, people can learn to alter certain physiological functions if they are given feedback signals (reinforcement) as to their psychological activity. In this way, people have been taught to slow down their heart rate, lower their blood pressure, stop headaches due to tension, and so on.

Studies of conditioning, usually with the ubiquitous bar-pressing laboratory rat, produced a number of laws of learning that were believed to be universal. They were thought to apply to all cultures, all ages, all types of behavior—motor, cognitive, emotional, and social—

and to both animals and humans. Here are examples of such universal laws.

1. The more quickly reinforcement occurs after the response, the more effective the reinforcement is.

2. A response made in the presence of one stimulus generalizes to similar stimuli.

3. Behavior that is reinforced only part of the time takes longer to extinguish than behavior that has been reinforced continuously.

Although learning theorists still believe that some laws of learning are universal, they consider other laws specific to certain species or even to a particular developmental level within a species. An example of the latter is verbally mediated learning that can occur only in older children and adults.

For learning theorists, development involves the accumulation of operantly and classically conditioned responses. In Bijou and Baer's words, "The developing child may be adequately regarded, in conceptual terms, as a cluster of interrelated responses interacting with stimuli" (1961, p. 15). Both operant and classical conditioning can be established within the first few days of birth, although with classical conditioning, this learning is accomplished only after a large number of trials. Thus, learning changes behavior, and thereby causes development, from birth.

## Modern Social Learning Theory

Social learning theorists retained the focus on learning, but broadened the notion of learning in two main ways. First, they were especially interested in social behavior and the social context of behavior. They argued that learning theories based on animal research are inadequate to account for human behavior, which occurs in a social milieu. Although children solve discrimination-learning problems and undergo classical and operant conditioning, they also act aggressively, share, play with peers, learn sex-typed behaviors, and develop independence. Much of the socialization of children involves the shaping of behaviors directed toward other people. Thus, social learning theorists broadened the *content* of learning theory by proposing that even social behaviors could be explained by principles of learning. Even behaviors that are not social in nature are influenced by the social *context* in which they occur. A boy's attempts to learn to play the piano may be reinforced by his parents, but actively discouraged by his baseball teammates. As children grow older, others' expectations of them become greater. A 4-year-old who cannot add is not a cause for alarm to adults, but a 7-year-old who cannot add faces a social environment in school directed toward learning this concept.

Second, social learning theorists broadened the *types of learning* to be explained. They saw the importance of observational learning: acquiring new skills or information or altering old behaviors simply by watching other children and adults. In fact, Bandura (1986) claims that most learning comes from observational learning and instruction rather than from overt, trial-and-error behavior. Years ago Aristotle commented, "Imitation is natural to man from childhood, one of his advantages over the lower animals being this, that he is the most imitative creature in the world, and learns at first by imitation."

Imitation of the model's behavior when the model is no longer present is an especially important learning skill. The behavior acquired may be an interpersonal behavior, a perceptual-motor skill, or a conceptual rule. The critical features are that the child need not produce the behavior right away and the model need not be reinforced in order for the observer to learn. Thus, observational learning differs from operant conditioning and classical conditioning in significant ways. Although all three types of learning are important, observational learning is particularly important for explaining how novel, complex behaviors are acquired during development. Operant conditioning can gradually produce relatively new behaviors by shaping, but cannot explain how complex new behaviors emerge suddenly after watching peers play a new game or watching the antics of superheroes on television. Observational learning is especially important for acquiring behaviors in areas where mistakes are costly or life-threatening. There cannot be much trial-and-error learning in studying brain surgery or learning to drive a car.

How observational learning occurs is now illustrated by a real-life example and a laboratory study. One skill acquired by many boys and girls today is playing soccer. This skill includes a complex set of conceptual and perceptual-motor skills. It is doubtful that this skill could be taught simply by telling the child how to play the game, though this type of instruction is important. Much of the learning comes from observing models playing—older children, parents, coaches, and professional soccer players on television. These models are particularly likely to be modeled because they are perceived as having high status, competence, and power—characteristics that encourage modeling (Bandura, 1986). Books on how to play soccer provide symbolic models. These various types of models demonstrate how to travel with the ball, pass, attempt goals, make corner kicks, and express elation appropriately after scoring a goal.

To a great extent, an understanding of the game is acquired through what Bandura calls *abstract modeling*: abstracting a general rule from observing specific behaviors. The child gradually extracts general concepts of group action in the game: team defensive strategy, the prediction of where one's teammates will be at a particular moment, strategies concerning how to play one's position, and so on.

During the course of observational learning, the child tries to reproduce the behaviors he has seen and receives feedback regarding how closely his behavior matched that of the model. A skillful pass meets with success when it reaches another player. Also, this behavior may be praised by the coach. An attempt to score that misses the goal gives immediate feedback to the player, and he may adjust the angle of his kick next time or seek further verbal instruction or demonstration from others. Note that this reinforcement or nonreinforcement serves primarily as a source of information to the child concerning his behavior. This feedback also serves as an incentive, encouraging the child to seek future self-satisfaction, achievement, competence, or attention from others by participating in soccer. Unlike operant conditioning and classical conditioning, there is not an automatic "stamping in" of an association via reinforcement. Furthermore, there is much more than trial-and-error learning. Learning comes more from observing, listening to instruction, and remembering than from trial and error with reinforcement.

Social learning theory contributed the notion of *vicarious reinforcement*. Observing that others are reinforced for a particular behavior may impart to the child the information that the behavior is desirable in that situation and may encourage him to imitate that behavior. Seeing others punished has the opposite effect. It should be noted, however, that Bandura found that reinforcement or punishment to the model or the child is not necessary for observational learning to occur. Of the numerous laboratory studies that illustrate observational learning, an early influential one by Bandura, Ross, and Ross (1961) is described here. Preschool children saw an aggressive adult model punch a large, inflated Bobo doll and hit it on the head with a hammer, saying "Sock him in the nose" and "Pow." In a comparison group, the model played nonaggressively with Tinkertoys, and in a control group there was no model. Later, the children were taken to a room that contained a variety of aggressive toys (Bobo doll, dart guns, tetherball with a face painted on it) and nonaggressive toys (tea set, teddy bears, trucks), including the toys the adult model had used aggressively. The children who had observed the aggressive model were more aggressive than the children who had seen an unaggressive model or the children who had not seen a model.

It is clear that Bandura and Freud give us opposite predictions concerning the effects of watching aggression in other people. Freud would see such an activity as a way of reducing aggressive tensions, thus lessening subsequent aggression. In contrast, Bandura would predict that viewing aggression, especially if the aggression is not punished, is likely to cause imitation, thereby increasing aggression.

We can conclude that children become more aggressive as a result of observing an aggressive model. But how, exactly, does the model cause aggression? A model can cause imitative behaviors in several ways.

1. Teaching new behaviors. Perhaps the children in Bandura's study learned new forms of aggression: hitting a Bobo doll over the head with a hammer.

2. Strengthening or weakening children's inhibitions. Although the children presumably had been taught by their parents not to be aggressive (and the comparison groups were not aggressive), the aggressive model may have disinhibited the children's aggression. Disinhibition is especially likely because the model was not punished. Evidence for a general disinhibition of aggression comes from the fact that some of the aggressive behaviors differed from those presented by the model, for example, firing imaginary shots at objects in the room and saying "Stupid ball" and "Knock over people."

3. Drawing attention to particular objects and thereby increasing their use in various ways.

4. Increasing emotional arousal, which typically increases responsiveness.

A further result in this study is noteworthy. Boys were physically more aggressive than girls. Thus, characteristics of the child influence imitation. However, other studies (for example, Bandura, 1965) revealed that one must make a distinction between learning and performance. We know that girls *learn* as much aggression from the model as do boys, because they can produce the aggressive behaviors when asked to or rewarded for doing so. However, they typically do not *produce* as much physical aggression, presumably because there are stricter inhibitions of this behavior in girls than boys. The finding that children learn and remember what they observe even if it is not reproduced immediately is of interest to those concerned with violent models on television shows watched by children. Even if the child does not immediately reproduce the aggression, he may have stored it for future use.

The basic paradigm of Bandura's study has been used to examine a variety of models (filmed, symbolic, real) and a variety of behaviors (prosocial behavior, styles of information processing, conservation of number). It is clear that observational learning is widespread during childhood. Much of the enculturation of children involves exhibiting desirable social behaviors and strategies of problem solving. Many of the behaviors pervasive within a culture reflect the fact that children in that culture are exposed to the same or similar models. Thus, considering observational learning greatly extends traditional learning theory's narrower portrayal of learning.

Observational learning also accounts in part for differences in personality among cultures. For example, cultures vary in how much effort they put into teaching aggression. The Dugum Dani, a warrior society in the New Guinea highlands, have a training program that brings boys closer and closer to real warfare (Gardner and Heider, 1969). War games include skewering the enemy (berry seeds) on a sharp stick, spearing a hoop tossed by the opposition, battling with grass "spears," and watching real battles from a distance. In contrast, the Polynesians of the Society Islands actively discourage aggression and rarely provide aggressive models (Levy, 1969). They teach their children that spirits punish aggression with illness and injury. Observational learning not only is a process of normal socialization, but also can be a therapy for problem behaviors. For example, observational learning can help children overcome fears. In another study by Bandura (1967), nursery-school children who were afraid of dogs watched a child happily approach a dog gradually and play with him. After the therapy and even 1 month later, most of the previously fearful children would hand-feed a dog and even climb into a playpen with it. Showing the modeling sequence on film also proved effective in reducing fears.

## Emphasis on Environmental Control of Behavior

I imagine the mind of children as easily turned, this or that way as water itself.

[John Locke]

### Traditional Learning Theory

The belief that changes in behavior are largely brought about by experience is closely linked with the belief that the environment controls behavior. Skinner claimed that "a person does not act upon the world, the world acts upon him" (1971, p. 211). The environment is viewed as a set of stimuli. Stimuli can play several roles. They can serve as signals for the onset of reinforcement if the proper response is emitted; become linked with unconditioned stimuli and eventually elicit conditioned responses; become associated with responses, as in the verbal learning of pairs of nonsense stimuli; or serve as punishment or reinforcement. Thus, stimuli control behavior by determining which behavior occurs, when and where it occurs, and how frequently it occurs. In this way, a child's development takes a particular course.

It is interesting that learning theory's emphasis on the role of the environment fits so well with American democratic ideals. If all men are created equal and the environment offers equal opportunity for all, then all humans can achieve lofty goals. A strong version of this belief in the influence of the environment is expressed in a famous quote from Watson:

Give me a dozen healthy infants, well-formed, and my own specified world to bring them up in and I'll guarantee to take any one at random and train him to become any type of specialist I might select—doctor, lawyer, artist, merchant, chief, and yes, even beggar-man and thief, regardless of his talents, penchants, tendencies, abilities, vocations, and race of his ancestors.

[Watson, 1924, p. 104]

It should be noted that Watson goes on to say: "I am going beyond my facts, and I admit it, but so have the advocates of the contrary and they have been doing it for many thousands of years."

The importance of reinforcement in controlling behavior is a central concept in learning theory. As already mentioned, the occurrence of reinforcement increases the frequency of the behavior it follows. Conversely, of course, a behavior not followed by reinforcement decreases in frequency. It undergoes extinction. Skinner even kept a cumulative record of his writing output as a way of providing self-reinforcement (Skinner, 1967).

Another way that reinforcement controls behavior is by *shaping* behavior. Pigeons do not naturally play table tennis. However, by beginning with the table-tennis-related behaviors they do have, it is possible to slowly modify these behaviors into a chain of movements appropriate to table tennis. The experimenter "ups the ante" (raises the requirement for obtaining reinforcement) as the behavior gradually comes to approximate the desired behavior. Early in training, moving toward the ball might be sufficient to receive reinforcement, but later on it may be necessary to make the ball drop onto the opponent's side in order to receive reinforcement.

Skinner has described his first attempt to use shaping on a human subject:

I soon tried the procedure on a human subject—our 9-month-old daughter. I was holding her on my lap one evening when I turned on a table lamp beside the chair. She looked up and smiled, and I decided to see whether I could use the light as a reinforcer. I waited for a slight movement of her left hand and turned on the light for a moment. Almost immediately, she moved her hand again, and again I reinforced. I began to wait for bigger movements, and within a short time, she was lifting her arm in a wide arc—"to turn on the light."

[Skinner, 1980, p. 196]

In natural settings, shaping may occur unintentionally. If their mothers do not immediately attend to them, preschoolers rapidly become noisier and more insistent until their mothers reinforce them with attention. Thus, the child's rapidly escalating negative behavior is shaped. Patterson notes that "rapid escalation is thought to be an important component in the repertoire of the trained fighter and well practiced coercive children" (1980, p. 7).

## Modern Social Learning Theory

Although social learning theorists agree that the environment exerts a great deal of control over behavior, they consider this only one of many forces operating in any situation. The entire learning context includes characteristics of the person, the person's behavior, and the environment. These three factors are highly interdependent. They influence and control each other via a process that Bandura calls *reciprocal determinism*. Consider a situation in which a child observes another child giving some of her pennies to help poor children. Several characteristics of the child influence whether she will imitate this behavior. Is she cognitively and socially developed enough to understand what it means to be poor? What are her standards of fairness or social justice? Is she even attending to the model's behavior at all? Has she observed her parents contributing to charities in the past? The environmental factors might include the social attractiveness of the model, whether the model was praised after she gave, and the salience of the model in that situation.

Although many theories acknowledge that personal and environmental factors such as these interact, the main contribution of Bandura's reciprocal determinism is that it recognizes that the child's behavior affects, and in a sense "creates," her environment. In the sharing situation just described, the child who has habitually shared in the past and thereby elicited warmth and gratitude from others has created a positive, supportive milieu for herself. In contrast, the child who is obnoxious to others creates a hostile world for herself, as others react negatively toward her. Another example of how behavior creates an environment is that children who watch television a great deal expose themselves to a different set of models from that of children who usually play with friends instead. Or the child may perfect a skill, such as drawing or ballet dancing, that creates an environment of social reinforcement in the form of praise from others. Thus, children act on the environment through their behavior and often change the environment in significant ways. Unlike earlier conceptions of learning, which viewed people as passive, social theory views people as active agents in their environments.

Evidence that a child's behavior can change his social environment comes from a study by Brunk and Henngeler (1984). Two 10-year-old child actors exhibited either anxious-withdrawn or aggressively noncompliant behavior in a setting in which mothers attempted to engage each boy in a game of checkers. The mothers used more helping and rewards with the anxious-withdrawn child and more ignoring, commands, and discipline with the aggressively noncompliant boy. Thus, the boys "created" two different social environments.

It should be noted that in reciprocal determinism, behavior can affect thinking as well as environment. Behavior causes certain experiences, which in turn affect how the child thinks and what he expects, which in turn affects behavior. The child may become skilled at playing board games and discover that this accomplishment earns the respect and admiration of others. He then begins to view himself as a good game player and comes to expect success and social reinforcement from this pastime.

In Bandura's theory, the influence of the environment becomes cognitive as the child symbolically represents the relationship among the situation, his behavior, and the outcome. The essence of reinforcement is that it provides information about what effect one's behavior has in the environment. The child may learn that physical aggression leads to favorable outcomes in certain situations — when playing football or getting an attractive toy from another child — but not when parents or teachers are nearby. Children develop a set of expectations concerning which events lead to which other events. These correlations among events are learned by direct experience, by instruction from others, and by observing others.

Social learning theorists consider the entire system of reinforcement in which one particular event is embedded. This systematic approach is nicely illustrated by a study on coercive systems in families (Patterson and Reid, 1984). Patterson analyzed the network of behaviors among members of the family during hostile interchanges, essentially providing a description of which behaviors lead to which other behaviors. Various "reinforcement traps" are typically found in family interaction. For example, the mother asks the child to clean his room, the child whines, the mother intensifies her command, the child resists, and the conflict rapidly escalates. When the behavior of the child becomes unbearably aversive for the mother, as when the child throws a temper tantrum, the mother gives up and the child stops his aversive behavior. Each person has ended the aversive behavior of the other. The mother has increased the chances that the child will act aversively in the future to obtain negative reinforcement (removing an aversive stimulus). The mother has been negatively reinforced (the temper tantrum stopped), which increases the likelihood that she will give in on future occasions. This pattern of reinforcement should also increase the likelihood that a rapid escalation of conflict will occur in their future interactions.

Another example of a complex set of contingencies occurs when a young sister's teasing of her older brother leads to his hitting her, which in turn leads to punishment from the parents, which finally may even escalate the boy's aggression. The family can become a coercive system, in which each family member learns to cope with aversive behavior from others, such as hitting, teasing, ignoring, verbal abuse, and requests to do work, by counterattacking, which often ends the aversive behavior. Thus, aggressive behavior works. Each family member is periodically reinforced for behaving aggressively and coercively when overpowering another family member through negative behaviors. The difference between normal and problem families lies in how intense and frequent these interchanges are. After the problem family is made aware of these correlated events, an attempt is made to reduce the amount of aversive behavior with which the child must cope and lower the "payoff" for the child's coercive behaviors. If the child is old enough, the family may write a contract that includes the child, specifying what behaviors will be punished by withdrawal of rewards. Thus, the expectations for behavior and the consequences of disobeying are presented in a clear and consistent way that can be easily grasped and represented symbolically by the aggressive child.

One critical way that social learning theory departs from traditional learning theory is that reinforcement — direct or vicarious — is not even considered necessary for learning in many cases. In fact, as Bandura concludes, "After the capacity for observational learning has fully developed, one cannot keep people from learning what they have seen" (1977, p. 38). Children observe, encode information, and retain it. However, even if reinforcement is not necessary for learning, it has considerable influence on *performance*. For instance, reinforcement (or lack of punishment) of the model is likely to be necessary for imitation when the model's behavior breaks a social rule, as when the model cheats or aggresses.

## Breakdown of Behavior into Simple Units

### Traditional Learning Theory

Behavior is complex. People learn to play chess, write computer programs, organize governments, and create soufflés. Learning theorists' strategy is to break down complex behavior into simple units, study these units, then put the behavior back together again. They believe that in this way complex behavior can eventually be understood. The simplest units are associations — the atoms of psychology. The research strategy, then, is to study simple associations, then chains of S–R associations, and perhaps even hierarchies of chains. Metaphorically, many simple units of Tinkertoy sticks and joiners are combined to form a larger structure.

Building upon simple units of behavior also accounts for development. During development, S–R associations can be strengthened, weakened, or chained with other associations. Associations can also be placed in competition, as when a given stimulus has formed associations with several responses at different times. The strength of these associations determines response. When handed a book, a child may say "book," look at the pictures, ask a parent to read it, or read it herself.

The breakdown of complex concepts into simpler parts and the sequencing of units to be learned also characterize programmed instruction. This technique, inspired by Skinner's analysis of operant learning, sometimes uses teaching machines. The child reads a short passage, answers a question, then turns a knob to see if he is correct. The child of today follows similar procedures, but with computers.

In contrast to learning psychologists, Freud and Piaget claim that a simple behavior has meaning and can be understood only in its structural context. By the reduction of complex behavior into simpler elements, the structure is destroyed and consequently the behavior is destroyed, in a sense. For example, the toddler's relationship with his parents involves a complex, organized set of behaviors, attitudes, expectations, and so on. A learning theorist would claim that such a complex phenomenon can best be studied at first by examining simple behaviors one at a time. The investigator might begin by finding out what stimuli cause smiling or crying to occur. In contrast, structural theorists would claim that smiling and crying can be understood only by understanding the overall structure of the parent – child relationship and the child's organized perception of this relationship

## Modern Social Learning Theory

After children acquire new behaviors by observing various models, they can combine these behaviors to form more complex behaviors. A girl may become sex-typed by imitating specific behaviors of her mother, older sister, female teachers, and females on television. A child may at various times observe other children drawing houses and creatively synthesize these different styles into his unique style of drawing houses. Learning to play basketball requires integrating a number of simpler subskills, such as dribbling, guarding, and shooting baskets. This integration of simpler behavior into more complex units differs from traditional learning in important ways, however. For social learning theory, the integration has more cognitive involvement. Rather than a simple chaining of responses, there is an active reorganization of behaviors learned earlier. By mentally manipulating symbols, children can form unique combinations of these behaviors.

In addition to forming complex behaviors by drawing on various previously observed behaviors, it is possible to learn whole complex behaviors all at once, without needing to reduce them to subunits. Observational learning is not restricted to simple behaviors. The young child may be able to reenact a play after seeing it only once. Acquiring large chunks of behavior by observation is more efficient than traditional learning theory's time-consuming learning of small units of behavior by trial and error and combining them into larger units.

### Focus on Observable Behavior

What is Matter? — Never mind.
What is Mind? — No matter.

[*Punch, 1855*]

## Traditional Learning Theory

When the behaviorists revolted against the introspectionist psychologies of the early 1900s, they carved out what they believed to be the proper object of study: observable behavior rather than mental structures or conscious experience. Just as physical scientists could observe physical events, psychologists could now point to physical events (behaviors) as the content of their science. Rats press bars, children push buttons, and adults say words. Observable behavior is available to public inspection and can be objectively measured. Definitions of learning or thinking refer to observable behavior rather than mental events. In a recent article entitled "Whatever Happened to Psychology as the Science of Behavior?" Skinner (1987) attacked the "cognitive restoration of the royal House of Mind" (p. 784). He argued, as he had throughout his career, that psychology should confine itself to its accessible subject matter, behavior.

Of course, there have always been some unobservable entities in learning theory. For example, no one has ever directly observed an "association" between a stimulus and a response. And over the years, learning theorists have added more and more hypothetical constructs to their explanations of behavior. The observable stimuli and responses went underground and became mental S–R associations. Mental S–R chains, expectations, concepts, and rules were added to the vocabulary of learning theory. Even today, however, an investigator with a learning-theory orientation relies as much as possible on observable behavior and adds few cognitive processes.

## Modern Social Learning Theory

Bandura's social learning theory is a synthesis of earlier versions of social learning, which focused on overt, imitative behaviors, and cognitive theory, particularly information-processing theory (see Chapter 4). According to Bandura, models mainly influence us by providing information rather than by eliciting matching behavior. Thus, in observational learning, there can be learning without performing the model's behavior even once. Overt behavior is important but is only one aspect of learning—often an unnecessary aspect. There is even evidence that for children, observational learning can be more effective than learning by direct participation (Kessler, White, Rosenthal, and Phibbs, 1973).

Watching another person solve a problem may provide a better overall idea of the nature of the problem than being thoroughly immersed in it oneself.

Figure 3.1 presents Bandura's (1986) outline of the cognitive processes underlying observational learning and, to provide a context, the other component processes involved in observational learning. Much like a computer, the child selects and processes information, applies general rules or principles, weighs information, and makes a decision. Information-processing theory stresses both attention and retention processes. The model must be attended to in order to have an influence, and the important features of his behavior must be attended to, while unimportant features are ignored. Characteristics of both the model and the observer control attention. Certain models command attention because of their attractiveness, based on their high status or power. Certain behaviors of models, such as aggression, are more salient than others. Models appearing on television in adventure-filled programs are particularly effective at capturing attention. Even the consequences to the model affect attention. Children are more likely to attend to behavior that leads to either reward or punishment (Yussen, 1974), presumably because both highlight the model's behavior. As summarized in Figure 3.1, attention to the model and its behavior is most likely if the model is salient and regarded favorably (affective valence), if the model's behavior is not too complex, if there are many opportunities to see the behavior (prevalence), and if the model's behavior has proved to be effective (functional value).

The child's ability to attend selectively and his past experiences influence which models he attends to and how effectively he attends. Mature perceptual capacities and an optimal level of arousal encourage attention to important aspects of the model's behavior. The child's perceptual set (what he expects to see), his cognitive ability to comprehend the event, and his preferences (interests) also influence which features are selected for processing.

Even if the model's behavior is attended to, it has little influence unless it is retained for future use when the model no longer is present. The event must be translated into symbols, integrated into the child's cognitive organization, and rehearsed. Cognitive rehearsal, or visualizing oneself successfully carrying out the desired sequence of activities, is a skill developed to a high degree in outstanding athletes as they mentally prepare for competition. Enactive rehearsal refers to activities

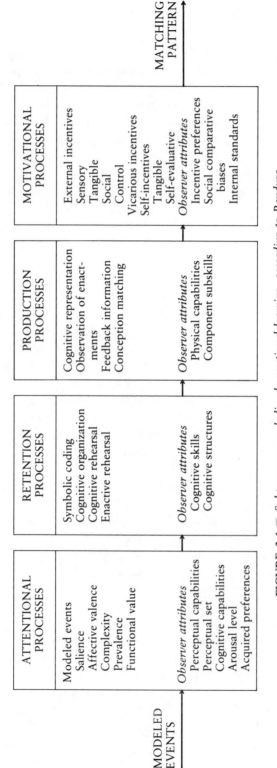

**FIGURE 3-1** ■ *Subprocesses underlie observational learning, according to Bandura.*
*[From Albert Bandura, Social Foundations of Thought and Action, © 1986, p. 52.*
*Reprinted by permission of Prentice-Hall, Inc., England Cliffs, N.J.]*

such as actually practicing the modeled activity or verbally rehearsing it. Symbols are either visual images or verbal codes, depending on the behavior modeled and the child's developmental level. Bandura emphasizes that the representation of the model need not be structurally similar to the model's behavior. It may be a conception, rule, or set of propositions that abstracts the underlying conceptual structure rather than the concrete event itself.

The two remaining component processes, production processes and motivational processes, refer to the performance of behaviors once they are learned by observation. Both components have been topics of interest for learning theory throughout its history. Social learning theory, however, gives them a cognitive interpretation. During production, the person mentally selects and organizes responses to serve as a representation model by which to compare the performed behavior. As a result of receiving feedback while monitoring this performance, the child may modify his initial response. Finally, motivational processes refer to the fact that children tend to reproduce behavior they see resulting in desirable outcomes. In contrast to Piaget, who examines only the cognitive development underlying imitation, Bandura is interested also in why a child is motivated to imitate only certain actions of certain models at certain times and places.

Bandura's notion of abstract modeling, described earlier, is a radical departure from traditional learning theory. Bandura proposes that children can formulate an abstract rule by pulling out the relevant elements from a number of specific episodes of observational learning. Abstract modeling is the main mechanism for explaining language learning. As the child observes that the past tense is usually formed by adding *-ed*, he abstracts this as a general rule and correctly says "walked" and "talked" and incorrectly says "hitted" and "doed." He may even make very complex incorrect utterances such as "He was disingappeared."

To summarize our discussion of Bandura's theory, two points can be made. First, the traditional focus on observable behavior has been supplemented by a concern with the cognitive components underlying observational learning. However, compared with Piaget's theory of cognition, thinking stays near the surface. That is, external events are translated into a symbolic form and combined with other symbolically represented events or used as information to develop a more general rule; however, the theory does not specify a complex reworking of the information into broad cognitive structures of the type described by Piaget. Second, a child's failure to imitate a model's behavior is due to one or more of the four component processes: inadequately attending to the behavioral events, inadequately encoding and retaining these events, failing to perform because of physical limitations, or possessing low motivation. Stated differently, cognitive factors influence what is observed, how that person or event is perceived, how this new information is organized for the future, whether the observational learning has a lasting effect, and what this effect is.

A final important way in which Bandura sees cognition as mediating behavior is that self perceptions influence which available behaviors a person will produce. He emphasizes *self-efficacy*: a person's perception of his competence in dealing with his environment. Any type of behavior—academic, social, or recreational—is affected by self-efficacy. Children may have the necessary skills for mastering a task, but if they do not perceive themselves as capable of actually using their skills to master the task, they may fail or may not even attempt the task. For example, Collins (1982) gave difficult math problems to children with high or low math self-efficacy within each of two groups, differing in levels of math ability. Although math ability obviously influenced their performance, significant effects of self-efficacy were found as well. Within each ability level, children who perceived themselves as efficacious solved more problems, more quickly rejected strategies that did not work, more willingly reworked failed problems, and displayed more positive attitudes toward mathematics. This positive reaction to failure among highly efficacious children reflects their attributions of their failure to insufficient effort. In contrast, low-efficacy children attribute their failure to low ability, an attribution that does not encourage them to try again.

The work on self-efficacy has two particularly important implications for development. First, in Bandura's view, the efficacy judgments most conducive to development are slight overestimations, because these help motivate children to try moderately challenging tasks that could hone their present skills. The second implication concerns children's motivation to become self-directed learners. Adults can enhance children's intrinsic (internal) interest in an activity by rewarding them wisely. As Zimmerman (1985, p. 152) concludes, "It is not so much *what* one gives as rewards that determines children's intrinsic motivation, it's *how* the reward is given that matters." When rewards are given to a child because he has achieved a certain level of competence on a task, he will feel efficacious, value the activity, and choose it on further occasions. Rewards given for simply engaging in the activity are less likely to have this positive effect. In fact they can even destroy intrinsic interest (Lepper, Greene, and Nisbett, 1973).

During development, children gradually construct their self-knowledge about their efficacy in various situations from four main types of information. The most authentic and direct source of information is the success or failure of previous similar attempts. A second source is vicarious experiences of observing others fail or succeed on similar tasks. If a child perceives herself as similar to a model who succeeds, her self-efficacy is enhanced. In addition, children can acquire new coping strategies by observing successful others. A third source of information is verbal persuasion: others talk the child into believing she has the ability to achieve her goal. An example is a coach's locker room halftime pep talk. Finally, information comes from one's physiological state: arousal, anxiety, fatigue, and physical pain.

For all four sources of information, developmental changes influence how accurately children can process the information. The acquisition of language, the broadening of social awareness, increased differentiation of internal states, and the development of self-appraisal skills all play a role. Another relevant developmental change is that the family is the main contribution to the young child's self-efficacy, whereas the peer group and school context become increasingly important thereafter. Bandura notes that throughout the lifespan, there are changes in which aspects of self-efficacy are most important. For example, adolescence and young adulthood bring new challenges to self-efficacy regarding heterosexual relationships, physical appearance, and occupational competence. During middle age, people may reevaluate their lives, doubt their efficacy concerning physical performance, and seek to achieve efficacy in new areas. A divorce or retooling for a new occupation may be the outcome. The elderly may face damaged self-efficacy as a result of perceived memory loss, slowed reactions, and lessened self-esteem because they no longer hold a job. A self-fulfilling prophecy can occur: if the elderly are insecure about their efficacy and expect to fail, they may limit their range of activities and invest little effort in any activity. Bandura argues that true declines as a result of aging can be offset to a great extent by real-world knowledge and coping strategies acquired throughout one's lifetime.

Self-efficacy is related to the processing of information outlined in Figure 3.1. Interesting processing biases may be at work. People who tend to attend to and recall the negative features of their performance may underestimate their efficacy. Thus, parents and teachers can enhance a child's self-efficacy by drawing attention to the positive aspects of his performance and thereby increasing the salience of those aspects.

## Methodology

### Traditional Learning Theory

Learning theory took the physical sciences as its model, an emphasis that has been called "physics envy." The preferred method of study, therefore, was the tightly controlled, small-scale laboratory experiment. This precision was an important step, historically. Researchers adopted William James' attitude: "I wished, by treating psychology like a natural science, to help her become one." The experiments focused on changes in simple, observable behaviors brought about by certain features of the stimulus environment. The stimuli and responses were described in an objective and precise way so that the experiment could be replicated in other laboratories. Learning was measured by the number of trials needed to solve the problem or to establish the conditioned response or by the number of responses per unit of time. Although these requirements have loosened in recent years, learning experiments are still quite rigorous.

The investigator's need to define and control the environment led to the development of certain apparatuses and paradigms suited to this purpose. One such apparatus is the Skinner box, a cage-box containing a lever that the animal presses, which delivers a food pellet to the tray below. These responses are automatically recorded on a cumulative record, so the experimenter need not be present. This apparatus has become so well known to the general public that "Skinner box" appears in *Webster's Third New International Dictionary*. The Skinner box has become standard equipment for studying operant conditioning in rats in laboratories across the country. It is simple, automatic, and flexible.

Skinner's concern with controlling the environment can be seen in another invention: a completely enclosed, temperature-controlled, soundproof "baby tender" (called a "baby box" by some), constructed for one of his own infants. This was not, as many people believed, a Skinner box for conditioning babies.

Most laboratory studies of learning include a number of subjects in each experimental condition and compare conditions by looking at group characteristics, such as the average number of trials required to learn a problem. However, studies of operant conditioning sometimes examine changes over time in single subjects. In behavior modification, a common design is the A – B – A design. After determining the child's usual frequency of hitting behavior (A), the experimenter causes a decline in hitting as that behavior is ignored and prosocial behaviors are rewarded (B). Then, to prove that the changed contingencies are responsible for the change in behavior, these new contingencies are discontinued (A) and hitting increases. Afterward, of course, the desirable behavior is reinstated by further behavior modification.

One way investigators often ensure control over the environment of human subjects is to establish new associations or create new responses. In early experiments on associating two verbal units, researchers used nonsense syllables (for example, WIC – GAF) rather than words, so that previous associations were less likely to influence learning. Similarly, in the early social learning studies of imitation, by showing children an adult wearing a funny hat and marching around, it could be concluded that imitation actually reflects learning acquired in that setting rather than in the child's previous learning history.

## Modern Social Learning Theory

Social learning theory retains the methodological spirit of traditional learning theory: rigorous, well-controlled laboratory experiments that determine which variables affect learning. The content has broadened to include social behaviors, social reinforcers, and abstract concepts, such as conservation or moral reasoning, but the methodology has changed little. Although most studies with a social learning orientation take place in the laboratory, there has been some research on social learning in natural settings. An early study by Bandura and Walters (1959) examined the puzzling fact that adolescent boys who exhibited antisocial aggression often came from "privileged," middle-class families in neighborhoods where law-abiding behavior was supported. Bandura and Walters discovered that the parents of the boys discouraged their sons' aggression toward them. However, the parents encouraged the boys to use aggression to solve their problems with their peers and with adults outside the home. The nature of this encouragement of aggression is illustrated in the following interchange between the interviewer (I) and a mother (M):

I: Have you ever encouraged Earl to stand up for himself?

M: Yes, I've taught young Earl, and his Dad has. I feel he should stand up for his rights, so you can get along in this world.

I: How have you encouraged him?

M: I've told him to look after himself and don't let anybody shove him around or anything like that, but not to look for trouble. I don't want him to be a sissy.

I: Have you ever encouraged Earl to use his fists to defend himself?

M: Oh yes. Oh yes. He knows how to fight.

*[1959, p. 115]*

These lessons were learned well. One of the boys interviewed mentioned his pride in his prowess at "stomping," fighting with his feet: "Like my Dad, he said, 'If you know how to fight with your feet, then it's in your hands, you've got it made,' or something like that. 'You never need to be afraid of anybody'" (1959, p. 122). This information is consistent with laboratory studies of reinforcement and modeling, but provides insights into real-life aggression that could not emerge in a controlled laboratory setting.

## MECHANISMS OF DEVELOPMENT

There is controversy as to whether social learning theory or any current learning theory is truly a developmental theory. Is developmental change the same as short-term change accumulating over a longer period of time? Are the central laws of learning the same, regardless of the child's cognitive level? If development is merely accumulated learning, then it should be possible to speed up the rate at which children develop.

Learning and social learning theorists focus on *processes* of change, in contrast to Piaget and Freud, who focus on *structural* change as the child goes through the stages. Bandura has stressed nonverbal processes of change. His main concern, especially in the 1960s, was to determine which variables other than age or cognitive level encourage or discourage observational learning. There has been much less interest among social learning theorists in how observational learning differs from one point in development to another.

Bandura's current model of observational learning, described in the previous section, identifies a number of developmental variables that social learning theorists have only recently begun to examine. These developmental variables are highlighted in this section. Development occurs because of three main factors: physical maturation, experience with the social world, and cognitive development. The first, *physical maturation*, holds little interest for social learning theorists. Its main relevance is that the child may not have the physical maturity to reproduce certain motor patterns he observes. The other two factors are much more important.

*Experience with the social world* causes development in two main ways. First, the child acquires a repertoire of behaviors, learns the appropriate situations for these behaviors, and, because these behaviors are reinforced by others, becomes motivated to perform these behaviors. Thus, with increasing age, the child has a larger and increasingly differentiated set of behaviors. Much of this increased exposure to social behaviors comes from the growing number and types of models the child encounters from television, movies, books, school, and his neighborhood.

Second, as the child becomes older, his social environment changes simply because society, ranging from his parents to the legal system, changes its expectations of the child. This fact of life has received little attention from developmental theorists, with the exception of Erik Erikson, in his account of cogwheeling. By observing a model, older children are expected to learn complex new skills quickly, with a minimum of verbal instruction. A teacher provides much more help when showing a first-grader how to write out addition problems than when showing a third-grader how to write out division problems. In short, children of different ages face different social environments.

Although the importance of experience has long been recognized by learning theorists, Bandura's concern with the third factor, *cognitive development*, provides new possibilities for explaining developmental changes in learning. Children's conceptions of the world and of themselves are developed through four processes: Direct experience of the effects produced by their actions, vicarious experience of the effects produced by other's actions, judgments articulated by others, and inference of new knowledge from their preexisting knowledge.

All four component processes in Bandura's model in Figure 3.1 undergo changes as the child's thinking develops. As described in the next chapter, on information processing, the child's attention, memory, and cognitive organization undergo dramatic changes during development. For example, older children have much better comprehension and recall of characters, behaviors, motivations, and outcomes of the behaviors in a television story (Newcomb and Collins, 1979). Young children often do not even make a connection between the model's behavior and the consequences of that behavior later on. Another relevant developmental change is that older children are more likely to rehearse verbally what they have observed than are younger children. Motor reproduction and motivational processes also become more complex, differentiated, and efficient as children become more able to integrate several pieces of information, accurately interpret feedback, develop standards for their own performance, and so forth.

Bandura points out one particularly critical developmental change in thinking: the growing ability to translate observations into symbols and to recombine these symbols. Very young children must rely heavily on visual images to represent past observations. Once the child can use symbols, his observational learning is much more flexible and enduring. Symbols can be rehearsed and thereby stored in memory more efficiently than can visual images. Hypotheses about physical or social events can be formulated and tested. An increasingly sophisticated symbolic ability also makes it possible to model behavior by reading a description of it or listening to instruction rather than by having to see the behavior and try to reproduce it. The modeling can be symbolic rather than behavioral. Even the effect of vicarious reinforcement is influenced by the observer's symbolic ability. The young child may be most influenced to imitate by seeing another child rewarded with candy or toys, whereas the older child can infer more subtle consequences, such as the model's feelings of self-worth and achievement. The important role of using symbols in incentive processes can be seen when the child represents future consequences of his imitative behavior and relates those consequences to his personal standards and goals. If they are compatible, he is likely to perform the observed behaviors.

The experimental study of symbolic functioning is illustrated in an experiment by Bandura, Grusec, and Menlove (1966). A group of

7-year-olds recalled more of the behavior they observed on film if they were told to verbally describe the model's actions rather than told simply to watch the film carefully. There was even lower recall if the children counted while viewing the film—an activity that interferes with symbolization. Thus, verbal encoding facilitates observational learning. However, in interpreting this study, we should note that the adults' or children's verbalizations may have increased attention to the model as well as encouraged symbolic representation.

Social learning theory's mechanisms of development become clearer when contrasted to those of structuralists, such as Piaget, in two content areas: moral reasoning and conservation. These two areas have served as the battleground concerning development for social learning theory and other theories, especially Piaget's. In both content areas, Piaget posits structural changes—changes in the organization of thought. With respect to moral reasoning, the child moves from an objective perspective, in which the amount of damage and degree of punishment are considered, to a subjective perspective, in which intentions and extenuating circumstances (such as fatigue or life-or-death factors) are taken into account. With respect to conservation, Piaget proposes that the child develops an organized set of mental operations that can be applied to many content areas, including conservation. For Piaget, the mechanism responsible for these changes is the equilibration process, which bring into harmony social experience, experience with physical objects, and physical maturation. Learning, for Piaget, is a sort of "applied cognition" as one's cognitive structure is used to interpret new situations. What the child can learn depends on his cognitive level.

Rosenthal and Zimmerman (1978) object to the structuralists' account on several grounds. A primary objection is that structuralists tend to classify children as "being" in a particular stage. Consequently, structuralists ignore the many differences among children of a given age and the many differences in how a particular child performs in different content areas. Bandura states that "greater progress can be achieved in identifying the developmental determinants of complex abilities by analyzing the prior competencies needed to master them, than by categorizing people into fill-fitting types" (1977, p. 47). Social learning theorists propose that the acquisition of new knowledge, rather than internal disequilibrium, is the main mechanism for development. Rosenthal and Zimmerman also note that structuralists are primarily concerned with the underlying cognitive structures and thus do not have a robust theory of *performance*. That is, they do poorly at explaining how the child's knowledge is expressed in behavior and establishing which situational variables determine whether the knowledge is expressed in a particular situation. Social learning theorists carefully consider how the particular situation, the child's previous history of observational learning, and the particular content area determine the child's judgments on moral issues or conservation tasks. Rosenthal and Zimmerman also present evidence that stages can sometimes be skipped, that sequences do not seem to be universal, and that regression can occur. None of these outcomes should occur, according to a strict structural viewpoint.

## Moral Reasoning and Behavior

Social learning theorists account for developmental changes in moral judgments by changes in a child's criteria for judgments, such as intentions, clumsiness, amount of damage, long-range consequences, the child's personal standards, adults' prohibitions, expected punishment or reward, and peer influence. The particular factors the child thinks are important vary from situation to situation, depending on variables such as which situational factors are operating, which causes are most salient, and what the child's perceptual set is. Moral judgments involve a complex process of considering and weighing various criteria in a given social situation. Thus, moral judgments are expected to be much more variable from time to time and from situation to situation within a social learning framework than within a Piagetian framework. In some situations the child makes subjective judgments (based on intentions) and in other situations makes objective judgments (based on amount of damage). This is true from preschool age through adulthood. Rosenthal and Zimmerman argue that there are not dichotomous, mutually exclusive types of moral reasoning. Rather, the frequency of using various criteria changes from situation to situation and from age to age.

The increase in making subjective judgments as a function of age reflects the increasing preponderance of models making subjective judgments, adults' heightened expectations of older children, older children's ease of inferring internal states from situational cues, the lessening effect of the salience of consequences, the more refined analysis of moral criteria by older children, and so on. For example, parents are more likely to explain to the child their reasons when disciplining an 8-year-old than a 3-year-old. The younger child is not impressed with arguments about fairness and equality and may respond better to physical controls. Similarly, parents' presentation of legal codes and societal punishment may be reserved for preadolescents and adolescents. It is known, for example, that young boys use moral-judgment rules that are similar in form and complexity to those of their mothers (Leon, 1984). Some mothers use a simple unidimensional rule based on damage alone, whereas others use a more complex integration that combines both intent and damage or even weighs damage differently, depending on the person's intent.

Piaget acknowledges the influence of parents and peers in providing experiences with authority figures and decision making that present conflicting ideas concerning morality, but the critical event is that these experiences spur a cognitive reorganization. Rosenthal and Zimmerman do not see the need to posit cognitive disequilibrium and a reorganization of logical structures during development as long as social experiences, particularly observational learning, provide a more parsimonious explanation. Even so, social learning theorists recognize that children must attain a certain level of cognition before they can comprehend certain types of moral reasoning.

The main evidence bolstering the social learning account is that children's moral judgments can be altered by a brief social experience in the laboratory. In a prototypic study (Bandura and McDonald, 1963), 5- to 11-year-old children were first assessed as having either an objective or a subjective moral orientation, based on Piaget's stories depicting moral dilemmas. As described in the chapter on Piaget, one actor has good intentions, but produces great material damage; whereas the other actor has bad intentions, but produces minimal material damage. The most extremely subjective or objective children were assigned to one of three conditions in the second phase.

1. In one group, first the model and then the child made judgments about stories. The model's judgment was always opposite that of the child's from the first phase. The experimenter praised the model's judgments and also praised the child's if he changed his decision after hearing the model.

2. A second condition was the same except that the child was not reinforced for changing his judgment.

3. In a third group, there was no model. The child was praised if his judgment changed from the first session.

A third phase tested for generalization. In another room, a different adult presented new stories that the child judged. There was no feedback. As predicted by social learning theory, the children adopted the model's moral standards, and this new moral perspective generalized to the new stories in the third phase. This generalization suggests that the children abstracted a general rule rather than imitated specific responses. These results occurred with or without verbal praise to the child. Thus, even without being reinforced, children observe and accept the moral judgments of others. There was no change in the group with no model. In a later study (Dorr and Fey, 1974), the same changes were maintained for at least one month.

According to social learning theorists, observational learning can both transmit new moral rules and influence which of the rules already in the child's repertoire are considered appropriate for the particular situation. With respect to the selection of appropriate rules, models can make certain morally relevant dimensions more salient, change the child's weighting of the various morally relevant dimensions, and encourage the child to express his moral beliefs.

One developmental acquisition central to social learning theory's account of moral reasoning is setting standards of conduct concerning one's own behavior. These are rules, goals, and expectations for one's own conduct abstracted from experiences such as observing other's standards of self-reinforcement or punishment and observing which behaviors of others occur in each situation. For example, after seeing a model criticize his own behavior as undeserving of a reward, children are less likely to reward themselves for similar behavior (Bandura, 1971). If the child's models are older, such as older siblings and parents, he may set impossibly high standards of conduct for himself. It is noteworthy, however, that when models require little of themselves, but much of others, their attractiveness and influence decrease (Ormiston, 1972). The hypocrisy is detected. There are clear implications for parents who do not practice what they preach.

Reinforcement can play a role in children's adopting the standards of conduct observed in others. Imitating statements of self-criticism is encouraged by reinforcement. When the child tells his mother that he was wrong to raid the cookie jar, he is less likely to be punished. A general set of standards is abstracted from the standards of conduct observed or expressed and rewarded in specific situations. These standards, retained in memory in the form of symbols, guide behavior via anticipatory self-pride and self-criticism. The child may be moved to share his cookies with another child if he expects to feel good about himself afterward.

These internal standards constitute what Freud would call the superego. However, social learning theorists stress that the parent of the same sex serves as only one of many models the child has learned from. These internal standards, along with self-reward and self-punishment, are especially effective because they can be applied to many situations; an external authority need not be present.

One critical difference between the Piagetian and social learning accounts of moral reasoning highlights a more general difference in the way the two theories explain changes in behavior as a function of age. As described earlier, Bandura proposes that at all ages children can use different features of the setting and the person to evaluate the morality of that person's behavior. As children get older, they become more proficient at weighing these various features in each situation. Piaget, however, proposes that the tendency to take these circumstances into account is itself an ability that is acquired as a result of cognitive development. The young child is unable to take extenuating circumstances into account. Thus, Piaget sees widespread cognitive changes underlying the effect of situational factors on moral judgments. Or, more generally, Piaget believes that stimuli have an influence only if they can be assimilated into the child's current cognitive structure.

## Conservation

We now turn to the second area of conflict between structuralists and social learning theorists: conservation. With respect to the acquisition of conservation, Rosenthal and Zimmerman (1978) argue that cognitive development involves the acquisition of a set of specific cognitive skills and knowledge rather than a uniform mental structure characterizing everyone in a particular stage. Cognitive skills are acquired primarily by watching others solve problems, listening to their verbalizations about the problem, and attending to instruction. In Rosenthal and Zimmerman's words: "Although there is hypothesis-formation during learning, the rules permitting hypotheses to be generated and tested can be traced to previous environmental experiences and usage norms. . . . Organizing structures can usefully be examined in terms of component rules and operating assumptions" (1978, p. 30). In other words, thinking involves specific rules that are created from experience and can be changed by experience. Each culture transmits certain ways of thinking considered appropriate for that culture. Because our culture values scientific thinking, there are numerous models of systematic problem solving.

In the conservation task, the child sees many physical changes as water is poured from one glass to another. What he needs to learn is which changes are relevant with respect to quantity and which are not. Tall things usually hold more than short ones, but this rule does not always work. The child learns which dimensions are relevant or irrelevant when adults explain the conservation rule ("It doesn't matter what you do to the material as long as you don't add to it or take some away"), show that material is conserved (by counting), or correct his conservation judgment.

During these experiences, abstract modeling may occur as the child extracts a general conservation rule. Although in this way the child plays an active role in acquiring the conservation concept, there is little of the spontaneous self-discovery that Piaget posits. For social learning theorists, conservation is a decision that children make in a social context, not while sitting alone counting pebbles. Rosenthal and Zimmerman (1972, p. 400) state the issue dividing the two theories as follows: "Do older children conserve because it is 'logical' to subordinate shape differences to quantitative equality, or because this is a high probability discrimination taught and supported by cognitive socialization to the dominant usages of the culture?"

Two theoretical differences clearly separate Piagetian and social learning views of conservation. First, for Piaget, experience specifically having to do with quantity is not the only sort of experience contributing to the development of conservation. Any sort of experience, social or physical, that facilitates the development of cognitive operations, such as compensation or reversibility, contributes to the development of conservation. Thus, social learning theory's narrow focus on conservation as content is somewhat misguided, according to Piagetians. Second, the two theories clash over the role of conflict. Piaget sees disequilibrium (cognitive conflict) as playing a critical role in learning. Social learning theorists, disputing this claim, have shown that the degree of cognitive conflict does not predict conservation performance (Zimmerman and Blom, 1983). This conflict about conflict may be resolved by Murray's (1983a) observation that conflict is sufficient but not necessary for learning. Cognitive conflict appears to be only one of several successful conditions for cognitive change.

An experiment by Rosenthal and Zimmerman (1972) illustrates social learning theorists' evidence concerning the social transmission of conservation. First-graders who did not conserve participated in a training study by observing a model conserve. In one condition, the model conserved ("There's just as much here as is there") and gave a logical explanation ("They were the same in the first place"). In another condition, the model conserved, but gave no explanation. In both conditions, half the children saw the model verbally reinforced ("good," "correct"), and half did not. Next, the children were tested again on these items. Finally, the children's generalization of conservation was tested on a new set of conservation items. Generalization tests are important because they show whether the children merely learned a specific response cued by a particular set of stimuli. The number of correct conservation judgments increased after observing the model and, importantly, later on the generalization tests. The control group, who did not see a model, did not show improvement. Whether or not the model was praised or gave an explanation had no effect. If the criterion for conservation included not only conservation judgments but also adequate explanations, the same results were obtained, except that hearing the model give an explanation led to more explanations from the children. However, even children who had not heard explanations gave more explanations than they had before the modeling phase. Rosenthal and Zimmerman concluded that children can learn conservation via observation and can even abstract a conservation rule when none is provided.

Of further interest is what happens when conservers are shown nonconserving models. As predicted by social learning theory, conservation declines. This result is important because Piaget claims that cognitive regression is not possible.

Later studies broadened the early observational learning studies of conservation by using conserving and nonconserving peers as models and including discussions with small groups of conservers and nonconservers. In addition, several researchers claim to have trained conservation in children as young as age 4 (for example, Denny, Zeytinoglu, and Selzer, 1977).

The structuralists, however, question social learning theorists' interpretation of these studies. First, structuralists are dubious that the previous nonconservers really believe in conservation after training. The children may have simply adopted the answer they observed the model making without having acquired the reasoning underlying the answer. Tests of the generality of the change and the new conserver's resistance to disconfirming evidence have not yielded results that clearly favor one interpretation over the other (Kuhn, 1974). Second, even if children actually have acquired a general rule that physical transformations do not change amount, this is not logical knowledge in the sense that Piaget defines it, because logical necessity is not involved. That is, conservation behavior in social learning training studies "may have nothing to do with conservation because it is one thing to know that one event is true and quite another thing to know that it has to be true" (Murray, 1983a, p. 57). Third, there are methodological problems with studies claiming to show that natural conservers give up their belief in conservation (Miller, 1976a).

Another disagreement concerns which children profit from instruction and observation. Structuralists claim that the child must show "readiness" to profit from this experience. That is, he must be in or near a state of transition to conservation. Social learning theorists, however, claim that children showing no evidence of being in a transitional state acquire conservation as a result of observational learning (Rosenthal and Zimmerman, 1972). This issue cannot be resolved until there are agreed-upon procedures to assess how close the child is to developing conservation, that is, what prerequisite cognitive skills he has.

One problem in designing a definitive test of structuralist versus social learning theories is that the differences become minimal when abstract modeling is considered. There appears to be little if any testable difference between a cognitive operation relevant for conservation and a general rule concerning conservation abstracted from observations of a variety of conservation-relevant experiences. Consider, for example, reversibility—the notion that a substance or collection of objects that has been physically transformed can be returned to its original state with no change in amount. In Piaget's view, this general mental operation is acquired as a result of years of social and physical interactions between the child and the environment, physical maturation, and equilibration. In contrast, Rosenthal and Zimmerman view reversibility as a rule gleaned from various direct and vicarious experiences. The rule can be transferred to a variety of situations if the child perceives that the situations are similar. The differences between reversibility as a mental operation and as a generalized abstract rule seem minimal and certainly are not easily tested.

There is a more general issue over how to interpret the demonstrations that conservation or moral judgments or other concepts can be acquired through observational learning. Showing that a concept *can* be acquired in this way does not necessarily mean that children naturally acquire the concept in this way. It is even possible that a concept can be developed in different ways by different children. Thus, it is not yet clear if studies of observational learning are damaging to, complementary to, or irrelevant to Piaget's theory.

Rosenthal and Zimmerman probably overstate Piaget's claims concerning stages and sequences and underestimate the role of experience in his theory. For instance, Piaget includes the social transmission of information as one source of influence on cognitive development and the neo-Piagetians have offered explanations for the lack of generalization to all domains. Still, Rosenthal and Zimmerman have drawn the battle lines clearly. The primary mechanism of development is the process of acquiring information through observational learning for social learning theorists, and it is structural reorganization for the structuralists. Social learning theorists view learning as a cause of development, whereas Piaget stresses that what can be learned is constrained by the child's level of cognitive development.

## POSITION ON DEVELOPMENTAL ISSUES

### Human Nature

For years, learning theory has served as textbook writers' favorite example of a theory with a mechanistic view of human behavior. The infant — "a lively squirming bit of flesh," in Watson's words — is material to be fashioned by parents and society. The learner is viewed as passive, nudged by the whim of the environment, influenced in a machinelike way by a chain of events. It was believed that there are "efficient causes," antecedent conditions or events that initiate or inhibit the child's behavior. This view of human beings has been called the "mechanical mirror" model (Langer, 1969): "The child is born empty of content into a world of coherently organized content. Like a mirror, however, the child comes to reflect his environment" (p. 51).

The mechanistic model, however, does not accurately represent the views of modern social learning theory. The main difference is that modern learning theory sees humans as active in many ways. The person actively operates on the environment, just as the environment acts on the person. People filter their experience through their current knowledge and expectations about the world, create their own environment as their own behavior influences the environment, and generate new behavior by reorganizing previously learned behaviors. People are also active in their self-regulation. They set their own standards, reinforce themselves when they act in accord with these standards, and use feedback to judge their success at observational learning.

Bandura certainly considers people more actively involved in their own development and learning than does Freud. Piaget, however, posits an even stronger role for activity than does Bandura. Although both Bandura and Piaget describe symbolic activity, this mental activity has a greater role in Piaget's theory. According to Piaget, the child does not simply learn more or less automatically by watching or listening to others. As he assimilates and accommodates to new information, there is distortion of the information and a slight reorganization of his present cognitive structure. Although Bandura occasionally refers to these processes, he does not stress them.

There is a more basic difference in the role of interaction in Piaget's and Bandura's theories. For Piaget, the interaction or exchange between the child and the environment forms a structure that later becomes an internalized cognitive structure. The actions of sucking, hitting, and feeling become mental schemes that serve as concepts. In contrast, for Bandura, the structure of the interchange between the child and the environment is not important. What is important is the new information acquired as a result of this interchange. The child observes a new behavior in the model or learns that certain behaviors in others lead to reinforcement.

Although, in Bandura's view, people are active rather than passive and are often internally motivated, his theory still falls more into the mechanistic camp than the organismic camp. He stresses antecedent causes more than inherent properties and goals, quantitative change rather than qualitative, and component behaviors more than holistic structures. In addition, he is concerned with external as much as with internal motivation.

A final point of comparison among social learning, Piagetian, and Freudian theories is the view of the human as rational or irrational. For Piaget, the essence of development is that the child becomes more logical as his mental structures gradually come to reflect reality. Adults, having achieved formal operations, possess equilibrated, logical thinking. Although all three theorists consider logical thinking important, both Freud and Bandura see a larger role for illogical, irrational thought than does Piaget. This may be due to their focus on social and emotion-laden events. Adults often ignore critical information when making judgments, believe what they want to believe about themselves, make snap judgments about others, follow their intuitions about whether to invest in a business venture, and so on. For Bandura, the child may think logically or illogically, depending on the types of models in problem-solving situations he has encountered. He acquires styles of processing information from others. Thus, children and even adults may show great variability in how logical they are.

## Qualitative Versus Quantitative Development

Both traditional and modern learning theories view development as a process of quantitative change, in which learning episodes gradually accumulate over time. Development simply involves a multitude of short-term changes. Observational learning may change somewhat from toddlerhood, when symbolic functioning is severely limited, to middle childhood, when thinking is more advanced. However, we do not find either rapid qualitative changes in movement from one stage to another or massive cognitive reorganization. Bandura does not explicitly deny that stages exist, but he considers the search for stages counterproductive because stages "tend to cast people into prefixed types, thus lending themselves readily to stereotyping people by stage classification" (1977, p. 183). After children are classified into stages, individual differences may not be noticed. Furthermore, a failure to learn may be dismissed as a lack of cognitive readiness. He thinks that an analysis of what subskills are needed to produce a certain behavior or knowledge is much more promising.

If smaller, more limited qualitative changes are considered, there are several candidates within social learning theory. Acquiring a new rule or adopting a new strategy of gathering information is more than a change in amount or strength.

## Nature Versus Nurture

A young branch takes on all the bends that one gives it.

[*Chinese proverb*]

The early militant environmentalism of traditional learning theory viewed the young mind in the way British empiricist John Locke viewed it: a blank slate on which experience writes. This extreme position has evolved into a more moderate position, which recognizes constraints on the effect of the environment. Bandura sums up the view of social learning theory:

> From a social learning perspective, human nature is characterized as a vast potentiality that can be fashioned by direct and vicarious experience into a variety of forms within biological limits. The level of psychological and physiological development, of course, restricts what can be acquired at any given time.
>
> [*1977, p. 13*]

Thus, the child is malleable, but within limits. Within the constraints of the child's biological makeup, experience provides data for forming rules through models and instruction and helps him polish the component skills needed for observational learning. The types of behaviors the child encounters in his models and the reactions of others to these behaviors influence the particular set of behaviors the child develops.

With increasing age, children usually encounter an increasing variety of models, many of them contradictory. An important developmental achievement, learning to read, further broadens the child's exposure to models by introducing him to symbolic models.

Bandura's view of the role of experience is captured in his notion of *reciprocal determinism*. The environment, the person, and the person's behavior are interdependent forces operating in any event. Freud and Piaget are centrally concerned with the interaction of biological maturation and experience with the physical world (especially Piaget) and the social world (especially Freud). To these concerns, Bandura adds the idea that one's behavior can change one's environment.

Biology not only constrains learning but also makes learning possible. As Skinner has pointed out, an organism's learning ability is innate. It has evolved as a way of surviving in a changing environment. The ability to learn from experience, especially the sensitivity to reinforcement, allows an organism to adapt to whatever demands the environment makes. The ability to process and store information, abstract general rules, and translate this information into behavior is obviously adaptive for humans.

## What Develops

Because what is learned depends greatly on what the environment has to offer, learning theorists propose few universal behaviors, those that we would be certain to find developing in every culture. Whereas Piaget, with certainty, would predict that all physically normal children in the world would develop concepts of object permanence, causality, and conservation and whereas Freud would predict universal concern with sexuality and aggression, social learning theory appears to be almost content-free. Investigators have directed their energy toward process rather than content. One culture may encourage aggressive behavior, whereas another may discourage it. Superstitious behavior may be valued and nurtured in one culture, whereas scientific, analytic thinking may be fostered in another. In other words, there is no universal goal or endpoint to development. Piaget, in contrast, sees development moving toward a particular way of thinking: formal operations. And Freud sees mature sexuality and freedom from excessive anxiety as the goal of development.

What is universally developed is a skilled ability to learn by observing or listening to other people or by attending to characters on television and in books. This learning allows the child to acquire large chunks of behavior. In essence, we see development of the four component abilities: attention, retention, production, and motivation. By symbolically representing models' behaviors, the child can predict which behaviors will be punished or rewarded, and he acquires a standard against which to evaluate his own behavior. A representational system also allows the child to combine symbols in novel ways to form and test out new rules, hypotheses, and behaviors.

## THEORETICAL NATURE OF THE THEORY

Most recent work in social learning theory falls into the category of functional theory. There is interchange between modest, limited hypotheses and empirical data. Questions are closely tied to a particular experimental problem, such as the observational learning of conservation. Bandura's theory is not a formal set of postulates in a deductive system. Rather, it is a loosely organized set of hypotheses that have been modified as a result of experimental evidence.

Although functional-theory construction dominates current learning theory, the other modes of theory construction (Introduction) arise from time to time. Hull's theory, of course, is the standard example of a deductive theory in psychology. The operant-conditioning movement, led by Skinner, is an inductive approach. Research leads to summary statements of the empirical relationships observed. For example, some statements describe the rat's behavior under a particular reinforcement schedule. In its extreme form, there is a one-way relationship between data and these summary statements. These statements do not contain hypothetical constructs that would lead to new theoretical questions. Finally, there is use of an implicit model in the notion of S–R associations. It is an analog to the reflex arc described by nineteenth-century neurologists. The reflex arc is a connection between a stimulus and a response in the central nervous system. The model implies that learning is linear (straight in and out) and automatic. This model created a scientific aura for the basic learned associations.

# EVALUATION OF THE THEORY

This evaluation does not rehash the now-familiar list of strengths and weaknesses of traditional learning theory, for which there are several excellent sources (Bowers, 1973; White, 1970). Because most of learning theory's current influence on developmental psychology lies within Bandura's modern social learning theory, the evaluation centers on this version. As in the previous chapter on psychoanalytic theory, the focus is on what the theory can contribute to present and future research and theory building in developmental psychology. Learning theory, including Bandura's work, has recently been criticized and eclipsed somewhat by the Piagetian and information-processing approaches. Still, it has several strengths that developmentalists should not ignore: its focus on situational influences on behavior, its focus on the interface of cognition and society, and its testability. At the same time, two main weaknesses limit the theory: an inadequate account of cognitive development and an inadequate description of development in natural settings.

## Strengths

### Focus on Situational Influences on Behavior

One characteristic of structural, trait, and organismic theories is that they locate the causes of behavior primarily in the person and therefore predict that a person will act similarly in different situations. Thus, Freud would expect a child with a strong superego to be overly controlled in most situations. Similarly, Piaget was relatively uninterested in the fact that conservation is acquired for certain content areas (substance) before others (weight) or that a newly acquired piece of knowledge might be exhibited in one situation but not in another. Learning theory, in contrast, has taken the stance that a person's behavior in fact varies from situation to situation, depending on which eliciting stimuli and reinforcers are found in each situation and on what the person's previous experiences in these situations have been. In Bandura's version, the person, his behavior, and the situation all exert an influence, but most of his research has analyzed situational variables, such as the type of model present or the consequences to the model. More generally, social learning theorists today are part of a movement toward a contextualist account of cognitive functioning that emphasizes interaction between the person and the environment. This attention to situational variables is sorely needed in current work on children's thinking, remembering, and learning. It is now common to find that the child applies a given concept to some materials but not others, that a concept is acquired earlier in one culture than another, and that teaching the child a concept or strategy does not ensure that it will be transferred to another task. There is, however, no generally accepted explanation of these results. As described in Chapter 1, neo-Piagetians tried to address this problem. Following social learning theory's analysis of situations, investigators could determine in which situations a behavior is most likely to occur and identify the social or physical features that affect the occurrence of the behavior. More specifically, it is necessary to analyze what demands on information processing each task makes, what style of information processing is modeled in the child's social environment, what instruction (if any) has been offered the child, whether reinforcement is given for performing the behavior, and so on.

As noted in Chapter 1, one limitation of Piaget's theory is that it deals more with describing the child's knowledge and how it develops than with explaining how this knowledge is actually applied in a specific situation. Considering situational factors would be one step toward filling this gap. To illustrate, we turn again to Rosenthal and Zimmerman's (1977) account of conservation. They suggest several situational factors that may underlie the décalage among the various types of conservations. They maintain that some conservations are more frequently modeled and reinforced than others. Thus, it is expected that conservation would be demonstrated for some materials before others. They suggest that Piagetians have underestimated the role of observational learning in the acquisition of conservation. Children observe others comparing quantities by counting in many settings from very early in life. Learning to count to 10 before kindergarten is a heavily valued and reinforced skill in Western middle-class societies. Comparing the weights of objects is considered a less critical skill. It is used less in a child's day-to-day living and thus is less salient. A related reason for décalage, according to Rosenthal and Zimmerman, is that it is much easier to keep track of the number of objects than the amount of a continuous substance, because counting can be used to verify the former. Information concerning the number of objects is readily available. Children count pennies, keep track of the number of days until their birthday, and make sure that they are given the same number of cookies as their siblings receive. In summary, whether a child conserves quantitative features such as number, substance, weight, or volume depends in part on (1) the opportunities for observing others use these concepts, (2) the opportunities for practicing conservation-related skills such as counting, and (3) the importance assigned to each type of conservation in a given culture. By analyzing these factors, we can acquire a fuller understanding of developmental changes in how children think.

### Focus on the Interface of Cognition and Society

Although most theorists recognize that thinking develops in a social context, they do not provide a comprehensive account. This limitation is a serious problem. There are two central questions here. First, how does social experience affect cognitive development? Second, how does cognitive development influence children's understanding of social events? With respect to the first question, social learning theory describes how modeling, instruction from others, and vicarious learning about reinforcement and punishment impart information to the child. Much new information comes from others rather than from direct trial-and-error experience with the physical world. Even styles of processing information, such as impulsive decision making, can be imitated. With respect to the second question, Bandura's answer is that cognitive development influences social comprehension in the following way: as the child becomes increasingly skilled at attending selectively, representing events symbolically, using memory strategies, and reorganizing previous knowledge, he becomes more efficient at understanding the behavior he observes.

Although Piaget lists social experience as one of several factors underlying cognitive development, he gives much more attention to experience with physical objects, equilibration, and maturation. He does cite disagreements among peers as a source of conflict that might help overcome egocentrism. Also, adults verbally convey information about the world that may or may not be understood, depending on whether the child can assimilate it to his present level of cognitive development. Still, Piaget's handling of social experience is limited because he does not consider observational learning, expectations concerning punishment, and other phenomena described by social learning theory. In addition, Piaget does not consider social influences on how children verify their beliefs. In his theory, children test their beliefs by performing experiments on the environment, much as a scientist would, or by examining the logic of an argument. Bandura includes these forms of verification but also believes that children verify their ideas by observing the effects produced by the behavior of concrete or symbolic models or by comparing their own ideas with those of others.

Freud emphasizes social influence, in that the prohibitions of society force the child to develop structures of thought that can bring ultimate satisfaction and help him deal with anxiety. This view stresses the negative more than the positive influence of society—learning new behavior by observing others. Two of Freud's key concepts are given a new perspective by social learning theory. First, identification with the same-sex parent involves a great deal of observational learning. Freud's notion that the child "incorporates" the parent and acquires a super-ego actually may involve the child's observing or inferring, from observation, the parent's values, beliefs, and behaviors. The child also controls his own behavior by repeating to himself the parent's approving or disapproving statements. Second, defense mechanisms, such as displaced aggression, projection, or regression, can be acquired by observing others use these defenses, especially if these behaviors appear to ward off punishment or unhappiness. Freud does not seriously consider how cognitive development affects the comprehension of social behavior, except that the development of ego functions, such as memory and logical thought, brings the child closer to perceiving social reality.

Bandura's social learning theory has one distinct advantage over Piagetian and information-processing theories of cognition. It considers what has been called "hot" cognition (Zajonc, 1980), as opposed to "cold." Hot cognition refers to the emotional, motivational aspect of thinking; cold cognition includes the nature of thinking but not its emotional aspects. Examples of hot cognition include children's thinking about how to please their parents, experiencing sadness when they fail at a task, and feeling disappointed in themselves when they do not meet their own standards of conduct. Also the child is much more interested in some activities than others and thus applies his knowledge inconsistently. Motivation is a critical part of learning in real life, but has been virtually ignored by Piagetian and information-processing theories. For Freud and Erikson, of course, motivation is a central concern.

In Bandura's (1986) most recent comprehensive account of his theory, he applies his work to a wide range of social concerns. Examples are terrorist tactics, sexual and racial stereotypes, transcultural modeling through satellite telecasting, pornography, deterrents to crime, and encouragement of healthy behavior.

In summary, social learning theory broadens other accounts of cognitive development by considering the social context of this development. It specifies how, through observational learning and symbolic representation, thought interfaces with society.

## Testability

Even those who have attacked learning theory admit that it is probably the most testable theory in psychology. Throughout the theory's history, learning researchers have defined terms clearly, stated hypotheses precisely, and kept unobservable, intervening variables to a minimum. Parsimony is highly valued. As mentioned earlier, learning theory was largely responsible for making developmental psychology an experimental science. This testability has led to disconfirmations that have caused the theory to change over the years. In response to disconfirming evidence, learning theorists added fruitful modifications, such as mediation and observational learning. For example, when there was evidence that children learned and performed behaviors they had observed, even with no practice and even when the model was not reinforced, it was clearly necessary to modify the original social learning theories. The theory is likely to continue to change as well. It should be noted, however, that purist S–R psychologists have criticized Bandura's addition of cognitive variables.

There is a greater proportion of difficult-to-test concepts in Bandura's theory than in earlier learning theories, but fewer than in Piaget's or Freud's theory. Symbolic representation, abstract modeling, and expectations are not unambiguously related to observable behavior. Given the cognitive zeitgeist of the field of developmental psychology, Bandura's theory will probably acquire even more cognitive terms. Although an increasing emphasis on cognition would enhance the theory (as noted in the next section), it is desirable to have a theory that reminds us that we are interested in behavior as well as in thinking. Thus, social learning theorists can serve as watchdogs on cognitive psychologists, who sometimes seem to have forgotten about behavior. We must remember that schemes, object cathexes, secondary-process thought, associations, and rules derived from abstract modeling ultimately refer to behavior.

## Weaknesses

### Inadequate Account of Cognitive Development

As we saw earlier, two strengths of social learning theory are its concerns with the way situational variables influence whether a behavior occurs and with how cognition interfaces with social settings. The theory helps to explain the apparent inconsistency from situation to situation in whether the child conserves, uses logical, information-processing strategies, uses high-level moral reasoning, shares, or aggresses. All these matters refer to the child's actual *performance*—the application of his knowledge about the physical and social world to behavior. This is an important theoretical contribution. It is less clear, however, whether social learning theory will successfully explain how this knowledge is acquired in the first place. What cognitive skills must the child acquire before he can conserve, conceptualize another person's problem-solving strategies, infer the causes of another person's behavior, and reorganize his memory of previous models?

Bandura's theory is more complete than earlier learning theories because it emphasizes that the environment and a person's behavior are connected through the person's cognitive system. However, the nature of this cognitive system, how it develops, and how this development affects observational learning remain to be worked out. Although the theory has loosely adopted information-processing theory's account of thinking, only the general features are included, such as symbolic representation, attention, storage, rule construction, and verification. Furthermore, these processes seem to work almost automatically. Children observe an event and learn it. To some extent, social learning theory seems to have a "copy" theory of knowledge. A sequence of events in the world is more or less copied as it is represented in symbols and retained. Knowledge seems to consist of a storehouse of observed, empirical regularities. Bandura is only beginning to work out exactly how this happens and how changes in cognitive development change observational learning.

One such problem to be worked out is how children's thinking is organized and how that organization changes during development. Bandura clearly does not endorse complex cognitive organizations that characterize a particular stage and change in a qualitative way as the child moves from one stage to another. However, he does not take the opposite view, from traditional learning theory, that specific associations, chains of associations, or specific facts are acquired piecemeal and joined together in very simple ways during development. He allows for an integration of various knowledge; abstract modeling, as common features are abstracted from several related events; creative modeling, as previous knowledge is reorganized to produce a novel behavior; and the construction of schemes, such as gender schemes. Thus, Bandura seems to allow for simple cognitive organization and restructuring, but stops far short of Piaget's equilibrated, highly organized structures. The exact nature of these developmental changes, however, is not yet described.

This description of cognitive changes is important because the way the child's knowledge is organized surely influences how an observed behavior is interpreted at each point in development. For example, watching another child share a toy with a friend may be regarded as an isolated behavior by a 4-year-old but may imply a set of meanings concerning fairness and reciprocity for an 8-year-old. What is learned from this observation differs for the two children. Furthermore, the child's cognitive level limits on his observational learning. A 4-year-old does not learn the rules of division after watching a 1-year-old do division problems. Social learning theorists recognize that one's developmental level influences what is learned during observation, but do not have a detailed account of this process.

A specific portrayal of developmental changes in cognitive reorganization is also necessary for evaluating the criticism that for social learning theory, development is simply learning accumulated over a long period of time. If children organize their thoughts differently over the course of development, then the theory is more clearly a developmental theory.

Finally, an account of developing cognitive organization would indicate whether the process of observational learning itself changes during development. Bandura proposes that the ability to imitate develops very early in life. There is, in fact, evidence that even the young infant can imitate responses, at least if they are already in his repertoire (Meltzoff and Moore, 1983). Bandura proposes that with further cognitive, perceptual, and motor development, this ability becomes more efficient and abstract. However, there is little experimental evidence concerning these changes. Which cognitive ability must be developed before children can form a cognitive representation of what they have observed or read about? What differences underlie the infant's ability to copy his mother when she sticks out her tongue and the 10-year-old's ability to operate a computer after reading the instruction manual? Investigators other than Bandura have begun to study this important developmental issue (Parton, 1976; Yando, Seitz, and Zigler, 1978).

Another issue concerning cognition is whether the concepts of social behavior and physical events are actually as similar as Bandura seems to believe. Observational learning may underlie both conservation and aggression but play a different role in the two cases. Most nonsocial events have either logical or empirical necessity. If stick A is taller than stick B and if stick B is taller than stick C, then it is logically necessary that stick A is taller than stick C. It could not be otherwise. An example of empirical necessity is that in our world a rock, when released, falls downward rather than upward. Logically and empirically necessary concepts are not violated in our experience. Most social events, however, are another matter. A child learns that hitting a peer usually, but not always, leads to disapproval. He learns that one should say "thank you" when given a gift, but that people do not always say this. Most social concepts involve conventions — social customs or rules of social interaction agreed upon by one's culture — rather than logically necessary rules. Even within the social realm, there may be important distinctions. There is evidence that school-age children distinguish between social conventions, such as wearing clothes in public, and logic-based moral judgments (Weston and Turiel, 1980).

The differences between physical and social concepts surely influence exactly how these concepts are acquired during observational learning. A theory that seeks to explain how children acquire both social and physical concepts must make a careful conceptual analysis of the similarities and differences between these concepts. For example, one hypothesis might be that expectations about physical events and logical reasoning are easier to develop than expectations concerning social events because the former are more consistent in the real world. Another question might be whether décalages occur in both the physical and the social realm. Certain physical concepts such as conservation of displaced volume, which are usually not acquired until early adolescence, may not be acquired through observation as easily as such concepts as conservation of number, which are acquired about five years earlier. The observational learning of interpersonal behavior may not have these limitations. Another difference between these concepts may be that children rely on different ways of verifying physical and social rules. It may be that children check the truth of physical rules primarily by logical tests or physical experiments, but check their developing rules of social behavior by observing other people.

## Inadequate Description in Natural Settings

Robert Sears, one of the pioneers of social learning theory, concluded a history of developmental psychology with the observation that the field is long on process research and short on substantive research (Sears, 1975). The former leads to universal principles, whereas the latter leads to principles applicable when a particular set of circumstances exists. We know much more about the variables that *can* affect the learning of social behaviors than about what variables *actually* operate in the lives of children or what behaviors actually occur at various ages. We know how variables operate to produce short-term changes in the laboratory but not how they operate in natural environments. We do not know the ecology of aggressing, sex typing, or dependency. For example, laboratory studies stimulated by social learning theory have identified many processes, such as imitation, abstract modeling, reinforcement, and concept formation, that mold sex-typed behaviors. Which processes, in fact, are most important in particular natural settings? We need a taxonomy of the various situations in which children typically find themselves in each developmental period. The theory's contribution would be much greater if investigators would examine the models and reinforcement contingencies usually found in the typical environments of each phase of development. Our culture presumably rewards different behaviors at different developmental levels. It appears, for instance, that the elderly, in order to obtain reinforcements, often must learn "old, sick, helpless" behaviors and unlearn independent behaviors (Baltes and Barton, 1979).

It is true that there are some observational studies of various behaviors in natural settings. However, these observed behaviors have not been tied systematically to social-ecological variables, such as mothers' working, an increasing divorce rate, urbanization, racial unrest, and changing sex roles. A complete account of social learning must also take into account demographic variables, such as socioeconomic level, race, sex, and geographic location.

In summary, the approach proposed here is that the processes of observational learning and the variables affecting modeling, such as characteristics of the model, should be related to each point in development, taking demographic and other contextual variables into account. For instance, we need a description of developmental changes in aggression that takes into account the type of television programming seen by children in various subgroups of the population, the type of day care the child has, and the father's role in child rearing.

A study of interpersonal coercive behaviors demonstrates that the approach recommended above is feasible. Patterson (1980) observed interactions between mothers and their children in their homes and in laboratory settings. These observations led him to label mothers of preschoolers as "unacknowledged victims" in our society. They are exposed to high densities of aversive events, such as crying, yelling, whining, noncompliance, and hitting. The younger the preschooler, the higher the density of these events. Families differ in how well they cope with these aversive events. In distressed families, the mother and siblings, but not the father, have an unusually large number of extended aversive interchanges with the problem child. In these families, the mother must take on the additional role of crisis manager. The mother adopts behaviors that remove the aversive events (giving in to the child's demands, punishing the child, leaving the situation). These coping behaviors become less necessary when the child is older. Thus, it is possible to study principles of social learning as they are embedded in a particular set of circumstances, such as the child's level of maturation, the roles of mother and father, and the relative frequency of aversive and pleasant stimuli in the environment.

The point is that we have data about social learning but lack an accompanying ecologically based description of developmental change. In addition, in some instances, we have the description but not the data; that is, we have rich descriptions of developmental changes tied to a social context, but the processes underlying these changes have not been analyzed from a social learning point of view. For example, there is much recent interest in interaction between toddlers and their mothers and fathers. The nature of this interaction appears to be influenced by such variables at the parent's sex, socioeconomic class, and race. If this descriptive information were combined with social learning theory's principles of learning, we would have a powerful descriptive and explanatory account of development. The types of models available for verbal and nonverbal behavior, the vicarious reinforcement and punishment, and the degree of encouragement for abstract modeling certainly influence the nature of the parent–child interaction.

## SUMMARY

Social learning theory is a natural outgrowth of the S–R learning tradition. It retains the spirit of the behaviorist movement: the experimentally rigorous study of how basic learning occurs as a result of environmental forces. The spotlight, however, has switched from a hungry rat pressing a bar to a child interacting with other people. First, the evidence mounted that children learn new behaviors by imitating others and that the effect of environmental influences is cognitively mediated, as seen in children's verbal mediation and strategies during problem solving and in their expectations concerning reinforcement. This evidence converged to form the most influential current version of social learning theory — Albert Bandura's.

Bandura broke away from early social learning's interest in psychoanalytic concepts and its preoccupation with how imitation is maintained by reinforcement. He made social learning theory a more convincing explanation of learning by contributing three key concepts:

1. Observational learning can be much broader than mimicking another person's behavior. The child can symbolically construct a new behavior by listening to another person or simply by reading. Complex new behaviors as well as simple modifications of previously acquired

behaviors can be learned in this way. Furthermore, overt behavior is not even necessary in order for learning to occur.

2. The child is self-regulatory. Although reinforcement is not necessary for learning, it is helpful for self-regulation. The child observes which behaviors occurring around him led to reinforcement and punishment and uses these observations as sources of information to help him abstract rules, evaluate his performance, develop standards of conduct, set goals, and decide in which situations to use the observed behavior.

3. Reciprocal determinism provides a model of behavior change. Three sources of influence—the person, his behavior, and the environment—interact. The environment does not always exert the greatest control.

The most novel feature of this three-pronged model is that the child's behavior helps shape his environment, which in turn acts on him.

During development, children become more skilled at the four component processes of observational learning: attention, retention, production, and motivation. In particular, the growing ability to use visual and verbal symbols boosts the child's observational learning. Much of social development results from the accumulation and integration of episodes of observational learning. Although social learning theory has examined a wide variety of developmentally important behaviors, the most vigorously studied topics today are aggression, concept formation (especially conservation), language, and moral development (especially moral judgments and self-regulating standards of conduct). Rosenthal and Zimmerman's work in social learning theory has challenged Piaget's structural theory of development.

Bandura's theory is testable, flexible, and integrative. It is flexible in that it continues to change in light of research outcomes. It is integrative in that it brings together several areas that, by themselves, are somewhat limited. These areas include operant conditioning, information processing, reinforcement processes (direct and vicarious), and socialization processes. Social learning theory holds great promise for correcting several shortcomings of Piagetian and information-processing theory, currently the most influential cognitive approaches. First, the theory provides a way to conceptualize why the child's behavior or demonstrated knowledge might vary from situation to situation. Second, it shows that focusing on physical concepts and ignoring the social context in which they are acquired has resulted in an unrealistic view of how concepts are learned.

There are two needed directions for further developing social learning theory. First, the interface between cognitive development and observational learning must be worked out in greater detail before the theory can be considered a truly developmental theory. Second, the theory could become much more powerful in predicting and exploring behavior if it acquired a broader ecological base. The theory has shown us that processes of social learning can guide development; the next step is to discover how these processes are tied to the environments typically found at various points in development, in various types of families, and in various socioeconomic niches.

## SUGGESTED READINGS

Bandura systematically presents his theory in the following volume.

Bandura, A. Social foundations of thought and action. Englewood Cliffs, N.J.: Prentice-Hall, 1986.

The following article applies a social learning – social interaction perspective to social interaction within the family.

Patterson, G. R., and J. B. Reid. Social interactional processes within the family: The study of the moment-by-moment family transactions in which human social development is imbedded. *Journal of Applied Developmental Psychology*, 1984, 5, 237–262.

The following chapter covers much of the experimental work on social learning theory in the area of moral development.

Casey, W. M., and R. V. Burton. The social-learning approach. In G. L. Sapp, ed., *Handbook of moral development*. Birmingham, Ala.: Religious Education Press, 1986.

# 4

# Information-Processing Theory

1PDV1   ((*GOAL GETREL BLUE RED) (HEARD (BIGGER)) (VALUE RED)
        (VALUE BLUE) (HEARD BLUE) (HEARD RED) NIL NIL NIL NIL NIL)
2P4     ((*GOAL COMPARE BLUE RED) (*GOAL GETREL BLUE RED)
        (HEARD (BIGGER)) (VALUE RED) (VALUE BLUE) (HEARD BLUE)
        (HEARD RED) NIL NIL NIL NIL)
        *[Performance on a conservation task, Klahr and Wallace, 1976, p. 137]*

*The contents of the sixth-grader's rehearsal sets are much more
varied than those of the younger child. The sixth-grader
repeats the presented word, and then draws two other items
from the pool of words which have been presented,
sometimes repeating the two previously presented words
and sometimes sampling from items which have been
presented much earlier in the list. In contrast, the third-
grader tends to combine the present word with the same
two other words from the list. Often as in this example,
these two other words are the first two words presented.*
*[Naus, Ornstein, and Aivano, 1977, pp. 249–250]*

**I** n the last two decades, the information-processing approach has spread quietly through the field of cognitive development. It arrived with little fanfare and, surprisingly, with only moderate clashes with Piagetian theory. Both approaches currently stimulate research, but the information-processing viewpoint continues to grow in influence, while the Piagetian influence has leveled off or, in the opinion of some, is even waning.

The Piagetian, Freudian, and learning theories are easily recognized as theories, and most psychologists who adhere to these theories are aware of their allegiance. In contrast, many developmental psychologists who study memory, attention, and problem solving are not aware that they have accepted certain assumptions and methods of the information-processing approach. They feel they are simply performing empirical, atheoretical studies of various aspects of thinking. This chapter makes explicit this implicit agreement about what thinking involves, what aspects of thought change during development, what questions are worth asking, and how these questions should be studied. We begin with a brief description of the information-processing approach, then continue with a historical sketch, a general orientation, descriptions of major developmental approaches, and an account of mechanisms of development. Later sections describe the position of information processing on developmental issues and the theoretical nature of the theory. The chapter ends with an evaluation and some thoughts on what developmental psychology has contributed to the information-processing approach, which arose from research on adults.

Information processing is not a single theory, but rather a framework characterizing a large number of research programs. As Kendler (1987, p. 364) states, "Cognitive psychology was never born; it gradually coalesced." Information-processing investigators study the flow of information through the cognitive system. This flow begins with an *input*, usually a stimulus, into the human information-processing system. The flow ends with an *output*, which could be information stored in long-term memory, physical behavior, speech, or a decision. Mental operations occur between input and output; for example, the information may be attended to, transformed into some type of mental representation, compared with information already in long-term memory, assigned meaning, and used to formulate a response. These mental processes are similar in some ways to the workings of a computer as it takes in information, performs certain operations on it, and stores it. More generally, both humans and computers manipulate symbols and transform input into output. The correspondence is, of course, only partial. The circuitry of a computer is quite unlike the anatomy of the brain. However, as we shall see later, the computer metaphor served as a valuable heuristic for developing the field of information processing.

To illustrate this description of the information-processing approach, consider what happens when a young child first encounters the Dr. Dolittle story with the pushmi-pullyu, a horselike creature with a head at each end. The delighted child attends to the picture of the creature while ignoring other objects on the page and encodes it visually, as an image, or verbally, as a "pushmi-pullyu" or "two-headed horse." He processes this visual or verbal representation further as he compares it with previously stored information about horses or fantastic creatures such as unicorns. Furthermore, the child may derive certain implications about having two heads ("How does it know if it's coming or going?"), store the new information in a way that allows him to recognize pushmi-pullyus on future occasions, and finally laugh, ask his father to reread the page, or look ahead in the book for more pictures of the pushmi-pullyu.

Thus, the child transforms information over a period of time. An information-processing psychologist (who specializes in pushmi-pull-yus?) might ask the following questions: Did the child process the input superficially, noting only its physical characteristics, or deeply, relating it to a system of meaning? How fast did he process the information? Did he process the pushmi-pullyu's features simultaneously or successively? Were there limits to how much information he could analyze during the time he could see the picture? Did he "rehearse" the label "pushmi-pullyu," by repeating it several times aloud or to himself? How is the pushmi-pullyu as it is finally stored in long-term memory different from the input, the physical stimulus? If he is shown another picture of a pushmi-pullyu, how does he retrieve the relevant information from memory and "recognize" the picture? If a theorist can answer these questions, he can write a set of rules describing how the child can process information.

The pushmi-pullyu example illustrates similarities and differences in learning, Piagetian, and information-processing theories. All three theories would ask how this new object, the pushmi-pullyu, fits into or contradicts previous concepts such as that of the "horse." However, the emphasis differs. A learning theorist might look at stimulus generalization. That is, the pushmi-pullyu as well as the horse can elicit the previously learned response, "horse." Piaget would be interested in how the concept of horse or a horselike creature fits into the child's overall cognitive structures. For example, Piaget might ask if the concept is part of a class-inclusion relationship (horse – mammal – animal). Finally, an information-processing theorist would analyze the processing demands of this particular situation. He would look at what mental processes the child applies to the information and, as a result, how he transforms, manipulates, and uses that information. In other words, an information-processing theorist is primarily interested in how the processing system actually operates in a particular situation — how the system changes external objects or events into a cognitively useful form according to certain rules. In general, Piaget focuses on the acquisition of general logical concepts and their organization with other concepts, whereas learning theorists focus on the shaping of specific concepts and the influence of environmental events in this process. Finally, information-processing theorists focus on how information is encoded and stored in the particular task at hand.

Although the pushmi-pullyu example illustrates the "style" of information-processing psychologists, it masks the diversity of approaches within the field. The main division is that the approaches vary in the type of role that computers play in research and theorizing. At one extreme, we have *computer simulation,* in which the goal is to develop computer programs that model human thought. The "cognitive scientists" adopt the formal language used by computers and in fact see both computers and humans as examples of physical symbol systems. A sample of this formal language appears at the beginning of this chapter.

At the other extreme, the computer serves as a loose metaphor to help researchers think about the processes the subject uses to represent, store, and solve problems about words, pictures, objects, or events. This "soft-core" (Klahr, in press) information-processing approach is much more common than the "hard-core" simulation model among developmental information-processing psychologists. The researcher adopts the informal, but not the formal, language of computer science. That is, he talks about "information," "capacity," and "rules," but does not translate cognitive processes into a formal language in a computer program. He accepts many of the assumptions and concepts of computer science. However, he tends to study cognition using the experimental method, much as experimental psychologists have for years in the study of processes such as verbal learning or discrimination learning. A simple example would be a study in which some children see a group of pictures and some other children see a list of words for those pictures. The psychologist compares the children's memory in the picture-only and word-only conditions. By looking at the relationship between different inputs (visual-pictorial or visual-verbal) and their outputs (types of errors, order in which the objects were recalled), he tries to infer what mental processes the children in the two groups applied over time to the input. These processes might include verbal rehearsal, organizing the objects into categories, or constructing visual representations.

In between computer-simulation approaches and approaches that use the computer as a loose metaphor, we find other information-processing psychologists. Some investigators develop flow diagrams (see Figure 4.1, which is described later), diagrams that depict stages of processing and that could be used, at least in principle, to develop

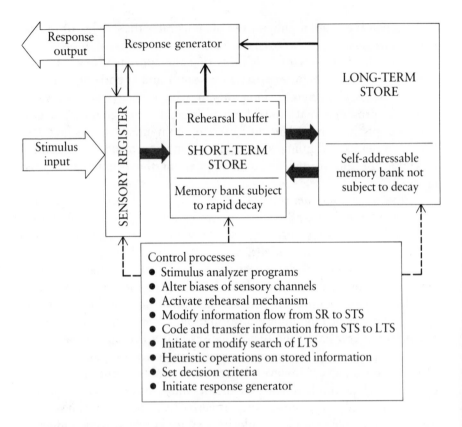

FIGURE 4-1 ■ *A flow diagram of the memory system. SR = sensory register. STS = short-term store. LTS = long-term store. [From "Storage and Retrieval Processes in Long-Term Memory," by Richard M. Shiffrin and Richard C. Atkinson, in* Psychological Review, 1969, 76, 179–193. *Reproduced by permission of the authors.]*

computer simulations of thought. (We look more carefully at such simulations later.)

## HISTORY OF THE THEORY

### Adult Information Processing

Once developmentalists entered the domain of experimental psychology en masse in the early 1960s, they felt reverberations from every significant event in adult experimental psychology. Information processing is the first major theory of adult cognition to arise since developmental psychology became an experimental science. This minirevolution within adult experimental psychology gradually changed the prevailing view of thinking in children. The attraction of information-processing theory for developmentalists can be understood only if we trace the chain of events within adult experimental psychology that led from neobehaviorism to the information-processing approach. After this historical account, we look at the much briefer history of the information-processing approach within developmental psychology.

Two general developments in the 1940s and 1950s eventually transformed adult experimental psychology. First, a crisis occurred within neobehaviorism. Second, technological advances in society crept into the lives of psychologists. The first development, the crisis in neobehaviorism, is described in the previous chapter. This crisis arose partly because many psychologists lost confidence that verbal-learning research, the hallmark of neobehaviorism, was actually advancing our understanding of adult learning (Lachman, Lachman, and Butterfield, 1979). Studying how people remember nonsense syllables, such as GAV–HIG, and systematically varying parameters in learning tasks, such as the length of the list to be remembered and the degree of prior association between words, led to many experiments. The approach did not, however, lead to promising theories and an understanding of human thought in day-to-day living outside of the laboratory.

At about the same time, the feeling of crisis was increased by a serious challenge to the theory from outside psychology. A young linguist named Noam Chomsky attacked the learning account of language acquisition, particularly in his now-famous review (1959) of Skinner's book *Verbal Learning*. Chomsky argued that learning theory is subjective rather than objective in its definitions and observations. Furthermore, its account of language acquisition is wrong in principle because language is actually a complex set of abstract rules rather than a simple set of specific conditioned associations. Chomsky contended that the essence of language—the underlying rules that generate sentences—is unobservable and must be inferred from the relations between language input and output.

The second influential development was the exposure of psychologists to conceptions of the human implicit in much of society's new technology. Lachman, Lachman, and Butterfield (1979) described several of these influences. First, World War II drew psychologists out of the laboratory because they were needed to improve the human operation of wartime equipment and weapons. Psychologists began to think of humans as information transmitters and decision makers when they examined how military personnel divided their attention between a plane's controls and instructions from a radio, detected blips on a radar screen, interpreted a plane's instrument readings, and made decisions about when to open fire on the enemy. A human and a machine (plane or weapon) operate together as a unit. It is desirable that this unit operate efficiently to avoid unfortunate errors, such as plunging into the ocean.

Another technological influence came from communication engineering and information theory. Engineers working on communication systems, such as the telephone, telegraph, radio, and television, developed the notion of "communication channels," which came to serve as a metaphor for human thought. Psychologists began to speak of "limited-capacity channels," "serial" (successive) and "parallel" (simultaneous) processes, "coding information" into large units, "uncertainty" (ambiguous information), and "structures."

Computer science formed yet another technological influence on psychology. Digital computers, robots, and other symbol-manipulating systems suggested to psychologists that people might also be considered symbol-manipulating systems. Newell and Simon (1961), in particular, argued convincingly that the logical capabilities of people could be simulated by appropriate computer programs.

The crisis of confidence within psychology and the technological advances outside psychology produced a generation of psychologists who, unlike the behaviorists, are willing to talk about the mind. Several landmark works advanced the young field, which would soon be called "information processing." George Miller's (1956) famous paper, "The Magical Number Seven Plus or Minus Two," suggested that humans are limited to remembering approximately seven items (plus or minus two) in their immediate memory. However, by "chunking" items into larger units, a large amount of information could be contained in seven units. For example, 149217761918 is beyond our memory span until we chunk it into 1492, 1776, and 1918 — familiar dates in history (Lachman, Lachman, and Butterfield, 1979).

Two years later, Broadbent, in *Perception and Communication* (1958), proposed that humans have a limited capacity to process information. Therefore, they must filter out the less important information while transmitting the more important information to higher levels for further processing. The next year, a study by Peterson and Peterson (1959) provided support for the notion that there are two kinds of memory states. A short-term memory system requires verbal rehearsal to prevent forgetting, and a long-term memory system receives an item after it has been rehearsed. Miller, Galanter, and Pribram (1960) suggested that humans solve problems by using strategies — plans that consist of goals and subgoals in a hierarchic arrangement. In the 1960s, influential publications by Waugh and Norman (1965) and Atkinson and Shiffrin (1968) outlined the important issues in the field in their account of how information moves through several distinct stages involving attention and memory (see Figure 4.1). These *stages of processing* were later challenged by Craik and Lockhart (1972), who claimed that memory should be characterized by many *levels of processing*, rather than separate stages. The more deeply material is processed, the more likely it is to be placed in long-term memory and recalled at a later time. Thus, thinking about how the pushmi-pullyu resembles and differs from the horse is deeper processing than simply noticing its color and shape. Processing the meaning of the stimulus more deeply requires more attention and effort. Finally, a recent trend is the emergence of a field labeled *cognitive science*, an amalgamation of cognitive psychology, computer science, and psycholinguistics. One interest of cognitive scientists is problem solving. A typical problem is the "missionaries and cannibals" puzzle. Three missionaries and three cannibals need to cross a river, but their boat holds only two people at a time. Given their food preferences, cannibals can never be allowed to outnumber missionaries on either bank of the river. How can all be transported across the river without anyone being consumed? A "dog–cat–mouse" problem, presented to preschoolers, requires moving each animal to its favorite food (Klahr, 1985). Only certain types of moves are permissible. A child's series of moves to place the dog with the bone, the cat with the fish, and the mouse with the cheese reveals her strategies of problem solving.

Today, information-processing research encompasses a wide variety of activities, such as laboratory research on memory for simple materials (words or pictures) or the comprehension of complex materials (prose), and computer simulation of problem solving. One branch not yet mentioned, *artificial intelligence*, develops robots, computer programs, or other devices that can play chess or other games, translate texts, serve drinks, perform mathematical calculations, keep track of a store's inventory, and move documents from one office to another. The goal is to produce maximally efficient and intelligent systems. Such devices typically do not model human intelligence and in some cases surpass average mental skills, as anyone who has been humiliated by a computer in a chess game can attest.

Since the days of neobehavioristic studies of verbal learning, investigators have moved from the use of nonsense syllables to meaningful material (sentences and stories) for studying memory. They have also moved from a focus on behavior to a focus on thinking and from the notion of a passive learner to the notion of an active learner. Whereas investigators used to believe that previous knowledge and strategies contaminated any "pure" measure of memory or association, they now consider these nuisance variables objects of interest. Psychologists changed their minds about what is worth studying. More important, they have dared to be mentalistic, to consider behavior as merely an indicator of the more interesting underlying mental events. After causing an initial tremor in the field of psychology, the information-processing approach is quietly maturing into a well-developed field. The 1970s and 1980s truly were the era of the mind.

## Child Information Processing

Although most developmental psychologists merely served as spectators to these dramatic changes in adult experimental psychology, many soon recognized the possibilities of information processing for studying children's thinking. In the late 1960s, many developmentalists had misgivings about the ultimate value of discrimination-learning studies, along with uncertainty that Piagetian theory would ever explain cognitive change as well as describe it. The information-processing approach was appealing because it permitted controlled experimental studies, as had the learning theory orientation that used discrimination-learning tasks, but it also supplied a fruitful new methodology, language, and metaphor for studying the development of thought. In addition, there already was interest in some of the topics studied by information-processing psychologists. Developmentalists had studied attention in discrimination learning and were becoming increasingly interested in language because of Chomsky's work. Also, a growing number of young Ph.D.s trained in adult cognition were beginning to study children.

As a result of all of these factors, information processing entered the field of developmental psychology. The number of studies of children's memory and, to a lesser extent, attention, comprehension, and problem solving has increased exponentially in the last two decades, and no waning is in sight. Most of the early studies were simply direct translations of the adult research, using children as subjects. For example, children were given simpler versions of the memory and attention tasks given to adults. Eventually, as will be apparent later in the chapter, developmental research began to go beyond these simple translations and look at specifically developmental issues.

## GENERAL ORIENTATION TO THE THEORY

How do we recognize an "information-processing cognitive developmental psychologist" when we see one? Distinctive markings aid identification by "psychologist watchers." The following field guide describes several characteristics that are shared with information-processing psychologists who study adults: viewing humans as information-processing devices, conceptualizing development as self-modification, conducting task analyses, and using information-processing methodology.

### Humans as Information-Processing Devices

It is inevitable in this machine age that psychologists would ponder what people and machines have in common. Computers, hand calculators, electronic games, and people all deal with information in some form. More specifically, all manipulate symbols according to certain rules and store the results of these operations. Furthermore, we find striking correspondences in how people and machines process this input. We can compare perceiving with "input," thinking with a "computer program," storage capacity with number of "K," memory with a "memory bank," a decision with "output," and mental operations with "subroutines." In essence, the information-processing psychologist is asking "How is the human organism programmed to make sense out of the complicated world around it?" Using the computer analogy, information-processing psychologists try to track detailed changes in the flow of information over time. They make a step-by-step analysis of what the person does to the information. How this new orientation breaks with the past is illustrated in its language. For example, "input–output" connotes a different sort of being than does "stimulus–response" or "assimilation–accommodation."

The input to the information-processing device is information, which can come in many forms. It might be a word, a paragraph, a mathematical or logical symbol, a blip on a radar screen, or a mental image. The device performs certain operations on this information, such as comparing it with previously stored information or transforming it into a representation (*encoding*), for example, by transforming a written word into a mental image.

The adult mind can efficiently organize millions of pieces of information. How is such a remarkable device developed? Information-processing psychologists view children at various ages or cognitive levels as being in different states. Psychologists infer each knowledge state from the relationship between the input and output. Thus, each developmental level is characterized by a particular input–output relationship.

To illustrate, let us consider what happens when we show a child a two-pan balance scale and ask him to order a set of blocks according to weight. How does he gather information about the weights (input) and use this information to make a set of decisions as to how to order the objects (output)? Baylor and Gascon (1974) have used this situation to examine how children process information. They carefully analyzed the sequences of behavior of individual children: which block was placed on which pan, how many blocks were weighed at the same time, whether the heavier or lighter block was removed from the pan after weighing, and so on. Suppose we provide the same input, a set of seven blocks, to a 5-year-old and an 11-year-old. The differences in their output would lead us to infer how their states differ, that is, how they operate on the input. The 5-year-old may weigh one pair of blocks at a time, but weigh each pair only once. After the child completes the weighing, he knows which block of each pair is heavier, but does not know how the blocks from different pairs compare in weight. In contrast, the 11-year-old might compare one block with each of the other blocks and always leave the heavier block on the pan. After he identifies the heaviest block, he carries out the same process with the remaining blocks until no blocks are left. The child has seriated the seven blocks. From the behaviors and perhaps from the children's descriptions of what they were doing, we can infer the rules used in each state, or age. As we change the input in various ways and observe how the output changes at the different ages, we can more confidently describe the nature of the information-processing system at each state.

At a finer level of analysis, we must look at developmental changes at each step from input to output. As we will see later, developmental changes are apparent in nearly every phase of processing — from attention through encoding to recall and decision making. Any of these changes could be responsible for the differences in the strategies used by the younger and the older child on the weight-seriation task.

The way information-processing psychologists study the weight-seriation task contrasts with Piaget's approach to the same task. Although both are concerned with how the child reaches his answer, Piaget used the task to diagnose whether the child has underlying mental operations, such as reversibility and transitivity. (If A is heavier than B and if B is heavier than C, the A must be heavier than C.) Baylor and Gascon, in contrast, inferred what specific rules the child used for that task. They made a more detailed analysis of the child's actions and related them to the stimulus characteristics of the task, such as how the blocks are arranged and how many blocks there are. Finally, they wrote a program based on the inferred rules to see if they had generated the child's sequence of actions.

Now that we have noted the general nature of the human information-processing device and its development, let us look more specifically at the flow of information through this device. Information processing might be called the "psychology of boxes and arrows." A well-known example is the influential Atkinson and Shiffrin flow diagram in Figure 4.1. These flow diagrams are called "models." They communicate the theorist's claims about how humans process information. In this way, information-processing psychologists express their theories. A model outlines the temporal and functional relationships among the stages of processing in the information-processing system. As far as we know, these stages do not correspond to different areas of the brain.

The Atkinson and Shiffrin model is typical of the information-processing models in positing sensory registers, a short-term store (short-term memory), and a long-term store (long-term memory). *Sensory registers* in each modality retain all information reaching the sense organs, but only for perhaps a fraction of a second or several seconds, depending on the sense organ. Children's sensory registers appear to have as great a capacity as those of adults. However, children form sensory representations more slowly than do adults.

Any information selected for further processing continues to a short-term store. The *short-term store* can maintain a limited amount of information (perhaps 5 to 9 units in an adult) for up to approximately 15 to 30 seconds, or longer if the person verbally rehearses (repeats) or otherwise acts upon this information. Material that is not attended to further in short-term store and transferred to long-term store is quickly lost forever. Thus, we must either immediately dial the phone number we have looked up or keep repeating it. Information from the sensory register and the long-term store can be brought together to perform calculations or other activities in the short-term store. Thus, the short-term store is sometimes aptly called the "working memory." Finally, the *long-term store* of large capacity retains information indefinitely within a complex mental organization. During retrieval, information is summoned out of the long-term store and once again enters the short-term store.

The cognitive system performs various kinds of work. For example, when a first-grader reads, he filters out irrelevant information, such as the color of the letters, and performs preliminary analyses on information as he breaks the stimuli into letters or words and "recognizes" these letters and words. He also transforms the visual stimuli into a verbal code ("see Spot run") or a visual image (of Spot running) and searches his long-term store for related information about Spot. Anywhere along the way, the information may be lost and no further analysis is possible. Thus, in assembly-line fashion, a sequence of operations is applied to the input. Metaphorically, information follows the arrows and "goes" in and out of boxes.

A crucial set of processes listed in Figure 4.1, called *control processes*, are the "executives of the company." Like computer software, they direct the activities in each stage of processing, keep track of what is going on in all parts of the system, and make sure the entire system is working in harmony. Control processes help humans to overcome structural limitations on how much information can be handled. Some of the most impressive developmental changes in information processing occur in these control processes.

With respect to development, two questions could be raised about the stages of processing outlined in the flow diagram. First, in what way, if any, do the stages of processing differ in the various developmental states? Do they differ quantitatively or qualitatively? Second, what causes the child to progress from one state to the next? Are changes in how the child compares the weights of blocks due to an increase in the capacity of short-term store or the more efficient retrieval of a relevant rule from long-term store or both? This question concerning the cause of change is the ultimate challenge for the information-processing approach if it is to be a viable theory of development.

Developmental psychologists have used levels-of-processing models as well as stages-of-processing models. Levels models describe memory as a set of actions that may process information at any of several levels, ranging from a superficial analysis of perceptual features to a deep analysis of meaning. As A. L. Brown (1979) points out, the levels-of-processing approach is very congenial to developmental approaches because the child more and more actively relates the material to be remembered to his conceptual system and his goals.

## Development as Self-Modification

An important breakthrough in computer technology was the development of self-correcting, self-modifying programs (for example, Wallace, Klahr, and Bluff, 1987). Suppose a computer program simulates the cognitive state of a child at one point in time. Because a computer program can act on itself as a source of information, in principle it can change itself. Some computer simulations now consist of programs that ruthlessly reject procedures that turn out not to be useful, reorganize units already available, and increase or decrease the number of situations in which a particular operation will be used. These self-modifications, then, propel the program from state to state, or from one developmental level to another.

Many information-processing pscyhologists who use computers only metaphorically also posit self-correction through feedback. The child tries out various rules or strategies in her attempts to attend to, comprehend, and remember the events of daily life. She learns how to select the most promising routes to solving a problem. By rejecting useless methods and retaining helpful ones, the child gradually becomes a more efficient information processor.

We encountered the notion of modification through feedback earlier, in learning theory and Piaget's theory. All three theories view feedback as information to be evaluated and used to develop new concepts or behavior. However, information-processing theory and Piagetian theory essentially ignore learning theory's account of how this feedback can serve as reinforcement or punishment to increase or decrease the frequency of a response. Instead, they focus on acquisition.

## Task Analysis

One hallmark of the information-processing approach is the careful, almost compulsive analysis of the experimental or real-life task facing the child or adult. The investigator analyzes the task according to the various necessary and sufficient cognitive skills for performing it. This concern with the specific features of a particular task follows naturally from the approach's focus on the information available in the stimulus, the limits to the person's processing capacity, the goals of the task, and the person's processing skills. The unique demands of each particular task elicit different processing activities. For example, conceptually unrelated objects may be rehearsed verbally, but related objects may be categorized into "small and large kitchen objects" and "small and large living-room objects" and then only briefly rehearsed.

Information-processing psychologists point out that an accurate assessment of a child's cognitive structures depends on the investigator's thorough understanding of task demands: "Cognitive structures cannot be measured per se; they can only be measured by activating them and recording their behavioral consequences. Consequently, our understanding of these structures can only be as deep as our understanding of the procedures by which those structures become active" (Kail and Bisanz, 1982, p. 74).

This issue of task demands is of particular concern to developmentalists. Is there so much information that it exceeds the child's capacity and therefore cannot be comprehended, even though the child has the appropriate rule? If so, the child's knowledge may be underestimated. The child may be able to seriate weight if there are four blocks, but not if there are seven. Is there salient, but irrelevant, information that draws the child's attention away from the important information? For example, the child may attend to differences in the sizes of the blocks, thereby ignoring their weights. Are there developmental changes in what behaviors the child has available to apply toward the goal of the particular task? Weighing the blocks, comparing them, and placing them in a line are performed differently at various ages.

The concern with task analysis is related to a central issue among the neo-Piagetians: domain-specific versus domain-general knowledge. Information-processing investigators tend to propose that the child acquires a set of rules that is specific to a particular domain, that is, limited to a certain task or set of tasks. A careful analysis of various tasks clarifies why a child may apply a rule (for example, a counting rule) or set of rules to certain tasks (adding) but not others (class inclusion).

There is a common spirit in the information-processing and learning approaches. Both break down tasks or behavior into their simple components. In addition, both are very concerned with the nature of the task stimuli. The information-processing approach, however, allows for much more complexity in how the person operates upon stimulus information. He can, for example, relate it to an organized set of knowledge about objects, people, and events.

## Methodology

Information-processing psychologists investigate topics traditionally studied by experimental psychologists: memory, attention, text processing, language, and problem solving. However, the experiments tend to be microscopic, in that they often look at very brief events, such as detecting whether a particular design flashed briefly on a screen has been rotated from its earlier orientation. The studies often examine such temporal variables as the amount of time, in milliseconds, the stimulus is exposed and take temporal measures, such as reaction time (how long it takes the subject to decide whether a design has been rotated). It is assumed that any mental activity takes a certain amount of time. There may, however, be differences in speed of processing between different ages, between normal and mentally retarded children, and between good and poor readers (Stanovich, 1978). Such a concern with time is not surprising, given the focus on the flow of information over time. Under certain conditions, it can be assumed that the longer the time between input and output, the more cognitive activity taking place. Consequently, it can be assumed that if two tasks are identical, except that one additional cognitive operation is required for one of the tasks, the difference in the time required to perform the two tasks provides a measure of the time needed to perform the additional operation.

Another powerful method is error analysis. The pattern of correct and incorrect answers over various types of trials reveals the rule or rules the child is using to solve the problem. A classic example is Siegler's (1978) work with the balance-scale task, to be described later. Although Piaget also made considerable use of children's errors, he did not analyze them in the elegant, systematic way sometimes found in information-processing work. Still another assessment is eye-movement analysis. What children look at, how long they look at stimuli, and the order in which they examine stimuli provide clues to their processes of attention and encoding.

In addition to these traditional experimental methods, however, information-processing psychologists have developed two tools: models and computer simulation. We briefly discussed the simple flow-diagram model in Figure 4.1. It is a typical information-processing model, in that it is a schematic representation describing temporal and functional relationships among several stages of processing. Some models, however, are expressed in other forms, such as mathematical symbols, propositional logic, and formal grammars.

The use of models in the form of flow diagrams is not, of course, unique to the information-processing approach. As we saw in an earlier chapter, even Freud occasionally tried to express his theoretical notions through diagrams. However, no other approach has relied as heavily as the information-processing approach on schematic models for theory building.

The advent of the computer not only gave psychologists and other scientists an efficient way to analyze their data, but also provided a way to test theories of human thought. Computer simulation is an attempt to write a program that is specific enough, accurate enough, and complete enough to perform much as humans do. As information-processing psychologists pose the question: What would an information-processing system have to be like in order to behave as the child does? Psychologists develop a computer program that is intended to generate the child's performance on the task. Given the same input, do the computer program and the child produce the same output? Do they make the same errors and succeed on the same problems? The closer the correspondence, the better the simulation.

The development of a successful simulation can be a long and arduous task. Usually the psychologist begins by gathering descriptions of how people solve a particular problem. For example, he might describe the order in which the child weighs blocks on a scale. He might also have the child describe what he is thinking and doing as he solves this weight-seriation problem. These data make up the "protocol." The problem-solving session may be videotaped, so that it can be viewed many times. The researcher then tries to write a set of rules or procedures that the child or a group of children used to order the weights. He then writes a computer program that gives instructions based on this set of rules. The program must make specific statements about the capacity of the system, the representation of information, and the nature of the cognitive processes. If the psychologist has left out some steps in the rules he wrote into the program, if his instructions are logically inconsistent, or if he has incorrectly inferred a rule from the child's behavior, the program either will not run or will give an output that does not correspond to the child's. The psychologist then tries to correct the program and runs it again. Often, this cycle must be repeated many times. With each repetition, the number of unexplained behaviors of the child becomes smaller and smaller. Eventually a satisfactory correspondence between the outputs may be achieved. In other words, the program essentially reproduces the protocol from which it was generated.

At this point, the researcher applies more stringent tests. Can the program predict what other children of the same age or a different age would do? Can it predict what the child would do if there were fifteen blocks instead of seven or if the blocks were a different set of sizes? Can it predict what the child would do on a length-seriation task? Further modification of the program may be necessary to achieve this generalization.

At some point, the psychologist finds that he has a satisfactory model of how humans behave in a particular type of task, such as seriating weight or playing chess. Ideally, he then develops a more general model that explains behavior on a wider set of tasks, for example, a model of memory during problem solving. Thus, as further changes are made in the program, it may become both more specific and more general. A good model will generalize to more behaviors than the small set of protocols on which it was based but be specific enough to be supported or refuted by empirical findings. By the preceding process, a model becomes less limited and more convincing as a theory of thinking.

One unexpected bonus of computer simulation is that it can suggest new hypotheses to the psychologist. There may be implications of his simulation of which the psychologist was unaware. Unexpected output from the program may suggest that a new variable should be examined. For example, if the researcher found that the program predicted the same level of recall with 5 and with 10 items, he might look for a "chunking" mechanism that operates when there is a large number of items.

## MAJOR DEVELOPMENTAL APPROACHES

The study of information processing in children is a diverse, multi-faceted enterprise. Some information-processing psychologists use letters flashed briefly on a screen, while others make the stimuli available for half an hour. Some look at reaction time, while others look at the child's own explanation of how he solved a problem. The common orientation presented earlier should not mask this diversity. The following smorgasbord offers a sampling of current information-processing research programs or influential earlier studies. We look at the development of memory, representation, problem solving, and intelligence. This division into four areas is strictly for convenience of presentation. In actuality, all four make up an indivisible psychological process. The programs are described in some detail in order to illustrate which problems have been considered worthy of study, which theoretical concepts have been advanced, and how developmentalists have actually studied cognitive development from the information-processing point of view.

## Memory

Memory is a net; one finds it full of fish when he takes it from the brook; but a dozen miles of water have run through it without sticking.

[Oliver Wendell Holmes]

Children's memory is a fascinating phenomenon, but the area of study is fraught with contradictions. On the one hand, it is widely believed that young children have poor memories. On memory subscales of IQ tests or on laboratory memory tasks, they perform poorly compared with adults, and in more natural setting they find it difficult to memorize their phone numbers and street addresses. Yet parents or teachers who read stories to preschoolers know that children often memorize a story word for word after only a few readings. In fact, children become quite indignant if the reader inadvertently (or because it is past bedtime) leaves out a word or two.

A typical developmental information-processing psychologist conducts laboratory studies of memory in children. This recognition of the important role of memory in all phases of thought is shared with information-processing psychologists who study adults. Hundreds of these studies fill the developmental-research journals of the last 20 years. This investment of psychologists' time and energy has paid off handsomely in knowledge not only about children's memory but also, as a bonus, about the development of language, attention, and complex cognitive structures such as the organization of the knowledge base. Although psychologists do not yet have the whole picture, some generalizations have emerged. Four major conclusions from the massive body of memory research are now presented, along with a description of one or several studies that convey the flavor of the research.

### Acquisition of Appropriate Strategies Underlies Much of the Developmental Change in Memory

Some memory activities are effortless and seemingly automatic: a baby recognizes his father's face, a boy relates to his friend the plot of his favorite television show seen the night before, an adult hums "White Christmas" while Christmas shopping. The person is not conscious of trying to remember and does not make an effort to remember. These acts of memory "just happen." They involve simple recognition rather than active recall or involve recall as a by-product of a meaningful activity. There is little change in these types of memory during development. Simple recognition memory (indicating that an object or a picture has been seen before) is very good even in infants. It shows little improvement from infancy to maturity when possible differences in the efficiency of encoding are ruled out. By the end of the preschool years, coherent, comprehensible stories or past experiences that were of interest to the child are recalled fairly well.

When the material to be recalled is *not* part of a context that is meaningful to the child and memory itself must become the primary goal, then there *is* striking improvement in memory during development. Phone numbers, a group of unrelated objects, and the order in which pictures of toys were presented, all fall into this category. A. L. Brown (1975) is primarily responsible for bringing to our attention this distinction between involuntary and deliberate memory in children. The two types of memory have very different characteristics and require different theoretical explanations.

A commonsense explanation of improvement in deliberate memory would be that the memory span (the capacity of short-term memory) has increased. Memory span is sometimes measured by how many numbers in a string (for example, 3281734) a person can repeat in order. However, there is disagreement whether the apparent increase in memory span during development actually reflects an increase in memory capacity per se or shows instead increasingly efficient use of a constant amount of capacity. The problem is that it is almost impossible for a researcher to create a task that eliminates all possibility of strategy use.

It is clear that there are developmental changes in what children do when they are trying to remember. In order to store unrelated information, the person must do something special to the material. This "something special" is a strategy. Defined more formally, strategies are "subject-controlled activities that are employed in the service of a memory goal" (Ornstein and Naus, 1985, p. 118). For example, if the person wants to remember what to buy at the store, he could say the items over and over again to himself or put the items into categories such as "dairy products" and "vegetables." Or he could make up a silly story about the items ("The carrot swam through the sea of milk on the back of a tuna . . . "), mark the location of the items on his mental image of the supermarket, or simply write a list. These strategies are tools that humans have devised in their constant struggle to overcome their processing limitations.

In an early influential study of children's strategies, Flavell, Beach, and Chinsky (1966) asked young children to remember the order in which the experimenter pointed to several pictures of objects. During the delay between the presentation and the recall tests, a visor on a space helmet was lowered over the child's eyes so that he could not see the pictures. A trained lip reader noted any overt verbal rehearsal. Few 5-year-olds, over half of the 7-year-olds, and most of the 10-year-olds rehearsed. In a later experiment, Keeney, Cannizzo, and Flavell (1967) found evidence for a direct link between rehearsal and memory. First, those children who spontaneously rehearsed recalled more items than those who did not. Second, when the experimenter directed nonrehearsers to say the names of the objects during the delay between the presentation and the recall test, they successfully rehearsed. Consequently, they remembered the order of the objects. Two conclusions follow. First, the strategy of rehearsal is critical for this type of memory task. Second, although young children are capable of using rehearsal to aid memory if they are told to rehearse, they are deficient at spontaneously producing the strategy. Flavell dubbed this a *production deficiency*. Young children have appropriate strategies, but are deficient in knowing when, where, and how to use (produce) them effectively. This theoretical claim has stimulated much of the memory research in the last twenty years. Since the Flavell studies, a production deficiency has been rediscovered with many other memory tasks and many other strategies, such as leaving clues that will help in retrieval or classifying the items into categories (animals, furniture, and food). This research shows that older children are more likely than younger children to gain access to the higher-order relations among stimuli, such as categories.

Even after children develop and use strategies, they continue to refine them. Ornstein, Naus, and Liberty (1975) found that verbal rehearsal becomes more systematic and organized during development. During the memory task, the children were to say the words aloud as they were presented. Third-graders tend to say each word alone as it is presented or perhaps with the previous word. In contrast, eighth-graders rehearse cumulatively, including previously presented words as well as the new word.

By the preteen years, children typically can pick a strategy that fits the particular task and carry out the strategy spontaneously, quickly, and efficiently. Certain strategies, however, continue to develop during adolescence. An example is "elaboration," or constructing an image out of the materials to be remembered (Pressley, 1982).

A major developmental change during the grade school and adolescent years involves learning to make maximal use of one's limited capacity. For example, during the grade-school years, children become more efficient in their use of study time. Older grade-school children focus more on the important elements of the text, as reflected in their underlining and note taking (Brown and Smiley, 1978). Similarly, after age 11 or 12, children skillfully ignore irrelevant information (for example, distracting pictures) and process only relevant information (pictures to be recalled) during memory tasks (Hagen and Hale, 1973). A. L. Brown (1978) stresses the increase in the child's control of strategies and other cognitive processes. As if learning to conduct a great orchestra, the child eventually brings the parts into perfect harmony and increases his control over the whole. These control processes eventually mature into those found in adults, as in the model in Figure 4.1.

Three recent lines of research illustrate some of the current questions asked in studies of memory strategies. First, investigators recently have identified in toddlers and preschoolers such rudimentary strategies as looking at, pointing at, or naming objects to be remembered. These behaviors sometimes are "faulty strategies" (Wellman, 1988) because they are not appropriate for the task at hand and are not helpful, but still are strategic, in that they are systematic attempts to aid memory. For example, 3-year-olds faced with the task of hiding an object for later retrieval in one of 144 containers arranged in a 12 by 12 matrix simply hid it in the same place each time, most commonly in one of the inner boxes (Heisel and Ritter, 1981). This was a faulty strategy because it was not helpful. Five-year-olds, in contrast, hid the object in a distinctive location, such as a corner. Second, the study of memory strategies has broadened to become the study of strategies as a developmental phenomenon of interest in itself, independent of its facilitation of memory. Employing strategies is an important function of the control processes described earlier. Third, investigators recently have linked strategies to capacity. It is more effortful for a young child than for an older one to use a strategy (Guttentag, 1984). Thus, he has less remaining capacity to devote to memorizing per se than does an older child for whom the strategy itself requires less capacity-draining effort. Why are strategies so helpful? They may simply "pound in" the material by going over it again and again. On the other hand, they may convert the information into a more encodable and durable verbal form, "chunk" the material so that more can be processed, or make the material more meaningful by relating it to the child's previous knowledge. According to the levels-of-processing approach (Craik and Lockhart, 1972), all of these strategies are helpful because they cause the material to be processed at deeper levels and therefore made more memorable. A. L. Brown (1979) suggests that much of the development of memory comes from knowing when, where, and how to process relevant information at deep levels. She asserts that it is important that the young child engage in meaningful activity with respect to both the material to be remembered and the child's goal. Soviet theories of memory have a similar orientation in their view of memory as a natural by-product of engaging in a meaningful activity. Some of the contradictory observations about young children's memory may not seem so mysterious once we consider whether the task is meaningful to the child.

### Memory Limitations Can Restrict the Use of Available Logical Reasoning Skills

Memory and reasoning are intimately related. For example, when the child reasons, a set of information must be "kept in mind" long enough for the child to relate the pieces of information and make a decision. The child may have a certain mental operation or skill, but be unable to use it in certain contexts because there is too much information to relate simultaneously. Consequently, his thinking may be more advanced than it appears. Any general theory of cognition must consider the role of memory in cognitive performance.

Bryant and Trabasso (1971) challenged Piaget's claim that young children (under about age 7) do not have the cognitive ability to reason transitively. An example of transitive reasoning is the statement, If John is taller than Jack and Jack is taller than Bill, then John must be taller than Bill. Bryant and Trabasso used a set of sticks of various lengths. They extensively trained children 4 to 7 years of age to remember the set of relevant information: The green stick (A) is taller than the red (B), the red (B) is taller than the blue (C), and so on for five sticks. Thus, the children memorized the relative heights of all adjacent pairs. Subsequently, most of the children were able to demonstrate transitive reasoning. They could, for example, infer that stick B must be taller than stick D. They had not, of course, been told during memory training that B was taller than D; they had been trained only on adjacent pairs. Thus, Bryant and Trabasso concluded that young children's ability to reason transitively had been underestimated in the past because the relevant information was poorly remembered.

## Development of Memory Is Closely Tied to Acquisition of Knowledge

Memory is not a mental process separate from the rest of cognition. It is intermeshed in a broad system of thought. In fact, memory has been called "applied cognition" (Flavell, 1971a) because the cognitive system is simply directed to a particular set of problems, namely, storage and retrieval. There are two implications for development. First, children are more likely to remember material that is meaningful to them. When there is a match between what the child knows and what is to be remembered, there is what Brown (1975) calls "headfitting." The task fits the child's mental abilities. Second, as the developing child becomes "world-wise" and possesses a growing store of knowledge about objects, events, and people in the world, she should be able to remember a broader range of information.

There are numerous experimental demonstrations of the first phenomenon, remembering meaningful materials. For example, children who are skilled chess players have better recall of the locations of chess pieces on a chessboard, positioned as if in the middle of a game, than do adults who know less about chess (Chi, 1978). Another example concerns 6-year-olds, who typically do not group similar items together during recall. When they are asked to remember the names of classmates, they show a great deal of grouping according to seating arrangement, reading groups, and sex of the children (Bjorklund and Zeman, 1982). Examples from adults include better recall of a list of soccer terms among experienced soccer players (Naus and Ornstein, 1985) and very good recognition of rug patterns among Moroccan rug sellers with little formal education (Wagner, 1978).

Such cases of knowledge facilitating recall can be explained in several ways. First, a rich knowledge base may allow children to automatically access items to be recalled because these items have a rich network of associations with other items and with category labels (Bjorklund, 1987). Thus, items can be retrieved by many different cues; in Piaget's terminology, memory is facilitated because children can easily assimilate the material to their cognitive structures.

A second explanation is that the knowledge base may increase the likelihood that an appropriate strategy is used, which in turn facilitates recall. Thus, a strategy mediates the effect of the knowledge base. According to one version of this argument, because of the ability to quickly process the information by relating it to previous knowledge, capacity is freed and can be applied to deliberately using a strategy (Bjorklund, 1987). Thus, Siegler (1986, p. 251) concludes that "familiar contents may serve as a kind of practice field upon which children can exercise emerging cognitive skills such as new memory strategies." In addition to these two main explanations is the suggestion that a rich knowledge base may facilitate recall by enhancing motivation or increasing children's understanding of the goal of the task.

One problem with examining the relationship between the knowledge base and recall is that a researcher needs to be able to describe the child's knowledge base accurately and in great detail. A rare attempt at such description was a study of a 4-year-old obsessed with dinosaur lore (Chi and Koeske, 1983). He knew the names of 40 different dinosaurs, understood the differences between a pachycephalosaur and a rhamphorhyncus, and persuaded his patient mother to spend an average of 3 hours a week reading his dinosaur books to him. His semantic network concerning the subset of dinosaurs better known to him is illustrated in Figure 4.2. The diagram was generated by two procedures. First, Chi and Koeske observed which dinosaurs he named in succession when asked to recall all the dinosaurs he could. Second, they assessed his knowledge and organization of dinosaur properties in a game: one person named two or three properties, and the other person guessed which dinosaur it was. As the figure shows, the links or associations within a category are strong, numerous, and conceptually close (for example, armored species are grouped in the left-side shaded area, A, and giant plant eaters in the right-side shaded area, P). This structure was not found for less familiar dinosaurs; in other words,

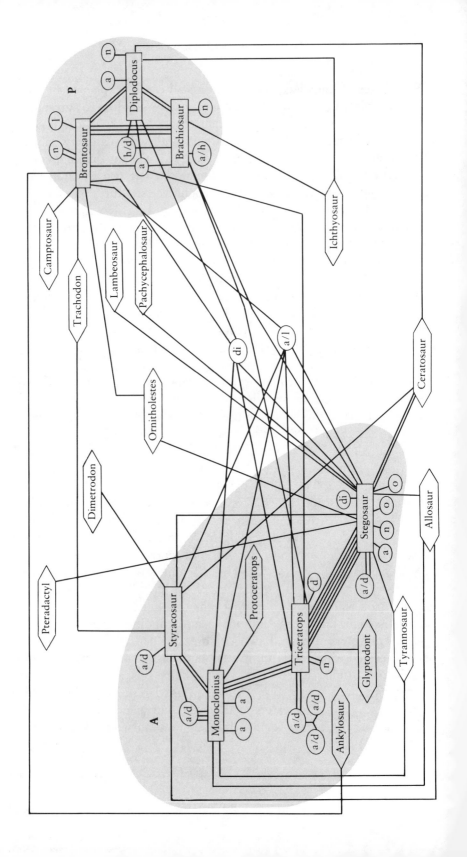

knowledge of seven familiar dinosaurs (in the areas A and P) was more organized than the knowledge about less familiar dinosaurs. For example, the boy could say that diplodocus and brachiosaur both eat plants but not that two relatively unknown dinosaurs do. The patterns of linkages, or semantic network, are the essence of the structuring of the knowledge base. The boy's knowledge of the properties were useful for forming subsets on the basis of diet, appearance, and other characteristics. As expected, the boy could remember more of the better-known than of the lesser-known dinosaurs, perhaps because the former had many links to other dinosaurs and the items were more structured conceptually.

The increase in amount of knowledge during development is important for memory development. But perhaps even more critical is *how* knowledge is represented, specifically, how it is organized, as illustrated in Chi's study of dinosaur knowledge. Young children may tend to form categories on the basis of perceptual features of objects, whereas older children may be more likely to use conceptual features. If a memory task is not represented in a way that taps the child's knowledge base, then his considerable knowledge about the materials may not be beneficial. For example, for Chi's subject, presenting categories of large plant eaters and armored dinosaurs, which are congruent with his own categories, should lead to greater recall than categories formed on some other basis, such as their aggressiveness or time of emergence during evolution.

A final observation about the relationship between knowledge and recall is that since the child's interests and knowledge differ from those of adults, his most salient memories may differ from those of adults. One 5-year-old, when asked if he remembered the home he had moved from 2 years earlier, answered: "I remember lots about Michigan. I

FIGURE 4-2 ■ *Semantic network representation of a child's knowledge concerning well-known dinosaurs (the seven enclosed in rectangles). The child's two categories are indicated by the two shaded areas: armored dinosaurs (A) and giant plant-eating dinosaurs (P). The characteristics include appearance (a), defense mechanism (d), diet (di), habitat (h), locomotion (l), nickname (n), and other (o). Other dinosaurs associated with the seven target dinosaurs are enclosed in hexagons. Adapted from "Network Representation of a Child's Dinosaur Knowledge" by Michelene T. H. Chi and Randi D. Koeske in* Developmental Psychology, 1983, 19, 29–39. *Reproduced by permission of the authors;* © 1983 by the American Psychological Association, Inc.

remember you left a piece of cheese at the back of the refrigerator and it got green stuff all over it."

The second claim mentioned about the knowledge base was that developmental progress in knowledge should bring about progress in memory. Piaget's studies of memory described in Chapter 1 provide vivid examples of this progress. Children drew pictures of seriated (size-ordered) sticks seen about half a year earlier. These pictures were more accurate, that is, more seriated, than were the drawings they made half a year before. Piaget's interpretation was that the memory image of the sticks was assimilated into a more advanced structure based on the child's growing understanding of seriation.

As the child increases his store of knowledge, he tends to make inferences that go beyond the information given to him. Hebb (1949) likens this feature of remembering to the way a paleontologist reconstructs a prehistoric creature. Just as a paleontologist generates a complete dinosaur from lone fragments and his general knowledge about the anatomy of dinosaurs, so does a person reconstruct an event by filling in among remembered fragments. For example, in one study (Paris and Carter, 1973), children were told "The bird is inside the cage" and "The cage is under the table." Later the children were presented with sentences, some new and some heard earlier. Children as young as 7 often believed, erroneously, that the sentence "The bird is under the table" had been presented earlier. They had spontaneously made a reasonable inference from the information they had been given.

Children's constructive memory also reflects their social beliefs, attitudes, and expectations. For example, school-age children with the most stereotyped views of gender-appropriate behavior recalled more pictures of traditional (for example, female secretary) than nontraditional (for example, male secretary) activities (Signorella and Liben, 1984). In addition, they sometimes even reconstructed the pictures, for example, recalling that a secretary was female when in fact the person was a male. In another study (Ceci, Caves, and Howe, 1981), 7- and 10-year-olds "remembered" that a character known to them to be powerful, such as "The Six Million Dollar Man," had been strong in a story heard 3 weeks earlier. In fact, the character had been weak in the story. This distortion of memory did not occur with unfamiliar characters.

Memory does not simply copy the world. Children "construct" a memory from inferences based on their knowledge. Younger children are less likely to make these inferences (Liben and Posnansky, 1977). In short, "creative memory" is a by-product of cognitive development. These illustrations of how memory is tied to knowledge should further clarify how involuntary memory differs from the deliberate, voluntary memory discussed in an earlier section. If children have the knowledge necessary to understand the material, then they are likely to remember it without further ado.

### Children Increase Their Understanding of Memory

"The horror of that moment," the King went on, "I shall never, *never* forget!"
"You will, though," the Queen said, "if you don't make a memorandum of it."

*[Lewis Carroll]*

Taking notes while listening to a lecture, underlining key points in a textbook on developmental theories, writing a shopping list before leaving for the supermarket, leaving one's completed homework by the front door the night before school, and mentally walking through the previous day in order to recall where a jacket might have been left, all reflect *metamemory*. Metamemory is knowledge about memory and is a special case of *metacognition*, which is knowledge about any aspect of human thought. During development, we acquire an understanding that sometimes it is necessary to make an extra effort or do something special in order to remember and that certain factors facilitate or hinder memory. These factors can include person, task, or strategy variables (Flavell and Wellman, 1977). Examples are knowing that there are limits to how much can be remembered (person variable), that recognition is easier than recall (task variable), and that verbal rehearsal aids recall (strategy variable). Thus, children become amateur psychologists.

It appears that preschoolers sometimes realize that simply looking at something does not ensure that it will be remembered. They know they must perform memory-related activities. In one study (Acredolo, Pick, and Olsen, 1975), the experimenter took a 4-year-old on a walk and, during the walk, dropped her keys and picked them up. Later, the child was asked to find the place where the keys had been dropped.

Children made more accurate responses if they had been told before the walk that they would be asked to remember where the keys had been dropped. These children had done something extra to remember the site. Beyond this simple kind of metamemory, preschoolers know little about memory. For example, they claim superhuman memory abilities, such as when they predict they can remember seven items though they can remember only three or four (Flavell, Friedrichs, and Hoyt, 1970).

The more sophisticated facets of metamemory develop later. In a study by Kreutzer, Leonard, and Flavell (1975), children were asked whether it mattered if, after being told a phone number, they made the call immediately or got a drink of water first. Approximately 40 percent of the kindergarteners, but more than 75 percent of the fifth-graders thought it would be better to phone first. Presumably, children become increasingly aware that short-term memory fades rapidly. That strategies are helpful becomes common knowledge during the grade-school years. For example, Kreutzer et al. posed a retrieval problem, in which a child is trying to remember which Christmas he received his dog. Nearly half of the kindergarteners were unable to suggest a way to recall the correct Christmas, but all of the fifth-graders could. The fifth-graders thought of aids such as taking a trip through the mind back to each Christmas and recalling the gifts received or trying to recall other things that happened when the dog was received in the hope that would provide a cue.

Kreutzer, Leonard, and Flavell found that children's thinking about strategies can become rather complex, as the following exchange with a third-grader demonstrates:

> Say the number is 633-8854. Then what I'd do is — say that my number is 633, so I won't have to remember that, really. And then I would think, now I've got to remember 88. Now I'm 8 years old, so I can remember, say, my age two times. And then I say how old my brother is, and how old he was last year. And that's how I'd usually remember that phone number. (Is that how you would most often remember a phone number?) Well, usually I write it down.
>
> *[1975, p. 11]*

An important theoretical question concerns the relationship between knowledge about memory and memory behavior. Intuitively, it seems that there should be a close relationship. If the child thinks that memory is automatic and does not realize that he needs to do anything special to remember, he is not likely to bother to rehearse the material, look for similarities among the objects, and so forth. Thus, the aforementioned production deficiency with respect to strategies may be caused by poorly developed metamemory. In addition, even after the child initiates a strategy, surely he must be sensitive to whether his chosen strategy is working before he can decide to continue or drop that strategy. It appears, however, that the relationship between knowledge about memory and memory performance is not so simple. Knowledge does not necessarily lead to the use of that knowledge. Children are more likely to continue to use a strategy if they attribute their success on the task to using that strategy (Fabricius and Hagen, 1984).

## Comment

Although memory has been the pet topic of the information-processing approach to studying children, the closely related topic of attention has also attracted great interest. Because humans are limited in their capacity to attend to stimuli, they must be selective in what they process, that is, they must attend to relevant information and ignore irrelevant information. Developmentalists report increases in the selectivity of attention but are less sure about increases in capacity. In addition, children increase their knowledge about attention, for example, that capacity is limited and that some attentional strategies are better than others (Miller, 1985).

## Representation

The research on memory we have described makes it clear that representational processes are closely tied to memory processes. *Representation* refers to the mental form in which information is cast. The child stores representations of external objects and events and then retrieves them when necessary. Knowledge can be represented in several ways, namely, words or sentences, actions, images, and abstract propositions (amodal "ideas" underlying statements). For the developmentalist, the issue is whether there are age-related changes in the ability and tendency to use these various types of representations. It is likely that 2-, 5-, and 10-year-olds differ in whether they represent a bicycle with the word "bicycle," a visual image of a bicycle, a nonverbal image of how it feels when riding a bicycle, or a set of propositions about the nature of bicycles.

Perhaps because adults rely heavily on language to represent knowledge, psychologists egocentrically have focused on how objects or events are verbally encoded and interpreted within a semantic network—the meaning system of language. (Because this research typically has used memory tasks, the results with children were summarized in the previous section.) With increasing age, children are more likely to rehearse verbally and make inferences about sentences based on an analysis of their meaning. This integration of language and thought is expressed by the term *semantic memory*—the storage of information represented in the language system (Tulving, 1972). In contrast, *episodic memory* refers to the memory of a personally experienced specific event in time and space, for example, what one did last Saturday night. It should be noted that psychologists disagree whether the episodic–semantic distinction is a useful one and whether semantic memory should be restricted to information expressed in language or should include all our general knowledge about the world stored in long-term memory.

Recently, psychologists have taken seriously the notion that people of any age, but especially infants and young children, may use nonverbal representations, such as visual images. These images are not necessarily static photographs of the world. They may be constructed on the spot, as needed, and may be distortions of the real objects they represent. Kosslyn (1978a) has proposed that people use imagery if they are asked a question about an object and the relevant information is not "filed" with respect to that particular object. Suppose we ask, "Do Volkswagen Beetles have vent wings (little triangular windows near the front of the door)?" Most people report that they have to conjure up an image of the car before they can answer the question. In contrast, "Do Chevrolet Novas have wheels?" does not require imagery to produce a correct answer. The adult deduces that since a Nova is a car and cars have wheels, Novas have wheels. Kosslyn predicts that since children have less information "on file" and are less skilled at making deductions, they rely heavily on imagery, but do so less with increasing experience and maturity. There is some evidence for this hypothesis (Kosslyn, 1978b).

An example of how children might use representations in problem solving comes from a study by Trabasso, Riley, and Wilson (1975) on transitivity of length. In this Piagetian task, the child is first told the premises concerning length (A is taller than B, B is taller than C, and so on). Then he must make inferences about the relative lengths of nonadjacent pairs (for example, B and D). Trabasso et al. argue that children solve length-seriation problems by representing the sticks in memory in an array ordered from tallest to shortest. The child need only locate the two sticks in question and choose the taller one. Thus, being asked about the height of two adjacent sticks, similar in length, should lead to a slower reaction time than would being questioned about two sticks clearly separated by other sticks. Trabasso et al. predicted that the further apart the sticks of interest in the line of sticks, the shorter the reaction time. Their predictions were supported at all ages tested (6, 9, and adult). Their hypothesis, that reasoning in seriation tasks utilizes linearly ordered arrays, contrasts with Piaget's explanation, that logical inference is necessary for solving the problem. Since there are alternative interpretations of Trabasso's studies of transitivity (Breslow, 1981), the main point here is simply to show how visual representation could be involved in thinking.

Children can also represent much larger arrays. It appears that the representation of visual space has to be developed. For example, young children had great difficulty using a set of pushbuttons to move a robot turtle from one point of the room to another (Gregg, 1978). Without training, the child was unable to map the appropriate buttons to the appropriate movements for the turtle, keeping in mind its particular orientation with respect to himself (the turtle's front, back, or side to him) and other objects in the room. Children do, however, have an accurate spatial representation in less demanding situations. Even young schoolchildren have reasonably accurate "cognitive maps" of their classroom, home, or other familiar places (for example, Hardwick, McIntyre, and Pick, 1976; Siegel and Schadler, 1977).

One type of representation of special interest to developmentalists is *scripts*, which were conceived of by information-processing psychologists studying adults (Minsky, 1975; Schank and Abelson, 1977). Scripts are coherent conceptual frameworks about a series of events that occur in a consistent temporal order and are based on experience with objects or events in daily life. These scripts lead the person to expect that certain events will occur in a particular order. They also allow the person to understand and interpret both old and new objects and events. As Nelson defines it, a script "(1) contains certain basic and obligatory events in sequence, (2) predicts open slots for options, objects and events and what they may contain, and (3) designates appropriate roles and actors" (1978, pp. 256–257). Nelson found that even young children develop scripts based on the order of events in familiar situations. To illustrate, a child might have a script for eating at a fastfood hamburger restaurant:

> I walk in there and I, I, I ask my daddy and then the daddy ask the lady and the lady gets it. One small coke, one cheeseburger. . . . They want to eat here so they don't need a tray. Then we go find a table. I eat it all up. All. And throw the . . . paper . . . the cheeseburgers in the garbage can. . . . Goodbye. Goodbye. Jump in the car. . . . Vroom! Vroom! Goodbye.
>
> *[1978, p. 260]*

Three features of this approach are noteworthy. First, both linguistic representation and nonverbal imagery of objects and events are likely to form these schemes or scripts. Thus, scripts are less verbal and less static than representations in semantic networks, which emphasize information about the meanings of words and concepts. Second, the script approach seems to correspond more closely than many of the other approaches we have considered to the way children represent complex events of their day-to-day lives. Third, the approach is immediately applicable to the social world of people and events. For these reasons, it is an interesting alternative to the approaches based more strictly on the computer metaphor.

This section has described several different types of representation: representations of single objects or events, complex images of a set of stimuli, networks of representations such as semantic networks of words or propositions, and scripted representations of a sequence of events in time and space. A distinction that cuts across these types of representations is whether we represent differently information that permits us to *know how* to do something (procedural knowledge) and information that allows us to *know that* something is true (declarative knowledge). For example, knowing how to subtract may be represented differently than knowing that first-grade teachers smile when children subtract correctly.

We have focused on the nature of representation rather than on how representations are organized in long-term memory. The latter issue is critical, however, for a satisfactory account of the development of representation. Two questions asked of adults by Collins and Quillian (1969) illustrate the problem of storage: "Is a canary yellow?" and "Does a canary have skin?" Adults take longer to answer the second question than the first. There must be differences in how the relevant information is stored in the two cases. Do children organize their representations in the same way as adults? Developmentalists have only recently begun to tackle this difficult question. The dinosaur study described earlier is one example of that effort.

## Problem Solving

Information-processing psychologists are interested in how people solve problems. How do people use stored representations to analyze a problem and seek a solution? And how is adult problem solving developed? We look at two approaches to these questions.

Siegler (1978) has examined the rules children use to solve problems about many physical phenomena studied by Piaget. A good example is Inhelder and Piaget's balance-scale (teeter-totter) problem. On each arm of Siegler's scale are four equally spaced pegs on which weights can be placed. The child is to predict which side, if either, will go down. Two pieces of information are relevant: the number of weights (all of equal weight) on each side and their distance from the midpoint (fulcrum). Siegler identified four rules.

1. The child considers only the number of weights, so he predicts that the side with the most weights will go down.

2. The child considers only the number of weights, unless they are equal on the two sides; then he also takes the distance into account.

3. The child examines both weight and distance, but does not know what to predict when one side has greater distance and the other side has more weights.

4. The child can assess the exact contribution of both weight and distance by multiplying the number of weights on each peg by that peg's ordinal distance from the fulcrum. (The ordinal position can be used because the pegs are an equal distance apart. The fourth peg from the midpoint is four times as far away as the first one.) By comparing the outcome of this computation for the two sides, the child can predict which side will go down.

Siegler could determine which rule a child was using by systematically varying the number of weights and their distance in a series of problems. Each rule would lead to a characteristic pattern of correct and incorrect predictions over the series of problems. This study is an example of the error-analysis method mentioned earlier. Consider, for example, a "conflict-weight problem," in which there is more weight on one side, but the weights are more distant on the other side. The configuration is such that the side with more weights goes down. The child using rule 1 or 2 always correctly predicts that the side with more weights will go down. Children using rule 3, however, are correct only about one third of the time, because they simply guess. They know that both distance and number of weights are important but cannot determine the exact contribution of each. Notice that the children's errors are as informative as their correct answers. The results were that the four rule models accurately described the pattern of predictions over the various types of trials of 89 percent of the children aged 5, 9, 13, and 17. Furthermore, as expected, the older children used more sophisticated rules than did the younger children. Siegler has conducted similar analyses on many other tasks, including conservation, projection of shadows, probability, speed, and mathematical calculations.

For several years Klahr, often in collaboration with Wallace, has been developing computer programs to simulate problem solving in children. He has examined class inclusion, conservation, transitivity, counting, balancing weights, as well as other concepts. Klahr has sought the "programmable Piaget" (Quillian, Wortman, and Baylor, 1964). The flavor of Klahr's approach can be conveyed by tracing the way that Siegler's four rules used to solve the balance-scale problem are translated into a computer program. A first step is to translate the four rules into the flow diagram in Figure 4.3. This diagram shows the steps involved in applying each rule. "Yes" and "No" answers lead to

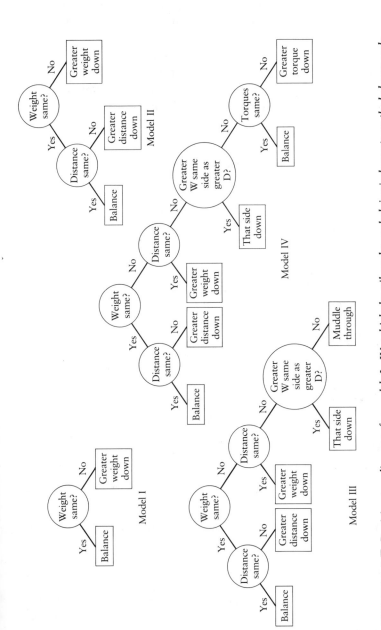

**FIGURE 4-3** ■ *Decision tree diagrams for models I–IV, which describe rules underlying judgments on the balance-scale task. Torque = downward force. D = distance. W = weight. [From "The Representation of Children's Knowledge," by David Klahr and Robert S. Siegler, in Advances in Child Development and Behavior, vol. 12, edited by H. W. Reese and L. P. Lipsitt. Copyright © 1978. Reproduced by permission of Academic Press, Inc., and the authors.]*

different events. Constructing a flow diagram is an intermediary step between rules stated in everyday language and rules stated in a production system in a language that can be fed into a computer. Figure 4.4 describes, in computer language, the production system for the four rules. Several terms must be explained at this point. Models I to IV correspond to the four rules described. A *production system* is a set of productions stored in long-term memory. *Productions* are condition –

```
Model I
    P1:((Same W) --> (Say "balance"))
    P2:((Side X more W) --> (Say "X down"))

Model II
    P1:((Same W) --> (Say "balance"))
    P2:((Side X more W) --> (Say "X down"))
    P3:((Same W) (Side X more D) --> (Say "X down"))

Model III
    P1:((Same W) --> (Say "balance"))
    P2:((Side X more W) --> (Say "X down"))
    P3:((Same W) (Side X more D) --> (Say "X down"))
    P4:((Side X more W) (Side X less D) --> muddle through)
    P5:((Side X more W) (Side X more D) --> (Say "X down"))

Model IV
    P1:((Same W) --> (Say "balance"))
    P2:((Side X more W) --> (Say "X down"))
    P3:((Same W) (Side X more D) --> (Say "X down"))
    P4':((Side X more W) (Side X less D) --> (get Torques))
    P5:((Side X more W) (Side X more D) --> (Say "X down"))
    P6:((Same Torque) --> (Say "balance"))
    P7:((Side X more Torque) --> (say "X down"))
```

|  | Productions | Transitional requirements Operators |
|---|---|---|
| I -> II | add P3 | add distance encoding and comparison |
| II -> III | add P4, P5 |  |
| III -> IV | modify P4; add P6, P7 | add torque computation and comparison |

**FIGURE 4-4** ■ *Production-system (P) representations for models I – IV, which describe rules underlying judgments on the balance-scale task. Written in a special language called PSG. Torque = downward force. D = distance. W = weight. [From "The Representation of Children's Knowledge," by David Klahr and Robert S. Siegler, in* Advances in Child Development and Behavior, *vol. 12, edited by H. W. Reese and L. P. Lipsitt. Copyright © 1978. Reproduced by permission of Academic Press, Inc., and the authors.]*

action rules for changing the set of information currently activated in the cognitive system. Productions take the following form: "If X is present, Y occurs." For example, in production 1 (P1), if the number of weights is the same, the child says that they balance. Thus, there is recognition (X is present) and then action (Y occurs). Recognition occurs if the conditions are satisfied, that is, if there is a match. If the conditions are not satisfied, that production does not "fire." If two productions are satisfied, then some conflict-resolution principle must decide which production should fire. As condition–action rules are applied for several cycles, they transform the initial knowledge state regarding the task into its final state by adding, deleting, or changing the elements of the state. As the production system goes through these cycles, it leaves a record, or "trace," of what it knew and did at each step. (Looking ahead to page 310, Figure 4.5 is a trace for one child.)

Let us look more closely at one of the models in Figure 4.4. Recall that in model II the distance is considered only if the weights are equal. Model II is a production system containing three productions (condition–action rules). The "condition" part of the condition–action rule refers to tests for the sameness or difference in weight or distance. The "action" part after the arrow in Figure 4.4 refers to a behavioral response. Thus, in P1 if the number of weights is the same on both sides (condition), the child says they will balance (action). P2 says that if side X has more weights than side W, then side X will go down. Finally, in P3 if the number of weights on each side is the same, but there is more distance on side X than the other side, then the child predicts that X will go down. At the bottom of Figure 4.4 is a list of what changes in the set of productions occur when the child moves from one model to the next during development.

The formal representation of production systems may make its greatest contribution by describing the behavior of individual children. Figure 4.5 shows how the production system runs for a 7-year-old child, Jan. For our purposes, we need not be concerned with most of the notations; the interested reader is referred to Klahr and Siegler (1978) for a detailed account. The important sections are the descriptions of the state of "working memory" (currently available information) after each cycle of applying the production system. For example, as cycle 2 begins, working memory (WM) has four elements: more distance on the right arm, more weights on the left arm, task is to predict, and criterion is weight. During recognition tests, P2 and P4

```
          (0003|0020)
Cycle 1
WM: ((PREDICT) (CRITERION WEIGHT))

Fire P8: ((PREDICT) (<DIMENSION.1>) ABS --> ATTEND)
     Output from ATTEND (input to WM) ::> (weight more left)(distance more right)

Cycle 2
WM: ((DISTANCE MORE RIGHT) (WEIGHT MORE LEFT) (PREDICT) (CRITERION WEIGHT) )
    CONFLICT.SET: (P2 P4)
Fire P4: ((PREDICT) (WEIGHT MORE) (DISTANCE MORE) --> FIND.BIG)
     Output from FIND.BIG (input to WM) ::> (distance big right)(weight big left)

Cycle 3
WM: ((WEIGHT BIG LEFT) (DISTANCE BIG RIGHT) (PREDICT) (WEIGHT MORE LEFT)
    (DISTANCE MORE RIGHT) (CRITERION WEIGHT))
    CONFLICT.SET: (P2 P4 P5 P6 P7)
    CONFLICT.SET: (P4 P5) AFTER SPECIAL.CASE.ORDER
    CONFLICT.SET: (P5) AFTER WM.ORDER
Fire P5: ((PREDICT) (CRITERION <DIMENSION.1>)(<DIMENSION.1> BIG <SIDE.1>)
         (<DIMENSION.2> BIG <SIDE.2.) --> (MADE **) (EXPECT <SIDE.1> DOWN) SAY.D)

********** LEFT down

Cycle 4
WM: ((EXPECT LEFT DOWN) (MADE (PREDICT)) (CRITERION WEIGHT) (WEIGHT BIG LEFT)
    (DISTANCE BIG RIGHT) (WEIGHT MORE LEFT) (DISTANCE MORE RIGHT))
Fire E1: ((EXPECT) --> LOOK)
     Output from LOOK (input to WM) ::> (see right down)

Cycle 5
WM: ((SEE RIGHT DOWN) (EXPECT LEFT DOWN) (MADE (PREDICT)) (CRITERION WEIGHT)
    (WEIGHT BIG LEFT) (DISTANCE BIG RIGHT) (WEIGHT MORE LEFT) (DISTANCE MORE RIGHT))
    CONFLICT.SET: (E1,E3)
Fire E3: ((EXPECT <SIDE.1> <DIRECTION>)
         (SEE <SIDE.1> <DIRECTION>) ABS (SEE) --> (DID **) (SEE ===> SAW)
(RESULT WRONG))

Cycle 6
WM: ((RESULT WRONG) (DID (EXPECT LEFT DOWN)) (SAW RIGHT DOWN) (MADE (PREDICT))
    (CRITERION WEIGHT) (WEIGHT BIG LEFT) (DISTANCE BIG RIGHT) (WEIGHT MORE LEFT)
    (DISTANCE MORE RIGHT))
Fire SW2: ((RESULT WRONG) (CRITERION WEIGHT) --> (OLD **) (WEIGHT ===> DISTANCE))

Cycle 7
WM: ((OLD (RESULT WRONG)) (CRITERION DISTANCE) (DID (EXPECT LEFT DOWN))
    (SAW RIGHT DOWN) (MADE (PREDICT)) (WEIGHT BIG LEFT) (DISTANCE BIG RIGHT)
    (WEIGHT MORE LEFT) (DISTANCE MORE RIGHT))
```

**FIGURE 4-5** ■ *Trace of 7-year-old Jan's production system (P) running on a conflict-distance problem in the balance-scale task. ABS = absent. WM = working memory. E = problem number. [From "The Representation of Children's Knowledge," by David Klahr and Robert S. Siegler, in* Advances in Child Development and Behavior, *vol. 12, edited by H. W. Reese and L. P. Lipsitt. Copyright © 1978. Reproduced by permission of Academic Press, Inc., and the authors.]*

(productions 2 and 4 in the particular model Jan uses) match (recognize) these elements, and since P4 happens to be a special case of P2, P4 fires. The output directs the system to find what is big (FIND BIG). After doing so, the production system moves on to cycle 3. The result of cycle 2 appears at the beginning of cycle 3, and the process continues. Notice that on some cycles the system recognizes conflict between two productions and attempts to resolve the conflict.

As if this model were not already complicated enough, there is additional information written into the model, such as the general problem-solving abilities and semantic knowledge that the child brings to the task at each developmental level. Also, the model becomes more complex as the child changes his strategies during the task as a result of training. Psychologists who do computer simulation have learned to live with this complexity for the sake of a complete and specific theory.

A formal model produces a detailed, explicit, moment-by-moment description of how the child solves a problem. Ideally, it contains all relevant information about the child and the task. The Klahr and Siegler work is perhaps the best example of the task-analysis approach described in the general orientation section. Note that one strength of this description is that it includes not only the formal structure of the way the child solves the problem, but also the demands of the experimental situation, for example, the nature of the feedback and the way the scale is presented. Since both the cognitive state and the situation affect performance, especially in children, it is important that they both be specified in any theory of problem solving.

The simple set of rules revealed by Siegler is an appealing model of development, yet this simplicity has been a focus of criticism. It has been suggested (Strauss and Levin, 1981) that these simple rules emerge because Siegler's methodology restricts children to these rules. Presenting the same task in an open-ended, rather than forced-choice, manner may produce more complex reasoning.

Although the research programs of Klahr and Siegler were chosen to illustrate the integration of the information-processing and Piagetian approaches with respect to problem solving, the research effort is much broader than that described here. There also are computer simulations of areas such as children's mathematical thinking (Greeno, Riley, and Gelman, 1984) and language acquisition (Hill, 1983). In addition, as described in the earlier chapter on Piaget, the neo-Piagetians have adopted information-processing constructs. It is not yet clear whether these attempts will strengthen Piaget's theory by making it more specific and gearing it more to performance or unearth so many weaknesses in Piaget's theory that it will gradually be abandoned in favor of the information-processing approach.

## Intelligence

Robert Sternberg's theory is an attempt to combine the best aspects of three frameworks. His focus on cognitive processes, capacity, and the time course of thinking, along with his careful task analyses, are in the tradition of the information-processing approach. The concern with individual differences reflects the psychometric (IQ testing, for example) approach. Finally, his interest in cognitive development and logical operations shows the influence of Piaget.

Sternberg (1985) characterizes intelligence as a set of components — elementary information processes that operate on internal representations of objects, events, or symbols. There are three types of components: *knowledge-acquisition components* (described later), *performance components*, and *metacomponents*. When the child does not have the knowledge needed to solve the problem, knowledge-acquisition components obtain relevant information. The metacomponents, which are used in planning and decision making in task performance, then combine this new information with previous knowledge to construct an appropriate problem-solving strategy from among the performance components. The performance components then actually solve the problem. Thus, the metacomponents, much like the control processes and metacognitive processes described earlier, orchestrate the other two components into goal-directed behavior. Metacomponents perform duties such as deciding how to best allocate mental capacity to the other components during the limited time for problem solving, keeping track of what one has done, and deciding how to respond to feedback. If the child already has the understanding required for solving the problem, then only the metacomponents and performance components come into play.

As an example of the performance components, consider the following analogy problem used by Sternberg (1979): N.J.:N.Y.::N.H.:(a.R.I., b.N.D.). The correct answer is R.I. The seven performance components for these types of problems include the following. The first involves *encoding*, identifying various attributes of the first two terms. For example, N.J. might be encoded as New Jersey and N.Y. as New York. Second, *inferring* specifies the relation between the first and second term; for example, both are abbreviations, are adjacent states, and begin with N. Third, in *mapping* the person compares the encoded attributes of the first and third terms; for example, both are states and begin with N. Fourth, *application* derives a relation between the third term and one of the possible answers that is analogous to the relation between the first and second terms. Fifth, *comparison* involves comparing and contrasting the possible answers. Sixth, *justification* entails comparing the chosen answer with one's notion of the ideal answer to decide whether the chosen option is good enough. And seventh is *responding*.

Although school-age children and adults use the same performance components to solve analogy problems, they differ in their allocation of cognitive resources to the various performance components (Sternberg and Rifkin, 1979). For example, adults spend more time encoding the terms than they spend in the subsequent steps. Seven-year-olds do the opposite. High-IQ children are more like adults in this respect.

The knowledge-acquisition components appear to provide a striking difference between average and intellectually gifted children. Gifted children are particularly adept at selective encoding (differentiating relevant and irrelevant information), selective combination (integrating information in a meaningful way), and selective comparison (relating newly encoded information to knowledge the child already has). More than average individuals, gifted persons are able to use these skills to deal with novel situations in insightful, original ways. Sternberg (1986) supported this claim in a study with insight problems such as this one:

> You have black socks and blue socks in a drawer, mixed in a ratio of 4 to 5. Because it is dark, you are unable to see the colors of the socks that you take out of the drawer. How many socks do you have to take out of the drawer to be assured of having a pair of socks of the same color?
>
> *(p. 213)*

Selective encoding is necessary for detecting that the ratio of the socks is irrelevant. Regardless of the ratio, taking out three socks would insure that a pair of socks was obtained.

The other two knowledge-acquisition components can be illustrated by examples of insight among famous scientists. Selective combination was crucial to Darwin's ability to combine facts, known to him for years, into a coherent framework that became his theory of evolution. Insight based on selective comparison can be seen in the chemist Kekulé's dream about a snake curling back on itself and catching its tail. Upon awakening he realized that this image was a metaphor for the structure of the benzene ring.

With respect to development, all three types of components become more available, accessible, and easily executed. In an older child or an expert, the increasing automaticity of the components in a particular domain frees capacity for other tasks. Sternberg proposes that retarded children have poor automaticity. If they are not able to automatize subskills such as recognizing letters or words, the higher-order skills needed for smooth reading will be very slow to develop. Probably the most important developmental change lies in the metacomponents, particularly in the acquisition of strategies for using one's information-processing skills. For example, inadequate metacomponents can be seen when a young child or a retarded child chooses the wrong performance and knowledge-acquisition components for his strategies or does not shift to an alternate strategy if the chosen one is not successful.

Sternberg calls his theory a "triarchic theory of intelligence" because it includes three subtheories. The "componential" subtheory refers to the components of intelligence described earlier. The "experiential subtheory" involves the abilities, discussed earlier, to deal with novel demands and to automatize information processing. The "contextual" subtheory emphasizes the cultural context of thinking. That is, intelligent behavior is social and practical behavior; it is adaptive in particular real-world environments and is influenced by social-cultural forces. For example, an intelligent person actively selects an environment that draws on her strengths or helps her to compensate for her weaknesses. Sternberg tests for everyday intelligence for example, by asking subjects to identify real couples and fake couples in photographs or by assessing their knowledge about career management. This broad, complex theory of intelligence has developed far from its start in Sternberg's seventh-grade science project: constructing an IQ test that has been referred to as the "less-than-widely-used Sternberg Test of Mental Abilities" (*American Psychologist*, 1982, p. 74).

## Comment

It is time to summarize these sections on memory, representation, problem solving and intelligence. Although model building in developmental psychology is far behind that in adult psychology, progress has been made. An adequate developmental model must do the following:

1. Account for both verbal and nonverbal encoding.

2. Express, through depth-of-processing or "stage" notions (sensory register, short-term store, long-term store), the operation of both involuntary and deliberate memory.

3. Specify the workings of the control processes.

4. Describe the interplay between memory and the knowledge system with its rules and organization.

5. Account for the development of these four aspects of the information-processing system.

The information-processing approach has contributed several new languages for representing the thinking of adults and children. As Siegler (1986) notes, although any type of information can be described by any of the four languages, each language is most appropriate for certain types of information. Semantic networks are most useful for modeling declarative knowledge (general world knowledge and basic concepts). Production systems and flow diagrams usually model procedural knowledge (how to play tennis, solve balance-scale problems, or do math problems). Finally, scripts are most useful for representing abstract-event sequences such as everyday social events.

## MECHANISMS OF DEVELOPMENT

Klahr and Wallace have voiced the research priorities of the field of information processing in children: "A theory of transition can be no better than the associated theory of what it is that is undergoing that transition" (1976, p. 14). Stated differently, "One never sees transitions, only by-products of transitions; so the empirical snapshots provide a major source of support for theories of transition" (Klahr, 1984, p. 106). Thus, the first task is to describe carefully each step in the acquisition of a concept, such as each of the four models in Figure 4.4. Only then is it possible to identify the sort of mechanisms that might cause the change. Most of the research programs outlined in the previous section have followed this sequence. At first, researchers compared processing at different ages. Some research programs are still at this descriptive level, while others have begun to look at mechanisms of development.

Investigators have identified both general and specific sources of changes in processing. Two general sources of change are the acquisition of particular cognitive skills and increases in capacity or rate of processing. Cognitive skills that may bring about changes in the way information is processed include the child's growing knowledge about various aspects of the physical and social world, knowledge about memory and other mental phenomena, representational abilities, and higher-order cognitive operations such as those suggested by Piaget. An 8-year-old faced with memorizing the multiplication tables—the ultimate terror of the third grade—has certain aids unavailable to a 5-year-old. She possesses the underlying mental operations, such as the necessary "groupings" in Piaget's theory, that provide a meaningful framework in which to fit the rote memorizing. Also she has more experience with abstract concepts, quantities of objects, addition, and so forth, in her daily life. Finally, as she studies the tables, she can rehearse the items, look for relationships in the materials ($6 \times 8 = 8 \times 6$), perhaps monitor her own progress through self-testing, and so on.

The other proposed general mechanism of development, increases in capacity or rate of processing, is much more ambiguous. It is difficult to differentiate, experimentally, increases in absolute capacity or rate of processing from increases in the efficiency of processing through the skillful use of strategies or the automatizing of mental processes. The more automatic (less effortful) a process, the less capacity it requires. Consequently, capacity is made available for other processes. Increase in either total capacity or in the efficiency of a constant capacity may provide new possibilities for the developing organism (Case, 1985; Pascual-Leone, 1970).

A satisfactory account of developmental change must go beyond these general mechanisms and identify specific mechanisms of change.

Investigators have used two main techniques to study specific mechanisms of development: training studies and self-modifying computer programs. Training studies that have brought about changes in processing suggest that changes in development may come about through certain kinds of experiences. The experiences include encountering conflict between different predictions, becoming more familiar with the task materials, trying out a strategy that works, and acquiring more knowledge about the physical and social world. These experiences lead to new rules or strategies, which in turn lead to better (or at least different) memory, representation, and problem solving. For example, Siegler (1978) found that teaching children what information to encode (both distance and number of weights) enabled them to learn from feedback regarding their predictions on the balance scale and subsequently to adopt new rules for problem solving.

A much smaller group of psychologists has used computer simulation to look at mechanisms of development. Although most computer simulations have simply (or not so simply!) described the behavior of children of various ages, recently there have been attempts to describe how changes in thinking occur. Most of these models have come from studies in which adults learn during a short period of time, the experimental session. However, in principle, similar models could describe developmental changes over longer periods of time (Klahr, 1982).

Klahr (1984) has proposed that learning occurs when children analyze their stored record of previous behavior and its results. This analysis involves such principles as detection of regularity, elimination of redundancy, organization of subsystems according to their similarity and relatedness, and global rather than refined processing in the initial stages of processing. These principles could lead the child to develop new rules for solving the problem, strengthen certain old rules, generalize old rules, and restrict the situations in which an old rule is used (Klahr, in press). More specifically, the child compares several related experiences (sequences of events), extracts a common feature from these events, and generalizes this feature to other related situations (Klahr, 1984). A very simple example is that on many occasions a child might count objects, move them, count them again, and compare the results of the two countings. The type of objects and the type of transformation would vary, but the constancy of the number before and after the transformation would be common to the situation. This rule gradually becomes more general to include, for example, larger numbers. Finally, redundancy is eliminated, for example, by removing the second counting because it is not needed if the objects are only moved. For more complex examples and a fuller account of these principles of change, the reader is referred to Klahr (1984). The essence of these principles is that they reflect the operation of a self-modifying system. The system works on itself to produce change.

Klahr argues that it is crucial to develop specific, explicit, formal accounts of mechanisms of transition, in contrast to vague verbal statements: "For 40 years now, we have had *assimilation* and *accommodation*, the mysterious and shadowy forces of equilibration, the 'Batman and Robin' of the developmental processes. . . . Why is it that after all this time, we know no more about them than when they first sprang upon the scene?" (1982, p. 80) The information-processing approach probably has better theoretical equipment for achieving this goal of *specific* accounts of cognitive change than do other theories.

# POSITION ON DEVELOPMENTAL ISSUES

## Human Nature

In an update of Newton's view that "man is a machine," man now is a computer. (Presumably, children are microcomputers.) In this mechanistic view, we have input, followed by a series of events and finally output. Although the information-processing approach is mechanistic in that it posits input–output machinelike devices, it is organismic in its emphasis on overall organization and on an active organism. The ultimate goal of the information-processing models is to characterize the organization of cognitive processing into a system, not just an aggregate of parts. Information-processing theorists believe this holism is achieved by control processes that organize and direct the varied cognitive components. Most adherents to the information-processing point of view do not, however, posit the tightly knit, organized set of underlying logical mental operations proposed by Piaget.

Like social learning theory, the information-processing approach has been criticized for positing a passive organism (Shaw and Bransford, 1977). However, this criticism is probably unfair to most investigators. This undeserved reputation for positing passivity may come from the flow diagrams, which sometimes seem to portray static structures nudged into activity by intruding arrows. There certainly is nothing inherent in the information-processing approach that would call for a passive organism. It is true that people react to input in what has been called "bottom–up processing"—from the stimulus "up" to the higher levels of the cognitive system. And when processing is automatic, the organism can be characterized as passive. However, there is also "top–down processing" as long-term memory interprets the input, applies rules and strategies, searches for further information in the environment, or even "constructs" information as it makes inferences based on the input and on previous knowledge. Humans are also active in that they are self-modifying cognitive systems. They bring about their own learning and development, with help from experience with the environment, of course. In addition, children become more active cognitively with increasing age as they develop control processes to enhance their memory by rehearsing, making written reminders, and relating new information to old.

## Qualitative Versus Quantitative Development

Information-processing theories allow for both qualitative and quantitative development. Most do not have the emphasis on the qualitative, stagelike development found in Piagetian and Freudian theory, but they do identify more qualitative change than does social learning theory. Examples of qualitative development are the emergence of new strategies for storage or retrieval, rules for problem solving, or modes of representation (for example, verbal representation after language is developed). Quantitative development appears in increases in the number of items remembered, in the amount of information in semantic memory, and in the increasingly efficient application of strategies. There is often interplay between quantitative and qualitative development, as when experience with weights leads to a new rule about balance scales, which then becomes more efficiently and consistently applied to a variety of situations.

## Nature Versus Nurture

Unlike most theories, information-processing theories have had little to say about this issue. There has been more interest in specifying the exact interplay between information from the environment and the state of the processing system at one or several points in time than in unraveling the nature and nurture influences. However, the implicit view seems to be that the two influences interact to produce change. The impact of the environment is obvious as it continually brings input to the cognitive system. On the nature side, examples of important influences are that neurological development increases the efficiency of the transmission of neuronal impulses and that the visual system limits how long information can stay in the visual sensory register. There has not been much interest, however, in studying the role of physical maturation in information processing. It has been suggested that certain ways of processing information are likely to be innate. For example, Klahr and Wallace (1976) suggest that the tendency toward economical, nonredundant, efficient processing is innate. The processing system also may be pretuned to process certain types of stimuli, such as linguistic input.

## What Develops

Stated most generally, cognitive processing develops. It becomes more efficient and organized in its operation and acquires more and more content as the child explores the world. More specifically, children acquire strategies, rules, scripts, representations, deeper levels of processing, or a broader knowledge base, depending on the particular approach. Another way to describe what develops comes from A. L. Brown (1975): "knowing" (development of knowledge about the world), "knowing about knowing" (metacognition), and "knowing how to know" (development of strategies). A major goal of current research is to map out the developmental relationships among these three areas.

## THEORETICAL NATURE OF THE THEORY

Information-processing theories are characterized by the use of models. The computer model as a formal theoretical model or as a loose metaphor has formed the main theme of this chapter. The various information-processing approaches discussed share this computer model but vary in whether they use flow diagrams, tree diagrams, and computer programs or merely use computer language metaphorically to describe laboratory studies of memory, representation, and problem solving. For the first time in this book, we must consider the possibility that models can be used for inductive, deductive, and functional theory building.

Most information-processing psychologists find the computer metaphor useful for conceptualizing laboratory research on basic cognitive processes. Following the traditional role of empirical psychologists, they either collect data from related studies and stay close to the facts (inductive theory building) or, more commonly, go back and forth between data and hypothetical constructs, such as short-term memory (functional theory building). The much smaller group of information-processing psychologists that develops detailed flow diagrams or computer programs follows the functional or deductive mode of theory building. The approach is functional when flow diagrams, tree diagrams, or computer programs are developed, tested in light of the data, corrected, and tested again through many cycles. On the other hand, the approach can become deductive, but in a new and curious way. Once all the psychological assumptions are stated in a formal language — a mathematical, logical, or computer language — the program can be "run" and thereby can generate the implications of, or make deductions from, these assumptions. Thus, a computer program can operate as a deductive theory. The possibilities of this approach are exciting because the computer can make the deductions much faster and more accurately than humans.

## EVALUATION OF THE THEORY

The information-processing approach to development not only dominates current laboratory research on cognition, but also is spreading to other areas. In social development, information-processing notions appear in Bandura's social learning theory and in accounts of the development of moral judgments (Leon, 1980), peer interaction (Dodge, 1986), and social scripts (Nelson, 1986). The study of the comprehension of stories or other texts, often called "discourse processing," has a distinct information-processing flavor. Finally, a number of information-processing psychologists continue to study reading and instructional techniques, with obvious relevance for the education of children.

Despite the growing influence of the information-processing approach to development, the theory is not often scrutinized with respect to its strengths and weaknesses as a developmental theory. The following evaluation considers the information-processing approach both as a developmental model or metaphor and as a method of research on development. The theory's strengths lie in its ability to express the complexity of thought, its specificity concerning performance, and its rigorous methodology. Its weaknesses include the shortcomings of the computer model, problems with accounting for development, and a lack of concern with the natural context of behavior.

## Strengths

### *Ability to Express the Complexity of Thought*

In the previous chapter, social learning theory was criticized for its oversimple account of thinking and learning. In contrast, the information-processing approach allows for a variety of cognitive processes, ranging from the simple detection of a stimulus to the development of complex rules. Furthermore, it attempts to characterize how perception, attention, memory, language, and abstract mental operations might be interrelated. The approach posits an intricate organization of thought in which control processes direct and supervise. For example, children learn to handle large amounts of information by "chunking" it or by relating it to what they already know.

Because both production systems and rules used to solve problems are often written for individual subjects, they can highlight subtle differences in how people of the same age process information. Thus, it is possible to study individual differences in problem solving and tailor instructional materials to fit the individual needs of students (A. L. Brown, 1978).

### *Specificity Concerning Performance*

Perhaps the greatest strength of information-processing theories is that they make specific predictions about the child's behavior from moment to moment, based on a fine-grained analysis of the task and the current state of the child's cognitive system. This statement is especially true for computer-simulation programs, which attempt to specify all assumptions and relevant variables. Psychologists are forced to clear up any muddled theoretical thinking.

Although the Piagetian and the information-processing approaches have much in common, the latter attempts to be more explicit about *how* the child uses his cognitive skills in a given situation. This is a theory of performance, which, as mentioned in Chapter 1, is lacking in Piaget's theory. Information-processing theories describe how attention, memory, strategies, representational processes, and logical operations "connect" with tasks. For example, if the task requires a decision about relative weights, the information-processing approach would specify how the child selects certain information about the objects or the scale, encodes it, and applies rules from long-term memory. Piaget's décalages (asynchronies in applying a concept to different but related tasks or content areas) become less mysterious when investigators analyze the information-processing demands of each task (Baylor and Lemoyne, 1975). It is not surprising that tasks with different information-processing requirements elicit different behaviors.

One outcome of this specificity is that many hypotheses generated by the theory are testable—a trait shared with social learning theory. However, because some information-processing accounts are more specific and closer to observable behavior than others, all are not equally testable. Still, most make clear empirical claims that can be supported or refuted.

### Rigorous Methodology

In comparison with other theories in this book, information-processing theory, along with learning theory, is marked by its stringent and precise experimental methods. As one psychologist comments, "Many of us have become methodological behaviorists in order to become good cognitive psychologists" (Mandler, 1979, p. 281). Laboratory research on basic processing often makes precise measurements of processing time. More molar behavior and larger units of time are also examined under controlled conditions. Computer simulation requires that all relevant information about the task or child be stated in the programs. Gaps, contradictions, and vague statements are not permitted. These strict requirements demanded by computers are not easy to meet.

For developmental research, error analysis has proved to be a particularly powerful assessment procedure. By cleverly designing different types of problems, researchers have discovered two kinds of limitations in young children. One, illustrated by Siegler's balance-scale experiments, is that young children are using simpler, less-complete rules, procedures, or strategies than are older children. The other limitation is different. Children basically are using the correct rule, but they have various "bugs" in the application of the rules, which lead to errors. For instance, after Brown and Burton (1978) used error analysis to detect bugs in students' application of the subtraction procedure, they wrote a computer program appropriately dubbed "Buggy," which taught prospective teachers to detect various bugs in their students' math work. One subtraction bug, for example, involves knowing how to borrow but not borrowing when the top number is zero.

## Weaknesses

The preceding short section on strengths is followed by a much longer section on weaknesses. This imbalance does not necessarily reflect an abundance of weaknesses in the theory. Rather, most of the strengths were mentioned earlier in the chapter, whereas weaknesses have not been mentioned and must now draw our attention.

### Shortcomings of the Computer Model

A basic problem with flow diagrams or computer simulations is that they may be analogous to, but quite different from, human processing. The model may adequately describe human output (behavior), given knowledge of the input, but still differ in important respects from the way people think. For example, a computer program might process the information sequentially, while a child might process all the information simultaneously, but both could arrive at the same decision (output) in the task. Similarly, it is possible for different programs to predict performance equally well. This is one limitation to the generally good testability mentioned earlier. However, Simon responds that "there may be several ways to skin a cat, but probably not dozens of ways. Hence if *one* way (not admitting magical processes) is found, it may be similar to the way in which cats are actually skinned" (1972, pp. 20–21). To help avoid the problem, Simon has proposed that models meet certain criteria. They should be consistent with what we know about the physiology of the nervous system and about behavior in tasks other than the one examined. They should also be sufficient to produce the behavior of interest, and definite and concrete. Still, it can be difficult to judge the psychological validity of a model that meets these requirements.

The use of information-processing models has been very productive but, like all models, is subject to abuse. Information-processing psychologists have perhaps been overenthusiastic in adopting models. In particular, memory metaphors, which are much less formal and complete than flow diagrams and computer models, abound in the literature. Roediger (1979) points out that memory metaphors usually are spatial metaphors, implying that we "search" our mental space for objects stored in physical space. There almost seems to be a "homunculus" (little man) who rifles through the files of memory until he finds that necessary paper. (Some models, however, avoid the homunculus problem by specifying a set of low-level processes that underlie executivelike behaviors.) In these files or in semantic networks, concepts are stored at different "distances" from each other. Even the levels-of-processing approach has us wandering deeper and deeper into the dark recesses of the mind. Examples of metaphors in Roediger's list include a workbench, a pushdown stack (of clean plates in a restaurant), an acid bath, a dictionary, and a subway map. In a spoof of memory models, Hintzman (1974) likened memory to a "cow's belly." Information (like food) is transferred from the "short-term stomach" to the "long-term stomach." In this way, we "ruminate" over ideas and "digest" information.

Memory metaphors are suggested by the technology of the times, beginning with Plato's notion that memory is like the impression of a seal on a wax tablet, which in his time was a method of storing information. Much later we find the gramophone, switchboard, tape recorder, computer, and holograph used as metaphors. It has even been suggested (Langlois, Cooper, and Woodson, 1985) that a bank automatic teller machine might be an appropriate metaphor for a child. It processes information, is somewhat interactive, and usually follows instructions but sometimes has a mind of its own! What metaphors will future technology bring? Today's computer metaphor may eventually seem as naive as Plato's wax tablet.

The use of such metaphors is not necessarily bad. They explain abstract cognitive structures and processes in terms of concrete objects already familiar to people. Furthermore, they have helped psychologists view cognition from a new perspective and have suggested new research. However, we should use them with caution because they are a potentially dangerous tool. As George Eliot cautioned: "We all of us, grave or light, get our thoughts entangled in metaphors, and act fatally on the strength of them." First, these metaphors, and even the more formal models, usually have excess meaning that was not intended. Thus, we may erroneously think of memory as passive, spatially organized, unaffected by emotion, and unrelated to other cognitive processes. For example, because flow diagrams are necessarily spatial representations, they may be interpreted in spatial terms. It must be kept in mind that a model is similar *only in certain ways* to the phenomenon to which it is applied.

Second, adopting a particular model may seriously limit our thinking. Once psychologists began to express memory as a series of discrete steps (boxes in a flow diagram), it took several years before the less discrete, more gradual levels-of-processing approach could be seriously proposed.

One problem specific to the computer-simulation models has to do with computer techniques. Undoubtedly the greatest impediment to the acceptance of this approach is the "language barrier." Although most psychologists use computers, few are truly bilingual, speaking both their native language and one of the computer languages used by the simulators. It can take hours for the neophyte to wade through the detailed description in computer language of a 30-minute experimental session with one child. Part of the problem is that in order to be complete and to run successfully, the program must contain much that is psychologically trivial, such as which block is picked up first. Although the underlying explanation of the behavior may be elegantly simple, the superficial complexity may alienate many psychologists potentially sympathetic to the computer-simulation approach. As psychologists become even more familiar with computers, this problem may lessen.

Aside from the problem of comprehending computer programs, however, is the problem of writing them. Even people skilled in writing simulations are faced with a time-consuming, often tedious task. One problem is that the obvious must be included in the program. An example (cited by Kendler, 1987) is a college campus computer dating program that contained only information about the students' interests and attitudes. The results were not considered successful by a brother and sister who were paired together. No one thought to instruct the computer that siblings should not be paired.

Another problem with computer models is that they tend to be highly specific, precise models of very limited, specific behaviors. Because they must consider all relevant variables, it is difficult to develop more general models that can run successfully.

## Problems with Accounting for Development

The information-processing approach has advanced our understanding of adult cognitive systems. How successfully has it addressed developmental issues? The introductory chapter proposed three tasks for a developmental theory: (1) to *describe* changes *within* one or several areas of behavior, (2) to *describe* changes in the relationships *among* several areas of behavior, and (3) to *explain* the course of development that has been described. With respect to the first task, the information-processing approach rates high marks for its careful, refined descriptions of the memory system at various cognitive levels. An exception is that there is little work on information processing in adolescents or infants and toddlers. This relative neglect of infancy is unfortunate because, to be a viable developmental theory, the information-processing approach must describe preverbal, cognitively immature humans. It is important, for example, to know what kinds of nonverbal representations infants are capable of and why their recognition memory is so advanced. An important question for developmentalists is how these nonverbal representational systems and the later verbal representational systems are related developmentally.

With respect to the second task—describing relationships among simultaneous changes in various areas—the information-processing approach has sketched out some of the relations among memory, language, higher cognitive processes, and perception in a limited way. These broad outlines require much filling in over the next few years. The most progress has come in the area of language and thought, for example, story comprehension, verbal rehearsal, and semantic memory. Less is known about nonverbal, or at least less verbal, thought, for example, the representation and memory of space and actions.

The largest gap in fulfilling these first two tasks is the paucity of knowledge about the links between cognition and emotions, motivation, and social development. In principle, there is no reason why this should be so. For example, information about people could be processed like nonsocial information. Important questions about the relationship between cognitive and socioemotional variables include the following: How does a child's emotional state affect his learning at various ages? Are encoding and retrieval strategies applied to social as well as physical objects and events? Does acquiring social experience and developing social scripts (Schank and Abelson, 1977) provide a framework for attending to, encoding, interpreting, and storing social events? Freud observed rampant memory distortions and repressions of childhood experiences, but information-processing theorists have virtually ignored these. A notable exception is recent work on distortions in the eyewitness testimony of adults and children. Focusing on scientific concepts may be a reasonable initial strategy for a young theory, but this limitation should be recognized and eventually corrected. Fortunately, there is a growing interest in the intersect of information processing and social psychology (Nelson, 1978).

The third task — explaining development — poses difficulties for the information-processing approach, as it has for each of the theories already examined. Important forces of change have been identified, including broader encoding, strategy construction, an increasingly complex knowledge base, automatization of skills, detection of regularities, generalization, metacomponential processes, and elimination of redundancy. Still, developmental changes in these mechanisms themselves and accounts of exactly how the mechanisms operate to effect change are not well specified. For example, it is known that young children have strategy-production deficiencies that disappear during the middle school years, but the causes of this production deficiency and its disappearance still elude investigators. Likewise, it is clear that strategies of problem solving become more sophisticated, but there is little information concerning the forces that propel this development. Although the developments of control processes and improved encoding appear to be important achievements for memory and problem solving, the information-processing approach has not yet explained how these developments come about.

Other problems also remain to be solved. Why are some dimensions, such as number of weights, easier for young children to encode than other dimensions, such as distance of the weights from the fulcrum? In natural settings, what causes children to encode previously ignored dimensions? Finally, it is not yet clear exactly how a complex, well-organized knowledge base enhances recall. The main problem is that the evidence is primarily correlational. An advanced knowledge base is associated with improved recall, but the causal relationship is not clear. An advanced knowledge base may lead to a strategy such as chunking, to increased speed of access in semantic memory, to greater understanding of the goal of the task or what information should be attended to because of contextual information, or to increased motivation. Thus, the knowledge base is a global variable that needs to be specified further.

A central theoretical issue arising from the research on the knowledge base is whether this change within the child is the same as the novice-to-expert shift in adults. That is, is developmental change in knowledge equivalent to analogous change in an adult as he becomes more knowledgeable about an area? A child, in a sense, is a "universal novice" (Brown and DeLoache, 1978), lacking knowledge in more areas than adults do. Adults, however, are likely to have more sophisticated strategies of learning that allow them to move from the novice to the expert stage more quickly and to generalize new knowledge to other situations.

Because information processing is the "new kid on the block" with respect to developmental theories, it is too early to judge its ultimate success as an explanatory theory. Because of its focus on task analysis and because of its demands for specificity, clarity, and fine-grained analysis in the account of behavior, it possesses considerable promise. On the other hand, its view of development is too closely tied to its view of change in adults. As in social learning theory, attempts to explain development seem to proceed on the assumption that change over weeks and months follows the same principles as change over minutes within an experimental session. This assumption may or may not be warranted. In many cases, when adults "learn" in an experimental session, they are simply learning to make efficient use of what they already know. For example, when learning to play chess, the adult may grasp the rules by generalizing from other games he knows and rearranging this previous knowledge to fit chess. In contrast, much change in children is due to the acquisition of *new* rules, concepts, or cognitive skills, rather than the rearrangement of old ones. Before the child can learn chess, he must develop the ability to mentally move the pieces according to certain rules, to form a cognitive map of the location of pieces on the board, and so on. It is not clear that studying change in adults would elucidate these kinds of changes in children.

A related problem is that it is difficult to relate the short-term changes examined by information-processing psychologists to the long-term, stagelike qualitative changes postulated by Piaget. It may be that these seemingly revolutionary changes from stage to stage can be reduced to short-term quantitative changes if the level of analysis is refined enough. Or it may be that the information-processing approach will need to add some principles of functioning that cause major qualitative changes in cognitive organization.

### Lack of Concern with the Context of Behavior

Critics (for example, Neisser, 1985) have attacked information-processing psychologists' insensitivity to the natural context of behavior. The image of the child is of a "rational, decontextualized isolated mind with limited knowledge, without interests, without feelings, attitudes, or views of the world" (Sigel, 1986, p. 99). The information-processing approach has focused on which processing mechanisms the person brings to a task or setting and on the task parameters more than the interplay between the demands or possibilities of the larger setting and the needs, goals, and abilities of the person. Shaw and Bransford point out that "we tend to forget that humans and animals are active, investigatory creatures driven by definite intents through a complex, changing environment replete with meaning at a variety of levels of analysis" (1977, pp. 3–4). They argue that the passive, purposeless computer provides a sterile model for human cognition. Similarly, as mentioned earlier, several developmentalists (A. L. Brown, 1978; Meacham, 1977) have pointed out that memory is an activity applied to the child's goals in real-life settings. This ecological attitude toward knowledge can be expressed as follows: "Ask not what's inside your head, but what your head is inside of" (Mace, 1977).

After reviewing much of the recent research on information processing, Craik (1979) concluded that the field is belatedly moving into its natural-history phase. Whereas most theories began with observations of people in natural settings, information processing began in the laboratory, with research on artificial situations. Only now is it looking at more realistic and ecologically valid materials and tasks. Information-processing psychologists can now be found studying reading, sign language, conversations, stories, social behavior in natural settings, and memory for events occurring years earlier. Sternberg's theory of intelligence considers social influences and the fit between a person's intelligence and the demands of everyday life.

## SUMMARY

The information-processing approach studies how human symbol-manipulation systems, of limited capacity, work. Investigators take the computer as a model — either as a metaphoric heuristic device or as a way of simulating and testing their views concerning the nature of human thought. There are developmental changes in how children attend to, represent, store, and combine information. These changes occur at various points in the system: the sensory store, short-term memory, and long-term memory. Much of this development occurs via self-modification, as children formulate rules of decision making and modify them as a result of feedback. Investigators often begin by performing a task analysis. They then either formulate a computer model of how the child solves a problem or stores information or test the efficiency of the child's processing.

Humans are limited in how much information they can process at a given time and in how fast they can process this information. Much of development involves learning how to overcome these limitations by acquiring efficient control processes. Research on memory, the most-studied area of development in information processing, has led to four conclusions.

1. The acquisition of appropriate strategies underlies much of the improvement in memory.

2. Memory limitations can restrict the use of available logical reasoning skills.

3. The development of memory and knowledge are intertwined.

4. Metamemory improves greatly during development.

Changes in the representation of information and the rules for problem solving also alter the processing of information. These highly dependent changes in memory, representation, and problem solving are closely connected to other aspects of cognitive change, such as the growing knowledge of the world and the acquisition of the Piagetian mental operations. Intelligence can be seen as the efficient and insightful application of information-processing components.

Information-processing theorists view humans as active, organized, self-modifying systems. Development involves both quantitative and qualitative change and both genetic and environmental influences. The essence of development is an increasingly efficient system for controlling the flow of information.

The strengths of the theory are its ability to express the complexity of thought, its specificity concerning performance, and its rigorous methodology. Weaknesses involve certain shortcomings of the computer model, problems with accounting for development, and a lack of concern with the natural context of behavior.

## SUGGESTED READINGS

The following books describe current research on specific topics in memory, attention, and problem solving.

Daehler, M. W., and D. Butkatko. *Cognitive development.* New York: Knopf, Chapters 1–8, 12.

Kail, R. *The development of memory in children.* 2d ed. San Francisco: W. H. Freeman, 1984

Siegler, R. S. *Children's thinking.* Englewood Cliffs, N.J.: Prentice-Hall, 1986.

For a look at programs of research directed toward the computer simulation of children's thinking, the reader is referred to the following source.

Klahr, D. Information processing approaches to cognitive development. In R. Vasta, ed., *Annals of child development.* Vol. 6. Greenwich, Conn.: JAI Press, in press.

# 5

# Ethological Theory

At the beginning of these experiments, I had sat myself down in the
grass amongst the ducklings and, in order to make them follow me,
had dragged myself, sitting, away from them. . . . The ducklings, in
contrast to the greylag goslings, were most demanding and tiring
charges, for, imagine a two-hour walk with such children—all the
time squatting low and quacking without interruption! In the
interests of science I submitted myself literally for hours on end to
this ordeal.
[Lorenz, 1952, p. 42]

The initial phase, that of protest, may begin immediately or may be
delayed; it lasts from a few hours to a week or more. During it the
young child appears acutely distressed at having lost his mother and
seeks to recapture her by the full exercise of his limited resources.
He will often cry loudly, shake his cot, throw himself about, and
look eagerly towards any sight or sound which might prove to be his
missing mother. . . . During the phase of despair, which succeeds
protest, the child's preoccupation with his missing mother is still
evident, though his behaviour suggests increasing hopelessness. The
active physical movements diminish or come to an end, and he may
cry monotonously or intermittently. He is withdrawn and inactive,
makes no demands on people in the environment, and appears to be
in a state of deep mourning.
[Bowlby, 1969, p. 27]

**D**evelopmental psychologists have not taken Shakespeare's advice, "Neither a borrower, nor a lender be." Some of the most fruitful ideas about development have been borrowed from other areas of psychology and even other sciences. Ethology is one example of this. Ethology is the study of the evolutionarily significant behavior of a species in its natural surroundings. As a subdiscipline of biology, it looks at the biological and evolutionary blueprints for behavior.

The theory had its start years ago in European biologists and naturalists and eventually reached developmental psychologists in the last two decades via John Bowlby's studies of infant attachment. Ethological theory now provides the main theoretical notions for the evolutionary perspective on development.

As Rousseau observed, "One needs to look near at hand in order to study men, but to study man, one must look from afar." Ethology places humans into a broad context, the animal world. It is humbling to contemplate the fact that there are more species of insects in a square kilometer of Brazilian forest than there are species of primates in the world (Wilson, 1975). The human is just one small part of the huge, evolving animal kingdom. We are one of an estimated three to ten million species.

This chapter focuses on the implications of ethology for human development. It must be emphasized that most ethological research examines nonhuman species. How comfortably psychologists can apply concepts from animal research to human behavior is a controversial issue we return to later.

The organization of the first part of the chapter follows that of earlier chapters: a history followed by a general orientation. After that, however, there is a section on main contributions of ethology to human developmental psychology. Then the usual order resumes: mechanisms of development, position on developmental issues, theoretical nature of the theory, and evaluation.

## HISTORY OF THE THEORY

Ethology is linked to the German zoologists of the 1700s and 1800s who scientifically studied innate behaviors. The concept of evolution was strengthened by Darwin's painstaking observations of fossils and variations in plant and animal life. He, along with Alfred Wallace, was forced to conclude that nature ruthlessly selects certain characteristics because they lead to survival: "What a book a devil's chaplain might write on the clumsy, wasteful, blundering, low, and horribly cruel works of nature" (Darwin, quoted in Shapley, Rapput, and Wright, 1965, p. 446). As a result of this selective force, species changed and sometimes were differentiated into subspecies. Thus, many animals, including humans, are related through common ancestors. Darwin proposed that intelligence and other behaviors, as well as physical structures, were products of evolution. If they increased the chances of survival, they were retained; if they did not, they disappeared. Darwin's claim of a common ancestry of humans and other primates was not received well in Victorian England: Montagu (1973) related an anecdote about a shocked wife of an English bishop. She said that she certainly hoped that the theory was false, but if it were true, that not many people would find out about it.

Darwin's careful observing and cataloguing of plants and animals were imitated by ethologists years later. Just as he carefully described animal and plant life, he also described his own infants' behavior, as in the following excerpt on fears:

Before the present one was $4\frac{1}{2}$ months old I had been accustomed to make close to him many strange and loud noises, which were all taken as excellent jokes, but at this period I one day made a loud snoring noise which I had never done before; he instantly looked grave and then burst out crying. . . . May we not suspect that the vague but very real fears of children, which are quite independent of experience, are the inherited effects of real dangers and abject superstitions during ancient savage times?

*[1877, p. 289]*

Ethology as a distinct discipline began in the 1930s with the European zoologists Konrad Lorenz and Niko Tinbergen. They developed, often in collaboration, many of the key concepts discussed in the next section. Tinbergen describes this new approach as having "started as a revolt by young zoologists against the dead animal" (Cohen, 1977, p. 316). Ethologists saw animals as active organisms living within a particular ecological niche, not as passive organisms prodded by stimuli, as in the tradition of learning theory. Their studies of species as diverse as ducklings, butterflies, and stickleback fish gave scientific meaning to the sometimes mystical term *instinct*. Many of Lorenz's observations were of wild animals that wandered freely in and around his home. Lorenz and Tinbergen's work was honored with the Nobel Prize in Medicine or Physiology in 1973, which they shared with another ethologist, Karl von Frisch. For psychologists, Eibl-Eibesfeldt's work, beginning in the 1950s and continuing in the present, is especially important, for he was one of the first to make a formal connection between psychology and ethology. This link with psychology fueled an interest in ethological accounts of human behavior.

Ethology has continued to influence studies of behavior in Europe and, more recently, in the United States. The ethological perspective guides observational studies, neurobiological and physiological studies, and laboratory studies of behavior. In recent years, ethology has merged with comparative psychology, which emphasized laboratory research on various animal species, to form a new synthesis in North America. Work on such topics as how infant rats find the nest by odor, how monkeys interact with their peers, and how mammalian mothers treat their infants immediately after birth combines experimental and observational methods. This work is more empirical and experimental and less speculative and theoretical than the earlier European "classical" ethological studies. The focus now is on the immediate causes of the behavior — for example, scent or temperature — rather than on the evolutionary origins of the behavior. Observation, however, continues to play an important role and has become scientifically respectable: "To have made 'inspired observation' respectable again in the behavioral sciences is, I believe, a positive achievement of ethology" (Tinbergen, quoted in Cohen, 1977, pp. 323–324).

Part of the broad appeal of ethology is due to popularized accounts accessible to the general public. *The Naked Ape* (Morris, 1967), *The Territorial Imperative* (Ardrey, 1966), and *On Aggression* (Lorenz, 1966) proposed exciting ideas about innate causes of human behavior but have been criticized for exaggerating the biological influence on human social behavior.

Recently, ethology has been joined by a new subarea of biology. *Sociobiology* is defined by its main spokesman, E. O. Wilson, as the "study of the biological basis of all social behavior" (1975, p. 4). Although these two fields overlap a great deal, sociobiology focuses on social structures, especially at the level of an entire society, rather than on the individual. It is a hybrid of ethology, ecology (the study of how organisms are related to their environment), genetics, and population biology. Sociobiologists' work on such topics as reproductive patterns, altruism, and social hierarchies is beginning to influence developmental research (MacDonald, 1988).

Developmental psychology was receptive to ethology because developmentalists have a tradition of observing children and considering the biological basis of development (Barker and Wright, 1955; Gesell, 1945; G. S. Hall, 1904). Many developmentalists continued to observe children even through psychology's behaviorist years. The first burst of ethological work on children came in Great Britain, and ethology has continued to be an important force there. The most important figure to bring ethology to the attention of developmental psychologists is John Bowlby. His turning from a Freudian to an ethological account of infant-caretaker social attachment in the 1950s in England laid the groundwork for subsequent research in this area in both Europe and North America. (His work is described later.) More recently, ethologically oriented psychologists have extended the approach to other areas of infant behavior, for instance, facial expressions and biases toward looking at certain objects, such as faces. With older children, the work focuses on peer interaction. It is interesting that one of the founding fathers of ethology, Tinbergen, has studied autistic children and interpreted their behavior as an extreme fear response to being looked at by other people (Tinbergen and Tinbergen, 1972).

It should be noted that much of the recent animal research by North American ethologists and comparative psychologists is developmental. This research on maternal and newborn behaviors in animals is beginning to influence human developmental research. The importance of human and animal developmental research has been expressed as follows: "The developmental point of view is basic to an understanding of how evolutionary and ecological parameters are achieved in individuals and groups. The gap between molecular biology and natural selection will be filled by developmental analysis of the nervous system, behavior, and psychology" (Gottlieb, 1979, p. 169). The study of the development of behavior is "the backbone of comparative psychology. Shortcomings in its study inevitably handicap other lines of investigation, from behavioral evolution and psychogenetics to the study of individual and group behavior" (Schneirla, 1966, p. 283).

## GENERAL ORIENTATION TO THE THEORY

Ethology is characterized by four basic concepts: (1) species-specific innate behavior, (2) the evolutionary perspective, (3) learning predispositions, and (4) ethological methodology. The theoretical notions described here are based primarily on "classical" ethology, that is, on the contributions of European ethologists, particularly Lorenz, Tinbergen, and Eibl-Eibesfeldt. These contributions have influenced ethological accounts of human development more than has the recent North American work by comparative psychologists. As ethology continues to change, the particular focus of developmental questions will also change. In particular, developmental studies of animal maternal and infant behavior are likely to become a dominant force.

### Species-Specific Innate Behavior

An animal lacking "instincts" altogether would be a complete slave of conditioning.

[Ghiselin and Scudo (1986, p. 194)]

Innate behaviors are considered similar to organs of the body, in that both are essentially the same in all members of a species, are inherited, and are adaptive (Lorenz, 1937). Just as physical structures are under genetic control, so are certain behaviors. Although no physical structures or behaviors are completely innate, because they are always expressed in a particular environment, ethology emphasizes the biological contributions to behavior.

Ethologists generally agree that a behavior is innate if it has these four characteristics (Cairns, 1979):

1. It is stereotyped in its form (that is, has an unvarying sequence of actions) across individuals in a species.

2. It is present without relevant previous experience that could have allowed it to be learned.

3. It is universal for the species (that is, found in all members).

4. It is relatively unchanged as a result of experience and learning after it is established.

For example, in certain songbirds, the same song appears in all members of the species at sexual maturity, even if they have never heard the song sung by other members of the species. As this example illustrates, some innate behaviors are not present at birth, but appear later as a result of physical maturation. In contrast to innate behaviors, learned behaviors, such as chimpanzees' use of sticks as "tools," vary in form from individual to individual, require relevant previous experience, usually vary in their occurrence among members of the species, and change as a result of subsequent experience.

Innate behaviors are termed *species-specific*, which means they occur among all members of the species or at least a particular subgroup, such as all the males or all the young. If other species also have the behavior, two inferences are possible. One is that the two species are related, perhaps having split into separate lines at some point in their evolution. That is, they have common ancestors. The other possible inference is that the behavior has evolved independently in the two species, perhaps because they had similar physical environments and needs. For example, in many species, the young cling to the mother's fur — a necessity for survival if the infant must travel with its mother as she moves throughout an area in search of food or flees from predators. Conclusions about similar behaviors in different species must be drawn cautiously, not only because they may have evolved independently, but also because the behaviors may have different meanings or functions in the two species. An example is tail wagging in dogs and cats.

Ethologists have identified three types of innate behaviors: (1) reflexes, (2) taxes (spatial orientations), and (3) fixed action patterns. *Reflexes*, simple responses to stimuli, have long been familiar to psychologists. Examples from the human infant are grasping a finger placed in the hand, spreading the toes when the bottom of the foot is stroked, and turning toward a nipple when it brushes the cheek. Any long-haired parent would agree with ethologists' interesting observation that infants are particularly likely to grasp hair, especially during feeding. Eibl-Eibesfeldt (1975) speculates that this reflex originally served to facilitate clinging to the mother's fur. Many of these reflexes are quite strong. A premature baby can grasp a clothesline and support his own weight, for instance. This ability is later lost. Less familiar reflexes are coordinated swimming, crawling, and walking movements when the body's weight is supported, in newborns or young infants.

*Taxes* are bodily movements that orient the organism to a particular stimulus. The grayling butterfly escapes from an enemy by flying toward the sun, a source of light; the pit viper moves toward a warm body; and a frog turns its snout toward an insect.

The third category of innate behavior, the fixed action pattern, has received the most attention from ethologists and psychologists. A *fixed action pattern* is a complex innate behavior that promotes the survival of the species. It is a "genetically programmed sequence of coordinated motor actions" (Hess, 1970, p. 7) that arises from specific inherited mechanisms in the central nervous system. Examples are squirrels burying nuts, birds performing courtship "dances," spiders spinning webs, and stickleback fish fighting to protect their territory. Fixed action patterns can become very elaborate, as when the male bowerbird spends hours building a love nest decorated with flowers, fruit, shells, and colorful beetles to attract a mate. He adjusts a twig here, adds a flower there, and seemingly stops to admire his work from time to time. The adaptive value of these fixed action patterns lies in the fact that they often end in eating, mating, or protecting the species from harm.

Two conditions set the stage for the elicitation of the fixed action pattern: a sign stimulus and action-specific energy. A *sign stimulus* is a particular stimulus whose presence automatically releases a particular fixed action pattern. Lorenz (1966) likens this process to a key opening a lock. A sign stimulus may be a simple quality, as when the odor of butyric acid given off by warm-blooded animals causes a tick to drop down from a twig onto its prey (Uexküll, 1909). Or a sign stimulus may involve more complex, relational cues, as when the red belly of a male stickleback fish venturing into another stickleback's territory triggers fighting behavior. A decoy that only vaguely resembles the stickleback in shape but is red on its lower half elicits this fixed action pattern, whereas an accurate decoy without the red area usually does not (Tinbergen, 1951). Thus, the sign stimulus is specific, and sometimes must be in a particular orientation or position. Tinbergen (1958) discovered this sign stimulus when he noticed that his sticklebacks in an aquarium near a window facing a street would become agitated at a certain time of the day. He eventually realized that a red mail truck passed by at that time, a stimulus that approximated the natural sign stimulus. A further example of the specificity of the sign stimulus is that a hen will not rescue a distressed, flailing chick she can see under a glass bell but cannot hear. However, she will rescue the chick immediately if she can hear the distress cries even if she cannot see it (Brückner, 1933).

When the sign stimulus is an appropriate exaggeration of the normal sign stimulus, it encourages the fixed action pattern. The ringed plover prefers to roll unusually large eggs to its nest, even if the egg is so large that it continually slides off. Fishermen take advantage of sign stimuli by using lures that exaggerate the natural prey (the sign stimuli) of the larger fish.

The ease with which a sign stimulus elicits the fixed action pattern depends on the second facilitating factor, the *action-specific energy*. According to Lorenz, energy for each of several drives gradually builds up in the central nervous system. This energy creates a readiness to act or a certain "mood." The need to discharge this energy periodically is met when the fixed action pattern occurs and thereby releases the energy. The longer the period of time since the behavior last occurred, the greater the buildup of energy and the more likely the sign stimulus will release the behavior. If the pressure becomes very great, the behavior can occur even without the sign stimulus. This is sometimes seen in animals kept in captivity, as when a hand-fed starling with no experience at hunting prey attacks invisible insects, makes killing movements, and appears to swallow them (Lorenz, 1937). Another example is that the female rat is in such a state of readiness to retrieve her young shortly after birth that if no young are present, she will repeatedly grasp her own tail or one of her hind legs and carry it back to the nest (Eibl-Eibesfeldt, 1975). A human example is that infants who do not get enough opportunity to suck during feeding because the hole in the nipple is too large will cry and make sucking movements even when no object is in the mouth (Spitz, 1957).

When drives operate simultaneously, ambivalent behavior results. For instance, the male stickleback fish's zigzag courtship dance is actually a result of two conflicting drives. The "zig" toward the female is due to the aggressive drive, whereas the "zag" away from her is motivated by a desire to lead her to the nest in order to mate. According to Lorenz (1966), this behavior has become ritualized into the innate courtship behavior of the species. Simultaneously aroused drives can also lead to irrelevant behavior that does not belong to either drive. For example, fighting cocks will suddenly stop and peck at the ground as if to feed (Lorenz, 1935), a behavior that ethologists attribute to a conflict between fear and aggression.

Sometimes drives must be satisfied sequentially. Cichlids must fight with other males before mating with females. If no males are available for satisfying the aggressive drive, the females are killed instead (Eibl-Eibesfeldt, 1975).

The notions of fixed action pattern, sign stimulus, and drive fit together as follows: "When the inner readiness to act coincides with the appropriate releasing stimulus situation then a particular fixed action pattern will run its course almost automatically" (Eibl-Eibesfeldt, 1975, p. 17). This process is linked to physiological mechanisms that have a genetic basis. Neurological pathways and hormonal changes are ultimate causes of this innate behavior (for supporting evidence, see Eibl-Eibesfeldt, 1975).

This buildup and release of biologically based energy is similar to Freud's conception of drives. In addition, in both theories, this energy can be displaced toward an object other than the intended target, as in displaced aggression. Whereas Freud is concerned with sexual and aggressive drives, Lorenz (1966) refers to the "big four" drives: hunger, reproduction, aggression, and flight. These drives are expressed through a number of more-specific fixed action patterns, such as sucking, nest building, attacking, and running. More recently, ethologists have suggested other basic drives, such as a drive to learn, expressed in curiosity behavior and play (Eibl-Eibesfeldt, 1975). A more important change, however, is that many ethologists have dropped the notion of drive completely. They argue that the concept is not a useful one because it is not easily tested, is confusing, and leads to oversimplistic explanations of behavior.

The concept of fixed action pattern has also been modified in several ways (Beer, 1973; Dewsbury, 1978). For instance, research has found that many fixed action patterns are more variable than originally thought. They are now sometimes called "modal action patterns." Furthermore, part of the requirement that the sign stimulus must be specific actually reflected the nature of the sensory system rather than innate mechanisms in the central nervous system. Finally, displacement activities may have alternative explanations, such as the removal of inhibitions from common behavior.

Innate reflexes, taxes, and fixed action patterns have developmental significance. These behaviors permit the young infant's survival, either by allowing him to seek food and hide from predators on his own or by binding him to an adult caretaker through behaviors such as crying, grasping, sucking, or smiling. For example, the infant graylag gosling calls "wi-wi," especially when alone, and elicits a reassuring reply from its mother. Furthermore, with physical maturation come new behaviors such as nest building, which allow even further adaptation to the environment. This fit between the organism's needs and the innate behaviors it possesses is not accidental, but the product of the long evolutionary history of its species.

The emphasis on innate behavior directed by drives should not leave the impression that ethologists think learning is unimportant. Rather, most ethologists simply argue that it is necessary to describe and understand innate behavior before studying how it is modified by the environment. Most behavior is viewed as an interweaving of innate and learned components. A raven innately knows how to build a nest, but through trial and error learns that broken glass and pieces of ice are less suitable than twigs for this purpose (Eibl-Eibesfeldt, 1975). A squirrel innately knows how to manipulate, gnaw, and crack nuts, but with practice learns how to integrate these individual behaviors into an efficient act. This gnawing skill can easily be adapted to new situations, as when English titmice quickly learned how to open milk bottles. The survival value of this interweaving of innate and learned behaviors seems clear: "The learned components are considered to lend a flexibility to behavior and to promote greater adaptability in various environmental conditions. The innate components ensure that certain reactions to specific stimuli will be made without the necessity of learning" (Hess, 1970, p. 7).

A further connection between innate and learned behaviors is that once a new behavior is learned, it can serve the innate drives. Lorenz describes how a learned act, "shaking hands," becomes an appeasement gesture:

Who does not know the dog who has done some mischief and now approaches his master on its belly, sits up in front of him, ears back, and with a most convincing "don't-hit-me" face attempts to shake hands? I once saw a poodle perform this movement before another dog of whom he was afraid.

*[1950, p. 178]*

## Evolutionary Perspective

A chicken is just the egg's way of making another egg.

*[Anonymous]*

Evolution involves *phylogenetic* change, or change in a species over generations, in contrast to *ontogenetic* change, or developmental change in a single lifetime. Darwin's evolutionary theory is outlined in *The Origin of Species* (1859): Given that there is a variation among members of a species and given the nature of the environment of that species, certain variations are more likely to survive than others. Because characteristics have a genetic basis and surviving animals are those who reproduce, the most adaptive characteristics are passed on to offspring. There have been changes in the specifics of the theory, particularly in light of modern genetics, and also disagreements such as whether evolution can involve sudden changes. However, the basic notions have not changed since Darwin's time.

From an evolutionary perspective, the human is an experiment in nature. He is viewed "as though seen through the front end of a telescope, at a greater than usual distance and temporarily diminished in size, in order to view him simultaneously with an array of other social experiments" (Wilson, 1978, p. 17). Each species, including the human, is a solution to a problem posed by the environment. These problems include how to avoid predators, how to obtain food, and how to reproduce.

The course of development within an individual follows a pattern that was acquired by the species because it facilitated survival. Just as certain physical characteristics, such as the upright stance and the hand with opposable fingers and thumb, facilitated making and using tools, so did certain behaviors — reflexes, taxes, and fixed action patterns — facilitate survival through mating, food gathering, caretaking, and so forth. Social behaviors, such as interindividual communication and cooperation, encourage group cohesion and thereby increase the chances of survival. Darwin saw the "struggle for existence" and the "survival of the fittest" operating at the level of observable behavior as well as in bodily structures. New behaviors arose through natural genetic variations or mutations and, if they allowed the organism to survive long enough to reproduce, were genetically transmitted to the next generation. These successful behaviors gradually became more common in the whole population over many generations.

Inferring the course of evolution is not so simple as it seems, however. It is not always obvious what the survival value of an innate behavior is. For example, a behavior may lead to the death of individuals, but increase the survival of the species. When an individual bird spots a predator, it gives a warning call to the flock, thus attracting the predator's attention and endangering the bird's life. The flock, however, survives. A further complication is that many existing behaviors, such as many of the reflexes in the human infant, are no longer necessary for survival; they are relics. Many of the early arguments about evolution illustrate the dangers of armchair speculation in this area. It was once claimed that flamingos are pink because that makes it difficult for predators to see them against the sunset (Thayer, 1909).

We cannot overemphasize the importance of evolutionary theory in ethological thought. When an ethologist asks why a particular behavior occurs, he is mainly asking how that behavior facilitates adaptation to the environment, and therefore survival, for that species. This type of explanation is not seriously sought by any other major theory of development. Eleanor Gibson (see Chapter 6) stresses that each species develops certain perceptual skills because of the demands of its environment, but few specific developmental hypotheses have come from this argument. Most theories seek explanations for development in the learning experiences or the physical maturation of individuals during their lifetimes. Thus, ethology provides a broader context for viewing development.

## Learning Predispositions

The biological control of behavior can be seen not only in innate behaviors acquired during evolution but also in predispositions toward certain kinds of learning. Species differ in which aspects of their behavior are modifiable, in what kinds of learning occur most easily, and in the mechanisms of learning. Learning predispositions include sensitive periods and general or specific learning abilities. *Sensitive*, or *critical, periods* are specific periods when the animal is biologically ready to acquire a new behavior. During those times, the animal is especially responsive to particular stimuli and has certain behaviors that are particularly susceptible to modification.

The most popular example from ethology of a sensitive period comes from Lorenz. Shortly after birth, usually in the first day or two, certain birds (for example, geese) are most able to learn the distinctive characteristics of their mother and therefore their species. During this sensitive period, the young learn to follow a stimulus and come to prefer that stimulus—a phenomenon called *imprinting*. Imprinting increases the survival of the young because it ensures that they stay close to the parent, that is, near food and shelter and far from predators and other dangerous situations. The stimulus to be followed must meet certain criteria, for example, make a certain call note or type of movement. The particular criteria vary from species to species, but the mother always meets these criteria. In the wild, a row of ducklings scurrying after their mother is a common sight. However, as Lorenz discovered, certain "unnatural" objects also meet the criteria. Young birds have become imprinted on flashing lights, electric trains, moving milk bottles, and a squatting, quacking Konrad Lorenz (see the excerpt at the beginning of this chapter). Horses and sheep have also become imprinted on humans. Lorenz considered imprinting critical because he thought it was irreversible; a duckling imprinted on a flashing light does not become imprinted on its real mother if she appears for the first time after the end of the sensitive period.

In many species, imprinting has a long-term effect on sexual behavior. Lorenz (1931) discovered that jackdaws raised by humans will join a flock of jackdaws but return to their first love, a human, during the reproductive season. They try to attract the human with their species' courting patterns.

Sensitive periods have also been identified for behaviors such as learning bird songs, learning to distinguish males and females of the species, developing a social relationship with humans, and forming a bond between the newborn and the mother. In this last case, for example, mother goats form a bond with their young in the first 5 minutes after birth. If the young are removed right after birth for 2 hours, the mother attacks them upon their return. Waiting 5 minutes after birth before removal, however, leads to their acceptance later (Klopfer, 1971).

The notion of a sensitive period has evolved somewhat in recent years. The statement that can be made with most confidence is that how experience affects the organism depends on the stage of development at which the experience occurred (Bateson, 1978). More specific sensitive periods, such as a clearly demarcated time for imprinting, seem to exist only in certain species, and sensitive periods can differ greatly even among closely related species. Moreover, there is disagreement whether the length of the sensitive period is determined solely by a genetic mechanism or is affected somewhat by the animal's experiences as well (Hess, 1973). For example, it may be possible to produce imprinting even after the sensitive period has ended if the appropriate stimulus is exposed for a long enough time (Bateson, 1973). Thus, it is clear that sensitive periods are much more complex than was originally thought.

Sensitive periods also constitute learning predispositions: in the case of imprinting, the young bird is biologically pretuned to notice certain types of objects, sounds, or movements, yet it links up a response to this stimulus as a result of experience, that is, of seeing the object then following it. Thus, biology prepares the bird to learn from experience. The learning involved in imprinting or other behavior acquired during sensitive periods should not be confused with operant conditioning (discussed in the chapter on learning). Imprinting is acquired with no reinforcement; it even increases when punishment in the form of an electric shock occurs, and it resists extinction.

The concept of a sensitive period, in a general sense, has been applied widely in developmental psychology. Its implications for human infant attachment are discussed later. Most generally, the sensitive period supports the argument that early experience is particularly important for adult behavior, as suggested by Freud and many researchers of early development. Furthermore, all stage theories claim that at each stage the child is particularly sensitive to certain experiences, such as motor exploration in the sensorimotor period (Piaget), the meeting of one's needs by other people in the stage of trust versus mistrust (Erikson), and the satisfaction or deprivation of anal drives during the anal stage (Freud). Even most nonstage theories use the concept of readiness—the idea that the child is most likely to learn from an experience if it comes at the optimal time. The child may not profit from being shown how to put objects to be remembered into categories when she is 3 years old but may have increased recall as a result of this experience at age 6. Finally, it should be noted that sensitive periods are a central notion in embryological development. A particular drug taken by a pregnant woman will have no effect or a devastating effect on the fetus, depending on its stage of development.

A second way in which biology indirectly controls behavior is found in *general and specific learning skills*. Particularly in humans, the genetic endowment includes a tremendous general ability to learn from experience. Humans are educable and highly adaptable. As Lorenz (1959) noted, humans are "specialists in nonspecialization." We have evolved a central nervous system that is capable of flexible thinking, hands that can perform many different actions, and a language system that permits symbolic thought and verbal communication. The advantage of this flexibility is that the organism can adjust to a changing environment. There is less reliance on fixed action patterns for survival, especially during adulthood. Another way in which a general learning ability is tied to innate factors is the ability to learn via reinforcement and punishment. This ability to be affected by the consequences of one's behavior must be built into the nervous system.

As a result of humans' biologically based general ability to learn, we have developed cultures to help us adapt. This culture is passed on to the next generation by imitation and other forms of learning. Thus, even cultural adaptation has its biological origins.

General learning abilities are complemented by specific learning skills. Specific learning skills reflect the fact that an organism does not learn everything equally easily. Each species has its own bias toward certain kinds of learning. Contrary to the claims of classical learning theory, it is not the case that all responses are equally easily conditioned to all stimuli. These specific learning skills are easily identified when various species are compared. The digger wasp, during its morning inspection of up to 15 nests, decides how much food is needed by each nest. This information is retained for the entire day. A well-known example of an amazing specific memory skill is the ability of salmon to return to their spawning ground by remembering the odor of the waters in which they were born. Rats, which normally live in burrows, will learn to make their way through a psychologist's maze faster than herons and frogs (Eibl-Eibesfeldt, 1975). Wild rats quickly learn, after an unfortunate experience, to avoid poisonous bait (Barnett, 1963). When new bait is presented, rats will eat very small quantities and, if they fall ill, the bait will be avoided. Even within a particular type of learning—for example, visual discrimination and recognition—learning may be specialized. For instance, herring gulls learn to recognize their own chicks, but not their own eggs, even though the eggs have distinctive markings that could easily be recognized (Tinbergen, 1951). Humans also have specialized learning skills. Chomsky (1965) and others have claimed that human infants are pre-tuned to process and acquire language. The rapid acquisition of language early in life, the culturally universal forms of early utterances, and the occurrence of babbling in infants born deaf, all point to this conclusion.

An interesting footnote to animal learning comes from Lorenz (1963), who suggests that once a behavior is learned, deviating from it often causes great fear. He offers the following anecdote to illustrate this point. A graylag goose that lived in Lorenz's room had developed a routine for entering the house every evening. At first she had always walked past the staircase to a window before climbing the stairs to her room. This detour was shortened until she merely turned toward the window at the foot of the stairs instead of going over to it. One evening Lorenz forgot to let the goose into the house. When he finally remembered as darkness approached, the goose ran in and immediately ascended the stairs:

> Upon this something shattering happened: Arrived at the fifth step, she suddenly stopped, made a long neck, in geese a sign of fear, and spread

her wings as for flight. Then she uttered a warning cry and very nearly took off. Now she hesitated a moment, turned around, ran hurriedly down the five steps and set forth resolutely, like someone on a very important mission, on her original path to the window and back. This time she mounted the steps according to her former custom from the left side. On the fifth step she stopped again, looked around, shook herself, and performed a greeting display behavior regularly seen in graylags when anxious tension has given place to relief. I hardly believed my eyes. To me there is no doubt about the interpretation of this occurrence: The habit had become a custom which the goose could not break without being stricken by fear.

*[Lorenz, 1963, p. 112]*

## Methodology

Ethologists rely on two general methods for studying behavior: naturalistic observation and laboratory experimentation. Their particular version of naturalistic observation ranks as one of their main contributions to psychology. On the other hand, laboratory experimentation is probably used in the majority of present-day ethological studies. Both are necessary to the theory.

### Naturalistic Observation

It may not seem revolutionary to argue that organisms must be observed in their natural surroundings. After all, a science begins by building a data base of observations describing the content area of that science. Perhaps this argument was threatening to the struggling young science of psychology in the 1930s and 1940s, a field dominated by behaviorists, who prided themselves on their objective laboratory experimental methods. Psychologists looked for universal laws of learning in rats and pigeons and seldom observed their spontaneous behaviors. Bar pressing in rats and table tennis in pigeons could hardly be considered typical species-specific behaviors. It is unlikely that interesting natural behaviors, such as defending a territory or building a nest, would occur often in barren laboratory cages. In the 1960s, however, learning psychologists began to realize that each species has its own predispositions toward certain kinds of learning and consequently began to question the assumptions of behaviorism. Thus, the door was opened to ethology. In developmental psychology, because there was a history of using the observational method and because Piaget's and Bowlby's observations of children were making an impact, the naturalistic observational method of ethology was soon regarded with interest.

Naturalistic observation is closely tied to the three characteristics of the theory mentioned earlier. If one wants to describe species-specific innate behaviors or learning predispositions that evolved because they led to survival in that species' natural habitat, there is no substitute for observing animals in their typical environments. In particular, the function of a behavior can be understood only if one sees how it fits into the species' natural environment in order to satisfy the animal's needs. A giraffe's long neck makes sense when he is observed eating leaves from tall trees; young gulls' innate "freezing" rather than fleeing in the face of danger is understandable when one notes that their nests are built on narrow ledges or steep cliffs (Eibl-Eibesfeldt, 1975).

Observations of animals in captivity are inadequate because their behavior may be abnormal. One cause of abnormal behavior in this setting is that animals are usually healthier in their natural environments and therefore are more likely to behave in ways typical of their species. Another cause is the absence of sign stimuli that would release the drive energy that has built up. Thus, behavior is often redirected. Particularly in the older zoos, where most animals are in cages, we see restless pacing back and forth, constant rocking, and killing of the young by the mother. These abnormal behaviors can often be avoided by a simple change in the environment. For example, an armadillo in the Amsterdam zoo made various abnormal, stereotyped movements until a layer of dirt was placed on the floor of its bare cage. The animal could then bury itself at night when it slept (Eibl-Eibesfeldt, 1975). Ironically, giving too much care to the animal may cause problems. Titmice in a zoo threw their young out of the nest soon after birth. The problem was that food was too readily available. The young quickly became full, stopped gaping, and consequently were taken for dead by the parents. Young titmice in the wild never stop gaping unless they are sick or dead, because the parents must hunt for food and the infants are never full (Koenig, 1951). In the human, abnormal behavior —for example, rocking—has been observed in children in unnatural environments such as orphanages and hospitals.

Ideally, ethologists follow a particular sequence of steps when studying an organism:

1. They develop an *ethogram*: an extensive, detailed description of the behavior of a species in its natural environment. An ethogram is like an inventory or a catalog. It includes the animal's behaviors, the characteristics of the environment, and the events immediately preceding and following each behavior. Of interest are not only the types of behaviors—for example, nesting and food gathering—but also their frequency, stimulus context, function, and ontogenetic development. Psychologists have been particularly oblivious to the frequency of a behavior in natural settings. The problem of not having scientific data about frequency was noted long ago by Thorndike: "Dogs get lost hundreds of times and no one notices it or sends a scientific account of it to a magazine. But let one find its way from Brooklyn to Yonkers and the fact immediately becomes a circulating anecdote" (1898, p. 4).

The descriptive labels must be refined until two or more observers can agree, in nearly every case, regarding what behavior occurred and when it began and ended. Did the child smile or grimace, and for how long? When a behavior is described, a main concern is with the structure of that behavior: what elicits it, what the components are, in what order these components appear, and what ends the behavior. Note that these "raw data" in the ethogram are not totally unbiased observations. The observations typically focus on fixed action patterns that have evolved as an aid to survival. Furthermore, ethologists historically have been particularly interested in observing fixed action patterns that involve social behavior.

2. They classify these behaviors according to their function, that is, which drives they serve or how they encourage survival. These categories—such as caretaking, mating, and defending territory—serve as working hypotheses rather than immutable facts. As one investigator has observed, "The investigator of behavior is faced with a potential paradox in that categories of behavior must be formed . . . but these categories are unlikely to be either homogeneous (i.e., indivisible) or mutually exclusive (i.e., functionally independent) on refined analysis. Stated briefly, and without much exaggeration, categories of behavior *must be formed*, but the investigator *must not believe them*" (Fentress, 1973, p. 163).

3. They compare how a given fixed action pattern functions in various species and how a given need is met by various fixed action patterns in different species. Of special interest are similar fixed action patterns in closely related species. If several closely related species of birds have a similar courtship dance, they may have a common ancestor. Such species comparisons, along with changes in behavior inferred from fossils (for example, an increase in brain size), provide evidence about the evolutionary course of a behavior.

4. They use laboratory experiments to determine the immediate causes of the behavior described in the first three steps. From the viewpoint of ethologists, psychology has worked backward historically by performing laboratory research before obtaining a sufficient data base of naturalistic observations.

Recently, ethologists have increased the power of the observational method by filming or videotaping their observations. There are two advantages. First, filming permits repeated viewing of the same behavioral sample. Thus, it is possible to compare how various observers describe the behavior. Do they agree that a particular facial expression in an infant is a smile? Do they agree that the courtship of a particular species of bird always begins by hanging upside down? Interobserver agreement increases our confidence in the observations. Multiple viewing also allows a single observer to return to his earlier observations to check a hypothesis formed after observations of many individuals. After observing many human babies, an investigator may notice that they seem to be less fearful of strangers when the stranger is kneeling down than when he is standing. By viewing all of the observations again, this hypothesis can be checked.

The second advantage of filmed observations is that the action can be sped up or slowed down. When this is done, previously unnoticed patterns of behavior sometimes emerge. For example, a flirting look often involves raising the eyebrows for only one-sixth of a second—a movement that becomes a noticeable invariant part of the flirting sequence only when the film is slowed down (Eibl-Eibesfeldt, 1975). By speeding up films, investigators have noted that people who eat alone look up and around after every few bites, as if scanning the horizon for enemies, as baboons and chimps do (Eibl-Eibesfeldt, 1975). This is much less obvious at a normal camera speed.

Filming humans poses special problems because their awareness that they are being filmed is likely to change their behavior. The one-way mirror, which makes unobtrusive filming possible in the laboratory, is obviously of little use in field settings. Eibl-Eibesfeldt has made use of one clever solution to this problem. A mirror prism inserted in his camera allows the camera operator to point his camera at a right angle to his target. The subject knows the camera is present but does not think he is being filmed.

## Laboratory Studies

For an ethologist, a behavior has both a phylogenetic cause and an immediate cause. A spider spins a web "because" that innate food-gathering behavior has allowed the species to survive. In addition to this phylogenetic cause, various types of immediate causes can be identified. Spinning a web may be caused by specific physiological events, particular inborn neurological pathways, the presence of a sign stimulus, certain aspects of motor experience, and so on. These various causes of behavior suggested by the observational studies can be clarified by controlled experiments.

The classical ethological experiment is the *deprivation study*, which determines whether a behavior is innate or learned. In this method, the animal is deprived of specific experiences that could be relevant to the behavior of interest. Obviously, the organism is not deprived of broad aspects of experience—a procedure that would cause widespread disruption of behavior or even physical deterioration. As an illustration of the deprivation study, an ethologist interested in the origin of nut-burying behavior raised squirrels in isolation in a cage with a bare floor and provided a diet of only liquid food. The squirrels had no exposure to other squirrels (who could serve as models), nuts, or earth (which could provide digging practice). Under these conditions, squirrels demonstrated a stereotyped sequence of nut-burying behaviors at the same age as do squirrels in the wild. When presented with a nut at this time, they ate until satiated, then dug an imaginary hole in the concrete floor, pushed the nut into the hole with their snouts, covered it with invisible soil, and carefully patted down the "soil" to finish the job (Eibl-Eibesfeldt, 1975). Thus, since there was no opportunity to learn this behavior, it must be an innate fixed action pattern of the species.

Deprivation experiments sometimes reveal that certain features of the behavior are innate, whereas others are learned. Chaffinches raised in a soundless environment produce a song with the same number of syllables and total length as do their species in the wild, but the song lacks the organization into three stanzas. They must learn this phrasing, but they innately know which song to imitate when presented with several recorded bird songs (Eibl-Eibesfeldt, 1975).

Other ethological laboratory experiments are not different in method from those of comparative psychology or physiological psychology. They clarify which variables influence behavior and what the underlying physiological mechanisms are. For example, by systematically varying stimuli, one can determine which attributes of a stimulus are critical for eliciting the response. The experiments examine a variety of responses, ranging from pupil dilation (which indicates interest or attraction) to the amount of time spent near the stimulus. Although the laboratory experimental method is shared with the mainstream of experimental psychology, ethology maintains its distinctiveness by the content it chooses to study: behaviors tailored to the survival of the species.

## CONTRIBUTIONS TO
## HUMAN DEVELOPMENTAL PSYCHOLOGY

Ethologists are interested in the same categories of adaptive behaviors in humans as in other animals: for example, feeding, communication, parent-child interaction, and reproduction. However, there is no unified ethological view of development. Instead, particular topics have been selected by ethologically oriented psychologists. The study of children has focused primarily on infant attachment but has expanded recently to include the organization of peer interaction, facial expressions, bodily movements, and problem solving. A look at representative research in each of these areas will show ethology's imprint on both the content and the methodology of developmental research.

### Infant – Caretaker Attachment

#### *Bowlby's Theory*

John Bowlby, a London psychoanalyst, is credited with bringing ethology to the attention of developmental psychologists. His observations of infants separated for a long time from their mothers led him to conclude that an early social "attachment" between infant and caretaker is crucial for normal development. A disrupted relationship between mother and infant often leads to the infant's protest, then despair, detachment, and finally, in some cases, psychopathology (see the excerpt at the beginning of this chapter). Evidence for the attachment bond in normal situations includes protest when the parent leaves and greeting behaviors, such as smiling and babbling, when the parent returns. A child also seeks his attachment figure when under stress.

Drawing on observations of mother-infant bonding in nonhuman primates, Bowlby (1969/1982) proposed that attachment to a caretaker has evolved because it promotes the survival of the helpless infant by protecting him from predators or exposure to the elements. Separation of the infant from its mother can be a fatal error in many animals. At birth and throughout early development, infants have a biological predisposition to maintain proximity to adults of the species. In animals other than humans, the young often use the mother's odor or the warmth of the nest to keep in contact with her (Moltz and Leon, 1983; Rosenblatt, 1976). Many of the human newborn's reflexes served this function during human evolution. One of these reflexes is grasping an object such as a finger or the hair when it contacts the infant's palm, just as many mammalian infants stay with the mother by clinging to her hair. Another reflex is an embracing movement in response to a sudden loud sound or a loss of support. This reflex may have prevented many ancestral infants from falling when the mother suddenly ran upon seeing a predator.

Of course, these reflexes have little value for attachment in the human infant, who need not physically attach himself to the parent in order to survive. Of more importance to human newborns are signaling mechanisms such as crying, babbling, and smiling — both the spontaneous "gas" smile present in newborns and the true "social" or "answering" smile that emerges several weeks later. These behaviors communicate the infant's needs and encourage the adult to come to him. The infant's immature motor system is compensated for by these signaling abilities. Just as following the imprinted object in ducklings maintains proximity, so do signaling behaviors serve this purpose in humans. The result is the same. The infant is protected and nurtured. These signaling behaviors are more complex than the simple reflexes and are often considered to be fixed action patterns. As the infant matures, other behaviors, such as crawling, walking, and talking, facilitate contact between parent and child.

There is support for Bowlby's notion that the signaling behaviors are innate. Even infants born blind or blind and deaf acquire a social smile at approximately 6 weeks, as do normal infants. In fact, children blind and deaf since birth reveal a wide range of normal behaviors, including laughing, crying, babbling, and pouting, and typical facial expressions of fear, anger, and sadness (Eibl-Eibesfeldt, 1975). For example, they throw back their heads when laughing and stomp their feet when angry. Thus, these naturally occurring deprivation situations show that visual and auditory experiences that would allow imitative learning are not necessary for these signaling or expressive behaviors to develop. Further evidence for the universality of the human smile and other expressions comes from observations of these behaviors in infants in many cultures (see Eibl-Eibesfeldt, 1975, for a review). Darwin long ago observed smiling in infants of every culture with which he had contact.

It is highly unlikely that these expressive behaviors could be taught to these normal infants or to blind and deaf children. Smiling and laughing involve a complex sequence of coordinated movements or sounds. Eibl-Eibesfeldt (1975) describes a deaf and blind 12-year-old with severe brain damage who was unable to learn simple actions such as bringing a spoon to her mouth, in spite of an intense training program. Yet she was able to smile, laugh, and cry. Even the possibility that blind and deaf children might learn facial expressions by touching the mother's face and imitating those movements was ruled out by a child deaf and blind since birth, who was born with no arms. Despite these handicaps, he showed normal facial expressions.

Bowlby proposed four principles, quoted below, which account for the development of the infant's bias toward humans in general and attachment to a particular adult, the caretaker:

1. An in-built bias towards looking at certain patterns in preference to others and at things that move.

2. Exposure learning, by which the familiar comes to be distinguished from the strange.

3. An in-built bias to approach the familiar (and later to withdraw from the strange).

4. Feedback of results, by which a behavioural sequence is augmented when it is followed by certain results and diminished when it is followed by others (1969, p. 273).

As a result of these principles of development, the attachment to adults in general evolves, usually around 6 to 9 months of age, into attachment to one or a few specific adults. This specific attachment can be seen in the infant's protest when separated from a particular adult, as opposed to all adults. This separation is an innate "cue to danger" that elicits signaling behavior intended to restore proximity.

The infant and adult behaviors eventually become synchronized into an "attachment behavioral system," according to Bowlby. The appearance and behavior of each member serve as sign stimuli for the fixed action pattern in the other. Each member of the system comes to expect that the other will respond to its own behavior in certain ways. The child's expectations are part of his "internal working models" — mental representations of the world, attachment figures, and the self. These models help the child to interpret and evaluate new situations, then choose a behavior such as playing or seeking the attachment figure for comfort. When the infant's expectation that the parent will respond to his cries or calls (his basic trust, in Erikson's theory) is shattered by the prolonged absence of the parent, anxiety arises. The infant's distress, angry protest, and rejection of others eventually turns into grieving for the lost parent and general detachment from humans. After a period of grieving, the infant may develop new specific attachments.

Between the ages of about 9 and 18 months, the infant's various individual behaviors, especially sucking, clinging, crying, smiling, and following, become incorporated into more complex, self-correcting "control systems." These systems have the goal of maintaining an acceptable proximity to the mother. These control systems are described later in the chapter.

Bowlby's theory of attachment includes many of the characteristics of the general theory of ethology. Species-specific reflexes and fixed action patterns, which are the products of evolution, ensure the proximity of the mother to the child. Lorenz's drives, however, are not used in the theory. Sensitive periods and general and specific learning abilities biologically predispose infants and caretakers to develop a system of synchronized interactions. Bowlby goes beyond general ethological theory by suggesting that a control system regulates the distance between the child and the caretaker. In keeping with ethological theory, Bowlby relies heavily on observations of children and animals. However, much of the observational research on attachment stimulated by his theory was conducted in laboratory settings.

The ethological account of attachment, with its focus on innate behaviors, obviously contrasts with learning theory's focus on the reinforcement value of food (or, in later versions, other stimuli, such as warmth and physical contact), which establishes the mother as a secondary reinforcer. Although it seems likely that pleasant interactions have a positive effect on the bond between child and adult, ethologists point out that attachment occurs even when the attachment object physically abuses the infant. Ethology also differs from Freudian theory in accounting for attachment. Although some ethologists think that drives are involved in attachment, these drives are not primarily sexual in nature. Finally, ethology differs from both traditional learning and Freudian theory in stressing the infant's effect on the parent as much as the parent's effect on the child.

Bowlby (1980) has incorporated into his theory some of the notions of information-processing theory. Unsatisfactory early social relationships, abnormally strong repression, and thinking disorders can be explained in part by general principles of selective attention and selective forgetting. For example, if a young child's attachment behavior is continually aroused, but not responded to, he eventually excludes from awareness sights, thoughts, or feelings that normally would activate attachment behavior.

## Adults' Responsiveness to Infants

One of the most important contributions of the ethological account of attachment is that adults, as well as infants, are biologically predisposed to develop attachment. In species in which the infant depends on the parents for survival, innate caretaking responses in adults should be retained over the course of evolution. Adult attachment behavior can be elicited by signaling behaviors or by the infant's babyish appearance. Many infants emit calls to which the mother responds. For example, ultrasonic sounds from a young mouse elicit nest-building behavior in the adult female mouse (Noirot, 1974). Human signaling behaviors, such as smiling, visually fixating the face, and babbling, elicit the parent's attention and interest.

The idea that the infant's babyish appearance also elicits caretaking was proposed by Lorenz (1943). He noted that the infants of many species, especially mammals, share certain physical characteristics, which are depicted in Figure 5.1. These characteristics include a head that is large in relation to the body, a forehead that is large in relation to the rest of the face, limbs that are relatively short and heavy, large eyes at or below the midline of the head, and round, prominent

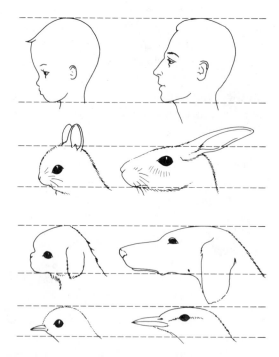

**FIGURE 5-1** ■ *Characteristics of babyishness or cuteness common to several species. [From "Die angeborenen Formen möglicher Erfahrung," by Konrad Lorenz, in Zeitschrift für Tierpsychologie, 1943, 5, 235–409. Reproduced by permission of Verlag Paul Parey.]*

cheeks. This description is simply an objective description of what is better known as cuteness. This babyishness is exaggerated in baby dolls for children and in young animals in the Disney cartoon films. Interestingly, Gould (1980) has observed that as Mickey Mouse became more lovable and well behaved over the years, his physical appearance became more babyish—a larger head with softer, more rounded features and larger eyes.

Studies of adults' and children's responses to pictures of infants or to live infants have included physiological measures (pupil enlargement or changes in heart rate), behavioral measures (amount of interaction with the infant), or self-reports (rating the attractiveness of faces). This research shows that people respond positively to infant faces. For example, 12- and 13-year-old girls who had begun menstruation rated pictures of infants more positively than did boys of the same age. In contrast, girls who had not begun menstruation did not differ from boys in their ratings (Goldberg, Blumberg, and Kriger, 1982). However, the responsiveness to the infants is not always greatest among females or during the childbearing years. The pattern of results depends on the type of response measure used, the physical and social nature of the testing situation, the person's experience with young children, and the person's cultural background (Berman, 1980). Thus, social factors, such as cultural expectations, appear to play at least some role in responsiveness to infants. Interpretation is also clouded by the fact that infants as young as 4 months also prefer looking at babies to looking at children or adults (McCall and Kennedy, 1980).

## Research Stimulated by Bowlby

Now that Bowlby's and Lorenz's accounts of human attachment have been described, we turn to recent empirical work on human attachment. Bowlby's portrayal of attachment stimulated novel and important research. Psychologists studied attachment from Uganda to Scotland to university laboratories in Baltimore.

The caretaker forms an emotional bond to the child in the first few days of life. This is called *bonding*. One of the most exciting discoveries from recent attachment research is that there may be a sensitive period for bonding during the first few hours after birth. It is tempting to draw an analogy with the sensitive period for imprinting in birds. Klaus and Kennell (1976) compared two groups of mothers and newborns. A control group followed usual hospital procedures, that is, a look at their babies at birth, brief contact at 6 to 8 hours, and 20 to 30 minutes of contact every 4 hours, when they fed their infants. An "extra-contact group" was given their nude babies for 1 hour of contact in the first 2 hours after birth and for 5 extra hours, compared with the control group, on each of the following 3 days. At the baby's examination 1 month later, the mothers from the extra-contact group held and soothed the infants more, showed more eye contact and fondling when they fed the infant, and reported they were less likely to leave the infant with another caretaker, in comparison to the control group. The differences were still present at 1 year. By 5 years of age, children in the extra-contact group had higher IQ and language-test scores. Although there is disagreement about the replicability of this research, its methodological adequacy, and its proper interpretation (Myers, 1984), the research does point to the importance of events occurring shortly after birth.

A different body of research points out the infant's bias toward attending to people early in life. Newborns prefer to look at human faces rather than inanimate objects. By the third week, the infant gurgles and makes various "pleasure sounds" in response to the sound of the human voice. Interpretations of this early predisposition toward social stimuli must be made very cautiously, however. On the one hand, these social stimuli may constitute sign stimuli that elicit the infant's innate responses. On the other hand, the responses may be mediated by the infant's preference for stimuli that are complex or involve movement and high black–white contrast (with respect to the eyes, hairline, and the like). Of course, this preference may be due to the nature of the nervous system, and ultimately may be as biological as the first explanation (see Cohen and Salapatek, 1975, for a discussion of these issues). Another type of facial preference is infants' preference for female faces that have been rated as attractive, rather than unattractive, by adults (Langlois et al., 1987).

Infants also appear to be predisposed to learn to discriminate their mother's odor from that of others. Two-week-old breast-fed infants turned toward a pad that had been worn in their mother's underarm area rather than a pad worn by some other lactating female (Cernoch and Porter, 1985). This was not true of bottle-fed infants. In addition, neither group of infants recognized their father's odor. Just as infants can recognize their mother's odor, so do mothers quickly recognize their infant's distinctive smell. Six hours after giving birth, and after only a single exposure to their babies, blindfolded mothers could pick out, by smell alone, their own baby from a set of three babies (Russell, Mendelson, and Peeke, 1983). Fathers could not do this.

One of Bowlby's colleagues, Ainsworth (1973), focused on the role of the attached parent as a "secure base" for exploration. The parent is a secure home port from which the child ventures to explore the next room or the next block and to which he returns from time to time for "emotional refueling" (Mahler, 1968). If, however, the responses to the child's signaling behaviors have been inappropriate (unpredictable, slow, abusive, or not matched to the child's needs), the child feels insecure and is less likely to use the mother as a base for exploring a strange environment (Ainsworth, 1973). Lamb (1978) also stresses the appropriateness of the adult's responses rather than the total amount of interaction. Thus, infants, become attached to fathers who respond appropriately to the child's signals, even when the total amount of time spent with the father is small.

A further controversy surrounds the issue of how parental physical abuse of the infant affects the attachment bond. After reviewing the effects of maltreatment of infants of various nonhuman species, Rajecki, Lamb, and Obmascher (1978) concluded that there is no evidence that maltreatment interferes with the development or maintenance of the social bond. Although this result seems to be counter to common sense, and certainly is counter to the predictions of learning theory, it makes some sense within an ethological framework. The physical assault causes distress in the infant, which leads him to seek proximity to his attachment figure, even when that figure is the source of the abuse. On the other hand, as Rajecki et al. point out, child abuse would not seem to be the "ordinarily expectable environment" for which evolution prepares the child.

The work on attachment spearheaded by Bowlby has grown to include not only the above issues, which are closely tied to ethology, but also much broader questions about early social relations. These topics include fear of strangers, individual differences in the course of attachment, the role of cognitive development in attachment, sex differences in parent-child attachment, and multiple attachments (day care, a kibbutz, peers, and fathers).

## Peer Interaction

Children's social interactions involve not only the family, especially the parents, as we have seen, but also the peer group. Ethological studies of animals' dominance hierarchies, aggression, play, altruistic behavior, and nonverbal communication led naturally to observations of these behaviors in groups of children in natural settings. Blurton-Jones (1972) and McGrew (1972) brought this approach into the mainstream of developmental psychology.

A basic feature of the organization of nonhuman primate groups is the *dominance hierarchy*: a pattern of social relationships involving the resolution of social conflict. It involves the distribution of power, especially access to resources such as food or mates, among group members by setting implicit "rules" as to who can control whom (Hinde, 1974). To illustrate ethologically oriented research on children's dominance hierarchies, we turn to a study by Strayer and Strayer (1976). They videotaped the free play of a group of preschool children toward the end of the school year, when the group had stabilized. The dominance relations could be inferred from the outcomes of three categories of naturally occurring social conflict between two children. These conflicts included physical attacks, threat gestures, and object or position struggles (physical or nonphysical struggles over a toy, standing at the front of the line, and the like). In response to these conflicts, a child could submit, seek help, counterattack, give up the object or position, or make no response. The child who wins in these encounters is considered to be the more dominant. These categories of initiated conflict and response to the conflict are quite similar to those used to study relations in nonhuman primate groups. The analysis of the videotapes revealed a relatively rigid and stable dominance hierarchy in the group. Although boys initiated more conflict than did girls, boys were not higher in the hierarchy than girls overall. It is interesting that there was a low frequency of counterattacks. Strayer and Strayer suggest that this indicates that the stable dominance hierarchy minimizes group aggression, just as in nonhuman primate groups. Other research, in agreement with this argument, shows that conflicts are high among humans when groups first form, then drop drastically (Savin-Williams, 1976).

The Strayer and Strayer study reflects the ethological approach in its content (dominance hierarchies observed in animals), method (observation of behavior in its natural context and subsequent categorization of this behavior), and theory (emphasis on behaviors adaptive for the species). The following sampling of research illustrates other areas of peer interaction of interest to ethologists: patterns of play in preschool children (Smith and Connolly, 1972), maintaining a preferred physical distance from other people (Peery and Crane, 1980), and children's appeasement behaviors, such as slumping the shoulders and bowing the head, which cause aggression to cease (Ginsburg, Pollman, and Wauson, 1977). The ethological approach clearly contrasts with social learning theory's focus on how a behavior (for example, aggression) in individual children is affected by reinforcement, punishment, and imitation.

It may seem strange that negative, aggressive, power-oriented social relationships have been of much greater interest than have positive, cohesive relationships. Indeed, Strayer (1980) reports that during a period of observation at a nursery school, there were fewer than 200 competitive or aggressive episodes in contrast to more than 1000 affiliative episodes. Strayer and his associates have recently tried to correct this bias toward examining negative behaviors by studying naturally occurring friendship groups in preschool children, stable patterns of proximity and contact behaviors among children, sharing, and helping. It is interesting that they found that the children's social preferences did not appear to be strongly related to the dominance hierarchy. That is, the more dominant children were not necessarily preferred for play and other contact. Finally, it should be noted that sociobiologists have been interested in developing genetic models to outline a biological basis of altruistic behavior.

One important aspect of social interaction at any phase in the life span involves obtaining resources from the environment. As Charlesworth (1988, p. 24) expresses it:

Whether it is an infant crying for attention, a preschooler struggling with a sibling over a toy, an adolescent trying to impress a peer, a graduate seeking a job, a scientist writing a grant proposal, or an octogenarian looking for someone to shovel snow, the possibility is always present of failing to acquire what one needs because of the competing needs of someone else. While all needs obviously do not have to be satisfied, a certain proportion of them must be if the individual is to carry out normal life functions.

Charlesworth (1988) has proposed a model for identifying which resources children seek, how they try to acquire these resources, and how successful they are in these attempts. A child often must compete with others in order to acquire and keep resources. Competitive behaviors can range from aggression and intimidation to manipulation, deception, and even cooperation (Charlesworth, 1988). Cooperation is a form of competition in at least two ways. First, two children may work together to obtain a resource sought by other children. Second, the contribution of one person may be greater than, but result in fewer resources than, that of the person with whom he is cooperating. Charlesworth refers to such "cheating" in lions. Male lions drive the prey downwind to an area where the females are waiting to kill the prey. Although the females have the more dangerous and demanding task, the males take the greater share of the kill (Trivers, 1985).

The task of obtaining resources changes developmentally. In most families an infant need only signal his needs through crying or fussing in order to obtain resources. Later, during socialization, children acquire a variety of skills for obtaining resources—aggressing, lying, threatening, frightening, flattering, helping, sharing, and working together. Through experience, children learn which strategy is most effective in various situations. The types of resources that are most important also change developmentally. Charlesworth suggests that Erikson's eight developmental crises, or tasks, can be seen as changes in which resources are needed most critically—such as access to food and attention in infancy, materials and tools during grade school, and a mate during late adolescence.

Charlesworth (1988) has examined preschoolers' resource-obtaining behaviors in a situation in which four children attempt to obtain a resource—viewing a cartoon movie. One child can view the cartoon only if a second child turns on the movie light and a third turns a crank to start the movie. A fourth child must simply be a bystander. The most successful strategy is to somehow get into the viewing position and then get others to turn on the light and crank the switch. Thus, a mixture of assertive, selfish, and cooperative behaviors is required. The tendency to adopt this strategy can be predicted from such factors as dominance rank in the classroom, gender, age, and friendship. An analysis of the videotapes of the children's interaction has led to an observational scheme that categorizes various types of preschool resources, resource-acquisition behaviors, reactions to such behaviors, and outcomes of the interaction. Resource-acquisition behaviors include several types of verbal behaviors, such as requests, appeals to take turns, and threats, and several types of physical behaviors, such as touches, blocks, and attacks.

More generally, Charlesworth has attempted to describe (1) the nature of the child's behavior and his resource environment and (2) how the interaction between the two changes developmentally and underlies individual differences in how well the child adapts to his environment. Some children have fewer resources available than others, and some are more skilled at obtaining them. Children who have mental or physical handicaps or who come from physically or psychologically impoverished environments may be at a disadvantage in obtaining resources necessary for satisfactory development.

### Facial Expressions and Bodily Movements

Certain facial expressions or bodily movements communicate emotions or intentions. Earlier we saw evidence from deaf and blind children that some of these expressions are innate. In addition, cross-cultural studies reveal certain universal behaviors. For example, Darwin and generations of explorers and anthropologists have observed that smiling indicates pleasure or appeasement. It has been suggested that the adaptive significance of an infant's smile is to make the tired, busy mother of the young infant feel that those difficult first months are worthwhile (Robson, 1967). Another expression, anger, is expressed by a forward stance (threatening attack), clenched fists, and a facial expression of rage in the bared teeth and the turning downward of the corners of the mouth (Eibl-Eibesfeldt, 1975). Eibl-Eibesfeldt reports "agreement in the smallest detail" in the flirting behavior of girls in nine different cultural groups studied. The flirting sequences include smiling, then lifting the eyebrows in a quick, jerky movement in such a way that the eye slit briefly enlarges, then a turning away, a lowering of the gaze, and a dropping of the eyelids. These universal expressions and movements should not, however, mask the many emotions and meanings that are expressed in different ways in different cultures. For example, "No" may be expressed by shaking the head, sticking out the tongue, or pointing the lips and pushing them outward.

Human nonverbal expressions have been compared with those of other animals. Certain monkeys have a "silent bared-teeth display," which indicates submission. This expression may be related to the human smile, which turns away aggression (Eibl-Eibesfeldt, 1975). A slightly different barring of the teeth, however, indicates aggressive intent. Bowing the head in chimpanzees, shaking the fist (waving a claw in crabs), and kissing and embracing upon meeting in chimpanzees all have their human counterparts. Like other primates, children some-times display lowered-brow expressions when being assertive during free play (Brannigan and Humphries, 1972). As zoo visitors know, chimpanzees even seem to laugh (at the human animals staring at them). These behaviors are often derived from a behavior that has some other function. It has been suggested that kissing in humans and other animals is ritualized feeding (Rothmann and Teuber, 1915). Ethologists have argued that these social signals permit communication of intent and thus enhance social interaction and stabilize the social group.

## Problem Solving

Cognitive ethology is a rapidly growing area. The ethological view-point concerning intelligence assumes that "intelligent behavior did aid survival over evolution — that the gene complexes responsible for the brain mechanisms generating such behavior were selected for positively by certain environmental factors during evolution because the behav-ior itself contributed to reproductive success" (Charlesworth, 1979, p. 510). As a result, the human brain is prepared for what is called an "evolutionarily expected environment." A child's cognitive system is designed to deal with a certain general type of environment, the type in which the species has evolved.

Although most ethological research on children reflects the theory's interest, historically, in social interaction, there are a few recent at-tempts to clarify the nature of cognitive development by observing naturally occurring problem-solving episodes. Charlesworth (1983) ob-served toddlers' responses to barriers (or "blocks") encountered in their everyday lives at home. Examples of these problems include being unable to reach a glass of juice (a physical block), being told by the mother to stop an activity (a social block), and being asked by someone to identify something (an informational block). In each case, the problem refers to a relationship between the child and his environment. A block can come from outside the individual or from the individual himself—his need or desire for something unavailable. Charlesworth recorded all blocks to the child's behavior and his response to each block, for example, compliance, ignoring, or hitting. The $3\frac{1}{2}$- to $4\frac{1}{2}$-year-olds, for example, encountered approximately 18 problems per hour and solved the problems 33 percent of the time. Social blocks occurred much more frequently than physical or informational blocks in these situations. It is striking that solving social problems is not assessed to any extent on standard intelligence tests or on Piagetian cognitive tasks. In addition, many of the problem-solving episodes lasted several minutes—much longer than the problems presented in intelligence tests. Charlesworth (1988) also has examined problem solving in a Down's syndrome girl and among preschoolers at nursery school in free play or instructional settings. In addition, he has documented the greater frequency of blocks, particularly informational and physical ones, among physically handicapped than among normal children. The handicapped children interacted with the teachers more than did the normal children, who were involved in significantly more peer interaction. Finally, his ethological analysis included undergraduate honor students who faced blocks such as deciding what to wear in cold weather, running out of eggs for breakfast, facing difficulty in finding library materials, being asked for advice by a friend, and forgetting how to make garlic bread.

The Charlesworth research illustrates the kind of information about cognition that we do not have from current approaches to studying this topic. The intelligence-testing approach views intelligence as a trait or disposition that is revealed by certain tests administered by an adult, usually in a setting unfamiliar to the child. Laboratory studies of problem solving examine a narrow range of tasks, which typically involve physical, nonsocial events. In contrast, Charlesworth's ethological research studies the function and ecological significance of the child's spontaneous use of his intelligence. The research tells us which features of everyday life pose problems, how they are usually handled, and how the child's reaction changes developmentally. Intelligence in action helps the child adapt to the physical and social problems created by parents, peers, his own body, furniture, and toys in his environment.

Although Piaget's account of the sensorimotor period came from his observations of his own children, most of his information about children past infancy came from semistructured interviews. He had little concern with the frequency of occurrence of various categories of behavior because his concern was with the underlying knowledge structures. He also did not ask which kinds of everyday environmental circumstances require the use of such knowledge as conservation or transitive reasoning and whether these circumstances are more frequent at some developmental levels than others. The main similarity between the Piagetian and the ethological approach to intelligence is their mutual concern with how an organism adapts to its environment. Both identify biological predispositions toward learning, for example, the assimilation–accommodation process (Piaget) and specialized learning abilities (ethology).

Before closing this section on applications of ethology to development, we should consider research on adults that has developmental implications. One topic of interest is aggression and wars. Lorenz, in *On Aggression* (1966), proposed that since there is evidence that aggression is innate in animals, aggression in humans may also be innate. There is much controversy over this conclusion. The fact that humans and other animals exhibit aggression does not necessarily mean that this behavior is primarily under genetic control in humans. Most human aggression has a cognitive component, which is lacking or less important in other animals.

Another social behavior of interest is the maintenance of a preferred distance between the self and another person, just as birds on a wire keep a certain distance from one another. The desire to prevent another person from coming too close has been observed in many cultures, but the preferred difference may vary from culture to culture. One experiment (Barash, 1973) examined the response to violation of one's territory. A person sat down close to another person in a library. The subject frequently turned away and sometimes built a barrier of books or other objects between the intruder and themselves. This preferred distance may be related to the establishment of group territories. These territories are common in many animal species and serve to spread out the population to avoid starvation and overcrowding.

## MECHANISMS OF DEVELOPMENT

Because ethologists have chosen to focus on behaviors with a strong biological component, they stress biological processes as mechanisms of development. Physical maturation, including hormonal changes, locomotor development, and increased efficiency of the nervous system, underlies the emergence of sensitive periods or of fixed action patterns at appropriate times. For example, the reproductive drive and nest-building behavior surface when a bird matures to the point where reproduction is possible. All of these biological mechanisms of behavior interact with experience, of course.

In addition to the biological changes over the life span are the innate general and specific learning abilities discussed earlier. The learning abilities, built into the nervous system, allow the organism to profit from its experience.

Although ethologists emphasize biological mechanisms, they also study learned behaviors that lead to adaptation. For example, even if it turns out that dominance hierarchies and altruism in children are entirely learned, such behavior patterns are still of interest because they lead to a socially cohesive group, which is considered an adaptive system.

## POSITION ON DEVELOPMENTAL ISSUES

### Human Nature

Human nature is just one hodgepodge out of many conceivable.

[*Wilson, 1978, p. 23*]

The human is a social animal with certain species-specific characteristics. He is a biological organism that has evolved within a particular environmental niche. Human intelligence, language, social attachment, and perhaps even aggression and altruism are part of human nature because they serve or once served a purpose in the struggle of the species to survive. The child's developmental level, therefore, is defined mainly in terms of the biologically based behaviors he possesses.

Asking whether humans are mechanistic or organismic highlights the differences among ethological theorists. As the later section on models indicates, Lorenz stresses the automatic, reflexlike nature of behavior, whereas Bowlby focuses on systems of behavior. The former view is primarily mechanistic; the latter, organismic. In the Lorenzian view, as in the Freudian view, humans are moved by biological drives to hunt for food, seek a mate, and run for safety. In addition, sign stimuli elicit fixed action patterns automatically. These notions are much less central in both Bowlby's theory and modern ethological theory, in which the human spontaneously acts to meet the demands of his environment. He actively searches for the parent, food, or a mate. Children explore, play, solve problems, and seek out playmates. In Bowlby's control-systems approach, the human seeks to maintain a certain state, for example, an acceptable degree of proximity to the caretaker. The child actively maintains that state by calling for the mother or crawling toward her. Thus, the child is self-regulating and active. This cybernetic system, in which the human interacts with the environment and uses feedback to maintain equilibrium, is reminiscent of Piaget's notion of the equilibration process.

## Qualitative Versus Quantitative Development

Ethology allows for both qualitative and quantitative change. It is not a stage theory and therefore does not posit large-scale qualitative changes in development. In a sense, there is qualitative change when biological maturation proceeds to the point where a sign stimulus triggers a fixed action pattern that has never appeared before. In this way, a new behavior appears in a more or less discontinuous fashion. There is also qualitative change when a drive or system is expressed in different behaviors as the child develops. One such instance is attachment, which is expressed at first by crying or smiling and later by crawling toward the mother or talking to her. The underlying attachment, however, is changing quantitatively, usually toward increased organization, security, and efficiency. More generally, there is quantitative change, in that the interweaving of innate and learned components becomes smoother and more efficient during development.

## Nature Versus Nurture

Although ethologists focus on the biological basis of behavior, like most of the theorists in this volume they are interactionists with respect to the effects of heredity and environment. The genotype and the environment operate together to produce changes in the child over his lifetime. One implication of this interaction is that a particular experience has more impact if it occurs during a relevant sensitive period rather than at another time.

Ethologists' view of how innate and environmental factors interact has changed over the years. Lorenz originally proposed an "instinct-training interlocking," or chaining of units of behavior that were either innate or learned. More recently, ethologists have rejected the distinction between innate and learned behaviors. Both heredity and environment contribute to all behavior, and there is a continual interweaving of these influences.

## What Develops

The most important behaviors to develop are species-specific behaviors that are important for survival. These include such behaviors as social attachment, dominance–submission, eating, mating, and infant care. In addition, what develops are drives (according to Lorenz), fixed action patterns, and systems (according to Bowlby). The theory seeks to explain similarities in what behaviors are acquired and how they develop in all humans and in both humans and other animals. Although interspecies differences in development are of interest, little attention is given to individual differences within a species.

## THEORETICAL NATURE OF THE THEORY

Classical ethology (Lorenz) draws loosely on the reflex model and the hydraulic or "flush toilet" model (Dewsbury, 1978). Sign stimuli, fixed action patterns, and reflexes are hallmarks of the reflex model. This model, as described in earlier chapters on Freudian and learning theory, is a mechanistic, stimulus–response model. It is based on early views of how the nervous system operates. The hydraulic energy model, also used by Freudian and learning theory, refers to the drive notion. As in physical systems, when pressure builds up, it must be released somehow. In Lorenz's account, this drive energy is released when the appropriate sign stimulus "opens the value." When the pressure becomes too great, the behavior is displayed in the absence of an appropriate sign stimulus.

Bowlby used control-systems theory from engineering as a model of how attachment forms an organizational system. Control systems are goal-directed and use feedback to regulate the system in order to achieve this goal. A simple control system is a thermostat, which maintains a particular room temperature (the goal) by comparing the actual temperature (the feedback) with the desired temperature. With respect to behavioral systems, Bowlby proposes that genetic action causes the behavioral system to develop, but the developed system is flexible enough to adjust to changes in the environment, within pre-scribed limits. Just as the human respiratory system works within a particular range of oxygen, a behavioral system operates efficiently within a certain range of variation in relevant features of the environment. The particular acceptable range of social and physical stimuli relevant for attachment varies from species to species. In human attachment, infants have a goal: an acceptable degree of proximity to the adult. When the infant detects that the adult is too far away (feedback), he corrects this state by crying or crawling, which reestablishes contact and reachieves equilibrium in the system. The limits of acceptable distance vary, depending on internal factors, such as hunger or illness, and external factors, such as the presence of an adult stranger or other cues of danger. The development of a secure attachment expands the distance acceptable by establishing the caretaker as a secure base from which the child can explore.

Ethologists have used various models of exactly how biological regulating mechanisms control the course of development, while allowing for the modification of development by the environment. One model, proposed by Waddington (1957), represents development as a ball rolling down an "epigenetic landscape." As the ball descends, this landscape becomes increasingly furrowed by valleys that greatly restrict the sideways movement of the ball. Slight perturbations from the developmental pathway can be corrected later through a "self-righting tendency," and the ball returns to its earlier groove. Thus, the general course of development is set, but some variation is possible because of particular environmental events.

Other models of the interactions of biological controls and environmental forces are discussed by Bateson (1976). One model, for instance, analyzes the costs and benefits of a behavior to a species

(McFarland, 1976). Although these models have developmental implications, they have had little impact on human developmental research thus far.

Because ethology seeks causes on many levels, the inductive, deductive, and functional modes of theory construction can also be seen. The development of the ethogram is primarily an inductive activity, in that the resulting description is little more than a listing of facts about the animal's behavior. The application of the theory of evolution is, on the other hand, a deductive process, in that hypotheses are generated from a set of propositions. Finally, as in most psychological and biological research, there is the functional mode of theory development in the close interplay between theory and data as hypotheses are formulated, tested, and modified.

## EVALUATION OF THE THEORY

### Strengths

With respect to its utility for developmental psychology, ethology has already demonstrated several strengths. In addition, some of its potential contributions have not been fully exploited by developmental psychologists. Both realized and potential advantages are explored in three areas: theory, method, and content.

#### Theoretical Contributions

Ethology broadens our perspective on what constitutes an explanation of development. We can fully "understand" the child's behavior only if we expand our vision to include a larger space (the larger social context) and a larger time span (the history of the species). Ethologists identify two basic kinds of explanations: the *function* of behavior and the *cause* of behavior. Each of these categories is divided into subcategories. There are two types of questions about function, both of which refer to the effects of behavior. First, what is the immediate function of a behavior? Second, what is the survival value of a behavior? The immediate function refers to the direct outcome of a behavior. The infant's cry brings the parent. The survival value of this behavior to the species is that the parent will care for the infant and protect him from life-threatening dangers.

Tinbergen (1973) has identified three types of questions about the causes of behavior, based in part on the time span involved, which varies from seconds to centuries. These causes are immediate, ontogenetic, or phylogenetic.

1. Immediate causes are the antecedent events that come directly before the behavior. The infant smiles after viewing a human face or cries as a result of hunger pangs. Physiologically based motivation states are a common immediate cause.

2. The second type of cause encompasses a longer time span. Ontogenetic causation refers to how the genotype and the environment interact to produce changes in behavior over the child's lifetime. In this process, earlier events contribute to later events, as when a secure attachment may later on allow the child to explore new environments confidently, and even later encourage various independent behaviors.

3. Finally, in phylogenetic causation, the cause of a behavior lies in the earlier forms of the behavior as it was shaped over generations as a result of the food supply, types of predators, mating patterns, and so on. Thus, a developmental psychologist seeking a phylogenetic cause of sex differences in behavior would consider environmental pressures in the early history of the human species.

Most developmental research has examined immediate causes or ontogenetic causes. Much less attention has been given to phylogenetic causes or to the behavior's functions (immediate function or survival value). Development cannot be completely understood, however, until all these functions and causes are identified. Most other theories either have ignored the larger context of behavior or have simply acknowledged its influence but have not studied it. Piaget and Gibson were concerned with adaptation to the environment, but developed few theoretical concepts to deal with this process. Erikson stressed the influence of society on the developing individual and made cross-cultural comparisons, but did not seriously consider phylogenetic adaptation.

Related to the notion that there are various valid types of causes is the belief that there must be various levels of analysis of behavior. The organism, with its genetic, physiological, psychological, and behavioral aspects, is part of a system that includes the environment, with its physical, interpersonal, and cultural aspects. Therefore, ethologists study each of these levels, with the ultimate aim of understanding the entire organism – environment system. Each level of analysis contributes to our understanding of behavior and has its own set of principles. Behavior can never be reduced to any single level, such as the physiological. Only a theory with multiple levels of analysis is likely to disentangle the complex interweaving of innate and environmental forces during development. Although human developmental research currently proceeds at all these levels, progress at relating the various levels has been very slow. Ethological principles, because they concern many levels and their interrelationships, are potentially a unifying force in developmental psychology.

Ethology's focus on the function of behavior helps the investigator relate the child's behavior to its natural context. The way an investigator thinks about children's aggressive behavior changes if he discovers that one of its functions is to increase the overall stability and cohesiveness of the group. The focus changes from a problem in the child to a less problematic feature of human groups. Thus, looking at function gives a broader context in which to embed a particular behavior.

Questions about function usually lead to questions about adaptation. Eibl-Eibesfeldt (1975) argues that ethology can fruitfully study cultural adaptation as well as the biologically based phylogenetic adaptation that is the theoretical core of ethology. Most human behaviors are not a matter of life and death. Few behaviors of the human child literally and directly avoid predators or avert starvation or exposure. Even the weak, ill, mentally retarded, and physically deformed are cared for and reproduce. In short, many of the evolutionary forces that operate on other species are less influential for human survival. Thus, the notion of adaptation in humans may be most fruitfully applied to the question of how behaviors taught by a society produce *optimal adaptation* (rather than biological survival). Optimal adaptation might include happiness, a feeling of competence at play, success at school, efficient use of tools (for example, eating utensils, scissors, and pencils), and so on. When Charlesworth studies how children solve problems, he does not see mistakes and inefficient problem solving leading to death, and success leading to survival. He does, however, see how the infant, by applying his intelligence, increases his control over his physical and social environment. If ritualistic behaviors, such as greeting, giving gifts, and communicating dominance or submission to others, lead to a more stable group, they are of interest to ethologists even if they turn out to be culturally based rather than biologically controlled adaptations. As these examples illustrate, looking at phylogenetic adaptation in other species can suggest hypotheses about cultural adaptation in humans.

Another central theoretical notion is that behavior and its development can be understood best from a comparative point of view. Although ethology typically compares species, its concepts apply equally well to comparisons across cultures and among developmental levels. Ethologists have much in common with anthropologists. The basic logic of the comparative approach is that contrast brings understanding. We begin to understand a behavior by seeing where in today's human and nonhuman world or in previous times the behavior appears and does not appear. It is just as important to know what an organism does not do as to know what it does do.

Comparisons tell us what is universal to all species or all human cultures or all ages, despite environmental differences. For example, does a child raised in a kibbutz develop attachment bonds with his parents? Does the swaddling of young infants in some cultures retard their physical and intellectual development? Are there limits to how far cognition can develop without formal schooling?

Comparative studies reveal not only universals, but also critical differences in the environments that lead to differences in behavior in different groups. Just as different gene pools are compared by studying different species, different environmental niches are compared by studying different groups within one species. A comparison of the environments of children from different cultures may highlight the importance of such factors as the degree of industrialization, the stability of the food supply, the degree of differentiation of sex roles, and the methods of child rearing.

Typically, comparative studies find universal, species-specific, and culture-specific characteristics. For example, one universal aspect of development is that the organism is "ready" for different experiences at different ages. The timing of experience is important. However, there may be specific critical periods only in certain species, and the particular culture may modify the outcome of the critical period. Also, comparative studies suggest certain universal tasks of development, at least among primates, for instance, establishing proximity to the mother, communication, play, parenting, and food gathering. All species have some mechanism of care for the embryo and newborn, but there are species differences and, within humans, cultural differences in the exact form these mechanisms take. A final example is that aggression is expressed in all human cultures, but what elicits aggression, how it is expressed, how often it occurs, and how it functions are factors that change throughout development and vary somewhat from culture to culture.

A final important theoretical contribution is ethology's interest in development throughout the life span. There are different behaviors required for adaptation at different developmental points: staying close to the mother in infancy, exploring and playing in childhood, and reproducing and finding a place in the social hierarchy in adulthood.

## Methodological Contributions

What can we learn from scientists who spend hours staring at crabs and birds? The most timely contribution of ethology is its method of observing behavior in its natural context. Although it is not new for developmental psychologists to observe children at school or at home (for example, Barker and Wright, 1955), ethology provides theoretically based observational methods that supplement the more common empirical, nontheoretical descriptions of ongoing behavior. Ethology suggests which behaviors are most important, stresses the need to note what environmental events precede and follow the behavior, and provides a detailed analysis of how the organism and environment interact. It also describes the structure of the behavior and suggests how behaviors can be classified and compared with other species, cultures, or ages. In particular, observing the two-way interaction between people is fruitful for developmental psychology. Developmental psychologists are incorporating the notion that the infant can affect the mother as well as be influenced by her (Bell and Harper, 1977). It is even recognized that three-way interactions — among infant, mother, and father — must be considered. Ethologists have developed observational techniques to examine these interactions (Hutt and Hutt, 1970). For example, a sequence analysis of social interaction records that if person A does X, then person B does Y. This can show exactly how an infant and her parents control and modify each other's behavior and can identify situations in which one person's behavior has multiple causes.

Ethological observations can fruitfully be combined with traditional developmental methods. Developmental psychologists, particularly those studying cognition during childhood, have relied too heavily on the questioning of children. As Charlesworth (1988, p. 298) comments, "As soon as a research subject has the appropriate Piagetian operations and can talk, researchers stop observing and start asking. It's less strenuous that way." Ethologically based observations can supplement these verbal methods in important ways. Another possibility, largely untapped, is ethologically based longitudinal research, in which the same children are observed over a period of months or years. This method could identify continuities and discontinuities not only in the child's behavior—the usual focus of longitudinal studies—but also in the child's environment and the interaction between the child and the environment. Ethology includes a changing physical and social world as well as a changing child in its account of development. The social environment, in particular, changes its demands on the child during development.

The criticism in an earlier chapter that information processing is lacking in ecological validity points to the need for observational studies of cognitive and perceptual development. As an illustration, consider what ethologically oriented observational studies might contribute to the understanding of the development of attention. Developmental psychologists nearly always examine attention in the laboratory. They typically examine children's attention to physical attributes, such as shape, color, or size, or attention to drawings of familiar objects. The experimenter presents a stimulus or a task, and the child responds to it in some way. The child sorts the objects or tries to remember them or say their names when they are exposed very briefly. An ethologist, in contrast, would ask the following questions: What types of objects or events does the child look at or listen to at home and at school? What events elicit attention, maintain it, and end it? What events distract the child? How often do distractions occur? Does efficient attention lead to efficient problem solving or other adaptive behaviors? How does attentional behavior differ from setting to setting? Does playful, exploratory attention resemble that observed in other primates, other ages of humans, and other cultures? Can the dominance hierarchy be inferred by who looks at whom and for how long?

Such questions are seldom, if ever, raised in studies of attention. The questions about how attention actually operates cause a shift in focus that makes previous research appear narrow and inflexible. Paralleling Charlesworth's ethological studies of intelligence, it is likely that many distractions and other events controlling attention are social and dynamic, rather than nonsocial and static, as is assumed by laboratory researchers. Laboratory studies tell us what *can* happen during the attentional process. Ethological studies tell us what in fact usually *does* happen, and they suggest new variables to be examined in depth in the laboratory. In a similar way, ethological methods could be applied fruitfully to the other theories examined in this volume. We know little about the natural context of the spontaneous occurrence of defense mechanisms, mathematical reasoning, ego-strengthening experiences, memory strategies, visual search for objects, and operant conditioning.

Ethologically based observational studies potentially could make a tremendous contribution to developmental research in the next few years because the field is moving toward an ecologically based approach. B. L. White (1969) described developmental psychology as "an edifice without a foundation" because the field has slighted its natural-history phase, which would have established a data base. It has been suggested that the field moved too quickly into its experimental phase. Bronfenbrenner characterized much of developmental psychology as the "science of the strange behavior of children in strange situations with strange adults for the briefest possible periods of time" (1977, p. 513). Bronfenbrenner, as well as others, has called for an ecological psychology of human development. There is recent interest in such topics as the effects of environmental noise, cognitive maps of large-scale environments, and the effects of changes in the role of the family in society. Ethology can play a heuristic role in this new interest in ecology. In addition, the recent interest in federal social policy relevant to children badly needs a description of the present environments of children and an understanding of how these environments enhance or disrupt development. Finally, current concerns about cognitive assessment could be addressed by ethological studies. Recent laboratory studies with young children show that whether a child demonstrates a particular competence, such as communicating nonegocentrically or comprehending social interactions, often depends on how familiar, meaningful, or ecologically valid the assessment task is for the child (for example, Shatz and Gelman, 1973). Thus, developmental assessment also has a need for information about children's natural environments.

## Content Contributions

Many of the theoretical and methodological contributions outlined here are potential rather than realized, with respect to developmental research. In terms of achieved contribution, ethology has had most of its influence on developmental psychology by bringing certain content areas to the attention of investigators. Although ethological methods and theory potentially cut across all content areas, the greatest influence has come through work on attachment. Bowlby's biologically based account of attachment challenged learning theory and stimulated hundreds of studies not only of attachment but also of such related topics as fear of strangers, parent-child interactions, the effects of early experience, and sensitive periods. Other behaviors considered to be universal and important for adaptation are peer interaction (for example, dominance hierarchies), nonverbal communication (facial expressions and bodily movements), and problem solving. Ethology brought new life to these areas, which previously had been limited mainly to the point of view of social learning theory and Piagetian theory. In addition, ethology pointed out certain behaviors that typically were overlooked. Examples of these are averting one's gaze, hunching one's shoulders, sticking out the tongue, and regulating the distance between the self and the mother.

## Weaknesses

It may be somewhat unfair to criticize ethology's account of human development, because the theory's influence on developmental psychology has been relatively recent. The theory is still in its translation stage. It seems important, however, to point out critical shortcomings in theoretical, methodological, and substantive areas that must be addressed by ethological theory if it is to fulfill its promise as a theory of development. Some of these shortcomings merely reflect a lack of developmental research in certain areas; others are more serious because they reflect the incompleteness of the theory itself.

## Theoretical Limitations

As is true of other theories, ethology describes more than it explains. Many of the ethological notions that are most useful to developmental psychology require further elaboration if they are to serve as specific explanations of development. These notions include sensitive periods, the development of innate behaviors in an attachment structure, and the two-way influence between the child and his social and physical environment. The need for more specificity can be illustrated by considering the notion of a sensitive period. Concluding that the child acquires a behavior "because" he is in a sensitive period is similar to concluding that the child acquires conservation because he is in the stage of concrete operations. These general descriptive notions are only a first step. Invoking a sensitive period does not explain why the organism is pretuned to certain experiences at one time rather than another. A sensitive period must be understood not as a particular period of time, but as a particular developmental level. A developmental level is a specific organization of capabilities that allows the child to interact with the environment in certain ways, but not other ways. We need to be able to specify in a detailed way the exact process by which sensitive periods operate. What causes them to begin, have their effect, and end? More generally, what moves development along? Are the effects of extra contact between mother and infant in the first few hours after birth due to biological, perceptual , or cognitive variables or all these variables in interaction? Although the many studies of sensitive periods in other animals are beginning to provide a specific explanation, theoretical and empirical work on sensitive periods in humans lags far behind.

This lack of detailed explanation also can be seen in an example drawn from a typical topic of ethological research: the dominance structure of peer groups. By what process do children detect and understand the existence of this hierarchy and their own place in it? How do they use feedback from their interactions with other children in order to adjust their subsequent behavior? A promising line of research suggests that the development of transitive reasoning (A > B > C, . . .) is related to the perception of the dominance hierarchy in groups (Edelman and Omark, 1973). Since most human behavior is cognitively mediated, we need an account of the cognitive processes involved when social cues in the environment are interpreted and influence subsequent social behavior. In other words, how is information about the environment assimilated and linked up with behavior?

In addition to the problem of the lack of specific mechanisms of development involving immediate and ontogenetic causes, there is a problem with phylogenetic causes and how a behavior functions as an aid to survival. Questions about phylogenetic development and the origins of the behavior in biological adaptation are useful when we try to form hypotheses about a behavior but in fact are unanswerable with respect to human behavior. The phylogeny of anatomical structures can be gleaned from fossils, but we have no fossils of human behavior. At best we can speculate about how an upright stance, enlarged brain area, and increasingly sophisticated tools reflect changes in human behavior in our history. The other potential source of information about phylogeny — similar behaviors in closely related species — is also suspect. With respect to adaptation, Bowlby can speculate that the function of attachment is to keep the infant and caretaker close together, but what kind of evidence could be gathered in support of this? This function of bonding in humans may or may not be the same as in other primates. It is tempting to note superficial similarities in human and nonhuman primates, such as showing the teeth, and claim a phylogenetic relationship, but the claim may not be valid. The general problem remains of making inferences about human behavior on the basis of the behavior of other animals.

## Methodological Limitations

One obvious limitation to applying ethological methods to humans is that the most critical experiments are unethical. We cannot perform deprivation experiments such as preventing an infant from seeing a human smile for the first few weeks of life in order to see if the social smile is innate. In an early misguided experiment, Frederick II (1194–1250) raised babies in silence and near isolation to find out if there is a "natural" human language. The babies, unfortunately, died before the outcome was clear (Wallbank and Taylor, 1960). Instead of deprivation experiments, we must rely on naturally occurring deprivation, such as infants born blind or deaf. Even simply observing people raises ethical and legal questions about the invasion of privacy. The ethical issues are especially problematic because human social environments are very complex and therefore need to be manipulated experimentally in order to tease apart the influence of each variable. Bowlby's hypothesis concerning the effects of disrupting the early bond between mother and infant cannot be evaluated adequately because this event is confounded with changes in the organization of the entire family, economic changes within the family, changes in the father's behavior, the mother's detachment from the infant when she returns because she has changed during her long illness, and so on. For ethical reasons, however, the necessary experimental manipulations cannot be performed.

Another limitation to applying the methods of ethology lies in four basic problems inherent in observational research. First, it is difficult, often tedious, research to do. Large investments of time and effort are required for filming, making detailed descriptions of the behavior, classifying the behavior, and establishing adequate interobserver reliability as to when the behavior begins and ends and how it should be classified. An example of the last item is the difficulty of agreeing when an infant shows fear. Furthermore, it may be necessary to observe children in many different settings to obtain a description of typical behavior because it is not clear what constitutes a "natural environment" for children in a highly technological society. Should we study children running through a meadow, sitting in a classroom, or playing with electronic games? Finally, so many events may be occurring simultaneously that not all the behaviors can be attended to and recorded. Even filming may miss certain important behaviors, such as facial expressions. In short, a comprehensive, detailed ethogram of a species is a large undertaking. As Charlesworth notes, "Unlike most tests, which throw out a small net with a small mesh, the present method throws out a big net with a small mesh and thereby catches many small fish. Herein, of course, lies a big problem of effort and cost. The net gets awfully heavy very quickly" (1979, p. 522).

A second problem with the observational method is that with children beyond infancy there is a danger that the very presence of the observer changes the child's behavior. This is less of a problem when children are involved in group activities of interest to them and have become used to the observer's presence. Eibl-Eibesfeldt's side-angle camera, which is not yet used widely, could facilitate observations.

Third, there are conceptual problems in dividing the stream of behavior into units. The investigator must choose an appropriate level of analysis — not so large a unit of behavior that critical features of the behavior are lost, but not so small that the overall structure of the behavior is lost. Furthermore, it is not always clear what behaviors are relevant. If one is interested in dependency behaviors, does one include touching others, looking at others, asking for help? A related problem is that many behaviors have multiple meanings. When one child hits another child, this behavior may function as a sign of aggression or affection or playfulness. It is almost inevitable that preconceived notions about what behaviors are relevant or irrelevant influence the choice of behaviors to describe and the language used to encode the behavior. An observer unfamiliar with Bowlby's work might well record that the infant crawled to the door of the adjoining room, but would probably not record the distance between the mother and the infant.

Fourth, although a main reason for observing behavior in its natural context is to discover the function of the behavior, the function cannot always be inferred. For example, one function of attachment is to establish the mother as a secure base for the child's exploration later on. In this case, the behavior has a delayed function that could not be validated until much later.

## Content Limitations

Certain developmental phenomena may not be easily studied from the ethological perspective. Many interesting psychological events are not consistently reflected in behavior. Charlesworth found it necessary to limit his investigation of intelligence to overt behaviors, such as removing a physical barrier blocking a desired object. Many other aspects of intelligence, such as the mental manipulations of symbols, are not so easy to observe. Since behavior becomes more mediated and motivation becomes more complex with increasing age, observation of overt behavior may in general be more informative in infants and toddlers than in older children. Another implication of mediated behavior in humans is that fixed action patterns, drives, and sign stimuli, which guide observation of animals, may be much less useful for observing children.

Another limitation to the content of ethological research has been the search for behaviors found in all members of a species rather than a focus on individual differences within a species. Both types of information are important for developmental research. Actually, there is nothing inherent in ethological theory or methods that would prohibit a focus on individual variation. For example, Ainsworth (1973) observed that infants vary in whether they have a secure or an anxious attachment. In addition, she noted variations in the age at which an attachment to a specific person is acquired. Variations between children in the form of a behavior, its time of acquisition, and its frequency could be due to genetic variability or environmental variability or both in interaction. By observing individual differences in naturally occurring behavior, ethology is in a position to supplement traditional sources of information about individual differences: standardized tests that measure personality, intelligence, academic achievement, and aptitude. This potential contribution has not been exploited.

Finally, certain aspects of the environment that are critical to developmental issues have not been studied in a detailed way. Although ethological methods could identify critical ways in which the social and physical environments change from one developmental phase or stage to another and from one generation to the next, they have not yet done so. A complete developmental theory must consider a changing individual in a changing world that both changes during the child's lifetime and has changed from that of the previous generation. During the child's lifetime, changes occur not only in what the child is allowed to do but in what the child's culture expects of him and prepares him for; expectations change as a result of generational changes, such as an increase in working mothers or in the divorce rate. Bronfenbrenner (1977) notes that developmentalists must consider whether society's institutions, such as family and school, are supporting each other or working against each other, in preparing the child for adulthood.

## SUMMARY

Ethology is one of zoology's main contributions to developmental psychology. Thousands of hours spent observing animals have revealed important concepts concerning behavior. Each species, including the human, has a set of innate behaviors, specific to that species. These behaviors have evolved phylogenetically because they have increased that species' chances of survival in its particular environment. Some of the most important behaviors are social, such as mating dances, imprinting, dominance behaviors, and some forms of communication. Of particular interest are fixed action patterns elicited by sign stimuli. Even learned behaviors have a strong genetic component because each species has particular learning predispositions in the form of sensitive periods or general and specific learning abilities. Behaviors are studied by both observations in natural settings and experimental studies in laboratories.

The ethological point of view is most influential within developmental psychology in work on attachment. There is some evidence that the very young infant and the adult are pretuned to respond to each other. This work has expanded to include the effects of separation from the mother, the role of the father, the mother as a base for exploration, and bonding in the newborn. Observation of dominance hierarchies in mammals and other animals has led to studies of the human peer group, especially in preschool groups. Other work has revealed commonalities and differences in the facial expressions and bodily movements of humans and other animals. Most recently, a few investigators have asked what kinds of problems children attempt to solve and how they try to solve them in natural settings.

With respect to developmental issues, ethologists see humans as a species that has evolved in order to survive within a particular environmental niche. Theorists vary in whether this adaptation is primarily passive, in response to drives or sign stimuli, or active and self-regulating. Behavior changes both quantitatively and qualitatively as innate and environmental factors interact during development. The result is an organism that can operate efficiently within its environment. Ethologists sometimes draw on models such as control systems or hydraulic drive-reduction systems.

Ethology has several strengths to offer the current field of developmental psychology. With respect to theory, it provides a broad evolutionary perspective on behavior that has encouraged investigators to look at the function of children's behaviors. Ethologists advocate more observational studies of children in natural settings in order to determine the function of particular behaviors. A final contribution is the identification of several content areas as particularly important in development: dominance hierarchies, attachment, nonverbal communication, and problem solving.

Ethology has certain weaknesses, however, that limit its usefulness for developmental psychology. Its theoretical notions, such as sensitive periods, have not yet reached an explanatory level. With respect to methodology, the observational method poses difficulties, and deprivation experiments are not possible with humans. Finally, certain aspects of development, such as language and abstract thought in older children, have not been given much attention by ethologists.

In conclusion, ethology is a fruitful source of working hypotheses about what behaviors are important and why they are acquired. An ethological attitude opens the investigator's eyes to a broad context that spans space and time and various levels of analysis. In particular, ethologically based observations in the early phases of a research project can give "the big picture" of the behavior that will later be studied in a controlled laboratory setting. Although the theory has certain limitations that probably can never be overcome, much of the potential of the theory has not yet been realized. Because of the renewed interest in ecological validity in developmental psychology, the time is right for drawing on ethology for inspiration.

## SUGGESTED READINGS

The following reading surveys ethological research on both humans and animals.

Hinde, R. A. Ethology and child development. In M. M. Haith and J. J. Campos, eds., P. H. Mussen, series ed., *Handbook of child psychology. Vol. 2. Infancy and developmental psychobiology.* New York: Wiley, 1983.

The breadth of recent research on attachment is illustrated in the following monograph.

Bretherton, I., and E. Waters, eds. Growing points of attachment theory and research. *Monographs of the Society for Research in Child Development*, 1985, *50* (1–2, Serial No. 209).

Lorenz delights us with this account of his life with animals.

Lorenz, K. Z. *King Solomon's ring.* New York: Crowell, 1952.

# 6

# Gibson's Perceptual-Development Theory

*We tested 36 infants ranging in age from 6 months to 14 months on the visual cliff. Each child was placed upon the center board, and his mother called him to her from the cliff side and the shallow side successively. All of the 27 infants who moved off the board crawled out on the shallow side at least once; only three of them crept off the brink onto the glass suspended above the pattern on the floor. Many of the infants crawled away from the mother when she called to them from the cliff side; others cried when she stood there, because they could not come to her without crossing an apparent chasm. The experiment thus demonstrated that most human infants can discriminate depth as soon as they can crawl.*
[Gibson and Walk, 1960, p. 64]

*Infants of 12 months were familiarized in the dark with an object of either a hard or an elastic (spongy) substance. Following 60 seconds of manipulation, a visual preference test was given with simultaneous presentation of two films of identical objects, one moving in a pattern characteristic of a rigid object and one moving in a pattern characteristic of an elastic object. Infants handled the two substances differently in an appropriate manner and looked preferentially with more and longer first looks to the type of substance familiarized . . . The results . . . suggest that quite young infants detect intermodal invariants specifying some substances and perceive the affordance of the substance.*
[Gibson and Walker, 1984, p. 453]

C hildhood is a time of perceptual discovery. The child learns to tell apart various faces, balls, juices, words, flowers, insects, seashells, and television heroes. He perceives and explores the wondrous objects and events in the environment occupied by his species. Although such discovery is exciting in itself, it is also necessary for adaptation to this environment. Humans must accurately perceive objects in order to learn to understand them and use them. Recognizing the importance of perception for adaptation, Eleanor Gibson has taken on a question largely ignored by other theorists we have met: How do we learn to perceive our world? Surely this is a basic question for psychology. Gibson's answer to this question is that children learn to detect information that specifies objects, events, and places in the world. As they perceive, they differentiate this information, rather than add to it. Thus, this view is in sharp contrast to other views of perception, which see perceptual learning as a process of adding meaning to sparse, ambiguous stimuli. For Gibson, the perceptual array is already rich, complex, and valid.

Gibson's theory of perceptual development is not a grand, wide-ranging theory of development as is Piaget's or Freud's. It has the more modest goal of explaining one area of behavior: perceptual learning and development. On the other hand, it is not simply a theoretical point of view shared by a group of people, as are information processing, learning theory, and ethology. It is one type of theory that emerges from time to time—an individual effort to develop a unifying, coherent view of one area of development. This effort includes many fruitful collaborations with students and colleagues, including James Gibson.

The organization of this chapter is as follows. First is a biographical sketch, followed by a general orientation to the theory, then a description of main developmental trends. Sections on the mechanisms of development, the theory's position on developmental issues, and the theoretical nature of the theory are followed by an evaluation.

## BIOGRAPHICAL SKETCH

Eleanor J. Gibson's studies in psychology began at Smith College, from which she graduated in 1931. She then stayed on as a teaching assistant and married a young faculty member, James Gibson, who was also to become an eminent psychologist. She earned her master's degree with a thesis on learning in 1933. Subsequently, she became an instructor at Smith and attended the Gestaltist Kurt Koffka's lectures regularly. Gibson moved on to Yale, hoping to study animal behavior, but instead studied people. In 1938, she obtained a Ph.D. under Clark Hull, the great learning theorist, at Yale. Gibson, however, did not feel intellectually comfortable in the S–R climate of Yale. Her career was interrupted by her husband's relocation for military service during World War II. The Gibsons returned to Smith and later to Cornell, where she became a research associate.

Gibson's work in the 1950s and 1960s developed the new fields of perceptual learning and perceptual development. At Cornell she studied goats and sheep at the "Behavior Farm," babies on "visual cliffs," and children in reading-related situations in the laboratory. She became a professor at Cornell in 1966. Her research and theorizing culminated in 1969 in *Principles of Perceptual Learning and Development,* which won the Century psychology prize. The book was hailed as one of the most influential books on development in the recent history of the field (Hartup and Yonas, 1971). In the next decade, she continued her wide-ranging research but turned her attention more and more to how children learn to read. Some of this work is summarized in *The Psychology of Reading* (1975), coauthored with Harry Levin. More recently, she can be found in the laboratory, studying perceptual development in infants. Cornell honored her with an appointment as the Susan Linn Sage Professor Emeritus of Psychology.

Gibson has been awarded many honors, including the Gold Medal Award and the Distinguished Scientific Contribution Award from the American Psychological Association and the Howard Crosby Warren Medal from the Society of Experimental Psychologists. In addition, she was elected to the National Academy of Sciences, the American Academy of Arts and Sciences, and the National Academy of Education. She also has served as president of the Eastern Psychological Association. Her influence on colleagues and students is demonstrated in a volume dedicated to her, *Perception and Its Development: A Tribute to Eleanor J. Gibson* (Pick, 1979).

## GENERAL ORIENTATION TO THE THEORY

Five characteristics of Gibson's theory place it in the proper place in our growing cognitive map of developmental theories. These characteristics include the notions that humans are active perceivers, that information for perception is specified in stimulation, and that ecology is an important consideration in our understanding of human perception. Two more characteristics are the claims that much of perceptual development depends on perceptual learning and that experimental methods should include simulations of natural environments.

### Humans as Active Perceivers

Gibson often refers to "the perceiver as performer" (Gibson and Rader, 1979). In her view, children and adults discover, explore, attend, extract information, and differentiate objects. These are the behaviors of an active organism who does something in order to learn about the world. For example, consider how young children perceive balls. Although even the infant can discriminate footballs, small rubber balls, basketballs, and other balls on the basis of obvious differences such as size or color, only after more experience with balls do young children detect more subtle differences in shape, texture, and so on. Young children not only detect differences among objects, but also abstract more complex information: A football that looks different when it is seen from different angles and distances is actually a unitary object; rolling a ball across the room is an event in time and space. By observing and playing with objects, children pull out more and more information about objects, events, and the spatial layout of the environment.

Both general and specific motivations underlie the perceptual activities of children. Humans, as a species, are inherently motivated to explore and learn about their world. There are, however, goals and needs specific to each task or situation. The girl putting together a puzzle attends to shape and color because these attributes are information she needs to achieve her goal of completing the puzzle. In contrast, the girl playing in a swing may be concerned with the pleasurable feeling of the wind blowing her hair and her body moving in space. In another setting, the baby learning to walk must be very attentive to the position of her body in space and the distance between furniture. Adults also have different goals relevant to perception in different situations. For example, Gibson points out that a mountain climber is more attentive to where he places each step than is someone taking a leisurely walk (Gibson and Rader, 1979). In short, perception is always motivated by goals that are important to the person. These goals, which give direction to the person's perceptual activities, may be as diverse as problem solving, amusement, and locomotion.

## Information Is Specified in Stimulation

Gibson's description of the active, self-motivated child exploring the world seems quite similar to Piaget's view of children. The theorists part, however, in their conceptions of how children "know" the world through activity. The Piagetian child "constructs" his knowledge by forming schemes based on his motor behaviors with objects. Because perception produces static images, it must be corrected by veridical, operational knowledge. Similarly, other approaches see perception as an act of enriching a sparse, ambiguous, uninformative retinal image. For instance, learning theorists propose that distinctive verbal labels added to objects make them more discriminable. The labels "beagle" and "foxhound" would increase the perceptual distinctiveness of these dogs. Information-processing approaches describe processes that add meaning to the stimulus by relating it to memories in the long-term store. They refer to going beyond the information given by making inferences based on knowledge of the world. The Piagetian, learning, and information-processing approaches consider perception and cognition to be an additive process. The child adds something—actions, words, meaning—to the stimulus.

In contrast, Gibson believes that stimulation is a rich source of information, which extends over space and time. The developmental issue, then, is how children learn to extract more and more information from stimulation. The assumption that information is inherent in stimulation is the most controversial claim in the theory. It is important, therefore, that we consider this claim carefully.

There is a spatiotemporal array in stimulation. That is, stimulation is not static and frozen in space and time. As Gibson (1988, p. 5) comments, "There is no shutter on the retina, no such thing as a static image." Stimulation specifies events, places, and objects. Thus, if the child can extract this information, he perceives events, places, and objects. The child does not perceive a single, discrete "stimulus," such as an object. Rather, from the entire spatiotemporal array, he perceives the information that specifies particular objects. In other words, stimulation is a field of available information.

Stimulation carries many levels of information. At the simplest and most concrete level, the child discriminates objects by one or several distinctive features, or attributes that differentiate them. Suppose the child moves near an ocean and for the first time in his life encounters hundreds of shells. He begins a collection and attempts to identify the shells with the help of a guidebook with photographs. Although he is perceptually capable of telling all of the shells apart if he places them side by side, he actually notices only a few distinctive features at first, perhaps the differences in color and size. Only after much playing with the shells and comparing them with the pictures in the book does he realize that the stimulus class of shells has a particular set of distinctive features that allows him to determine the appropriate label for each shell. Although size is a salient feature, it is seldom important. In contrast, slight differences in the shape of the "crown" at the top of the shell or subtle differences in the colored pattern on the shell are quite important. Although this information has always been in the light stimulating the eye, it was not really noticed or abstracted as a defining feature until the child had more perceptual experience with the shells.

At a more abstract level of analysis, we can perceive a higher-order structure to light or sound. A good example is the musical pattern we call a melody. We abstract a melody from a succession of notes on the piano. This melody is recognized as the same melody even if it is transposed to a different key or played at a different tempo or on a saxophone instead of a piano. The pattern is there in stimulation but may not be perceived at first. Thus, perceptual learning is a process of learning to perceive what has always been there. Gibson has noted that her theory might be called a "seek and ye shall find" theory (1977, p. 157). Young children, having limited experience with objects and events in the world, often do not perceive subtle differences in the appearance of objects or patterns (organized light). They must search out these differences.

It is instructive to carry the musical example to perceptual learning in adults. When we hear a new orchestral work, we have a relatively undifferentiated perception of the work after the first hearing. Only after listening to the work several times are we able to extract melodies and their transformations, grasp the overall structure of the piece, and perhaps even differentiate the various instruments of the orchestra. For most Americans, this task is more difficult with Eastern music or modern compositions using the 12-tone scale, which are less familiar, than with the first hearing of yet another Haydn symphony. In this musical example, stimulation has remained the same throughout the repeated playing of the record. What has changed is what information we have extracted. In the beginning we listened, yet did not hear. We gradually perceived more and more of what had always been there. Our perception becomes both more specific, as we became aware of subtle musical qualities, and more abstract, as we perceived musical patterns. Thus, the information is in the stimulation, but sometimes we must learn to perceive it. Our perception improves not by filling in the raw auditory stimulus by adding words or applying schemes, not by cognitively gluing together the notes, but by listening to the music and directing our attention. We attend to relational information— distinctive features and patterns concerning relationships among the parts—not to bits and pieces of information. In Gibson's words,

There is structure in the array, relational information that does not have to be pieced together because, like truth, it is already there. This is the assumption I want to proceed with. I do not want a construction theory, with processors at every stage like an assembly line.

[1977, p. 157]

## Importance of Ecology

More than most theories of perception, Gibson's theory stresses the natural behavior of the perceiver in a particular environment. People need to perceive objects, spatial layouts, and temporal events in order to adapt to the world: to walk around in it, find things in it, play in it, and even survive in it. These stimuli are complex relational units, not simple sensations of light or sound.

In recent years, Gibson's research and theorizing has centered around the notion of *affordances,* a concept introduced by James Gibson. Affordances are what an environment offers or provides for an organism. Humans' environments "afford" surfaces of support, objects to grasp, passageways allowing movement, and barriers preventing movement. Thus, the person and the environment form a whole, with a meshing of the person's activities and the environment's affordances. Gibson claims that these affordances are perceived directly: "We do not perceive stimuli or retinal images or sensations or even just things; what we perceive are things that we can eat, or write with, or sit down on, or talk to" (1982, p. 60).

As new motor skills are acquired during development, new affordances are discovered. When a child starts to walk, he learns to perceive if a surface affords solid support for walking. This affordance is irrelevant for, and unknown to, a younger infant. In one experiment (Gibson et al., 1987), infants faced a walkway raised 4 feet from the floor. Their smiling mothers stood 6 feet away on the other side of the walkway. The walkway for one condition was a rigid surface (strong plywood covered with a patterned fabric), and the other was a patterned fabric on a waterbed, which affords locomotion for a crawler, but not a walker. The infants who could walk looked at and felt the water bed before crawling onto it, much more than they did the rigid surface. The infants who could only crawl showed little, if any, differentiation of the two surfaces; they readily moved onto both of them.

We can look at ecological influences in two overlapping ways: by tracing our evolutionary heritage and by focusing on how specific environments mesh with the child's perception. Both are emphasized by ethologists as well. First, let us consider how the human species has evolved adaptive ways of perceiving the world. In Gibson's words, the search for information about complex relations among stimuli is

> so much a part of man's nature, evolved over millions of years, that it is as ingrained, strong, and unconscious as the functions of digestion and breathing and much more elaborately provided for. We have many windows on the world; systems for listening, looking, touching, tasting and accompanying patterns of exploration like scanning, palpating, and licking.
>
> *[1977, p. 157]*

Each species is specialized for perceiving critical information in its environment. For example, bats are pretuned to use acoustic information (interpreting feedback from sounds) to help them navigate in dark caves. Birds and primates rely heavily on their visual perception of the spatial layout, prey, and predators, and hands permit humans and other primates to detect whether an object can be grasped and manipulated. Thus, what information is extracted from the environment depend on the species. Affordances are directly perceived because the species has evolved a perceptual system that detects, or can learn to detect, the affordances that increase the likelihood of survival. The environment affords food, mates, and places to hide from predators.

Let us now look at ecological influences in the second sense: the fit between the child's immediate environment and his perceptual activities. His evolutionary heritage provides the perceptual equipment and the motivation to perceive — or learn to perceive — objects, events, and spatial arrays. By exploring and playing, children learn the affordances of objects, surfaces, and events. The particular information he attends to, however, depends on what the immediate environment provides and on what the child's goals are in that situation. A hungry 3-year-old notices another child's ice-cream cone, perceives hunger pangs, listens for the music of the neighborhood ice-cream truck, and looks for his mother. A young football player, however, attends to a different sort of information. He continually searches for and tracks the ball, perceives the spatial relationship between other players and the ball, and uses feedback concerning his attempt to kick the ball (falling down, kicking erratically, and so on). In these examples, there is a relationship — ideally, a match — between the child's goals and the information extracted from the environment. According to Gibson, attempts to study perception in isolation from any consideration of the ecology are misguided. Psychologists can understand perceptual development only by studying the correspondence between the child's perceptual activities, his goals, and what information is available to him. Recall that in a previous chapter the information-processing approach was criticized for focusing on the child's cognitive skills and giving little attention to how these skills "fit" with the child's goals in a particular environment. Gibson certainly would agree with this criticism.

## Primacy of Perceptual Learning in Perceptual Development

As the previous sections indicate, Gibson believes that much of perceptual development involves perceptual learning. Perception improves as the child explores, compares, searches, and abstracts information in a variety of settings. The process of perceptual learning is much the same in children and adults. An adult facing an unfamiliar task, such as reading the Russian alphabet or learning to play chess, must learn what to attend to, much as the child does in a larger number of situations. Overall, adults can pick up the needed information much more economically than children, partly because they understand what the task involves and what type of information in stimulation is relevant; however, children are quite efficient at extracting information in very familiar situations, such as looking through a new friend's toy collection.

## Methodology

Although Gibson's research, as well as other research stimulated by her theory, follows the experimental procedures of other areas of developmental psychology, it is unusual in one way. It tries to increase the ecological validity of the experimental setting. This does not mean that Gibsonians observe perceptual activities in their natural settings. It does mean that they attempt to simulate (mimic important features) in the experimental setting the stimulation, tasks, and goals of the child's natural environment. In an early experiment on depth, for instance,

Gibson, along with Walk (1960), constructed a "visual cliff," which simulates a cliff or drop-off in the real world. Gibson was inspired to create this miniature Grand Canyon after visiting the real Grand Canyon with her young child and pondering, with some concern, the child's ability to perceive it as a drop-off. The visual cliff is a table with a glass top that gives the impression of a solid surface on one half of the table; on the other half of the table, the floor is visible through the glass. Thus, the apparatus displays information specifying a drop-off. Some of the results were described at the beginning of the chapter. Infants will crawl on the "cliff" half, but refuse to crawl onto the half of the glass that hangs over the apparent "thin air." The visual-cliff experiments demonstrated that children perceive depth at an edge at least as early as 6 or 7 months, when they begin to crawl. Research using heart rate, indicates that even younger infants differentiate the cliff and noncliff sides (Campos, Langer, and Krowitz, 1970). The visual cliff has been used widely to study depth perception in many species.

## DEVELOPMENTAL TRENDS

From the seemingly diverse perceptual changes during childhood, Gibson (1969) identifies three developmental trends: (1) increasing specificity of correspondence between the information in stimulation and what is perceived, (2) optimization of attention, and (3) increasing economy of information pickup. These trends refer to three overlapping and interrelated aspects of perceptual learning. The trends arise from the child's ever-widening range of experiences as he explores different situations. All lead to the detection of affordances.

### Increasing Specificity of Perception

There is a growing correspondence between what the child perceives and what information is in stimulation. In order words, perception becomes more exact. The toddler may be insensitive to perceptual differences among members of the class "fish." The older child may discriminate among guppies, goldfish, and trout. Thus, perception has become more differentiated.

One well-known experiment demonstrates the increasing specificity of perceiving graphic patterns and nicely illustrates the type of research generated by the theory. Gibson, Gibson, Pick, and Osser (1962) presented letterlike forms—forms constructed on the same principles as printed capital letters in the English alphabet. On each trial the child's task was to select from a set of forms the two or three forms identical to the standard form. The nonidentical forms differed from the standard in several ways, for example, in orientation (reversed or rotated to an upside-down position) or shape (a straight line changed to a curve or vice versa). With increasing age, from 4 to 8, there is increased differentiation of the forms. That is, many of the forms that the younger children consider to be the same as the standard are, in fact, not the same. For example, the child might pick a reversal of the standard as a form that is the same as the standard. The older children's perception corresponds more closely to the forms. That is, they usually pick forms that are exactly the same as the standard. Their superior performance is presumably due to their greater experience with letters of the alphabet.

## Optimization of Attention

For Gibson, perceptual development is nearly synonymous with attentional development. Attention refers to activities that gather information, especially information about the affordances of objects. These attentional activities include peripheral exploratory activities, such as looking back and forth between two faces, turning the head to facilitate locating a sound, and sniffing a rose. In addition, there are central, nonobservable attentional activities, for example, attending to an object's color rather than its shape. As a result of all these activities, the child extracts certain information and ignores other information. How efficiently the child carries out these attentional activities depends to a great extent on his developmental level. Although to some extent children perceive selectively from the beginning, during development they learn to tailor their perception to the requirements of each situation.

Gibson (1988) posits a sequence of phases in the development of exploration (attention) during infancy. These phases are not strictly stages, because they overlap in time and vary across situations. In phase 1 (birth to about 4 months), the infant attends to (explores) *events,* particularly motions, in his immediate visual surround. By moving his head and eyes, he scans the visual layout and discovers rudimentary properties of objects and layouts. From information in the motion within the optic array, he can perceive depth, the unity of an object, and causal relations between events. He also can discriminate his own movement from that of other objects or their surroundings. During event perception, looking is somewhat coordinated with other systems, such as listening or exploring tactually. For example, when given a choice of two faces, infants prefer to look at a face where mouth movements match the vowel sounds heard rather than at a face where there is a mismatch (Kuhl and Meltzoff, 1982). Similarly, infants tend to look at a filmed event matching a sound track (a hand playing a rhythm with percussion instruments) rather than a filmed event that does not match (Spelke, 1976).

Phase 2 (around 4 to 7 months) involves attention to the affordances and distinctive features of *objects,* in part because physical maturation allows reaching and grasping, as well as improved visual acuity. The infant no longer has to depend on motion to provide information about objects, because his own actions with his hands reveal new affordances of objects. Objects can be squeezed, hit, banged, and thrown. The infant can identify objects and even show tactual recognition of an object first examined visually (Streri and Pecheux, 1986). He also detects both similarities and differences among objects. Finally, he detects a partly covered object as a unitary object. For example, an infant perceives a long stick protruding on either side of a rectangular object as a single unbroken stick, but only if he sees the stick move back and forth or in depth rather than remain stationary (Kellman and Spelke, 1983).

One of the most striking demonstrations of object perception is the perception of a living object in motion. For example, Fox and McDaniel (1982) presented a biological-motion light pattern—a videotape of 10 lights mounted on the joints of the arms, legs, and hips of a figure running in the dark. Another display included the same number of lights, but their movement was random. Infants of 4 and 6 months tended to look at the running pattern, which indicates both their ability to differentiate an object in biological motion from a random array and their preference for viewing a pattern of moving lights organized into a unitary object.

In phase 3 (around 8 to 12 months), attention expands to the larger *array* as the infant becomes ambulatory. He explores behind obstacles and himself, around corners, on top of furniture, and inside of cabinets. His perception of the layout guides his locomotion around obstacles, through openings, and onto safe, solid surfaces. A toddler crossing a room needs a great deal of affordance information in order to crawl under a table, over rather than around a blanket on the floor, and around rather than over the dog. Toddlers even make compensatory, or righting, responses when they have to walk around obstacles down a hallway that appears to move (Schmuckler, 1987). Objects' affordance of being carried seems to fascinate toddlers, who often carry objects from one place to another, just for the sheer joy of doing so. Gibson (1988) notes that this affordance may take a while to be learned, for there are reports that toddlers sometimes try to carry a toy or piece of furniture almost as large as themselves.

During development, attention becomes more efficient in several ways. It becomes more exploratory and less captive: the child can actively scan an object rather than only passively react to a bright light or sudden movement that "catches" his attention. Attention also becomes more systematic and less random, more selective in the information picked up, and more exclusive, in that irrelevant information is ignored. For instance, if children are asked to decide if two drawings of houses are the same or different, older children, more than younger children, use efficient attentional strategies (Vurpillot and Ball, 1979). They actively and systematically look back and forth between corresponding parts of the two houses, attending to relevant features, the windows, until a decision can be reached. Younger children settle for a few random glances before making their decision. Similarly, if children are asked to remember the locations of several pictures of objects, but distracting pictures are also present, young children attend to both the pictures they are to remember and the distractors. In contrast, older children ignore the distractors (Miller, Haynes, DeMarie-Dreblow, and Woody-Ramsey, 1986). As these examples suggest, older children extract a more useful set of information because of their more efficient selection of information.

As children learn more about themselves and the world, they learn what kind of attention each setting requires. For instance, they attend differently when crossing a street, looking for a particular brand of cereal in a store, playing basketball, and reading a book. Scanning from left to right, for example, would be efficient for reading, but inefficient for shooting a basket. Much of the improvement in fitting attention to the setting comes from feedback that the child himself evaluates. The child probably will not learn to shoot baskets if he does not learn to look at the basket. It is likely, however, that some of the improvement comes from instruction, such as "Keep your eye on the ball" and "Look both ways before crossing the street."

Let us look more carefully at the changes in attention that are illustrated in these examples. The fit among perceiving and moving and thinking during development is reflected in several ways:

1. There is more specific correspondence between what information the children attend to and its utility for the task. This progress comes as they learn to define each task more precisely and detect what information is relevant for that task. The child learns, for example, that when looking for a particular brand of cereal in a store, he should first look for the cereal section and then systematically search each shelf.

2. Children become more flexible in their attention as they learn to choose, from among alternative ways of performing, the most efficient way of performing. The child might look for a bright orange box of cereal, a particular cartoon character on the front, or a very small box, whichever is most efficient for that set of objects.

3. Children become more "prepared" — ready for expected events. With increasing experience, children learn what to expect and, consequently, what to look for and attend to. The child may know from past experience that sugary, highly advertised cereals are separated from granola or oatmeal in the cereal aisle.

4. Children's attention becomes more economical as they look for structure and order in stimulation and apply that information to their performance. This increasing economy of attention allows them to attend to more information. The child may simultaneously attend to the color, size, and front design of boxes of cereal. This increasing economy of attention is one aspect of a more general trend in perceptual development: the increasing economy of information pickup.

## Increasing Economy of Information Pickup

Although the mechanisms for extracting information are the same throughout the life span, they become more efficient, or economical. Children achieve this economy by detecting distinctive features in stimulation, extracting invariants over time, and processing larger units of structure.

1. *Distinctive features* were introduced earlier in this chapter. They are critical features that can be used to discriminate between objects. Imagine, for example, that a practical joker mixed up the container labels on the entire stock of ice cream in a 48-flavor ice-cream store. An efficient way to tell the flavors apart and group together identical flavors would be to pick out the minimal set of distinctive features that distinguish the types of ice cream. The set might include the following: color, nuts versus no nuts, sherbet versus nonsherbet, flavor (fruit-based, chocolate-based, or other), and smooth versus textured.

Faces are another group of objects that can be differentiated by distinctive features. Artists take advantage of striking facial character-istics by exaggerating them in caricatures. Distinctive features of faces — a toothy grin or large nose — can bring instant recognition.

2. A second aid to economy of information pickup, the extraction of *invariants,* is the search for relations that remain constant over change. A child extracts information for the constant size and shape of objects despite changes in their appearance as they move toward or away from him. It is clearly more economical to perceive a single, constant mother of a particular size and shape than a succession of different mothers that expand and shrink.

One invariant examined experimentally by Gibson, Owsley, and Johnston (1978) is the perception of the rigidity, or lack of malleability, of a moving object. They asked whether the property of rigidity could be extracted when the object underwent various kinds of movement. Infants 5 months of age saw a round, disklike piece of foam rubber move in three ways, for example, rotation in the frontal plane, rotation around the vertical axis, and movement toward or away from them. Each infant watched these movements in succession until he habi-tuated, that is, stopped looking at the object. Then the infant saw, in succession, a fourth rigid motion, perhaps rotation around the horizontal axis, and a nonrigid, elastic motion. The latter was accomplished by having an experimenter continually squeeze and release the spongy disk. Infants showed little interest in the new rigid motion, but much interest in the nonrigid motion. Thus, the infants discriminated rigid motions from nonrigid motions. The invariant property, rigidity, was extracted from the stimulus flux during the three types of movement. The authors concluded that the nonrigid movement "was perceived as different, presumably because it offered information about a new property of the object, that object being otherwise unchanged" (p. 414).

Studies using eyeglasses with prism lenses illustrate the detection of invariants in adults. These glasses move the entire visual field several degrees to the left or right, change straight lines to curves, and add color fringes to certain contours, among other transformations. Since these biases are consistent, relational information is unchanged. Thus, adults still perceive people, buildings, furniture, depth, and size (Gibson, 1969).

3. A third route to economical perception is the extraction of large units of perceptual *structure,* "the embedded relations constituting subordinate units or clusters" (Gibson, 1969, p. 466). A basic tenet of Gibson's theory is that the world is structured and that we gradually become more aware of this structure. We do not impose structure on an unstructured world; the structure is extracted by our perceptual systems. As mentioned earlier, music has a melodic structure that we may or may not detect immediately. Furthermore, much of learning to read is a process of detecting the structure in written discourse. Words have structure, or rule systems. The structure is apparent when we break words into letter clusters *(-ed, -ing, -ight)*. In addition, there are regularities in the spelling-to-sound correspondences, as in the unit *-ing* and the sound associated with that unit. Gibson, Shurcliff, and Yonas (1970) demonstrated that pronounceable pseudowords presented tachistoscopically are easier to recognize than unpronounceable pseudowords. The pronounceable words have a structure typical of English. Gibson has been particularly interested in the role of the perception of the structure of written language in learning to read. She states her position as follows:

Extracting this order from written language is the mark of economical perception in the skilled reader. The difference between a reader who uses the redundancy given by all these kinds of structure efficiently and automatically, and a beginning scholar who stumbles along decoding letter by letter into speech sounds cannot be exaggerated. The accomplishment of reading and comprehending the text of *War and Peace* is as wonderful as reading the score of a symphony, which does not come through note by note any more than the former comes through letter by letter.

[*Gibson, 1978, p. 748*]

The child is perceiving economically if he picks the most useful level of analysis: distinctive features, invariant relations, or higher-order structure. Once the appropriate level of analysis is chosen, the child is economical if he extracts the minimal number of properties necessary to accomplish his goal. If the child needs to discriminate the letters *b* and *d*, it is sufficient, and therefore economical, to note only their orientation, not their color or size.

Recently, Gibson (1988) has modified her views. She used to consider distinctive features, invariants, and higher-order structure the essence of perceptual learning, but she now sees them mainly as a source of information that leads to the discovery of the affordances of objects. In addition, she considers the detection of higher-order structure as only one aspect of the more general process of differentiating various levels of structure and discovering their relations. The parts are related to the whole; for example, infants eventually abstract both the overall intonation of a voice and the more subtle aspects within that pattern.


## MECHANISMS OF DEVELOPMENT

We have seen that perceptual development brings specific perception, optimal attention, and economical information pickup. The next step is to identify the mechanisms causing these changes. Gibson originally (1969) proposed three mechanisms, all having to do with attention: abstraction, filtering, and peripheral mechanisms of attention.

1. *Abstraction* is the extraction of distinctive features, invariant relations, or higher structure from an object, a set of objects, or an event. As children or adults encounter various objects and events in different settings, they discover certain constants among the change. William James described this process a century ago:

> What is associated now with one thing and now with another tends to become dissociated from either, and to grow into an object of abstract contemplation by the mind. . . . Why the repetition of the character in combination with different wholes will cause it thus to break up its adhesion with any of them, and roll out, as it were, alone upon the table of consciousness, is a little of a mystery.
>
> *[1890, pp. 506–507, emphasis in original]*

For example, children abstract the relations of up–down and left–right and the dimensions of color, weight, and height from objects. These general characteristics are information that, although already specified in stimulation, must be discovered and "pulled out" of the total stimulation.

2. *Filtering* is the other side of the coin. Abstraction cannot occur unless random, irrelevant, or nonessential stimulation can be ignored, or filtered out. A rose is a rose is a rose, regardless of its color, orientation, or size. There is a history of research on filtering in studies of attention by non-Gibsonian psychologists. Filtering is illustrated in the "cocktail-party phenomenon" (or "birthday-party phenomenon" in children), in which all background noise is ignored in order to hear a single voice. There is abundant evidence that filtering is a skill that develops. In one test of filtering, the child must repeat the message from one voice when two voices are heard simultaneously. This procedure has revealed a developmental improvement in the ability to filter out the irrelevant message, although even preschoolers do fairly well (Maccoby, 1969).

3. Finally, *peripheral mechanisms of attention* make perceptual development possible. Abstraction and filtering are internal processes by which information is accepted or rejected, but peripheral mechanisms of attention also deal with information. The child moves his eyes to the television, turns his head toward the sound of a distant call, moves his hands over sap dripping down a tree, sniffs when his mother is cooking

bacon, and cautiously rolls a brussels sprout over his tongue. By exploring, the child exposes his receptors to selected stimulation. This exposure, in turn, may lead to the detection of features, relations, and higher-order structure. Some perceptual mechanisms of attention exist at birth, for example, turning the eyes toward a sound.

Gibson later (1984) added a different set of three activities that are essential for development because they facilitate the pickup of information. In the infant, *exploratory activity* of the perceptual systems includes active looking, listening, and reaching as well as mouthing objects. Exploratory activities make possible the *extraction of invariants* from information in the array, as we saw earlier. Finally, *observation of consequences* of exploratory activity permits the detection of contingent relations, as when reaching for a rattle leads to an interesting noise. These three activities together lead to the discovery of affordances.

These processes of perceptual development are closely related to cognitive development. Using the manipulation of objects as an example, Gibson (1988, p. 34) proposes "a spiraling process, beginning with perception of the simplest affordances, such as separability and contractability, then moving on to chewability and graspability, then to reachability, to hideability, and eventually to all the refinements of transportability. With each new coil of the spiral, new properties of surfaces, objects, and events are perceived as consequences of perceptual activity, building an ever richer cognitive world."

Although Gibson would include physical maturation as an underlying mechanism of change, she gives little attention to it. There is more concern with experience of a variety of objects and events, growing cognition that helps the child learn what perceptual information is relevant for accomplishing each goal, and intrinsic motivation that keeps the child actively exploring his environment in an attempt to understand it and adapt to it.

## POSITION ON DEVELOPMENTAL ISSUES

### Human Nature

Gibson's view of human nature is much like Piaget's. In their organismic view, people are inherently motivated creatures who actively explore and try to make sense out of their world. Ideally, this is an organized and efficient process in which the child's needs and goals mesh with the nature of the environment. In their view, the child has a tremendous capacity to learn from experience and adapt to the environment. Both Gibson and Piaget describe complex organisms who are sensitive to the complex structure of the environment. The theorists differ, however, in the source of this structure. Gibson believes that in stimulation there is structure, which specifies the information available to be perceived. The child learns to detect this structure. In contrast, Piaget believes that to a great extent the nature of the interaction between the child and the world provides the structure.

## Qualitative Versus Quantitative Development

Gibson's three trends in perceptual development described earlier imply that development is gradual. Just as perception in adults can gradually improve with practice, so does perception in children gradually improve as a result of experience. Perceptual development is not stagelike. There may, however, be specific qualitative changes in the attentional strategies children use. For example, the child's systematic visual comparison of two objects may replace his earlier random looking at the two objects.

## Nature Versus Nurture

Gibson sees little need to contrast nature and nurture influences because "an organism only survives in an environment and in fact has evolved in it" (Gibson and Levin, 1979, p. 242). In other words, the species' genetic nature is influenced by the species' environment. There is a fit between the two. Thus, what information the child extracts from the environment depends on his endowment from the human species, in addition to his developmental level, immediate goals, and unique set of learning experiences. As we have seen, Gibson has been primarily interested in describing and explaining how children learn from experience and what they learn, especially affordances.

## What Develops

During development, by exploring our world we refine and learn to make optimal use of the perceptual activities of abstracting, filtering, and attending. As a result, we can detect the perceptual structure of the world, including affordances, and learn how to apply this knowledge to our goals.

## THEORETICAL NATURE OF THE THEORY

Unlike the previous theories in this volume, Gibson's theory makes almost no use of models. In our taxonomy, it is best characterized as a functional theory. The approach is research-oriented, and there is close interplay between research and theorizing. The theoretical notions, such as differentiation, distinctive features, and filtering, stay close enough to observations to be testable, but are general enough to organize and given meaning to a wide variety of empirical observations.

## EVALUATION OF THE THEORY

Gibson's theory is less ambitious than the others in this volume. She has limited her field of inquiry to one area: perceptual learning and development. Within that area, however, she has searched for unifying principles that tie together diverse phenomena. In her 1969 book, topics range from reading to controlled early experience in rats, from the perception of faces to the perception of causality.

Although Gibson's theory is the most well known theory of perceptual development, it does not dominate research efforts in that area. In fact, however, no theory does. Most perceptual researchers appear to be on a fact-finding mission, gathering basic descriptive information about the perceptual capacities of children, especially infants. Perhaps the most common issues are what young infants can discriminate and to what they attend. Given the empirical orientation of work on perception in children, it is particularly important to consider the potential of Gibson's theory to guide perceptual research and tie it to other areas of development. Thus, the following list of strengths and weaknesses is not intended to be an overall evaluation of her theory.

Such an evaluation would be premature. Rather, it is intended to highlight those aspects of the theory that speak to certain critical needs of current developmental theorizing and research. The strengths of the theory are its focus on the ecological context of perception and the interaction of knowledge and perception. The main weakness is the unclear relationship between perception and cognition.

## Strengths

### Focus on the Ecological Context of Perception

The differing assumptions of Gibson's theory and information-processing theory make them basically incompatible. Gibson herself emphasizes this incompatibility and criticizes the assumption of information-processing researchers that "input" consists of bits and pieces. In Gibson's words, "Such a conception requires them to invent 'processing mechanisms' to put the world together" (1977, p. 156). In contrast, her view is that objects are perceived directly, with no need for inferences or other forms of cognitive mediation. Stimulation consists not of bits and pieces, but of an entire array that changes over time.

Despite the impossibility of integrating the two theories because of the basic incompatibility of their underlying assumptions, there are several features of Gibson's theory that could fruitfully guide current research on cognitive development. In particular, Gibson's theory could bring researchers into the world beyond the laboratory. Recently, many developmental psychologists have called for ecological validity in research with children (for example, Bronfenbrenner and Crouter, 1983). For years, Gibson has been concerned with how perception serves us in our daily lives. She studies the perception of meaningful stimulation — patterns, objects, and events — rather than points of light or brief, static stimuli. In James Gibson's words, she works on "perception outdoors under the sky instead of perception of points in a darkroom" (1979, p. xii). The perception of natural units is essential for adapting to the environment. Children perceive by selecting information, especially affordance information, about the spatio-temporal environment, information that allows them to walk, run, grasp, and throw within an environment.

Gibson's ecological orientation could enrich the information-processing approach. Although the information-processing approach emphasizes the selection of information and analyzes the demands of the particular task, it has not successfully described and explained how the child's skills "fit" with the demands of the real-life environment. In other words, information-processing researchers tell us *how* children attend, encode, and recall, but not *what* they attend to, encode, and recall as a result of the environment in which they are developing. For instance, although there are hundreds of studies on the development of attentional and memory processes in children, we know little about what children attend to or remember in different situations, how this processing is guided by the child's goals and the possibilities in the setting, and how the obtained information helps them function in the setting. Do children attend to and encode people or materials in various school settings, at home, and when watching television? How do searching for a particular toy, trying to tell if two words are the same or different, and learning to do a cartwheel lead to different kinds of information-seeking activities? By asking these questions, Gibson changes the focus from the child's processing skills to the child-environment interface. The child actively seeks ecologically significant information in a complex, changing world of objects, places, and events.

Another way in which attention to Gibson's theory could increase the ecological validity of information-processing approaches is to take seriously her concern with the processing of events that occur over time: a rapidly approaching object, a ball rolling across the floor, one object striking another, liquid being poured out of a glass. This change in focus would broaden our understanding of processing based on the typically studied static stimuli, such as pictures, letters, objects, and written words. Most real-life events involve the movement of one or several objects or people—a complex set of information, to be sure.

Finally, Gibson's theory could correct the focus on verbal skills found in most work on memory and thinking. In particular, this focus is inappropriate for studying infants. Gibson's nonverbal distinctive features and invariants are a promising basis for correcting these verbal models.

### Focus on the Interaction of Knowledge and Perception

A recent chapter by Gibson (1988) bears the title "Exploratory Behavior in the Development of Perceiving, Acting, and the Acquiring of Knowledge." The links among these activities is a theme that runs through Gibson's theory. We gain knowledge of the world by perceiving it through active exploration. The detection of surfaces, events, and objects—and their affordances—is the foundation of knowledge about the world. Through perceptual learning we discover categories of objects or events, abstract properties such as number, and causal relations among objects or events, and we develop cognitive maps of the extended environment.

Another aspect of the interface is that our knowledge of the world guides our exploratory activities. As children learn more about tasks and goals, they learn what information is relevant and how to gather this information efficiently. They know, for example, that size may be an important distinctive feature for differentiating balls for sports, but not for differentiating capital letters.

Gibson's theory of perception is not the first to claim a close link between knowledge and perception. Most of these theories, however, have viewed knowledge as a way of correcting perception (Piaget) or enriching perception (Jerome Bruner). In contrast, in Gibson's view, the child discovers a complex, structured world; he does not create that complexity and structure. Knowledge is merely a way of directing perceptual activities in a way that leads to the efficient and accurate extraction of information from the visual array.

## Weaknesses

### Unclear Relationship Between Perception and Cognition

Although Gibson's focus on the interplay between perception and knowledge about tasks and goals was selected as a strength of the theory, in other respects this relationship remains both frustratingly unclear and unconvincing. The basic problem is that Gibson proposes a theory of the *direct* perception of the environment, but then includes some behaviors that seem to involve indirect, interpretive cognition. For instance, Gibson's examples of perceptual learning include reading maps, interpreting x-ray and aerial photographs, identifying material under a microscope, perceiving causality, and perceiving conservation as an invariance over time and over an event sequence (1969, pp. 8–9, 388). Furthermore, children are said to perceive affordances such as swinging (on swings), warmth and light for reading (from a fire), and hiding (behind a screen). Many psychologists seem uncomfortable designating these psychological activities as "perceptual." For example, Horowitz (1983) argues that instead of proposing that a chair affords sitting, one could propose more parsimoniously that the perceiver, because of previous experience, associates a chair with sitting. Although perceptual processes certainly are heavily involved in these cases, much of the learning concerns the interpretation and categorization of the information. Gibson has jumped from the perceptual discrimination of objects to the relating of objects to a rich network of abstract concepts.

Even if we agree with Gibson that much of perception does not depend on cognitive processes, it is necessary to examine the relationship between perceiving and thinking in a detailed way. Of course, it must be admitted that "perceptual" and "conceptual" processes are arbitrary divisions that psychologists sometimes impose on an underlying continuum from sensory to higher-order cognitive processes. Still, it is confusing to treat discrimination, identification, and interpretation similarly and claim that they all involve the abstraction of information already in the stimulus array. Deciding whether a shadow seen on an x-ray should be diagnosed as tuberculosis (Gibson, 1969, p. 9) seems to go far beyond direct perception of the x-ray. The main point being made here is that the theory needs to specify more clearly the similarities and differences among these activities along the perceptual–cognitive continuum. Stated differently, it is not clear what is *not* perception. What are the limits to direct perception? Perhaps further developments within the theory will address this question.

To illustrate the problem, it is not clear how perceptual learning is related to memory processes: a main focus of current cognitive research. In Gibson's account of the interrelationships of perceptual learning and cognitive processes (1969, Chapter 8), she proposes that the detection of distinctive features and invariant patterns precedes the formation of representations and concepts. She points out that representations and concepts typically exaggerate the distinctive features of objects rather than simply copy the object. She goes on to propose that representations, concepts, and language in turn aid further perceptual learning by directing attention to new differences or similarities between objects. These general two-way influences, however, have never been worked out more specifically. There are a number of questions we might ask: How do we retain the results of perceptual learning (for example, distinctive features, patterns, and objects) and recall this information when it is needed at a later time? Is there a relationship between the number of distinctive features abstracted and the likelihood of recall of the object or event? Are distinctive features and patterns stored in the same way in infants, children, and adults? These questions are not asked by those working within the Gibsonian framework because of their focus on direct perception. However, the theory's account of perception will not be complete until it examines how perception interfaces with other psychological activities.

## SUMMARY

Gibson asks an old question: How do we perceive our world? Her answer, however, is new. We learn to perceive by extracting, from stimulation, information that specifies objects, events, and places and their affordances for the child's actions. Thus, humans are active perceivers who directly perceive distinctive features, invariant relations, and higher-order structure. Perceptual development is largely a process of increasing the efficiency of perception as a result of experience. This is perceptual learning. The ecological context of this learning is important because children learn to perceive information that helps them adapt to this environment. In each setting, the child's goal—whether playing or reading or climbing over a fence—guides his pickup of information. In general, the fit between the goal and perception improves during development.

Gibson identifies three main developmental trends. First, perception becomes more specific as children learn to differentiate stimulation. Second, attention becomes more optimal as it becomes more active and selective. Children abstract information, filter out irrelevant information, and refine their peripheral mechanisms of attention. Third, there is an increasing economy of information pickup as perception becomes more efficient. Children learn to extract information at the most useful level of analysis: distinctive features, invariant relations, or higher-order structure.

On developmental issues, Gibson views humans as active, self-motivated creatures who develop primarily quantitatively but who also develop qualitatively. Nature and nurture interact to produce an efficient, adaptive perceptual system. The strengths of the theory are its focus on the ecological context of perception and its recognition of the role of knowledge in perception. An area of the theory needing further development is the relationship between perception and other psychological activities, particularly memory and decision making.

## SUGGESTED READINGS

The best source book on Gibson's earlier work is her own book.

Gibson, E. J. *Principles of perceptual learning and development.* New York: Appleton-Century-Crofts, 1969.

Two recent chapters describe changes in Gibson's theory since the publication of the 1969 book.

Gibson, E. J. Perceptual development from the ecological approach. In M. E. Lamb, A. L. Brown, and B. Rogoff, eds., *Advances in developmental psychology.* Vol. 3. Hillsdale, N.J.: Erlbaum, 1984.

Gibson, E. J. Exploratory behavior in the development of perceiving, acting, and the acquiring of knowledge. In M. R. Rosenzweig and L. W. Porter, eds., *Annual review of psychology.* Vol. 39. Palo Alto, Calif.: Annual Reviews, Inc., 1988.

# Reflections

*The beginnings and endings of all human undertakings are untidy,
the building of a house, the writing of a novel, the demolition of a
bridge, and, eminently, the finish of a voyage.*
[John Galsworthy]

$\mathbf{A}$ lthough it is tempting to tidy up the assortment of theories presented here by offering an orderly set of conclusions, that aim is not realistic. Developmental psychology is a huge, multifaceted discipline that has produced a diverse group of theories. Some theories are bold and speculative, others are cautious and precise; some are large-scale and rambling, others are modest and systematic. Furthermore, they ask different questions about development. Consequently, they address different levels of reality, ranging from a simple motor response to a complex personality structure. Any attempt to integrate all the theories would be foolish at best, and misleading at worst.

This chapter, then, offers several "untidy" thoughts that linger after we have delved into the theories of this book. The first section summarizes the theories' positions on the four developmental issues that were raised in each chapter. The second section views the history of developmental theory from two points of view. In the traditional view of scientific progress, research and theories build on previous work and thereby increase our knowledge base in a linear fashion. An opposing view, proposed by Thomas Kuhn, sees successive theories as supplanting previous theories rather than building on them and improving them. Third appears a list of common shortcomings of the theories that seem most serious in light of current needs of the field of developmental psychology. Critical areas for future theoretical and empirical work are identified. A final section proposes what roles theories of development can, and should, play today.

## DEVELOPMENTAL ISSUES REVISITED

### Human Nature

The distinction between organismic and mechanistic was a useful heuristic for understanding developmental theories, even though some theories do not fall neatly into one category. In particular, the dimension of active versus passive helped clarify the theories. All contemporary versions of the theories portray children as active agents in their own development, to varying degrees. The child assimilates, accommodates, and equilibrates (Piaget); strengthens ego processes (Freud); constructs a sense of identity (Erikson); and modifies his environment and develops self-regulatory mechanisms (social learning). In addition, he activates control processes (information processing), searches his environment and elicits reactions from others (ethology), and extracts new information from stimulation (Gibson). Some of the theories, however, include passive behaviors as well. Children are somewhat at the mercy both of drives (Freud, Erikson, ethology, early social learning theory) and of environmental stimuli (models and reinforcers in social learning theory, sign stimuli in ethology).

Another dimension separating mechanistic and organismic approaches ranges from antecedent causes of isolated behaviors to inherent causes within a whole structure. The former causes include S – R associations (learning theory), fixed action patterns (ethology), and input – output procedures (information processing). The latter are illustrated by cognitive structures (Piaget), the organization of the id, ego, and superego (Freud), the knowledge base or system of processing information (information processing), intrinsic motivation (Gibson), and control systems of behavior (Bowlby's ethological theory).

Overall, Piaget's theory is the most clearly organismic theory, whereas traditional learning theory is the most clearly mechanistic. Later, learning theory added some organismic features, especially as a result of Bandura's theoretical work.

In addition to the distinction between mechanism and organism is a striking difference in the theories' views of human nature: whether humans develop into rational, efficient "scientists" or into irrational beings whose thinking is colored by emotions. Piaget, Gibson, and information-processing theorists emphasize the former; Freud and Erikson emphasize the latter. Social learning theorists and ethologists are neutral on this issue. That is, they believe that motivation influences thinking but also recognize that logical thinking is encouraged by models who present logical methods of solving problems (social learning) or by the problem solving required for survival in most environments (ethology).

Our theorists' view of human nature is not a trivial matter, because it influences their theorizing. Developmentalists are influenced by their culture and need to be aware that both the field of developmental psychology and the definition of development are sociological phenomena, to some extent. For example, society's emphasis on technology and interindividual competition encourages developmentalists to study the development of the child as a solitary, scientific thinker who accumulates knowledge (Meacham, 1983).

## Qualitative Versus Quantitative Development

All the theorists see a number of ways in which development increases quantitatively — in amount, frequency, or degree. With increasing age, children strengthen and generalize their cognitive skills (Piaget), increase their ego strength (Freud and Erikson), imitate more accurately (social learning theory), process information more efficiently (information processing), refine the interweaving of innate and learned components (ethology), and detect more distinctive features (Gibson). Although all the theories posit at least minor qualitative change, only Piaget, Freud, and Erikson — the stage theorists — make qualitative change a central part of their theory. In the other theories, the most common qualitative change is a new strategy of learning or problem solving. A major current question regarding the issue of qualitative, stagelike change concerns the apparent unevenness in a child's cognitive performance across tasks or content areas. Domain specificity, which is addressed by neo-Piagetian and information-processing theorists, poses a major challenge for developmental theorizing during the next decade.

## Nature Versus Nurture

All the theorists agree that development springs from a complex interweaving of innate and experiential influences. However, they vary in their degree of concern with this issue and in which influences they choose to study. Piaget's theory most clearly is an interactionist theory. He sees development as an interaction of two innate factors (physical maturation and equilibration) and two types of experience (social and physical). Erikson also stresses both biological and social changes, showing that as drives change, they mesh (or conflict) with social institutions. Moving from the middle of the spectrum toward one end, we see that social learning theory and Gibson's theory examine the effects of experience. Toward the other end of the spectrum, ethologists, and to a lesser extent Freud, emphasize the effects of innate factors. In the remaining theory, information processing, this issue is seldom addressed. Neurological development obviously increases the potential efficiency of the information-processing system, and problem-solving experience leads the child to adopt new strategies when she receives feedback during attempts at problem solving.

## What Develops

The diverse answers to this question illustrate why an integration of theories is so difficult. The theorists attend to very different levels of behavior and select different content areas. The stage theorists look at stage-defining characteristics and therefore operate at a general level. In their view, the most important developments are cognitive structures (Piaget) or personality structures (Freud and Erikson). The other theorists focus on more specific acquisitions, often limited to certain situations or types of stimulation: rules (information processing and social learning theory), the perception of affordances and distinctive features (Gibson), and adaptive behaviors (ethology). With respect to content, the theories range from stressing social behaviors and personality (Freud, Erikson, social learning theory, ethology) to thinking (Piaget, information processing) to perception (Gibson). Development proceeds on several levels and in many content areas simultaneously. No one theory has unraveled this complex process.

# HISTORICAL PROGRESS OF DEVELOPMENTAL THEORIES

A succession of developmental theories has waxed and waned in influence. Are we left with a sense of scientific progress? Has each successive theory been better than the one before it? The traditional view of scientific progress, also the commonsense view, sees the history of a discipline as a cumulative enterprise. Each new discovery or theory builds on previous work and is a refinement of it in the search for ultimate truth. Each theory stands until empirical observations cast doubt on its validity. It is believed that the evaluation of facts is totally objective: "There is only one established dogma in science — that scientists do not blindly accept established dogma" (Brush, 1976, p. 68).

Clearly, there is continuity and a sense of theory development between Freud and Erikson within the psychoanalytic tradition or between classical learning theory and social learning theory within learning theory. Over a longer period of time, however, the historical progression of theories in this volume does not seem to follow this pattern. One is struck more with discontinuity than with continuity in moving from Freud to learning theory to Piaget to information processing. Each theory challenged a previous one and proposed an attractive alternative conception of development more than it refined the earlier theory. Furthermore, there is less than complete objectivity to science, as when a theory is used to guide observations and interpret facts. This general view of the growth of scientific knowledge is proposed by Thomas Kuhn (1970).

Kuhn proposes the following historical sequence within any scientific discipline. First is a "preparadigmatic phase," in which no one theory or generally agreed-upon way of studying the discipline's subject matter has emerged. There is debate over fundamental issues within the discipline. Next comes a period of "normal science," in which one paradigm dominates the field or at least an important subarea of the field. A paradigm is a generally accepted set of assumptions as to what should be studied, what questions should be asked, how these questions can be studied, and how the results should be conceptualized. For example, the information-processing approach emerged from a general agreement among developmental psychologists to study the flow of information through a processing system that resembles a computer and, furthermore, to ask how that information is stored, not how it is repressed as a result of anxiety. An investigator using this paradigm therefore is likely to measure reaction time, types of errors, or number of items correct but probably not the frequency of the response during a particular time period or the mean length of an utterance, measures used by learning theorists. Thus, a paradigm serves as a working model of how to do science.

A paradigm is larger than a theory. It is both an intellectual framework and a sociological phenomenon. Examples of this intellectual framework are the organismic and mechanistic world views. One holding a mechanistic world view, for instance, would be more likely to develop a theory that posits external rather than internal cognitive causes of behavior. With respect to the sociological aspect of paradigms, Kuhn points to a "community" of scholars who share certain assumptions or ground rules. The scholars can make rapid progress during the period of normal science because, instead of questioning the assumptions of the approach, they can concentrate their efforts on gathering data and solving problems identified by the paradigm. It is a time for "mopping-up operations" (Kuhn, 1970) to tidy up the paradigm. The paradigm is maintained by training students to carry on the tradition. They absorb the conventions for solving problems in the field and thereby "step into the circle" of that paradigm. An old paradigm never dies immediately; it just fades away, as students trained in the new paradigm enter the field and believers in the old paradigm are ignored and left behind.

The change from one paradigm to another follows a typical pattern. At some point a crisis arises. Phenomena may be discovered that cannot be explained by the current paradigm and consequently cause a crisis of confidence in the paradigm. If a more promising alternative paradigm appears on the scene, it may win the allegiance of the field and begin its own phase of normal science. Thus, after a first paradigm emerges in a discipline, there is a continual back-and-forth movement between normal science (a time of stability) and scientific revolution (a time of change). The history of a science is cyclic more than continuous, according to Kuhn.

Obvious examples of scientific revolutions are Darwinian theory, Einstein's theory of relativity, and the Copernican revolution, which brought the view that the sun rather than the earth is the center of the universe. Each of these paradigms brought a gestaltlike shift in the way scientists looked at facts.

Kuhn's view has been extended and modified by others. In particular, Lakatos (1978) has proposed "research programs," a progressive series of related theories with a common hard core of shared commitments (world view). Each theory is more complex and adequate than those before it. As a result of research, each theory is modified and thereby improved, or it is replaced. The core commitments are kept, but dispensable features are changed. At any one time there are competing research programs. If a scientific research program has not made progress, then it should be abandoned in favor of a more efficacious program.

Psychologists disagree about the value of Kuhn's model for the social sciences and about where to locate psychology in this history-of-science model. Is psychology in a preparadigmatic phase, or has it entered the cycle of paradigms and scientific revolutions? There has never been a paradigm that was accepted by the entire field of psychology or even developmental psychology. Today, there is still a questioning of basic assumptions about development. However, a paradigm can be restricted to a subarea within the field. From this perspective, there are several candidates for paradigms in developmental psychology. In fact, each of the theories described in this book has won over a group of scholars who have accepted the assumptions and gone about the business of solving problems defined by these assumptions. The general-orientation section of each chapter in this book roughly defines the paradigmatic characteristics of the theory. Each theory has had its community of productive investigators. One example is the Piagetian group in Geneva. A group of investigators accepted Piaget's intellectual framework and proceeded as though they were working out the details of this framework. Piaget's theory never quite reached this status among American researchers in cognitive development. Other paradigmatic communities can be identified for the computer-simulation approach at Carnegie – Mellon University and the Massachusetts Institute of Technology, for ethology in Germany, for psychoanalysis in certain clinical-psychology or psychiatry departments, and for learning (discrimination learning and social learning theory in the early 1960s in certain academic developmental psychology programs and in the early behaviorist movement in the United States). If one had to identify the most widespread paradigm in developmental psychology today, it would probably be information processing, in the general rather than the more specific, computer-simulation sense. The view of humans as organisms that represent, store, and reorganize information permeates much of the research on cognition, learning, and social behavior. It by no means encompasses the field, but it guides a sizable group of developmental researchers.

Whether future generations look back on this period as a time preparadigmatic or paradigmatic science, Kuhn's view of science as both continuous and discontinuous seems to have some validity in the history of theories of developmental psychology. Both continuity and discontinuity are apparent in information processing. It built on the precision and analytic posture of learning theory but won followers in part because of dissatisfaction within the ranks of learning researchers, rather than simply because it produced a better version of learning theory. Qualitative change came when Piaget challenged learning theory rather than modified it. Quantitative change came when Erikson built on, rather than replaced, Freudian theory.

The history of developmental psychology supports Kuhn's claim that when a theory cannot be modified satisfactorily, the stage is set for a revolution. A discipline seems to have a particular need at some point in history and embraces a new theory that offers a more satisfactory view of that discipline.

## SHORTCOMINGS OF THE THEORIES

All of the theories were evaluated, in part, in terms of their potential contributions to future developmental research. Although the theories vary in their strengths, there are common weaknesses that should be remedied in future research and theory construction. These weaknesses are (1) the failure to include all relevant sources of influence on development, (2) low ecological validity, and (3) the lack of adequate mechanisms of development.

### Failure to Include All Relevant Influences

Each theory identifies several sources of influence on development and then proceeds to emphasize one or two of these influences. Earlier chapters pointed out the ways in which each theory is incomplete. A useful framework for conceptualizing the influences on development is provided by various "contextual" approaches (for example, Lerner and Kauffman, 1985) that identify multiple influences on development and emphasize their dynamic interaction. The critical unit of analysis is the *transaction* between the organism and its context (social, historical, and physical). Unlike many approaches, the contextual view emphasizes that the developing person plays a role in her own development by choosing, interpreting, and modifying her environments, as they in turn influence her. One contextual account, "dialectical psychology," is a movement launched by Klaus Riegel. The term *dialectic* refers to the continual resolution of contradictions. In this view, development involves a changing individual in a changing world. Riegel (1976) identifies four sources of developmental change: (1) inner biological, (2) individual psychological, (3) cultural sociological, and (4) outer physical. Conflict can occur within each dimension, for example, parent-child conflict in the individual-psychological dimension or conflict between racial groups in the cultural-sociological dimension. In addition, as each of these four factors undergoes change, it affects and is affected by changes in the other three factors. These various causes are not simply added together; they interact. A serious illness (inner-biological change) may thwart one's career and cause family tensions (individual-psychological dimension). Changing a child's schooling from a traditional classroom to an "open" classroom (cultural-sociological change) may cause confusion and insecurity (individual-psychological dimension).

At any point in time, the four factors may be in or out of synchrony, but a lack of synchrony is much more common. Development is a lifelong process of trying to resolve the inevitable conflicts among these factors and within each factor. An active individual tries to cope with an active world and learns to live with a certain amount of contradiction. In fact, conflict plays a major role in bringing about successful development: "Rather than regarding these critical episodes in a negative manner or from a fatalistic point of view, they provide the fundamental basis for the development of the individual and for the history of society" (Riegel, 1976, p. 695).

Riegel emphasizes that life is a sequence of *concrete* interacting events and episodes as the individual grows within a sociohistorical context. He argues that theories should not treat development as though it occurs in a historical vacuum. A person who grew up during the Depression has had a different social and physical environment from that of a person who grew up in the more prosperous 1950s. More recently, the civil-rights movement and women's liberation movement surely have affected children's social development.

The idea that there is continual conflict punctuated by momentary stable structures is similar to Piaget's notion of equilibration. However, Piaget does not include a changing society or changing physical environment as possible sources of disequilibrium. That is, he sees an active organism but a passive environment. He emphasizes the child's interactions with the physical environment, but he virtually ignores interactions between developing individuals.

The dialectic view points out various developmental influences ignored in the other theories as well. Of the various theorists, Bandura alone emphasizes that an individual's behavior can change his environment. A cheerful, friendly child creates a positive, supportive social environment. Like Piaget, however, Bandura ignores sociohistorical changes. In fact, Freud, Gibson, the ethologists, and the information-processing psychologists also ignore the role of sociohistorical change. They all acknowledge or even emphasize that the environment influences development, but they see this influence as constant, or unchanging. Ethologists emphasize changes in the physical environment but have not conceptualized the effect of changes in the social environment as well. Erikson comes closest to dealing adequately with sociohistorical changes. He points out that these changes lead to changes in social institutions, which in turn lead to changes in society's expectations of the child at each point in development. For this reason, he found it necessary to compare development in different cultures.

An adequate theory should include an account of the effects of past and current social change. Both technological innovations and changing social structures obviously have an impact on children. The automatic washing machine and disposable diapers made early toilet training less important to busy mothers. Television and child-care centers brought a wider set of models to children. In particular, the television series "Sesame Street" brought academic instruction into the home of nearly every preschooler. Computers have made new forms of instruction and recreation possible. Mothers' employment outside the home, an increasing divorce rate, later first marriages, and the trend toward smaller families create a different environment from that of a child 25 years ago. Today only a minority of children live in a home with two parents, in which the father works outside the home and the mother does not. Will attachment, identification, independence training, and other aspects of socialization proceed in the same way as they have before? It seems unlikely. Future theory building should take a broad perspective on development. Even if a theorist chooses to cover only one aspect of development — such as cognitive development — to be complete, the theory should consider the interaction of physical maturation, psychological development, the changing physical environment, and the changing social environment over the entire life span.

## Low Ecological Validity

A second common shortcoming of developmental theories is a lack of serious concern with the ecological validity of research. Bronfenbrenner argues that "the properties of the environmental context in which research is carried out influence the processes that take place within that context and thereby affect the interpretation and generalizability of the research findings" (1977, p. 516). Although developmentalists acknowledge the importance of studying developmental tasks and problems as they actually operate in the lives of children, most of the research does not reflect this attitude. There is an understandable reluctance to give up the control and precision possible in the laboratory.

That low ecological validity can limit our understanding of a behavior is illustrated in the area of memory. The most common laboratory task is to recall a list of unrelated objects. Although there are some demands for rote memory in school or at home, it is likely that most material children need to remember is more meaningful. Todd and Perlmutter (1980) found that preschoolers accurately recall a substantial number of events in their lives, particularly social encounters.

Although Piaget's theory is high in ecological validity, in that he studied children interacting with objects commonly found in their environments, he paid less attention to the social context in which this learning takes place. Other people affect the child's motivation to learn, and the social world itself consists of events that are interpreted by the child. Psychoanalytic accounts of the emotional relationships between parents and their child must be supplemented with information about the child's relationship with peers and teachers. Ethological theory emphasizes the need to examine carefully the meshing of the demands of the environment and the child's attempts to adapt to that environment. Thus far, however, this theory has been applied to a very narrow range of child behavior, primarily infant attachment and dominance in peer groups. Ethologists typically study the immediate environment, but not the larger social settings, such as the school system or the economic system, which also influence children's development.

Bronfenbrenner (Bronfenbrenner and Crouter, 1983), among others, has urged developmentalists to consider the ecological context of behavior when doing their research. He views the environment as several levels nested in a hierarchy.

1. At the lowest level, a child operates within an immediate environment: the home, school, or immediate neighborhood. For instance, the way the father interacts with his infant is affected by whether the mother is present (Parke, 1977). In addition, the child in a one-parent family has a different set of experiences in the home than does the child in a two-parent family. In either type of family, if the mother decides to work outside the home, the family interaction changes.

2. At an intermediate level, we must consider the interrelationships among the child's major social settings. What happens in one setting influences another. For example, we might ask if the peer group and school system support or contradict the parents' value system.

3. An even higher level consists of the major institutions of society, such as the economic system, the transportation system, and the mass media. Bronfenbrenner notes that economic stress is one condition associated with child abuse. Another example is that watching television may interfere with family interaction.

4. The fourth and highest level "constructs" these first three levels. This level refers to general cultural "blueprints" that help to design the social structures and activities occurring at lower, more concrete levels. There is consistency within a culture among the important settings in that culture. To illustrate, Bronfenbrenner points out that within a given society, one elementary school classroom looks and operates much like every other. The nature of the prototypic classroom reflects unstated beliefs of the society.

These four levels form a system in which changes at one level affect the other levels. A recession may cause a father to lose his job. This leads to tension at home, which in turn causes the child to have problems at school. Such rippling effects can move in the opposite direction as well and bring about social change.

Psychologists have taken an interest in the view of Vygotsky (1978), another theorist who emphasizes the social context, that culture, particularly as represented by parents and teachers, guides and encourages development. He proposed that a child can be pulled from his current level of functioning through his *zone of proximal development* to his optimal level of functioning. This is accomplished, for example, during a problem-solving task when an adult or peer makes suggestions, gives hints, demonstrates the correct procedure, gives encouragement, or in some other way provides a supportive environment. For example, a mother helping her child construct a puzzle identical to a completed model might direct his attention to particular puzzle pieces in the model, point to corresponding pieces in his puzzle, and say the names of parts of the puzzle (Wertsch, McNamee, McLane, and Budwig, 1980). As children move through their zone of proximal development, they gradually take on more responsibility and become more self-regulated rather than other-regulated. That is, they eventually internalize the mode of problem solving that was first supported socially. As Vygotsky (1978, p. 88) expressed it, "Children grow into the intellectual life of those around them." Thus, thinking and learning are inherently social and dynamic. They are social in that they occur within, and are influenced by, a sociohistorical context. For instance, a society that existed before the invention of paper probably made different demands on children's memory than does modern society. One feature of social interchange, language, is a main way of communicating concepts. Thinking is dynamic in that it is defined in terms of the child's potential for progressing—his readiness for learning—rather than his current achieved level; process is more important than product.

These accounts of the importance of social context suggest that both laboratory and naturalistic studies are needed because they can converge to make an ecologically valid statement. Laboratory studies show that X *can* cause Y, whereas studies in natural settings determine whether X and Y *are* in fact correlated. That is, are high levels of X associated with high levels of Y, and are low levels of X associated with low levels of Y? Better yet, a longitudinal study examines whether children naturally develop X before Y. To complete the picture,

X is introduced into a naturalistic or quasi-naturalistic setting to see whether it leads to Y.

An example of converging laboratory and naturalistic research comes from studies of whether viewing violent models on television (X) increases aggression (Y) in children. Work by Bandura and others documents that viewing aggressive models increases subsequent aggression in the laboratory. Other investigators, working in natural settings, have obtained a positive correlation between watching violent programs and exhibiting aggression. Some of these studies, in contrast to the laboratory studies, reveal a bidirectional pattern of cause and effect (Huesmann, Lagerspetz, and Eron, 1984). Viewing violence encourages aggression, and aggressive children tend to view violence. Finally, the few studies that have introduced X into natural settings by controlling the type of television viewed modify the conclusions drawn in the other types of studies. For example, Friedrich and Stein (1973) found that a preschool group that was shown Batman and Superman cartoons subsequently exhibited higher levels of aggression. But this was true only of the children who were high in aggression to begin with.

Such a program of research has ecological validity, in that it examines a problem of great concern to society and studies this problem in natural situations. The laboratory studies suggest that the television programs have their influence through modeling, the naturalistic studies show bidirectionality, and the final experimental-naturalistic phase adds qualifiers to the results of the other studies. Both laboratory and naturalistic studies are needed.

Even cognitive-assessment research performed in a laboratory setting can have greater ecological validity than it often does. The situation need not be artificial and unfamiliar. First of all, the task chosen can be familiar or meaningful to the child. Shatz and Gelman (1973) found that young children's communications are less egocentric when they are explaining how a toy works (for example, a truck-dumping station) than if they are to communicate about less familiar objects or events. Another way to increase ecological validity in experimental tasks is to allow the usual situational variables to operate. If children sometimes rely on parents to remind them of what to take to school or what activity they are to do after school (Kreutzer, Leonard, and Flavell, 1975), then perhaps the development of this strategy should be studied in addition to the usual laboratory memory strategies, such as verbal rehearsal.

In summary, one requirement for future theories of development is to form a research base of ecologically valid studies. Thirty years ago, eminent developmental psychologists (McCandless and Spiker, 1956; Zigler, 1963) made a plea for more rigorous experimental work. This plea was answered with an explosion of laboratory studies. It is time now to test whether these results hold up in more natural settings, where many variables are operating at the same time and where the child and the environment are influencing each other.

## Lack of Adequate Mechanisms of Development

A third common weakness of developmental theories is the lack of an adequate account of mechanisms of development. It was stated in the Introduction that a developmental theory must *describe* development within one domain and the relationship among simultaneously developing domains, and it must *explain* the course of development that has been described. Piaget, Freud, and Erikson have given us a rich description of development, but their mechanisms of development — equilibration and the invariant functions for Piaget, drive for the psychoanalysts — are vague. These mechanisms are not easily observed and studied. In contrast, social learning theory, information processing, ethology, and Gibsonian theory emphasize processes of change but are weaker at describing development. Even these process theories, however, do not provide satisfactory mechanisms of development. Social learning theory posits observational learning, which includes verbal instruction and imitation of models. However, it is not clear how these processes actually operate. The processes have been given labels, but do not really serve as explanations of development. Acquisition of a new behavior by observing a model, listening to instructions, or reading involves a number of further processes that themselves are changing during development. These further processes include symbolically representing the sequence of behaviors to be imitated, constructing an image of a new behavior from printed words, integrating new information into previous knowledge, and translating new information into a course of action. One must still explain how these processes operate. In other words, it is not enough to identify the conditions facilitating observational learning and list the components involved (attention, retention, motor reproduction, and motivation). The identification step merely pushes the explanation back to another level.

The same problem arises with information processing, ethology, and Gibsonian theory. Exactly how do we acquire new strategies, develop control processes, overcome production deficiencies, integrate individual innate behaviors into a system, and abstract distinctive features? The precise cognitive, neurophysiological, or perceptual processes are still unspecified.

Future theories need to examine two roles of developmental mechanisms: (1) to lead to the acquisition of new skills and (2) to make these skills readily accessible. Any given mechanism may play one or both roles. Examples of mechanisms proposed by theorists to explain acquisition are the equilibration process, changes in biologically based drives, identification, ego development, observational learning, acquisition of strategies of information processing, automatization, and perceptual learning. Theorists have given much less attention to how these new acquisitions become readily accessible and expressed in performance. This is a critical issue, particularly in the area of cognitive development, because recent research suggests that much of development involves the child's learning to *use* the skills he has already acquired. Children can verbally mediate long before they spontaneously verbally rehearse a list of items to be remembered. Young children have a rudimentary understanding of number, but are easily diverted from using this understanding by distracting stimuli or a large amount of information to process. Adolescents use formal operations in some content areas, but not others. Social learning and information-processing theorists have identified a number of situational variables that facilitate or discourage the application of knowledge, but have not explained why or how these variables have an effect on performance.

Thus, the study of developmental processes involved in both acquiring new behaviors or skills and using them appropriately should be a central concern of future research and theorizing. It may even be that at different points in development, different mechanisms are important.

On a more optimistic note, recent theoretical and empirical advances in the study of mechanisms of development may preview exciting breakthroughs in the next few years. Siegler (1989) identifies five types of mechanisms of developmental change and provides examples of each.

1. Neural pathways: increasing the number of synapses (connections between neurons), strengthening heavily used synapses while pruning others, and differentiating one neural pathway into two. These changes have been related to cognitive and perceptual changes during infancy.

2. Associative competition: strengthening associations between various aspects of input (for example, syntactic information) and output (for example, German articles for nouns). Learning in areas such as language, recall, and problem solving may involve changes in this pattern of associations.

3. Encoding: increasing the encoding of relevant information and relational information (for example, heavier rather than heavy) and forming new encodings; these are involved in developmental changes in problem solving.

4. Analogy: transferring knowledge from a familiar problem to a novel, but related, problem. As children grow older, they make this leap with fewer or more subtle cues and less perceptual similarity.

5. Strategy choice: adapting to the particular task by choosing from among several available strategies. Children may select faster strategies when these can yield accurate performance, but slower strategies on certain problems that require these strategies for an acceptable level of accuracy.

Siegler concluded that underlying all these mechanisms is some type of competition, whether among synaptic connections, associations, information, cognitive rules, or strategies. Just as the fittest survive, the most adaptive processing units are retained. It is important that developmental psychologists understand mechanisms of change because, as Siegler notes, these mechanisms increase the generalizability of theories by showing that apparently unrelated developmental acquisitions may reflect the same underlying mechanisms of development.

## CURRENT VALUE OF DEVELOPMENTAL THEORIES

A knowledge of the developmental theories in this volume can prevent tunnel vision in researchers or professionals working with children. A rigid, egocentric perspective on children's behavior can be avoided if one shifts from theory to theory in an attempt to understand this behavior. There are many examples of this amalgamated approach. Freud's rich accounts of unconscious, irrational thinking made Piagetian-based research on logical concepts of physical phenomena seem incomplete. We have little work on the cognitive development underlying the defense mechanisms, emotional relationships with parents or peers, and identification. More generally, combining Freud's concern with emotions, Piaget's concern with cognitive structures, and learning theory's concern with performance in specific situations would produce a powerful perspective for understanding children's behavior.

Another example of how a multitheoretical approach broadens our view is the application of ethologists' methodology to social learning theory. By observing children in the environments to which they must adapt, we can see what role imitation plays. Is imitation most likely in situations where the child is uncertain about what the social environment is demanding? Does a peer dominance hierarchy involve imitation of the children higher in the hierarchy by children lower in the hierarchy?

It is important to realize that our use of some of the earlier theories may require certain modifications. Freud's notion of the powerful unconscious can be accepted without also accepting his claim that it is primarily sexual impulses that are repressed in the unconscious. As cultural conditions change and new information about development comes to light, we must select what is useful from the theories and ignore other parts.

As Beilin (1984, p. 9) comments, "History makes every theory look deficient in some way." Because no one theory satisfactorily explains development, it is critical that developmentalists be able to draw on the content, methods, and theoretical concepts of many theories. The various theories supply multiple levels of analysis, from the physiological to the sociological level. This proposed eclectic approach would most likely lead to small-scale, problem-oriented research and theories: a set of organized hypotheses concerning one area—for example, attachment, identification, or reasoning about quantity. Ideally, within this problem area, the concepts and methods selected would capture most of the diverse variables. There probably will be few large-scale, grand theories of development in the future, but there could be a number of minitheories with a broad perspective.

In summary, it is proposed that developmental researchers and practitioners use various theories as heuristics to guide their problem solving. This does not mean, however, that there is no place for developmentalists who operate within a single theory. There is value to pushing a single theory to its limits. As Kuhn noted in his discussion of paradigms, sometimes rapid progress is most likely when the investigator does not question the assumptions of his field. Finding out where a theory breaks down can be very informative. As the English logician Augustus De Morgan commented, "Wrong hypotheses rightly worked from, have produced more useful results than unguided observation." Given the current level of knowledge in developmental psychology, we need both eclectics and true believers.

"Where shall I begin?" asked the White Rabbit.
"Begin at the beginning," the King said gravely, "and go on till you come to the end, then stop."

[*Lewis Carroll*]

# Bibliography

Acredolo, L. P., H. L. Pick, and M. G. Olsen.
  1975    Environmental differentiation and familiarity as determinants of children's memory for spatial location. *Developmental Psychology, 11,* 495–501.

Ainsworth, M.D.
  1973    The development of infant–mother attachment. In B. M. Caldwell and H. N. Ricciuti, eds., *Review of child development research.* Vol. 3. Chicago: University of Chicago Press.

*American Psychologist.*
  1981    *36,* 27–34.
  1982    *37,* 74–85.

Anastasi, A.
  1958    Heredity, environment, and the question "How?" *Psychological Review, 65,* 197–208.

Ardrey, R.
  1966    *The territorial imperative.* London: Anthony Blond.

Astington, J. W., P. L. Harris, and D. R. Olson, eds.
  1988    *Developing theories of mind.* Cambridge: Cambridge University Press.

Atkinson, R. C., and R. M. Shiffrin.
  1968    Human memory: A proposed system and its control processes. In K. W. Spence and J. T. Spence, eds., *Advances in the psychology of learning and motivation research and theory.* Vol. 2. New York: Academic Press.

Averill, J. R.
  1976    Patterns of psychological thought: A general introduction. In J. R. Averill, ed., *Patterns of psychological thought.* Washington, D.C.: Hemisphere.

Baltes, M. M. and E. M. Barton.
  1979    Behavior analysis of aging: A review of the operant model and

Baltes and Barton (*continued*)
  research. *International Journal of Behavioral Development, 2,* 291–320.

Bandura, A.
  1965　Influence of model's reinforcement contingencies on the acquisition of imitative responses. *Journal of Personality and Social Psychology, 1,* 589–595.
  1967　Behavioral psychotherapy. *Scientific American, 216,* 78–86.
  1971　Vicarious and self-reinforcement processes. In R. Glaser, ed., *The nature of reinforcement.* New York: Academic Press.
  1977　*Social learning theory.* Englewood Cliffs, N.J.: Prentice-Hall.
  1986　*Social foundations of thought and action.* Englewood Cliffs, N.J.: Prentice-Hall.

Bandura, A., J. E. Grusec, and F. L. Menlove.
  1966　Observational learning as a function of symbolization and incentive set. *Child Development, 37,* 499–506.

Bandura, A., and F. J. McDonald.
  1963　The influence of social reinforcement and the behavior of models in shaping children's moral judgments. *Journal of Abnormal and Social Psychology, 67,* 274–281.

Bandura, A., D. Ross, and S. A. Ross.
  1961　Transmission of aggression through imitation of aggressive models. *Journal of Abnormal and Social Psychology, 63,* 575–582.

Bandura, A., and R. H. Walters.
  1959　*Adolescent aggression.* New York: Ronald Press.
  1963　*Social learning and personality development.* New York: Holt.

Barash, D. P.
  1973　Personal space reiterated. *Environment and Behavior, 5,* 67–72.

Barker, R. G., and H. F. Wright.
  1955　*Midwest and its children: The psychological ecology of an American town.* Evanston, Ill.: Row-Peterson.

Barnett, S. A.
  1963　*A study in behaviour.* London: Methuen.

Bateson, P. P. G.
  1973　The imprinting of birds. In S. A. Barnett, ed., *Ethology and development.* Philadelphia: Lippincott.
  1976　Rules and reciprocity in behavioural development. In P. P. G. Bateson and R. A. Hinde, eds., *Growing points in ethology.* Cambridge: Cambridge University Press.
  1978　Early experience and sexual preferences. In J. B. Hutchison, ed., *Biological determinants of sexual behavior.* London: Wiley.

Baylor, G. W., and J. Gascon.
  1974　An information processing theory of aspects of the development of weight seriation in children. *Cognitive Psychology, 6,* 1–40.

Baylor, G. W., and G. Lemoyne.
  1975　Experiments in seriation with children: Towards an information processing explanation of the horizontal decalage. *Canadian Journal of*

Baylor, G. W. (*continued*)
   *Behavioral Science, 7,* 4–29.
Beer, C. G.
   1973   Species-typical behavior and ethology. In D. A. Dewsbury and D. A. Rethlingshafer, eds., *Comparative psychology: A modern survey.* New York: McGraw-Hill.
Beilin, H.
   1971   The training and acquisition of logical operations. In M. F. Rosskopf, L. P. Steffe, and S. Taback, eds., *Piagetian cognitive-developmental research and mathematical education.* Washington, D.C.: National Council of Teachers of Mathematics.
   1980   Piaget's theory: Refinement, revision, or rejection? In R. H. Kluwe and H. Spada, eds., *Developmental models of thinking.* New York: Academic Press.
   In   Jean Piaget: The old theory and the new. In R. Vasta, ed., *Annals of*
   press   *child development.* Vol. 6: *Developmental theory.* Greenwich, Conn.: JAI Press.
Bell, R. Q., and L. V. Harper.
   1977   *The effect of children on parents.* Hillsdale, N.J.: Erlbaum.
Berkowitz, M. W., ed.
   1985   *Peer conflict and psychological growth.* San Francisco: Jossey-Bass.
Berlyne, D. E.
   1965   *Structure and direction in thinking.* New York: Wiley.
Berman, P.
   1980   Are women more responsive than men to the young? A review of developmental and situational variables. *Psychological Bulletin, 88,* 668–695.
Bijou, S. W., and D. M. Baer.
   1961   *Child Development.* Vol. 1. New York: Appleton-Century-Crofts.
   1978   *Behavioral analysis of child development.* Englewood Cliffs, N.J.: Prentice-Hall.
Bjorklund, D. F.
   1987   How age changes in knowledge base contribute to the development of children's memory. *Developmental Review, 7,* 93–130.
Bjorklund, D. F., and B. R. Zeman.
   1982   Children's organization and metamemory awareness in their recall of familiar information. *Child Development, 53,* 799–810.
Blurton-Jones, N.
   1972   *Ethological studies of child behavior.* Cambridge: Cambridge University Press.
Bower, T. G. R.
   1974   *Development in infancy.* San Francisco: W. H. Freeman and Company.
Bowers, K. S.
   1973   Situationism in psychology. *Psychological Review, 80,* 307–336.
Bowlby, J.
   1958   The nature of the child's tie to his mother. *International Journal of Psychoanalysis, 39,* 350–373.

Bowlby, J. (*continued*)
1980    *Attachment and loss.* Vol. 3: *Loss.* New York: Basic Books.
1982    *Attachment and loss.* Vol. 1: *Attachment.* 2nd ed. New York: Basic Books (1969).
Brainerd, C. J.
1973    Judgments and explanations as criteria for the presence of cognitive structures. *Psychological Bulletin, 79,* 172–179.
1978    The stage question in cognitive-development theory. *Behavioral and Brain Sciences, 1,* 173–181.
Brannigan, C. R., and Humphries, D. A.
1972    Human nonverbal behaviour, a means of communication. In N. G. Blurton Jones, ed., *Ethological studies of child behaviour.* Cambridge: Cambridge University Press.
Breland, K., and M. Breland.
1961    The misbehavior of organisms. *American Psychologist, 16,* 681–684.
Breslow, L.
1981    Reevaluation of the literature on the development of transitive inferences. *Psychological Bulletin, 89,* 325–351.
Bringuier, J.
1980    *Conversations with Jean Piaget.* Chicago: University of Chicago Press.
Broadbent, D. E.
1958    *Perception and communication.* London: Pergamon Press.
Bronfenbrenner, U.
1977    Toward an experimental ecology of human development. *American Psychologist, 32,* 513–531.
Bronfenbrenner, U., and A. C. Crouter.
1983    The evolution of environmental models in developmental research. In W. Kessen, ed., *Handbook of child psychology.* Vol. 1: *History, theory, and methods.* 4th ed. New York: Wiley.
Brown, A. L.
1975    The development of memory: Knowing, knowing about knowing, and knowing how to know. In H. W. Reese, ed., *Advances in child development and behavior.* Vol. 10. New York: Academic Press.
1978    Knowing when, where, and how to remember: A problem of metacognition. In R. Glaser, ed., *Advances in instructional psychology.* Vol. 1. Hillsdale, N.J.: Erlbaum.
1979    Theories of memory and the problem of development: Activity, growth, and knowledge. In L. S. Cermak and F. I. M. Craik, eds., *Levels of processing in human memory.* Hillsdale, N.J.: Erlbaum.
Brown, A. L., and J. S. DeLoache.
1983    Skills, plans, and self-regulation. In R. S. Siegler, ed., *Children's thinking: What develops?* Hillsdale, N.J.: Erlbaum.
Brown, A. L., and S. S. Smiley.
1978    The development of strategies for studying texts. *Child Development, 49,* 1076–1088.

Brown, J. S., and R. B. Burton.
1978    Diagnostic models for procedural bugs in basic mathematical skills. *Cognitive Science, 2,* 155–192.

Brückner, G. H.
1933    Untersuchungen zur Tiersoziologie, insbesondere der Auflösung der Familie. *Zeitschrift für Psychologie, 128,* 1–120.

Bruner, J. S.
1957    On perceptual readiness. *Psychological Review, 64,* 123–152.
1987    The artist as analyst. A review of *A way of looking at things: Selected papers from 1930 to 1980,* by E. Erikson. *The New York Review,* Dec. 3, 8–13.

Brunk, M. A., and S. W. Henggeler.
1984    Child influences on adult controls: An experimental investigation. *Developmental Psychology, 6,* 1074–1081.

Brush, S. G.
1976    Fact and fantasy in the history of science. In M. H. Marx and F. E. Goodson, eds., *Theories in contemporary psychology.* 2nd ed. New York: Macmillan.

Bryant, P. E.
1986    Theories about the causes of cognitive development. In P. L. C. Van Geert, ed., *Theory building in developmental psychology.* Amsterdam: North Holland.

Bryant, P. E., and T. Trabasso.
1971    Transitive inferences and memory in young children. *Nature, 232,* 457–459.

Cairns, R. B.
1979    *Social development: The origins and plasticity of interchanges.* San Francisco: W. H. Freeman and Company.

Campos, J. J., A. Langer, and A. Krowitz.
1970    Cardiac responses on the visual cliff in prelocomotor human infants. *Science, 170,* 196–197.

Case, R.
1984    The process of stage transition: A neo-Piagetian view. In R. J. Sternberg, ed., *Mechanisms of cognitive development.* New York: W. H. Freeman.
1985    *Intellectual development: Birth to adulthood.* Orlando, Fla.: Academic Press.

Case, R., S. Hayward, M. Lewis, and P. Hurst.
1988    Toward a neo-Piagetian theory of cognitive and emotional development. *Developmental Review, 8,* 1–51.

Cassirer, E.
1951    *The philosophy of the enlightenment.* Boston: Beacon Press.

Ceci, S. J., R. D. Caves, and M. J. A. Howe.
1981    Children's long-term memory for information that is incongruous with their prior knowledge. *British Journal of Psychology, 72,* 443–450.

Cernoch, J. M., and R. H. Porter.
1985    Recognition of maternal axillary odors by infants. *Child Development,* *56,* 1593–1598.

Charlesworth, W.
1979    Ethology: Understanding the other half of intelligence. In M. von Cranach, K. Foppa, W. Lepenies, and D. Ploog, eds., *Human ethology: Claims and limits of a new discipline.* Cambridge: Cambridge University Press.

1983    An ethological approach to cognitive development. In C. Brainerd, ed., *Recent advances in cognitive developmental theory.* New York: Springer-Verlag.

1988    Resources and resource acquisition during ontogeny. In K. B. MacDonald, ed., *Sociobiological perspectives on human development.* New York: Springer-Verlag.

Chi, M. T. H.
1978    Knowledge structures and memory development. In R. S. Siegler, ed., *Children's thinking: What develops?* Hillsdale, N.J.: Erlbaum.

Chi, M. T. H., and R. D. Koeske.
1983    Network representation of a child's dinosaur knowledge. *Developmental Psychology, 19,* 29–39.

Chomsky, N.
1959    A review of *Verbal Behavior,* by B. F. Skinner, *Language, 35,* 26–58.
1965    *Aspects of the theory of syntax.* Cambridge, Mass.: MIT Press.

Cohen, D.
1977    *Psychologists on psychology.* New York: Taplinger.

Cohen, L. B., and P. Salapatek.
1975    *Infant perception: From sensation to cognition.* Vol. 1. New York: Academic Press.

Cohen, R., ed.
1985    *The development of spatial cognition.* Hillsdale, N.J.: Erlbaum.

Collins, A. M., and M. R. Quillian.
1969    Retrieval time from semantic memory. *Journal of Verbal Learning and Verbal Behavior, 8,* 240–247.

Collins, J. L.
1982    *Self-efficacy and ability in achievement behavior.* Paper presented at the annual meeting of the American Educational Research Association, New York, March.

Cote, J. E., and C. Levine.
1987    A formulation of Erikson's theory of ego identity formation, *Developmental Review, 7,* 273–325.

Craik, F. I. M.
1979    Human memory. In P. H. Mussen and M. R. Rosenzweig, eds., *Annual review of psychology.* Vol. 30. Palo Alto, Ca.: Annual Reviews.

Craik, F. I. M., and R. S. Lockhart.
1972    Levels of processing: A framework for memory research. *Journal of Verbal Learning and Verbal Behavior, 11,* 671–684.

Darwin, C.
1859    *The origin of species.* New York: Modern Library.
1877    A biographical sketch of an infant. *Mind, 2,* 285–294.
Decarie, T.
1965    *Intelligence and affectivity in early childhood.* New York: International Universities Press.
Dekker, E., and J. Groen.
1956    Reproducible psychogenic attacks of asthma: A laboratory study. *Journal of Psychosomatic Research, 1,* 58–67.
Denny, N. W., S. Zeytinoglu, and S. C. Selzer.
1977    Conservation training in four-year-old children. *Journal of Experimental Child Psychology, 24,* 129–146.
Dewsbury, D. A.
1978    *Comparative animal behavior.* New York: McGraw-Hill.
Dodge, K. A.
1986    A social information processing model of social competence in children. In M. Perlmutter, ed., *Cognitive perspectives on children's social and behavioral development.* Hillsdale, N.J.: Erlbaum.
Dollard, J., L. W. Doob, N. E. Miller, O. H. Mowrer, and R. R. Sears.
1939    *Frustration and aggression.* New Haven, Conn.: Yale University Press.
Dollard, J., and N. E. Miller.
1950    *Personality and psychotherapy.* New York: McGraw-Hill.
Dorr, D., and S. Fey.
1974    Relative power of symbolic adult and peer models in the modification of children's moral choice behavior. *Journal of Personality and Social Psychology, 29,* 335–341.
Edelman, M. S., and D. R. Omark.
1973    *The development of logical operations: An ethological approach.* Paper presented at meetings of Society for Research in Child Development, Philadelphia, March.
Eibl-Eibesfeldt, I.
1975    *Ethology: The biology of behavior.* 2nd ed. New York: Holt, Rinehart and Winston. 1st ed., 1970.
Elkind, D.
1968    Giant in the nursery—Jean Piaget. *New York Times Magazine,* May 26.
Erikson, E. H.
1950a   *Childhood and society.* New York: Norton. 2nd ed., 1963.
1950b   In M. J. E. Senn, ed., *Symposium on the healthy personality.* New York: Josiah Macy, Jr., Foundation.
1951    The California loyalty oath: An editorial. *Psychiatry, 14,* 244–245.
1958    *Young man Luther.* New York: Norton.
1959    Identity and the life cycle. *Psychological Issues,* Monograph 1. New York: International Universities Press.
1968    *Identity: Youth and crisis.* New York: Norton.
1969    *Gandhi's truth.* New York: Norton.

Erikson, E. H. (continued)
1973      The wider identity. In K. Erikson, ed., *In search of common ground: Conversations with Erik H. Erikson and Huey P. Newton.* New York: Norton.
1977      *Toys and reasons.* New York: Norton.
Erikson, E. H., J. M. Erikson, and H. Q. Kivnick.
1986      *Vital involvement in old age.* New York: Norton.
Eron, L. D.
1987      The development of aggressive behavior from the perspective of a developing behaviorism. *American Psychologist, 42,* 435–442.
Evans, R. I.
1967      *Dialogue with Erik Erikson.* New York: Harper and Row.
1973      *Jean Piaget: The man and his ideas.* New York: Dutton.
Fabricius, W. V., and J. W. Hagen.
1984      Use of causal attributions about recall performance to assess metamemory and predict strategic memory behavior in young children. *Developmental Psychology, 20,* 975–987.
Fattu, N., D. Auble, and E. Mech.
1955      Partial reinforcement in a bar pressing situation with preschool children. *Journal of Genetic Psychology, 87,* 251–255.
Feldman, D. H.
1980      *Beyond universals in cognitive development.* Norwood, N.J.: Ablex.
Fentress, J. C.
1973      Specific and nonspecific factors in the causation of behavior. In P. P. G. Bateson and P. H. Klopfer, eds., *Perspectives in ethology.* Vol. 1. New York: Plenum.
Fischer, K. W.
1980      A theory of cognitive development: The control and construction of hierarchies of skills. *Psychological Review, 87,* 477–531.
Fischer, K. W., and S. L. Pipp.
1984      Processes of cognitive development: Optimal level and skill acquisition. In R. J. Sternberg, ed., *Mechanisms of cognitive development.* New York: W. H. Freeman.
Flavell, J. H.
1963      *The developmental psychology of Jean Piaget.* Princeton, N.J.: Van Nostrand.
1971a      First discussant's comments: What is memory development the development of? *Human Development, 14,* 272–278.
1971b      Stage-related properties of cognitive development. *Cognitive Psychology, 2,* 421–453.
1982      On cognitive development. *Child Development, 53,* 1–10.
1984      Discussion. In R. J. Sternberg, ed., *Mechanisms of cognitive development.* New York: W. H. Freeman.
1986      The development of children's knowledge about the appearance–reality distinction. *American Psychologist, 41,* 418–425.

Flavell, J. H., D. R. Beach, and J. M. Chinsky.
1966     Spontaneous verbal rehearsal in a memory task as a function of age. *Child Development, 37,* 283–299.
Flavell, J. H., A. G. Friedrichs, and J. D. Hoyt.
1970     Developmental changes in memorization processes. *Cognitive Psychology, 1,* 324–340.
Flavell, J. H., and J. Hill.
1969     Developmental psychology. In P. H. Mussen and M. R. Rosenzweig, eds., *Annual review of psychology.* Vol. 20. Palo Alto, Calif.: Annual Reviews.
Flavell, J. H., and H. M. Wellman.
1977     Metamemory. In R. V. Kail and J. W. Hagen, eds., *Perspectives on the development of memory and cognition.* Hillsdale, N.J.: Erlbaum.
Flavell, J. H., and J. F. Wohlwill.
1969     Formal and functional aspects of cognitive development. In D. Elkind and J. H. Flavell, eds., *Studies in cognitive growth: Essays in honor of Jean Piaget.* New York: Oxford University Press.
Fox, R. and C. McDaniel.
1982     Perception of biological motion by human infants. *Science, 218,* 486–487.
Freud, S.
1900*    The interpretation of dreams. Vols. 4 and 5.
(1953)
1901     The psychopathology of everyday life. Vol. 6.
(1960)
1905a    Fragment of an analysis of a case of hysteria. Vol. 7.
(1953)
1905b    Three essays on the theory of sexuality. Vol. 7.
(1953)
1909a    Analysis of a phobia in a five-year-old boy. Vol. 10.
(1955)
1909b    Notes upon a case of obsessional neurosis. Vol. 10.
(1955)
1913     Totem and taboo. Vol. 13.
(1955)
1914     The Moses of Michelangelo. Vol. 13.
(1955)
1915     Instincts and their vicissitudes. Vol. 14.
(1957)
1916     Introductory lectures on psycho-analysis. Vols. 15 and 16.
and

*The first date given is that of the original edition in German. The second date (in parentheses) is that of the translation: J. Strachey, ed. and trans., *The standard edition of the complete psychological works of Sigmund Freud.* 24 vols. London: Hogarth Press, 1953–1966.

Freud, S. *(continued)*
  1917
  (1963)
  1918     From the history of an infantile neurosis. Vol. 17.
  (1955)
  1920     Beyond the pleasure principle. Vol. 18.
  (1955)
  1923     The ego and the id. Vol. 19.
  (1961)
  1925a    An autobiographical study. Vol. 20.
  (1959)
  1925b    Some psychical consequences of the anatomical distinction between the sexes. Vol. 19.
  (1961)
  1927     The future of an illusion. Vol. 21.
  (1961)
  1928     Dostoevsky and parricide. Vol. 21.
  (1961)
  1930     Civilization and its discontents. Vol. 21.
  (1961)
  1933a    New introductory lectures on psycho-analysis. Vol. 22.
  (1964)
  1933b    Why war? Vol. 22.
  (1964)
  1940     An outline of psycho-analysis. Vol. 23.
  (1964)
Friedrich, L. K., and A. H. Stein.
  1973     Aggressive and prosocial television programs and the natural behavior of preschool children. *Monographs of the Society for Research in Child Development, 38* (4, Serial No. 151).
Furth, H. G.
  1987     *Knowledge as desire.* New York: Columbia University Press.
Garcia, J., and R. A. Koelling.
  1966     Relation of cue to consequences in avoidance learning. *Psychonomic Science, 4,* 123–124.
Gardner, R., and K. G. Heider.
  1969     *Gardens of war: Life and death in the New Guinea stone age.* New York: Random House.
Garmezy, N., and Tellegen, A.
  1984     Studies of stress-resistant children: Methods, variables and preliminary findings. In F. Morrison, C. Lord, and D. Keating, eds., *Applied developmental psychology.* Vol. 1. New York: Academic Press.
Gelman, R.
  1969     Conservation acquisition: A problem of learning to attend to relevant attributes. *Journal of Experimental Child Psychology, 7,* 167–187.

Gelman, R. (*continued*)
1972    Logical capacity of very young children: Number invariance rules. *Child Development, 43,* 75–90.
Gelman R., and C. R. Gallistel.
1978    *The child's understanding of number.* Cambridge, Mass.: Harvard University Press.
Gelman, R., and D. H. Weinberg.
1972    The relationship between liquid conservation and compensation. *Child Development, 43,* 371–383.
Gesell, A.
1945    *The embryology of behavior.* New York: Harper and Row.
Gewirtz, J. L.
1967    Deprivation and satiation of social stimuli as determinants of their reinforcing efficacy. In J. P. Hill, ed., *Minnesota symposia on child psychology.* Vol. 1. Minneapolis: University of Minnesota Press.
Gewirtz, J. L., and D. M. Baer.
1958    The effect of brief social deprivation on behaviors for a social reinforcer. *Journal of Abnormal and Social Psychology, 56,* 49–56.
Ghiselin, M. T., and F. M. Scudo.
1986    The bioeconomics of phenotypic selection. (Comment on D. Vining, *Social versus reproductive success: The central theoretical problems of human socio-biology.*) *The Behavioral and Brain Sciences, 9,* 194–195.
Gholson, B., D. E. Theobald, and S. T. Yarbrough.
1980    Strategic problem solving among kindergarten children of three cognitive levels. In B. Gholson, ed., *The cognitive developmental basis of human learning.* New York: Academic Press.
Ghuman, P. A. S.
1981    An evaluation of Piaget's theory from a cross-cultural perspective. In S. Modgil and C. Modgil, eds., *Jean Piaget: Consensus and controversy.* New York: Praeger.
Gibson, E. J.
1969    *Principles of perceptual learning and development.* New York: Appleton-Century-Crofts.
1977    How perception really develops: A view from outside the network. In D. LaBerge and S. J. Samuels, eds., *Basic processes in reading: Perception and comprehension.* Hillsdale, N.J.: Erlbaum.
1982    The concept of affordances in development: The renascence of functionalism. In W. A. Collins, ed., *The concept of development.* Hillsdale, N.J.: Erlbaum.
1984    Perceptual development from the ecological approach. In M. E. Lamb, A. L. Brown, and B. Rogoff, eds., *Advances in developmental psychology.* Vol. 3. Hillsdale, N.J.: Erlbaum.
1988    Exploratory behavior in the development of perceiving, acting, and the acquiring of knowledge. In M. R. Rosenzweig and L. W. Porter, eds., *Annual review of psychology.* Vol. 39. Pala Alto, Calif.: Annual Reviews, Inc.

Gibson, E. J., J. J. Gibson, A. D. Pick, and H. Osser.
1962     A developmental study of the discrimination of letter-like forms. *Journal of Comparative and Physiological Psychology, 55,* 897–906.

Gibson, E. J., and H. Levin.
1975     *The psychology of reading.* Cambridge, Mass.: MIT Press.
1979     Afterword. In A. D. Pick, ed., *Perception and its development: A tribute to Eleanor J. Gibson.* Hillsdale, N.J.: Erlbaum.

Gibson, E. J., C. J. Owsley, and J. Johnston.
1978     Perception of invariants by five-month-old infants: Differentiation of two types of motion. *Developmental Psychology, 14,* 407–415.

Gibson, E. J., and N. Rader.
1979     The perceiver as performer. In G. Hale and M. Lewis, eds., *Attention and cognitive development.* New York: Plenum.

Gibson, E. J., A. Riccio, M. Schmuckler, T. Stoffregen, D. Rosenberg, and J. Taormina.
1987     Detection of the traversability of surfaces by crawling and walking infants. *Journal of Experimental Psychology: Human Perception and Performance, 13,* 533–544.

Gibson, E. J., A. Shurcliff, and A. Yonas.
1970     Utilization of spelling patterns by deaf and hearing subjects. In H. Levin and J. P. Williams, eds., *Basic studies on reading.* New York: Basic Books.

Gibson, E. J., and R. D. Walk.
1960     The "visual cliff." *Scientific American, 202,* 64–71.

Gibson, E. J., and A. S. Walker.
1984     Development of knowledge of visual-tactual affordances of substance. *Child Development, 55,* 453–460.

Gibson, J. J.
1979     Foreward: A note on E. J. G. by J. J. G.. In A. D. Pick, ed., *Perception and its development: A tribute to Eleanor J. Gibson.* Hillsdale, N.J.: Erlbaum.

Gill, M. M.
1959     The present state of psychoanalytic theory. *Journal of Abnormal and Social Psychology, 58,* 1–8.

Gilligan, C.
1982     *In a different voice: Psychological theory and women's development.* Cambridge, Mass.: Harvard University Press.

Ginsburg, H., and S. Opper.
1979     *Piaget's theory of intellectual development.* 2nd ed. Englewood Cliffs, N.J.: Prentice-Hall.

Ginsburg, H. J., V. A. Pollman, and M. S. Wauson.
1977     An ethological analysis of nonverbal inhibitors of aggressive behavior in male elementary school children. *Developmental Psychology, 13,* 417–418.

Goldberg, S., S. L. Blumberg, and A. Kriger.
1982      Menarche and interest in infants: Biological and social influences. *Child Development, 53,* 1544–1550.
Gottlieb, G.
1979      Comparative psychology and ethology. In E. Hearst, ed., *The first century of experimental psychology.* Hillsdale, N.J.: Erlbaum.
Gould, S. J.
1980      *The Panda's thumb.* New York: Norton.
Greco, P.
1967      Logique et connaissance. In J. Piaget, ed., *Encyclopédie de la Pléiade.* Paris: Gallimard.
Greeno, J. G., M. S. Riley, and R. Gelman.
1984      Conceptual competence and children's counting. *Cognitive Psychology, 16,* 66–94.
Gregg, L. W.
1978      Spatial concepts, spatial names, and the development of egocentric representations. In R. S. Siegler, ed., *Children's thinking: What develops?* Hillsdale, N.J.: Erlbaum.
Grinstein, A., ed.
1956–    *The index of psychoanalytic writings.* Vols. 1–14. New York: Interna-
1971      tional Universities Press.

Guttentag, R. E.
1984      The mental effort requirement of cumulative rehearsal: A developmental study. *Journal of Experimental Child Psychology, 37,* 92–106.
Gzesh, S. M., and C. F. Surber.
1985      Visual perspective-taking skills in children. *Child Development, 56,* 1204–1213.
Hagen, J. W., and G. A. Hale.
1973      The development of attention in children. In A. D. Pick, ed., *Minnesota symposia on child psychology.* Vol. 7. Minneapolis: University of Minnesota Press.
Hall, C. S.
1954      *A primer of Freudian psychology.* New York: World.
Hall, C. S., and G. Lindzey.
1957      *Theories of personality.* New York: Wiley.
Hall, G. S.
1904      *Adolescence.* New York: Appleton.
Hardwick, D. A., C. McIntyre, and H. L. Pick.
1976      The content and manipulation of cognitive maps in children and adults. *Monographs of the Society for Research in Child Development, 41* (3, Serial No. 166).
Harris, B.
1979      Whatever happened to little Albert? *American Psychologist, 34,* 151–160.

Harris, F. R., M. M. Wolf, and D. M. Baer.
1967 Effects of adult social reinforcement on child behavior. In W. W. Hartup and N. L. Smothergill, eds., *The young child: Reviews of research*. Washington, D.C.: National Association for the Education of Young Children.

Hartmann, H.
1958 *Ego psychology and the problem of adaptation*. New York: International Universities Press.

Hartup, W. W., and A. Yonas.
1971 Developmental psychology. In P. H. Mussen and M. R. Rosenzweig, eds., *Annual review of psychology*. Vol. 22. Palo Alto, Ca.: Annual Reviews.

Hebb, D.O.
1949 *The organization of behavior*. New York: Wiley.
1960 The American revolution. *American Psychologist, 15,* 735–745.
1980 *Essay on mind*. Hillsdale, N.J.: Erlbaum.

Heisel, B. E., and K. Ritter.
1981 Young children's storage behavior in a memory-for-location task. *Journal of Experimental Child Psychology, 31,* 350–364.

Hess, E. H.
1970 Ethology and developmental psychology. In P. H. Mussen, ed., *Carmichael's manual of child psychology*. Vol. 1. 3rd ed. New York: Wiley.
1973 *Imprinting: Early experience and the developmental psychobiology of attachment*. New York: Van Nostrand.

Hicks, V. C., and H. A. Carr.
1912 Human reactions in a maze. *Journal of Animal Psychology, 2,* 98–125.

Hilgard, E. R.
1965 *Hypnotic susceptibility*. New York: Harcourt.

Hill, J. C.
1983 A computational model of language acquisition in the two-year-old. *Cognition and Brain Theory, 6,* 287–317.

Hinde, R. A.
1974 *Biological bases of human social behavior*. New York: McGraw-Hill.

Hintzman, D. L.
1974 Psychology and the cow's belly. *Worm Runner's Digest, 16,* 84–85.

Hoffman, M.
1975 Developmental synthesis of affect and cognition and its implications for altruistic motivation. *Developmental Psychology, 11,* 607–622.

Horney, K.
1967 *Feminine psychology*. New York: Norton.

Horowitz, F. D.
1983 A behavioral alternative to an ecological approach to understanding the development of knowing in infancy: A commentary. *Developmental Review, 3,* 405–409.

Huesmann, L. R., K. Lagerspetz, and L. D. Eron.
1984    Intervening variables in the TV violence-aggression relation: Evidence from two countries. *Developmental Psychology, 20,* 746–775.
Hutt, S. J., and C. Hutt.
1970    *Direct observation and measurement of behavior.* Springfield, Ill.: Thomas.
Inhelder, B., H. Sinclair, and M. Bovet.
1974    *Learning and the development of cognition.* Cambridge, Mass.: Harvard University Press.
Inhelder, B., and J. Piaget.
1980    Procedures and structures. In D. R. Olson (ed.), *The social foundations of language and thought: Essays in honor of Jerome S. Bruner.* New York: Norton.
James, W.
1890    *Principles of psychology.* New York: Holt.
Johnston, M. K., H. N. Sloane, and S. W. Bijou.
1966    A note on the measurement of drooling in free-ranging young children. *Journal of Experimental Child Psychology, 4,* 292–295.
Jones, E.
1953    *The life and work of Sigmund Freud.* New York: Basic Books. Vol. 1.
1955    Vol. 2.
1957    Vol. 3.
1961    Ed. and abridged by L. Trilling and S. Marcus.
Jones, M. C.
1924    A laboratory study of fear: The case of Peter. *Pedagogical Seminary, 31,* 308–315.
Kail, R., and J. Bisanz.
1982    Information processing and cognitive development. In H. W. Reese, ed., *Advances in child development and behavior.* Vol. 16. New York: Academic Press.
Keeney, T. J., S. R. Cannizzo, and J. H. Flavell.
1967    Spontaneous and induced verbal rehearsal in a recall task. *Child Development, 38,* 953–966.
Keil, F. C.
1986    On the structure-dependent nature of stages of cognitive development. In I. Levin, ed., *Stage and structure.* Norwood, N.J.: Ablex.
Kellman, P. J., and E. S. Spelke.
1983    Perception of partly occluded objects in infancy. *Cognitive Psychology, 15,* 483–524.
Kendler, H. H.
1987    *Historical foundations of modern psychology.* Chicago: Dorsey Press.
Kendler, H. H., and T. S. Kendler.
1962    Vertical and horizontal processes in problem solving. *Psychological Review, 69,* 1–16.
Kendler, T. S.
1979    The development of discrimination learning: A levels-of-functioning

Kendler, T. S. (*continued*)

    explanation. In H. W. Reese and L. P. Lipsitt, eds., *Advances in child development and behavior.* Vol. 13. New York: Academic Press.

Kessler, K., G. M. White, T. L. Rosenthal, and J. Phibbs.

    1973    *Modeling and overt practice in training a rule-creating rubric.* Paper presented at meetings of Rocky Mountain Psychological Association, Las Vegas, May.

Kimble, G. A.

    1961    *Hilgard and Marquis' conditioning and learning.* 2nd ed. New York: Appleton-Century-Crofts.

Klahr, D.

    1982    Nonmonotone assessment of monotone development: An information processing analysis. In S. Strauss, ed., *U-shaped behavioral growth.* New York: Academic Press.

    1984    Transition processes in quantitative development. In R. J. Sternberg, ed., *Mechanisms of cognitive development.* New York: W. H. Freeman.

    1985    Solving problems with ambiguous subgoal ordering: Preschoolers' performance. *Child Development, 56,* 940–952.

    In

    press    Information processing approaches to cognitive development. In R. Vasta, ed., *Annals of child development.* Vol. 6. Greenwich, Conn.: JAI Press.

Klahr, D., and R. S. Siegler.

    1978    The representation of children's knowledge. In H. W. Reese and L. P. Lipsitt, eds., *Advances in child development and behavior.* Vol. 12. New York: Academic Press.

Klahr, D., and J. G. Wallace.

    1976    *Cognitive development: An information-processing view.* Hillsdale, N.J.: Erlbaum.

Klaus, M. H., and J. H. Kennell

    1976    *Maternal-infant bonding.* St. Louis: Mosby.

Klausmeier, H. J., and T. S. Sipple.

    1982    Factor structure of the Piagetian stage of concrete operations. *Contemporary Educational Psychology, 7,* 161–180.

Klein, G. S.

    1970    *Perception, motives, and personality.* New York: Knopf.

Klopfer, P. H.

    1971    Mother love: What turns it on? *American Scientist, 59,* 404–407.

Koenig, O.

    1951    Das Aktionsystem der Bartmeise (*Panurus biarmicus* L.). *Oesterreichische Zoologische Zeitschrift, 1,* 1–82.

Kohlberg, L.

    1969    Stage and sequence: The cognitive-developmental approach to socialization. In D. A. Goslin, ed., *Handbook of socialization theory and research.* Chicago: Rand McNally.

Kosslyn, S.
1978a    Imagery and cognitive development: A teleological approach. In R. S. Siegler, ed., *Children's thinking: What develops?* Hillsdale, N.J.: Erlbaum.
1978b    The representational-developmental hypothesis. In P. A. Ornstein, ed., *Memory development in children.* Hillsdale, N.J.: Erlbaum.
Kreutzer, M. A., C. Leonard, and J. H. Flavell.
1975    An interview study of children's knowledge about memory. *Monographs of the Society for Research in Child Development, 40* (1, Serial No. 159).
Kris, E.
1952    *Psychoanalytic explorations in art.* New York: International Universities Press.
Kuenne, M. R.
1946    Experimental investigations of the relation of language to transposition behavior in young children. *Journal of Experimental Psychology, 36,* 471–490.
Kuhl, P., and A. N. Meltzoff.
1982    The bimodal perception of speech in infancy. *Science, 218,* 1138–1141.
Kuhn, D.
1974    Inducing development experimentally: Comments on a research paradigm. *Developmental Psychology, 10, 590–600.*
Kuhn, T.
1970    *The structure of scientific revolutions.* 2nd ed. Chicago: University of Chicago Press. 1st ed., 1962
Lachman, R., J. L. Lachman, and E. C. Butterfield.
1979    *Cognitive psychology and information processing: An introduction.* Hillsdale, N.J.: Erlbaum.
Lakatos, I.
1978    *The methodology of scientific research programs.* Cambridge, England: Cambridge University Press.
Lamb, M.
1978    Social interaction in infancy and the development of personality. In M. E. Lamb, ed., *Social and personality development.* New York: Holt, Rinehart and Winston.
Langer, J.
1969    *Theories of development.* New York: Holt, Rinehart and Winston.
Langlois, J. H., R. G. Cooper, and R. H. Woodson.
1985    The child: Many views, many fields. A review of *Handbook of child psychology,* by P. H. Mussen, ed. *Contemporary Psychology, 30,* 357–369.
Langlois, J. H., L. A. Roggman, R. J. Casey, J. M. Ritter, L. A. Rieser-Danner, and V. Y. Jenkins.
1987    Infant preferences for attractive faces: Rudiments of a stereotype? *Developmental Psychology, 23,* 363–369.

Leon, M.
1980    Integration of intent and consequence information in children's moral judgments. In F. Wilkening, J. Becker, and T. Trabaso, eds., *Information integration by children.* Hillsdale, N.J.: Erlbaum.
1984    Rules mothers and sons use to integrate intent and damage information in their moral judgments. *Child Development, 55,* 2106–2113.
Lepper, M. R., D. Greene, and R. E. Nisbett.
1973    Undermining children's intrinsic interest with extrinsic rewards: A test of the "overjustification" hypothesis. *Journal of Personality and Social Psychology, 28,* 129–137.
Lerner, R. M. and M. B. Kauffman.
1985    The concept of development in contextualism. *Developmental Review, 5,* 309–333.
Levy, R. I.
1969    On getting angry in the Society Islands. In W. Caudill and T. Y. Lin, eds., *Mental health research in Asia and the Pacific.* Honolulu: East-West Center Press.
Liben, L. S.
1977    Memory from a cognitive-developmental perspective: A theoretical and empirical review. In W. F. Overton and J. M. Gallagher, eds., *Knowledge and development.* Vol. 1. New York: Plenum.
Liben, L. S., and C. J. Posnansky.
1977    Inferences on inferences: The effects of age, transitive ability, memory load, and lexical factors. *Child Development, 48,* 1490–1497.
Looft, W. R., and C. P. Svoboda.
1971    Structuralism in cognitive developmental psychology: Past, contemporary, and futuristic perspectives. Unpublished manuscript, Pennsylvania State University.
Lorenz, K. Z.
1931    Beiträge zur Ethologie sozialer Corviden. *Journal für Ornithologie, 79,* 67–127.
1935    Der Kumpan in der Umwelt des Vogels. *Journal für Ornithologie, 83,* 137–413.
1937    Über die Bildung des Instinktbegriffes. *Die Naturwissenschaften, 25,* 289–300, 307–318, 325–331.
1943    Die angeborenen Formen möglicher Erfahrung. *Zeitschrift für Tierpsychologie, 5,* 235–409.
1950    *So kam der Mensch auf den Hund.* Wien: Verlag Borotha-Schoeler.
1952    *King Solomon's ring.* New York: Crowell.
1959    Psychologie und Stammesgeschichte. In G. Herberer, ed., *Evolution der Organismen.* Stuttgart: Fischer.
1963    *Das sogenannte Böse.* Wein: Verlag Borotha-Schoeler.
1966    *On aggression.* New York: Harcourt, Brace and World.
McCain, G., and E. M. Segal.
1969    *The game of science.* Belmont, Ca.: Brooks/Cole.

McCall, R. B., and C. B. Kennedy.
1980    Attention to babyishness in babies. *Journal of Experimental Child Psychology, 29,* 189–201.
McCall, R. B., R. D. Parke, and R. D. Kavanaugh.
1977    Imitation of live and televised models by children one to three years of age. *Monographs of the Society for Research in Child Development, 42* (5, Serial No. 173).
McCandless, B. R., and C. C. Spiker.
1956    Experimental research in child psychology. *Child Development, 27,* 75–80.
Maccoby, E. E.
1969    The development of stimulus selection. In J. P. Hill, ed., *Minnesota symposia on child psychology.* Vol. 3. Minneapolis: University of Minnesota Press.
MacDonald, K. B., ed.
1988    *Sociobiological perspectives on human development.* New York: Springer-Verlag.
Mace, W. M.
1977    James J. Gibson's strategy for perceiving: Ask not what's inside your head, but what your head's inside of. In R. Shaw and J. Bransford, eds., *Perceiving, acting, and knowing.* Hillsdale, N.J.: Erlbaum.
McFarland, D. J.
1976    Form and function in the temporal organisation of behaviour. In P. P. G. Bateson and R. A. Hinde, eds., *Growing points in ethology.* Cambridge: Cambridge University Press.
McGrew, W. C.
1972    *An ethological study of children's behavior.* New York: Academic Press.
Mahler, M. S.
1968    *On human symbiosis and the vicissitudes of individuation.* Vol. 1: *Infantile psychosis.* New York: International Universities Press.
Mahler, M. S., F. Pine, and A. Bergman.
1975    *The psychological birth of the human infant.* New York: Basic Books.
Malinowski, B.
1927    *Sex and repression in savage society.* New York: Harcourt Brace Jovanovich.
Mandler, G.
1979    Emotion. In E. Hearst, ed., *The first century of experimental psychology.* Hillsdale, N.J.: Erlbaum.
Marcia, J. E.
1980    Identity in adolescence. In J. Adelson, ed., *Handbook of adolescent psychology.* New York: Wiley.
1967    Ego identity status: Relationship to change in self-esteem, "general maladjustment," and authoritarianism. *Journal of Personality, 35,* 118–133.

Marx, M. H.
1976    Formal theory. In M. H. Marx and F. E. Goodson, eds., *Theories in contemporary psychology*. 2nd ed. New York: Macmillan.

Meacham, J. A.
1977    Soviet investigations of memory development. In R. V. Kail and J. W. Hagen, eds., *Perspectives on the development of memory and cognition*. Hillsdale, N.J.: Erlbaum.
1983    Wisdom and the context of knowledge: Knowing that one doesn't know. In D. Kuhn and J. A. Meacham, eds., *On the development of developmental psychology*. Basel: S. Karger.

Meacham, J. A., and N. R. Santilli.
1982    Interstage relationships in Erikson's theory: Identity and intimacy. *Child Development, 53,* 1461–1467.

Meadows, S.
1983    An assessment of Piaget's theory of cognitive development. In S. Meadows, ed., *Developing thinking*. London: Methuen.

Meltzoff, A. N., and M. K. Moore.
1983    Newborn infants imitate adult facial gestures. *Child Development, 54,* 702–709.

Miller, G. A.
1956    The magical number seven plus or minus two: Some limits on our capacity for processing information. *Psychological Review, 63,* 81–97.

Miller, G. A., E. Galanter, and K. H. Pribram.
1960    *Plans and the structure of behavior*. New York: Holt.

Miller, N. E., and J. Dollard.
1941    *Social learning and imitation*. New Haven, Conn.: Yale University Press.

Miller, P. H.
1978    Stimulus variables in conservation: An alternative approach to assessment. *Merrill-Palmer Quarterly, 24,* 141–160.
1985    Metacognition and attention. In D. L. Forrest-Pressley, G. E. MacKinnon, and T. G. Waller, eds., *Metacognition, cognition, and human performance*. Vol 2. Orlando, Fla.: Academic Press.

Miller, P. H., V. F. Haynes, D. DeMarie-Dreblow, and J. Woody-Ramsey.
1986    Children's strategies for gathering information in three tasks. *Child Development, 57,* 1429–1439.

Miller, S. A.
1976a   Extinction of Piagetian concepts: An updating. *Merrill–Palmer Quarterly, 22,* 257–281.
1976b   Nonverbal assessment of conservation of number. *Child Development, 47,* 722–728.
1976c   Nonverbal assessment of Piagetian concepts. *Psychological Bulletin, 83,* 405–430.
1982    On the generalizability of conservation: A comparison of different kinds of transformation. *British Journal of Psychology, 73,* 221–230.

Minsky, M.
1975     A framework for representing knowledge. In P. H. Winston, ed., *The psychology of computer vision.* New York: McGraw-Hill.
Moltz, H., and T. M. Leon.
1983     The coordinate roles of mother and young in establishing and maintaining pheromonal symbiosis in the rat. In L. A. Rosenblum and H. Moltz, eds., *Symbiosis in parent-offspring interactions.* New York: Plenum.
Montagu, A.
1973     The new litany of "innate depravity," or original sin revisited. In A. Montagu, ed., *Man and aggression.* New York: Oxford University Press.
Morris, D.
1967     *The naked ape.* New York: McGraw-Hill.
Munn, N. L.
1954     Learning in children. In L. Carmichael, ed., *Manual of child psychology.* 2nd ed. New York: Wiley.
Murray, F. B.
1983a    Equilibration as cognitive conflict. *Developmental Review, 3,* 54–61.
1983b    Learning and development through social interaction and conflict: A challenge to social learning theory. In L. Liben, ed., *Piaget and the foundations of knowledge.* Hillsdale, N.J.: Erlbaum.
Myers, B. J.
1984     Mother-infant bonding: The status of this critical-period hypothesis. *Developmental Review, 4,* 240–274.
Naus, M. J., and P. A. Ornstein.
1985     An investigation of the effects of expertise upon mnemonic strategies. Unpublished manuscript, University of North Carolina.
Naus, M. J., P. A. Ornstein, and S. Aivano.
1977     Developmental changes in memory: The effects of processing time and rehearsal instructions. *Journal of Experimental Child Psychology, 23,* 237–251.
Neisser, U.
1985     Toward an ecologically oriented cognitive science. In T. M. Shlechter and M. P. Toglia, eds., *New directions in cognitive science.* Norwood, N.J.: Ablex.
Nelson, K.
1978     How children represent knowledge of their world in and out of language: A preliminary report. In R. S. Siegler, ed., *Children's thinking: What develops?* Hillsdale, N.J.: Erlbaum.
Nelson, K., ed.
1986     *Event knowledge.* Hillsdale, N. J.: Erlbaum.
Newcomb, A. F., and W. A. Collins.
1979     Children's comprehension of family role portrayals in televised dramas: Effects of socioeconomic status, ethnicity, and age. *Developmental Psychology, 15,* 417–423.

Newell, A., and H. A. Simon.
1961      Computer simulation of human thinking. *Science, 134,* 2011–2017.
Noelting, G.
1980      The development of proportional reasoning and the ratio concept. *Educational Studies in Mathematics, 11,* 217–253, 331–363.
Noirot, E.
1974      Nest-building by the virgin female mouse exposed to ultrasound from inaccessible pups. *Animal Behaviour, 22,* 410–420.
Ormiston, L. H.
1972      Factors determining response to modeled hypocrisy. Unpublished doctoral dissertation, Stanford University.
Ornstein, P. A., and M. J. Naus.
1985      Effects of the knowledge base on children's memory strategies. In H. W. Reese, ed., *Advances in child development and behavior.* Vol. 19. Orlando, Fla.: Academic Press.
Ornstein, P. A., M. J. Naus, and C. Liberty.
1975      Rehearsal and organizational processes in children's memory. *Child Development, 46,* 818–830.
Osherson, D. N.
1974      *Logical abilities in children.* Vols. 1 and 2. Hillsdale, N.J.: Erlbaum.
1975      Vol. 3.
Overton, W. F.
1984      World views and their influence on psychological theory and research: Kuhn-Lakatos-Laudan. In H. W. Reese, ed., *Advances in child development and behavior.* Vol. 18. Orlando, Fla.: Academic Press, 1984.
Paris, S. G., and A. Y. Carter.
1973      Semantic and constructive aspects of sentence memory in children. *Developmental Psychology, 9,* 109–113.
Parke, R. D.
1977      Parent–infant interaction: Progress, paradigms, and problems. In G. P. Sackett, ed., *Observing behavior.* Baltimore, Md.: University Park Press.
Parton, D.
1976      Learning to imitate in infancy. *Child Development, 47,* 14–31.
Pascual-Leone, J. A.
1970      A mathematical model for the transition rule in Piaget's developmental states. *Acta Psychologica, 32,* 301–345.
Patterson, G. R.
1980      Mothers: The unacknowledged victims. *Monographs of the Society for Research in Child Development, 45* (5, Serial No. 186).
Patterson, G. R., and J. B. Reid.
1984      Social interactional processes within the family: The study of the moment-by-moment family transactions in which human social development is imbedded. *Journal of Applied Developmental Psychology, 5,* 237–262.

Peery, J. C., and P. M. Crane.
1980       Personal space regulation: Approach–withdrawal–approach proxemic behavior during adult–preschool interaction at close range. *Journal of Psychology, 106,* 63–75.

Perner, J., S. R. Leekam, and H. Wimmer.
1987       Three-year-olds' difficulty with false belief: The case for a conceptual deficit. *British Journal of Developmental Psychology, 5,* 125–137.

Peterson, L. R., and M. J. Peterson.
1959       Short-term retention of individual verbal terms. *Journal of Experimental Psychology, 58,* 193–198.

Piaget, J.
1923*    *The language and thought of the child.* New York: Harcourt, Brace.
(1926)

1924      *Judgment and reasoning in the child.* New York: Harcourt, Brace.
(1928)

1926      *The child's conception of the world.* New York: Harcourt, Brace.
(1929)

1927      *The child's conception of physical causality.* London: Kegan Paul.
(1930)

1932      *The moral judgment of the child.* London: Kegan Paul.
(1932)

1936      *The origins of intelligence in children.* New York: International Universities Press.
(1952)

1937      *The construction of reality in the child.* New York: Basic Books.
(1954)

1945      *Play, dreams and imitation in childhood.* New York: Norton.
(1951)

1946a     *The child's conception of time.* London: Routledge and Kegan Paul.
(1969)

1946b     *The child's conception of movement and speed.* London: Routledge and Kegan Paul.
(1970)

1947      *The psychology of intelligence.* New York: Harcourt, Brace.
(1950)

1952      Autobiography. In E. G. Boring et al., eds., *A history of psychology in autobiography.* Vol. 4. Worcester, Mass.: Clark University Press.

1961      *The mechanisms of perception.* London: Routledge and Kegan Paul.
(1969)

1964      Development and learning. In R. E. Ripple and V. N. Rockcastle, eds., *Piaget rediscovered.* Ithaca, N.Y.: Cornell University Press.

---

*The first date given is that of the original edition in French. The second date (in parentheses) is that of the translation.

Piaget, J. (*continued*)
1970    *Psychology and epistemology: Towards a theory of knowledge.* Harmondsworth, England: Penguin.
(1972)
1971    The theory of stages in cognitive development. In D. R. Green, M. P. Ford, and G. B. Flamer, eds., *Measurement and Piaget.* New York: McGraw-Hill.
1974    *Experiments in contradiction.* Chicago: University of Chicago Press.
(1980)
1978    *The equilibration of cognitive structures.* Chicago: University of Chicago Press.
(1985)
1979    Correspondences and transformations. In F. B. Murray, ed., *The impact of Piagetian theory: On education, philosophy, psychiatry, and psychology.* Baltimore: University Park Press.
1981    *Possibility and necessity.* Vol. 1: *The role of possibility in cognitive*
(1987)    *development.* Vol 2: *The role of necessity in cognitive development.* Minneapolis, Minn.: University of Minnesota Press.
1983    Piaget's theory. In W. Kessen, ed., *Handbook of child psychology.* Vol. 1: *History, theory, and methods.* 4th ed., P. H. Mussen, series ed. New York: Wiley
1986    Essay on necessity. *Human Development, 29,* 301–314.
Piaget, J., and R. Garcia.
In
press    *Towards a logic of meanings.* Hillsdale, N.J.: Erlbaum.
Piaget, J., and B. Inhelder.
1968    *Memory and intelligence.* London: Routledge and Kegan Paul.
(1973)
Pick, A. D., ed.
1979    *Perception and its development: A tribute to Eleanor J. Gibson.* Hillsdale, N.J.: Erlbaum.
Poincaré, J. H.
1908    *Science and hypothesis.* New York: Dover.
(1952)
Pressley, M.
1982    Elaboration and memory development. *Child Development, 53,* 296–309.
Price-Williams, D. R., W. Gordon, and M. Ramirez, III.
1969    Skill and conservation: A study of pottery-making children. *Developmental Psychology, 1,* 769.
Quillian, M. R., P. M. Wortman, and G. W. Baylor.
1964    The programmable Piaget: Behavior from the standpoint of a radical computerist. Unpublished manuscript, Carnegie Institute of Technology.

Rajecki, D. W., M. E. Lamb, and P. Obmascher.
1978      Toward a general theory of infantile attachment: A comparative review of aspects of the social bond. *Behavioral and Brain Sciences, 3,* 417–464.
Rapaport, D.
1960      The structure of psychoanalytic theory: A systemization attempt. *Psychological Issues,* Monograph 6. New York: International Universities Press.
Resnick, L. B.
1987      Constructing knowledge in school. In L. S. Liben, ed., *Development and learning.* Hillsdale, N. J.: Erlbaum.
Reyher, J.
1967      Hypnosis in research on psychopathology. In J. E. Gordon, ed., *Handbook of clinical and experimental hypnosis.* New York: Macmillan.
Riegel, K.
1972      Influence of economic and political ideologies on the development of developmental psychology. *Psychological Bulletin, 78,* 129–141.
1976      The dialectics of human development. *American Psychologist, 31,* 689–700.
Robson, K. S.
1967      The role of eye-to-eye contact in maternal-infant attachment. *Journal of Child Psychology and Psychiatry, 8,* 13–25.
Roediger, H. L.
1979      Implicit and explicit memory models. *Bulletin of the Psychonomic Society, 13,* 339–342.
Rose, S. A., and M. Blank.
1974      The potency of context in children's cognition: An illustration through conservation. *Child Development, 45,* 499–502.
Rosenblatt, J. S.
1976      Stages in the early behavioural development of altricial young of selected species of non-primate mammals. In P. P. G. Bateson and R. A. Hinde, eds., *Growing points in ethology.* Cambridge: Cambridge University Press.
Rosenthal, T. L., and B. J. Zimmerman.
1972      Modeling by exemplification and instruction in training conservation. *Developmental Psychology, 6,* 392–401.
1978      *Social learning and cognition.* New York: Academic Press.
Rothmann, M., and E. Teuber.
1915      Einzelausgabe der Anthropoidenstation auf Teneriffa: I. Ziele und Aufgaben der Station sowie erste Beobachtungen an den auf ihr gehaltenen Schimpansen. *Abhandlungen der Preussischen Akademie der Wissenschaften Berlin,* 1–20.
Russell, M. J., T. Mendelson, and H. V. S. Peeke
1983      Mothers' identification of their infants' odors. *Ethology and Sociobiology, 4,* 29–31.

Samuel, J., and P. Bryant.
1984    Asking only one question in the conservation experiment. *Journal of Child Psychology and Psychiatry, 25,* 315–318.

Savin-Williams, R. C.
1976    An ethological study of dominance formation and maintenance in a group of human adolescents. *Child Development, 47,* 972–979.

Scarr, S.
1985    Cultural lenses on mothers and children. In L. Friedrich-Cofer, ed., *Human nature and public policy.* New York: Praeger.

Schank, R. C., and R. Abelson.
1977    *Scripts, plans, goals and understanding.* Hillsdale, N.J.: Erlbaum.

Schlein, S., ed.
1987    *A way of looking at things: Selected papers from 1930 to 1980. Erik H. Erikson.* New York: Norton.

Schmuckler, M.
1987    The effect of imposed optical flow on guided locomotion in young children. Paper presented at the meeting of the Society for Research in Child Development, Baltimore, April.

Schneirla, T. C.
1966    Behavioral development and comparative psychology. *Quarterly Review of Biology, 41,* 283–302.

Sears, R. R.
1975    Your ancients revisited: A history of child development. In E. M. Hetherington, ed., *Review of child development research.* Vol. 5. Chicago: University of Chicago Press.

Sears, R. R., L. Rau, and R. Alpert.
1965    *Identification and child rearing.* Stanford: Stanford University Press.

Shapley, H., S. Rapput, and H. Wright, eds.
1965    *The new treasury of science.* New York: Harper and Row.

Shatz, M., and R. Gelman.
1973    The development of communication skills: Modifications in the speech of young children as a function of listener. *Monographs of the Society for Research in Child Development, 38* (5, Serial No. 152).

Shaw, R., and J. Bransford.
1977    Introduction: Psychological approaches to the problems of knowledge. In R. Shaw and J. Bransford, eds., *Perceiving, acting, and knowing: Toward an ecological psychology.* Hillsdale, N.J.: Erlbaum.

Shiffrin, R. M., and R. C. Atkinson.
1969    Storage and retrieval processes in long-term memory. *Psychological Review, 76,* 179–193.

Siegel, A. W., and M. Schadler.
1977    The development of young children's spatial representations of their classrooms. *Child Development, 48,* 388–394.

Siegler, R. S.
1978    The origins of scientific reasoning. In R. S. Siegler, ed., *Children's thinking: What develops?* Hillsdale, N.J.: Erlbaum.

Siegler, R. S. (*continued*)

1986 *Children's thinking*. Englewood Cliffs, N. J.: Prentice-Hall.

1989 Mechanisms of cognitive development. In M. R. Rosenzweig and L. W. Porter, eds., *Annual review of psychology*. Vol. 40. Palo Alto, Ca.: Annual Reviews, Inc.

Sigel, I. E.

1986 Mechanism: A metaphor for cognitive development? A review of Sternberg's *Mechanisms of cognitive development*. *Merrill-Palmer Quarterly, 32*, 93–101.

Signorella, M. L., and L. S. Liben.

1984 Recall and reconstruction of gender-related pictures: Effects of attitude, task difficulty, and age. *Child Development, 55*, 393–405.

Simon, H. A.

1972 On the development of the processor. In S. Farnham-Diggory, ed., *Information processing in children*. New York: Academic Press.

Skinner, B. F.

1948 *Walden Two*. New York: Macmillan.

1967 Autobiography. In E. G. Boring and G. Lindzey, eds., *A history of psychology in autobiography*. Vol. 5. Englewood Cliffs, N.J.: Prentice-Hall.

1971 *Beyond freedom and dignity*. New York: Knopf.

1980 The experimental analysis of operant behavior: A history. In R. W. Rieber and K. Salzinger, eds., *Psychology: Theoretical-historical perspectives*. New York: Academic Press.

1987 Whatever happened to psychology as the science of behavior? *American Psychologist, 42*, 780–786.

Smith, P. K., and K. Connolly.

1972 Patterns of play and social interaction in preschool children. In N. G. Blurton-Jones, ed., *Ethological studies of child behavior*. Cambridge: Cambridge University Press.

Snarey, J., L. Kohlberg, and G. Noam.

1983 Ego development in perspective: Structural stage, functional phase, and cultural age-period models. *Developmental Review, 3*, 303–337.

Spelke, E. S.

1976 Infants' intermodal perception of events. *Cognitive Psychology, 8*, 553–560.

Spiker, C. C.

1966 The concept of development: Relevant and irrelevant issues. In H. W. Stevenson, ed., *Concept of development*. *Monographs of the Society for Research in Child Development, 31* (5, Serial No. 107).

Spitz, R. A.

1945 Hospitalism: An inquiry into the genesis of psychiatry conditions in early childhood. *Psychoanalytic Study of the Child, 1*, 53–74.

1957 *Die Entstehung der ersten Objektbeziehungen*. Stuttgart: Klett.

Stanovich, K. E.

1978 Information processing in mentally retarded individuals. In N. R. Ellis,

Stanovich, K. E. (*continued*)
ed., *International review of research in mental retardation.* Vol. 9. New York: Academic Press.

Stern, D.
1974 Mother and infant at play: The dyadic interaction involving facial, vocal, and gaze behaviors. In M. Lewis and L. Rosenblum, eds., *The effect of the infant on its caretaker.* New York: Wiley.

Sternberg, R. J.
1979 The nature of mental abilities. *American Psychologist, 34,* 214–230.

1985 *Beyond IQ: A triarchic theory of human intelligence.* New York: Cambridge University Press.

1986 *Intelligence applied.* San Diego: Harcourt Brace Jovanovich.

Sternberg, R. J., and B. Rifkin.
1979 The development of analogical reasoning processes. *Journal of Experimental Child Psychology, 27,* 195–232.

Strauss, S., and I. Levin.
1981 Commentary. *Monographs of the Society for Research in Child Development, 46,* (2, serial no. 189).

Strayer, F. F.
1980 Social ecology of the preschool peer group. In W. A. Collins, ed., *Development of cognition, affect, and social relations.* Hillsdale, N.J.: Erlbaum.

Strayer, F. F., and J. Strayer.
1976 An ethological analysis of social agonism and dominance relations among pre-school children. *Child Development, 47,* 980–999.

Streri, A., and M. Pecheux.
1986 Vision-to-touch and touch-to-vision transfer of form in 5-month-old infants. *British Journal of Developmental Psychology, 4,* 161–167.

Thayer, G. H.
1909 *Concealing coloration in the animal kingdom.* New York: Macmillan.

Thorndike, E. L.
1898 Animal intelligence: An experimental study of the associative processes in animals. *Psychological Review: Series of Monograph Supplements, 2* (4, Whole No. 8).

Tinbergen, E. A., and N. Tinbergen.
1972 *Early childhood autism: An ethological approach.* Berlin: Parey.

Tinbergen, N.
1951 *The study of instinct.* London: Oxford University Press.

1958 *Curious naturalists.* New York: Basic Books.

1973 *The animal in its world: Explorations of an ethologist 1932–1972.* Vols. 1 and 2, Cambridge, Mass.: Harvard University Press.

Todd, C. M., and M. Perlmutter.
1980 Reality recalled by preschool children. In M. Perlmutter, ed., *New directions for child development: Children's memory.* Vol. 10. San Francisco: Jossey-Bass.

Tolman, E. C.
1959      Principles of purposive behavior. In S. Koch, ed., *Psychology: A study of a science.* New York: McGraw-Hill

Trabasso, T.
1977      The role of memory as a system in making transitive inferences. In R. V. Kail and J. W. Hagen, eds., *Perspectives on the development of memory and cognition.* Hillsdale, N.J.: Erlbaum.

Trabasso, T., C. A. Riley, and E. G. Wilson.
1975      The representation of linear order and spatial strategies in reasoning: A developmental study. In R. J. Falmagne, ed., *Reasoning: Representation and process.* Hillsdale, N.J.: Erlbaum.

Trivers, R.
1985      *Social evolution.* Menlo Park, Cal.: The Benjamin-Cummings Publishing Company.

Tuddenham, R. D.
1966      Jean Piaget and the world of the child. *American Psychologist, 21,* 207–217.

Tulving, E.
1972      Episodic and semantic memory. In E. Tulving and W. Donaldson, eds., *Organization of memory.* New York: Academic Press.

Tumblin, A., and B. Gholson.
1981      Hypothesis theory and the development of conceptual learning. *Psychological Bulletin, 90,* 102–124.

Uexküll, J. von.
1909      *Umwelt und Innenwelt der Tiere.* Berlin: Springer.

Uzgiris, I. C.
1968      Situational generality of conservation. In I. E. Siegel and F. H. Hooper, eds. *Logical thinking in children: Research based on Piaget's theory.* New York: Holt, Rinehart & Winston.

van den Daele, L.
1969      Qualitative models in developmental analysis. *Developmental Psychology, 1,* 303–310.

Vurpillot, E., and W. A. Ball.
1979      The concept of identity and children's selective attention. In G. Hale and M. Lewis, eds., *Attention and cognitive development.* New York: Plenum.

Vuyk, R.
1981      *Overview and critique of Piaget's genetic epistemology, 1965–1980.* Vol. 1. London and New York: Academic Press.

Vygotsky, L. (and M. Cole, V. John-Steiner, S. Scribner, and E. Souberman, eds.)
1978      *Mind in society.* Cambridge, Mass.: Harvard University Press.

Waddington, C. H.
1957      *The strategy of the genes.* London: Allen and Unwin.

Wagner, D. A.
1978      Memories of Morocco: The influence of age, schooling, and environment on memory. *Cognitive Psychology, 10,* 1–28.

Wallace, I., D. Klahr, and K. Bluff.
1987    A self-modifying production system model of cognitive development. In D. Klahr, P. Langley, and R. Neches, eds., *Production system models of learning and development.* Cambridge, Mass.: MIT Press.

Wallbank, T. W., and A. M. Taylor.
1960    *Civilization past and present.* Chicago: Scott, Foresman.

Wason, P. C., and P. N. Johnson-Laird.
1972    *Psychology of reasoning.* Cambridge, Mass.: Harvard University Press.

Watson, J. B.
1924    *Behaviorism.* New York: Norton.
1928    *Psychological care of infant and child.* New York: Norton. Watson, J. B., and R. Rayner.
1920    Conditioned emotional reactions. *Journal of Experimental Psychology, 3,* 1–14.

Waugh, N. C., and D. A. Norman.
1965    Primary memory. *Psychological Review, 72,* 89–104.

Wegman, C.
1985    *Psychoanalysis and cognitive psychology: A formalization of Freud's earliest theory.* Orlando, Fla.: Academic Press.

Weir, M. W.
1964    Developmental changes in problem-solving strategies. *Psychological Review, 71,* 473–490.

Wellman, H. W.
1988    The early development of memory strategies. In F. Weinert and M. Perlmutter, eds., *Memory development: Universal changes and individual differences.* Hillsdale, N. J.: Erlbaum.

Wertsch, J. V., G. D. McNamee, J. B. McLane, and N. A. Budwig.
1980    The adult–child dyad as a problem-solving system. *Child Development, 51,* 1215–1221.

Weston, D. R., and E. Turiel.
1980    Act–rule relations: Children's conceptions of social rules. *Developmental Psychology, 16,* 417–424.

White, B. L.
1969    Child development research: An edifice without a foundation. *Merrill–Palmer Quarterly, 15,* 47–78.

White, R. W.
1963    Ego and reality in psychoanalytic theory: A proposal regarding independent ego energies. *Psychological Review,* Monograph 11. New York: International Universities Press.

White, S. H.
1965    Evidence for a hierarchical arrangement of learning processes. In L. P. Lipsitt and C. C. Spiker, eds., *Advances in child development and behavior.* Vol. 2. New York: Academic Press.
1970    The learning theory approach. In P. H. Mussen, ed., *Carmichael's manual of child psychology.* Vol. 1. 3rd ed. New York: Wiley.

1976 The active organism in theoretical behaviorism. *Human Development, 19, 99–107.*

Whiting, J. M., and I. L. Child.
1953 *Child training and personality.* New Haven, Conn.: Yale University Press.

Wilson, E. O.
1975 *Sociobiology: The new synthesis.* Cambridge, Mass.: Belknap Press of Harvard University Press.
1978 *On human nature.* Cambridge, Mass.: Harvard University Press.

Winnicott, D. W.
1953 Transitional objects and transitional phenomena. *International Journal of Psychoanalysis, 34, 89–97.*
1971 *Playing and reality.* New York: Basic Books.

Wohlwill, J. F.
1960 Developmental studies of perception. *Psychological Bulletin, 57,* 249–288.
1973 The concept of experience: S or R? *Human Development, 16, 90–107.*

Yando, R., V. Seitz, and E. Zigler, eds.
1978 Imitation: A developmental perspective. Hillsdale, N.J.: Erlbaum.

Yussen, S. R.
1974 Determinants of visual attention and recall in observational learning by preschoolers and second graders. *Developmental Psychology, 10,* 93–100.

Zajonc, R. B.
1980 Feeling and thinking: Preferences need no inferences. *American Psychologist, 35, 151–175.*

Zigler, E.
1963 Metatheoretical issues in developmental psychology. In M. Marx, ed., *Theories in contemporary psychology.* New York: Macmillan.

Zimmerman, B. J.
1974 Modification of young children's grouping strategies: The effects of modeling, verbalization, incentives, and praise. *Child Development, 45,* 1032–1041.
1985 The development of "intrinsic" motivation: A social learning analysis. In G. J. Whitehurst, ed., *Annals of child development.* Vol. 2. Greenwich, Conn.: JAI Press.

Zimmerman, B., and D. E. Blom.
1983 Toward an empirical test of the role of cognitive conflict in learning. *Developmental Review, 3, 18–38.*

# Index of Names

# Index of Topics